Cases on Information Technology Planning, Design and Implementation

Mehdi Khosrow-Pour, D.B.A.
Editor-in-Chief, Journal of Cases on Information Technology

IDEA GROUP PUBLISHING
Hershey • London • Melbourne • Singapore

Acquisitions Editor:	Michelle Potter
Development Editor:	Kristin Roth
Senior Managing Editor:	Amanda Appicello
Managing Editor:	Jennifer Neidig
Typesetter:	Sharon Berger
Cover Design:	Lisa Tosheff
Printed at:	Integrated Book Technology

Published in the United States of America by
        Idea Group Publishing (an imprint of Idea Group Inc.)
        701 E. Chocolate Avenue, Suite 200
        Hershey PA 17033
        Tel: 717-533-8845
        Fax: 717-533-8661
        E-mail: cust@idea-group.com
        Web site: http://www.idea-group.com

and in the United Kingdom by
        Idea Group Publishing (an imprint of Idea Group Inc.)
        3 Henrietta Street
        Covent Garden
        London WC2E 8LU
        Tel: 44 20 7240 0856
        Fax: 44 20 7379 0609
        Web site: http://www.eurospanonline.com

  Library of Congress Cataloging-in-Publication Data

Cases on information technology planning, design and implementation / Mehdi Khosrow-Pour, editor.
       p. cm.
    Summary: "This book brings together a variety of real-life experiences showing how companies and organizations have successfully, or not so successfully, planned, designed, and implemented different applications using information technology"--Provided by publisher.
    Includes bibliographical references and index.
    ISBN 1-59904-408-0 (hardcover) -- ISBN 1-59904-409-9 (softcover) -- ISBN 1-59904-410-2 (ebook)
   1. Information technology--Management--Case studies. 2. Information technology--Planning--Case studies. I. Khosrowpour, Mehdi, 1951-
    HD30.2.C383 2006
    004.068--dc22
                                    2006003568

British Cataloguing in Publication Data
A Cataloguing in Publication record for this book is available from the British Library.

Cases on Information Technology Series

ISSN: 1537-9337

Series Editor
Mehdi Khosrow-Pour, D.B.A.
Editor-in-Chief, *Journal of Cases on Information Technology*

- Cases on Database Technologies and Applications
  Mehdi Khosrow-Pour, Information Resources Management Association, USA
- Cases on Electronic Commerce Technologies and Applications
  Mehdi Khosrow-Pour, Information Resources Management Association, USA
- Cases on Global IT Applications and Management: Success and Pitfalls
  Felix B. Tan, University of Auckland, New Zealand
- Cases on Information Technology and Business Process Reengineering
  Mehdi Khosrow-Pour, Information Resources Management Association, USA
- Cases on Information Technology and Organizational Politics and Culture
  Mehdi Khosrow-Pour, Information Resources Management Association, USA
- Cases on Information Technology Management In Modern Organizations
  Mehdi Khosrow-Pour, Information Resources Management Association, USA & Jay
  Liebowitz, George Washington University, USA
- Cases on Information Technology Planning, Design and Implementation
  Mehdi Khosrow-Pour, Information Resources Management Association, USA
- Cases on Information Technology, Volume 7
  Mehdi Khosrow-Pour, Information Resources Management Association, USA
- Cases on Strategic Information Systems
  Mehdi Khosrow-Pour, Information Resources Management Association, USA
- Cases on Telecommunications and Networking
  Mehdi Khosrow-Pour, Information Resources Management Association, USA
- Cases on the Human Side of Information Technology
  Mehdi Khosrow-Pour, Information Resources Management Association, USA
- Cases on Worldwide E-Commerce: Theory in Action
  Mahesh S. Raisinghani, Texas Woman's University, USA
- Case Studies in Knowledge Management
  Murray E. Jennex, San Diego State University, USA
- Case Studies on Information Technology in Higher Education: Implications for Policy and
  Practice
  Lisa Ann Petrides, Columbia University, USA
- Success and Pitfalls of IT Management (Annals of Cases in Information Technology, Volume 1)
  Mehdi Khosrow-Pour, Information Resources Management Association, USA
- Organizational Achievement and Failure in Information Technology Management
  (Annals of Cases in Information Technology, Volume 2)
  Mehdi Khosrow-Pour, Information Resources Management Association, USA
- Pitfalls and Triumphs of Information Technology Management
  (Annals of Cases in Information Technology, Volume 3)
  Mehdi Khosrow-Pour, Information Resources Management Association, USA
- Annals of Cases in Information Technology, Volume 4 - 6
  Mehdi Khosrow-Pour, Information Resources Management Association, USA

 IDEA GROUP INC.

Cases on Information Technology Planning, Design and Implementation

Detailed Table of Contents

Suresh Chalasani, University of Wisconsin - Parkside, USA
Dirk Baldwin, University of Wisconsin - Parkside, USA
Jayavel Souderpandian, University of Wisconsin - Parkside, USA

This case focuses on the development of information systems for not-for-profit volunteer-based organizations. Specifically, it discusses an information system project for the Volunteer Center of Racine (VCR). This case targets the analysis and design phase of the project using the Unified Modeling Language (UML) methodology, database modeling, and aspects of project management including scope and risk management. Students must decide how to proceed, including recommending an IT solution, managing risk, managing scope, projecting a schedule, and managing personnel.

Nava Pliskin, Ben-Gurion University of the Negev, Israel
Marta Zarotski, Ben-Gurion University of the Negev, Israel

This case looks at Dead Sea Works, an international multi-firm producer of Potash and other chemicals whose sales for 1998 were about $500 million. In 1996, the Information Systems group convinced top management to pursue a big-bang ERP implementation of SAP R/3.

This case study provides a detailed account of an ill-fated initiative to centrally plan and procure an integrated applications suite for a number of British higher education institutions. It is argued that because systems are so deeply embedded in operations and organization, high-risk, 'big-bang' approaches to information systems planning and development must be avoided. In this context the case illustrates the level of complexity that unpredictable change can bring to an information technology project that aims to establish the 'organizationally generic' and the destabilizing effects it has on the network of the project's stakeholders.

This case study provides an overview of the process utilized in implementing a broad-based strategy to address the information technology needs of a large public university, the University of Memphis. It deals at length with the planning and creation of an IT governance structure and a strategic planning and management model. In this case, modern theories of organizational change and strategic planning were applied to the creation and improvement of the University's IT structure.

An information kiosk system is a computer-based information system in a publicly accessible place. Such a system was developed for a large public transport company to provide African commuters with limited educational background with up-to-date information on schedules and ticket prices while also presenting general company information in a graphically attractive way. The challenges regarding liaison with passengers are highlighted and the use of a touch screen kiosk to supplement current liaison media is justified in this case.

This case focuses on four essential components of a paradigm shift in technology and higher education at the University of Minnesota Crookston (UMC). This case describes how a paradigm shift model can help to promote a long-term technology cultural change in a higher education institution. The model consists of technology commitment, technology philosophy, investment priority, and development focus. It has been used at UMC to bring about a reengineering of the entire institution to support a ubiquitous laptop environment throughout the curriculum and campus.

During a field trial performed at the Norwegian telecom company, NetCom, a methodology for model-based risk analysis was assessed. The chosen methodology was the CORAS methodology, which has been developed in a European research project carried out by 11 European companies and research institutes partly funded by the European Union. This case describes the goal of the analysis, to identify risks in relation to an organization's application that offered customers access to their personal account information online.

This case study is based on a multi-year information systems plan for a marketing firm. The case describes the critical components of the enterprise system, including the software and hardware architectures.

This case details the implementation of the systems applications and products (SAP) production planning module at EA Cakes Ltd. The market forced the company to change its sales and production strategy from "make-to-order" to "make-to-stock." The decision to change the strategy involved not only the company's decision to invest much more money in accumulation and keeping stocks of finished goods, it required a complete redesign of its production planning system, which was an integral part of an ERP system that used SAP software.

Chapter X
Developing Effective Computer Systems Supporting Knowledge-Intensive Work: Situated Design in a Large Paper Mill 150
Martin Müller, University of Zurich, Switzerland
Rolf Pfeifer, University of Zurich, Switzerland

The case is a joint project between the University of Zurich and "Swiss Paper," a large paper mill in Switzerland. The objective of this case is to improve and to enhance the existing computer infrastructure in a way that the communication process about the energy issue will be improved.

Chapter XI
Power Conflict, Commitment and the Development of Sales and Marketing IS/IT Infrastructures at Digital Devices, Inc. 178
Tom Butler, University College Cork, Ireland

This article explores the political relationships, power asymmetries, and conflicts surrounding the development, deployment, and governance of IT-enabled sales and marketing information systems (IS) at Digital Devices, Inc. The study reports on the web of individual, group and institutional commitments and influences on the IS development and implementation processes in an organizational culture that promoted and supported user-led development. In particular, the article highlights the problems the company's IS function encountered in implementing its ad-hoc strategies and governance policies.

Chapter XII
Changing the Old Order: Sequencing Organizational and Information Technology Change to Achieve Successful Organizational Transformation 197
Chris Sauer, The University of New South Wales, Australia

This chapter describes the transformation of the motor vehicle registration and driver licensing business of the Roads and Traffic Authority of the Australian state of New South Wales. At the heart of this transformation which took place between 1989 and 1992 is a system called DRIVES. The project was innovative in the technology platform it devised and in the CASE technology it used to build the application. The new system has paid for itself at the same time as transforming the Roads and Traffic Authority's way of doing the business. In addition it has generated new strategic opportunities.

This case describes challenges in the adoption and implementation of IT in two public sector enterprises in the postal and distribution businesses respectively, in India. In spite of similarities in the scale of operations and the general cultural contexts, the IT adoption processes and outcomes of the two organizations were significantly different. While one failed to implement IT in its crucial processes, the other responded effectively to changes in external conditions by developing and using IT applications for critical functions.

This case describes Mobile Technology, a small/medium sized electronics manufacturer that has been very successful and has grown rapidly in recent years. The firm relies heavily on information technology and most of the staff has very sophisticated computer expertise, yet it has no IS department and has only just appointed an IS manager.

This study describes the strategy and information technology adopted by Peru's National Superintendent of Public Registries (SUNARP) to meet its organizational goals. SUNARP was created in 1994 to become the ruling entity of all public registry offices in Peru, which to that time had been working in an isolated fashion. The case describes the projects already completed, their respective success and their deployment across the organization's bureaus across the nation.

This case concerns an information systems and technology (IS/IT) action research intervention into a train operating company in the newly privatized rail industry in the UK. The project involved information management in the maintenance wing of the company.

Chapter XVII

This case study describes experiences of a successful regional law firm — an information intensive enterprise-with the design and implementation of an enterprise portal. The technology choice is explained in detail within the context of the needs of the information intensive small enterprise. The issues discussed are both technological and behavioral.

Chapter XVIII

The case study describes the implementation of ManuSoft, a generic MIS package, and enhancement of its effectiveness to the management with the development of object-oriented interfacing programs in a Melbourne-based job shop engineering company.

Chapter XIX

This case describes evolution of a small software company through three major phases of its life cycle. During the first phase, the business was founded within a subsidiary of a large multinational information technology (IT) company. In the second phase, the business evolved as a spin-off from the initial organization through a MBO (management buy-out) into an independent software vendor. Finally, in the third phase, the business has established itself as a vertically-focused business unit within a publicly-quoted company operating in software and consulting businesses.

Chapter XX

This case study examines the foreign banking sector's potential in transferring technology to the domestic banks in the People's Republic of China. Although the rationale of the Chinese government's admission of foreign banks into its domestic banking industry was to attract foreign capital and banking expertise, the case shows that foreign banks have not been employed fully for their potential in technology transfer.

Yuan Long, University of Nebraska - Lincoln, USA
Fiona Fui-Hoon Nah, University of Nebraska - Lincoln, USA
Zhanbei Zhu, Shanghai Bell Co., Ltd., China

This case describes the environmental and organizational context of Shanghai Bell Corporation, and the problems and challenges it encountered in developing an enterprise-wide strategic IT/IS plan. The issues covered include alignment of IT strategy with evolving business needs, application of a methodology to develop the strategic IT/IS plan, and evaluation of strategic planning project success.

Preface

Information technology has reformed and restructured the inner workings of companies, organizations and government agencies over the past several decades, and will continue to do so well into the future. Managers and administrators are constantly in search of new tools to be used in support of greater utilization and management of information technology applications in their prospective organizations. *Cases on Information Technology Planning, Design and Implementation*, part of Idea Group Inc.'s *Cases on Information Technology Series*, brings together a variety of real-life experiences of how other companies and organizations have successfully, or not so successfully, planned, designed, and implemented different applications using information technology. Cases included in this publication present a wide range of issues related to systems development, design and analysis of modern information systems applications without pitfalls.

The cases included in this volume cover many topics, such as volunteer center information systems' design, ERP implementation in a global company, the procurement of a integrated applications suite, a learning organization-oriented information technology planning and management process, an information kiosk's development, a paradigm shift in technology and higher education at a university, the analysis of a Web application, systems requirements and prototyping, implementing a planning module at a company, effective computer systems for a large paper mill, developing sales and marketing IS/IT infrastructures, a new technology platform for motor vehicle registrations, implementing IT in developing nations, mobile technology, public registries technological modernization, information systems and technology outsourcing, enterprise information portals in small to medium sized businesses, the evolution of a small software company, IT adoption in the Chinese banking system, and systems for telecommunications enterprises.

Professionals and educators alike will find this collection of cases very useful in learning about challenges and solutions related to the planning, design and implementation of information technology applications. *Cases on Information Technology Plan-*

ning, Design and Implementation will provide practitioners, educators and students with important examples of successes and failures in the implementation of information systems and technologies. An outstanding collection of current real-life situations associated with the effective utilization of IT, with lessons learned included in each case, this volume will be very instrumental for those learning about the issues and challenges in the field of information science and technology.

Note to Professors: Teaching notes for cases included in this publication are available to those professors who decide to adopt the book for their college course. Contact cases@idea-group.com for additional information regarding teaching notes and to learn about other volumes of case books in the IGI *Cases on Information Technology Series*.

ACKNOWLEDGMENTS

Putting together a publication of this magnitude requires the cooperation and assistance of many professionals with much expertise. I would like to take this opportunity to express my gratitude to all the authors of cases included in this volume. Many thanks also to all the editorial assistance provided by the Idea Group Inc. editors during the development of these books, particularly all the valuable and timely efforts of Mr. Andrew Bundy and Ms. Michelle Potter. Finally, I would like to dedicate this book to all my colleagues and former students who taught me a lot during my years in academia.

A special thank you to the Editorial Advisory Board: Annie Becker, Florida Institute of Technology, USA; Stephen Burgess, Victoria University, Australia; Juergen Seitz, University of Cooperative Education, Germany; Subhasish Dasgupta, George Washington University, USA; and Barbara Klein, University of Michigan, Dearborn, USA.

Mehdi Khosrow-Pour, D.B.A.
Editor-in-Chief
Cases on Information Technology Series
http://www.idea-group.com/bookseries/details.asp?id=18

Chapter I

Information System for a Volunteer Center:
System Design for Not-For-Profit
Organizations with Limited Resources

Suresh Chalasani, University of Wisconsin - Parkside, USA

Dirk Baldwin, University of Wisconsin - Parkside, USA

Jayavel Souderpandian, University of Wisconsin - Parkside, USA

EXECUTIVE SUMMARY

This case focuses on the development of information systems for not-for-profit volunteer-based organizations. Specifically, we discuss an information system project for the Volunteer Center of Racine (VCR). This case targets the analysis and design phase of the project using the Unified Modeling Language (UML) methodology, database modeling, and aspects of project management including scope and risk management. Students must decide how to proceed, including recommending an IT solution, managing risk, managing scope, projecting a schedule, and managing personnel. The rewards and special issues involved with systems for not-for-profit organizations will be revealed. This case can be used in a variety of courses, including systems analysis and design, database management systems, and project management.

ORGANIZATIONAL BACKGROUND

Jeff McCoy, project lead of a four-person project team, was finishing requirements and project status documentation related to an information system for the Volunteer Center of Racine (VCR). Jeff, the information systems team, and the client needed to make some important decisions concerning the future of the project. Jeff needed to formulate his own opinion, but it was getting late. He promised his fiancé that they would see a movie at the new cinema tonight. Recently, his promises have gone unfulfilled.

To this point, the VCR project had progressed smoothly. The focus of the project was the development of an application that helped the VCR place and track volunteers at various volunteer opportunities. The development team used the Unified Modeling Language (UML) to document the requirements of the system (Booch et al., 1999). A Gantt chart and a standardized project status report were used to record progress. The project status report contained fields to record the time, budget, people, process, and technology status of the project (Appendix B). A color code was used in each field: Green meant that the item was on task, yellow indicated concerns, and red signaled a danger. In addition to these fields, the team had an opportunity to specify their confidence in the project. A high score signaled that the project was moving along well and was within budget. The previously filed status reports were all very positive.

Jeff and the other development team members, themselves, were volunteers at the Information Technology Practice Center (ITPC). The ITPC is a consortium of IT professionals from the local university and industry. The ITPC provided consulting services for not-for-profit agencies and small businesses. Some of the consulting engagements, including the VCR engagement, were performed on a pro bono basis. Many of the engagements involved students so that the students could obtain experience with live IT projects. The project status reports were sent to the ITPC executive committee.

Jeff was concerned that the next status report would not be as positive. At the most recent team meeting, several issues emerged. First, the project team disagreed about the quality and adequacy of the UML documentation. Jeff made changes to the documentation produced by some members of the team, and these members took offense. Jeff wondered whether they had captured all of the key requirements and had accounted for these requirements in the project plan. Second, volunteer placement and tracking was not the only need of the VCR. Marilynn, the primary contact at the VCR, also needed a system to track donors and expenses. These additional features were part of the original project scope, but it was not clear whether the IS team could deliver a system with this functionality by the target delivery date in August. Third, other options emerged besides a custom-developed solution, including purchasing an off-the-shelf package. Jeff and the project team needed to recommend a particular approach. Finally, a recent problem emerged regarding the computer network. This problem must be solved before any solution is implemented. Could the team deliver the system within the target timeline?

Client Mission and Organization

The Volunteer Center of Racine (VCR) is a not-for-profit organization located in Racine, WI, a city with a population of 85,000. While it primarily serves the county of Racine, it also services occasional requests from nearby counties. Volunteer organizations have existed in Racine County for a long time, but were not formally managed. That is, it existed as a volunteer organization managed by volunteers, and with no full-time employees on its staff. Since there was no full-time management staff, it was difficult to coordinate activities of the volunteers and obtain the much-needed funds for volunteer activities. VCR emerged as a formal organization only three years ago. Within three years it grew rapidly to list and coordinate thousands of volunteers. It currently has 7,000 active volunteers. An active volunteer is one who has volunteered with VCR in the past 12 months. VCR finds volunteers and places these volunteers at various community events. The community events range from blood donation drives at hospitals to fundraising ceremonies for causes such as leukemia.

The mission of the VCR is stated on their Web site.

Mission: The Volunteer Center is a:
- **Leader** in our community that mobilizes people of all ages and backgrounds to volunteer by investing their resources of time & talent to make a difference in their own lives as well as the lives of those served.
- **Catalyst** for responding to community needs by creating, developing, implementing & supporting volunteer opportunities.
- **Connector** of people & resources with the needs & services in our community.
- **Advocate** for promoting the value of volunteerism.

Programs and services offered by VCR include:

1. **Retired and Senior Volunteer Program (RSVP).** This program involves adults, 55 and over. Volunteers use their life experiences and skills to help make the community stronger. These volunteers commonly work with children, adults, or help homeland security activities.
2. **Youth with a Mission.** This program serves several local organizations such as community centers, medical facilities, faith-based organizations, and schools. Volunteers who work in such programs are primarily from the youth population. The program strives to show how the power of community service can make a profound difference in their lives.
3. **Special Projects.** This program provides onetime volunteer opportunities for individuals, co-workers, families, or youth. Example special projects include Earth Day and Make a Difference Day, and walks to raise food to feed the poor and the hungry.
4. **Volunteer Recruitment.** VCR recruits volunteers and matches their interests, skills, and availability to a list of volunteer opportunities from local not-for-profit agencies, organizations, and schools in need of their support.
5. **Volunteer Training.** VCR provides quarterly training meetings for volunteer coordinators of not-for-profit groups and organizations.

Being a small not-for-profit organization funded completely by grants and donations, VCR has a very simple organization structure. It has a board of directors and an executive director. There are other coordinators and support staff as listed below.

Figure 1.

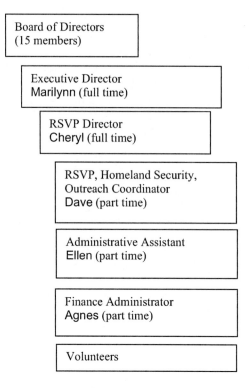

Marilynn, the executive director, believes that it is important that the organizational structure not be seen as a hierarchy. Rather, she pictures the full-time and part-time workers as a team working together to achieve the organization's goals (Figure 1).

VCR receives its funding primarily from federal/state grants, private companies, and individual donors. Its annual budget is approximately $278,000. Federal and state grants account for 65% of the budget. Corporate and private donations account for 27% and 8% respectively. The $278,000 annual budget is allocated to current employees, facilities, and programs. Additional expenditures, including funding for IT, can only be funded through new grants and donations.

Marilynn, Executive Director, and Cheryl, RSVP Director, are responsible for developing the strategic plan. This plan, as well as progress toward the plan's goals, is discussed with the board of directors. Consistent with VCR's mission, the strategic plan identifies activities that will support VCR's mission of finding, encouraging, and placing volunteers. Practically, the plan must also identify grant and other funding opportunities. Successful grant writing is critical to VCR's survival. Over the last year, VCR has focused on operational efficiency. As the size of VCR's volunteer base and opportunities have grown, the task of assigning and tracking volunteers has become more arduous. Success at grants has also resulted in significant administrative work. Grant writing, reports to funding agencies, and submitting reports to the state increasingly occupy Marilynn and

Cheryl's time. VCR believed that these tasks could be improved through the use of information technology.

Economic and Organizational Climate

The Wisconsin state budget and the budgets of local businesses, which are primarily manufacturing in nature, were adversely affected by the economy in 2003. These budgets are not expected to improve in the near future. The VCR and other not-for-profit agencies were increasingly under stress to find sources of revenue. Although the VCR has been successful in obtaining grants, the smaller pool of available funds is an ongoing concern.

As a result of the shrinking pool of money and their growth, Marilynn and Cheryl were eager to improve the operations of VCR. They met regularly with the ITPC group and were very appreciative of their efforts to date. Marilynn and Cheryl's support helped to motivate the other staff. In October, seven of VCR's employees and volunteers met with the ITPC group to discuss the features of the new information system.

SETTING THE STAGE

Project Team

The IS project team is composed of Jeff McCoy, Lyndsay Nash, Rick Harrington, Judy Taft, Bob Ferguson, and Zoya Alvi. Zoya Alvi is a graduate student in Computer Information Systems, while the remaining team members are senior students of Management Information Systems. In addition, both Jeff McCoy and Lyndsay Nash work full time for a major pharmaceutical company. Jeff has been with this corporation for more than 11 years, and is currently a senior computer software validation analyst. Lyndsay has been working for the pharmaceutical company for more than six years, and is currently a director's assistant. Just as in any project team, different members of the IS team have different abilities and personalities (Whitten, 2004). Jeff and Lyndsay both handled large-scale, complex projects in the past. Jeff is undoubtedly the most experienced person on the team and Lyndsay's experience is next. Jeff, based on his experience, was designated as the project manager. Jeff, by nature, is a very motivated person and seeks perfection from himself and others around him. Lyndsay is a dynamic, outgoing person who works hard to achieve the tasks at hand; however, she at times is not confident of her abilities, and some times has difficulty presenting even nice deliverables in a positive manner. Rick accomplishes tasks that are assigned to him, but lacks the skills to research an open problem and find solutions for it. Judy has no prior IS project experience, and requires an extensive amount of coaching on how to accomplish tasks in an IS project. Bob and Zoya are very well organized, responsible team members who follow any given task until it is satisfactorily completed. Bob and Zoya are recent additions to the project team.

In terms of capabilities, Jeff is skilled in project management, system analysis, system design, database development, and client-server programming. Lyndsay is skilled in project management, system analysis, and systems documentation. Rick is very comfortable with database development and client-server programming. Bob has expertise in implementation, troubleshooting, and network design. Zoya has expertise in project documentation, database design, client-server, as well as Web programming. Judy is skilled at system analysis and design.

The project team from VCR is primarily composed of Marilynn and Cheryl. Marilynn understands the high-level overview of the VCR operations, while Cheryl knows in detail the inner workings of the current systems and paper-based processes at VCR.

Project Initiation

Early in the project cycle, Jeff and his project team met with Marilynn and others from VCR to initiate the project. The VCR team was not familiar with the system development life cycle (SDLC) for constructing information systems (Dennis, 2002). Jeff and the project team explained the concepts behind SDLC and helped Marilynn create a system request (see Figure 2). Jeff forwarded a blank template of the system request to Marilynn, who then created a first draft. Jeff and Marilynn then sat together and refined the first draft into the system request document shown in Figure 2.

After the system request was developed, Lyndsay and Jeff conducted a feasibility study. The feasibility study focused on economic, technical, and organizational feasibility. Lyndsay and Jeff created extensive documentation to support the summary conclusions indicated.

- **Economic feasibility:** Based on the current available financial resources from the Volunteer Center, it has been determined that the proposed solution must be relatively inexpensive. Exact numbers were not available from the center; however, indications are that the Center can spend between $500 and $1,000 on this project. The Volunteer Center is in agreement that the value of this project greatly exceeds the allotted budget, but cannot support a larger budget at this time. Even with this budgetary constraint, the project team believed a solution can be obtained.
- **Technical feasibility:** With the young technical skills of the project team consisting of senior MIS students, a certain degree of risk appears to be evident. This risk is born out of the uncertainty in the skill-sets of the team (Ward & Chapman, 2003). The project team, however, is working closely with the ITPC members who have significant experience in building large-scale information systems. The faculty resources will guide the student project team in all aspects of the project.
- **Organizational feasibility:** An analysis of VCR staff indicates all end users are proficient with PCs. In addition, the VCR staff appears to be very open to accepting a new completely electronic system, as the current processes are highly inefficient.

Based on the above analysis, the project team concluded that the project meets the criteria for economic, technical, and organizational feasibility.

The Current System

Early in the system development process, the project team reviewed the current information systems at VCR. The VCR maintained and processed four general types of information: payroll, expenses, donors, and volunteer information. Agnes, the finance administrator, used a PC-based accounting application to process payroll and record expenses. Donors were recorded in a spreadsheet. Jeff and his team focused most of their time on the volunteer system. Information was manually gathered from each system to

Figure 2.

Date: September 18, 2003

SYSTEM REQUEST

Project Name: Information Systems for the Volunteer Center of Racine

Project Sponsor:
Name: Marilynn Pelky, Executive Director, Volunteer Center of Racine
Department:
Phone: 262-996-9612   Email: volunteer@bizwi.rr.com

Business Need:

VCR currently uses tools such as Excel to maintain information on the volunteers, organizations and the positions that the volunteers fill at different organizations.   VCR also uses an older system to keep track of volunteers 55 and older. However, these tools have several limitations and are unable to meet the growing requirements as the number of volunteers, organizations, and the funding agencies grow.

This project is aimed at obtaining a system that keeps track of the myriad pieces of information that VCR needs in a structured and organized database and provides the VCR employees a user-friendly interface to access the information and generate appropriate reports.

Functionality:

The VCR information system will:
- Maintain information on all volunteers in one integrated system.
- Maintain information on stations at which volunteers volunteer their time and the activities of the volunteers
- Maintain information on the donors to the VCR and the donations
- Generate reports for volunteer center management, and donors, which may include government agencies and private foundations
- Maintain and track expenses and budget

In addition, it is expected that all the above functions are integrated in one system with a user-friendly interface so that users with limited exposure to technology can use the system.

Expected Value:
Tangible:

- Because the quality of data on volunteers will improve with the new system, costs such as mailing costs can be reduced. An approximate estimate of this reduction is between $1,000 to $1,500.
- Since the new system will generate reports automatically, it is expected that the time to prepare reports for funding agencies will be reduced by 50%.

Intangible:

- Improved operations which will result in faster matching of volunteers with stations looking for volunteers.
- Improved satisfaction for the volunteers and for the stations.

Special Issues or Constraints:

- The VCR is new to project management methodologies. Hence, there may be a learning curve involved with different phases of the project.
- Since the project is to be carried out by students, ensuring the continuity of the student team is critical for the success of the project.

produce a variety of reports in preparation of grants and in fulfillment of state and national reporting requirements.

The VCR used terminology that was initially unfamiliar to the team. A *station* is a place where volunteers work by devoting their time and effort. Stations include local hospitals and schools where the volunteers work. A *job* refers to a specific activity that a volunteer performs at a specific station. Example jobs include driving seniors between a nursing home and a hospital or working at the reception desk at a blood-donation center. *Placement* is the process of matching volunteers, depending on their skills and interests, with specific jobs at stations.

Currently, VCR uses an electronic system for maintaining senior volunteers, 55 and older, and their activities under the Retired and Senior Volunteer Program (discussed below). Activities of all other volunteers (younger than 55 years) are maintained using paper processes. Jeff and his team documented the current business processes using UML documentation such as the use-case diagram. For a discussion of UML, the reader is referred to Arrington (2001). In addition, Appendix A provides an introduction to UML.

Jeff McCoy, leader of the project team, created the following use-case diagram to illustrate the different activities performed by the current electronic system.

The actors in the above use-case diagram include the following: 55-or-older volunteers, VCR-employees, station-coordinators. The current electronic system maintains information only on volunteers who are 55 or older. These volunteers fill out a paper application form to join VCR, indicate preferences on which station they would like to work, and respond to special-event mailings from VCR via phone or e-mail. In addition, volunteers can retire from VCR, and this activity is accomplished by phone or e-mail. VCR employees create volunteer records in the current electronic system for new volunteers who are 55 years or older. VCR employees may also update information on existing volunteers, and search for volunteers who might be interested in a specific job at a specific station. In addition, VCR employees may update volunteer activities including the number of hours spent by each volunteer in a job. Station coordinators communicate with VCR employees most often by phone, and they request volunteers for specific jobs at their stations. Station coordinators also communicate the number of hours spent by each volunteer at their stations in specific jobs by filling out a paper form. Most of these activities do not have any predetermined frequency and take place on-demand.

Note that the tasks performed by the volunteer and the station coordinator do not directly involve the current electronic system. However, the information obtained by performing these tasks is entered into the electronic system by the VCR employee.

The use-case diagram on the next page was also created by Jeff. This diagram includes all processes not integrated with the current electronic system. Some of the processes indicated in this use-case diagram do not necessarily involve "paper." However, they use manual processes such as using the typewriter or maintaining documents and spreadsheets that are not integrated with the electronic system described in the previous section (Figure 4).

The actors in the above use-case diagram include the following: VCR-employee and the donor.

As part of the "Generate Mailings" use case, VCR employees prepare word documents announcing opportunities to volunteers and mailing labels in Microsoft Word; they then mail them to volunteers. To accomplish the "Create Reports for Funding Agencies" use case, VCR employees obtain information on the number of hours spent

Figure 3. Use-case diagram for the current electronic system

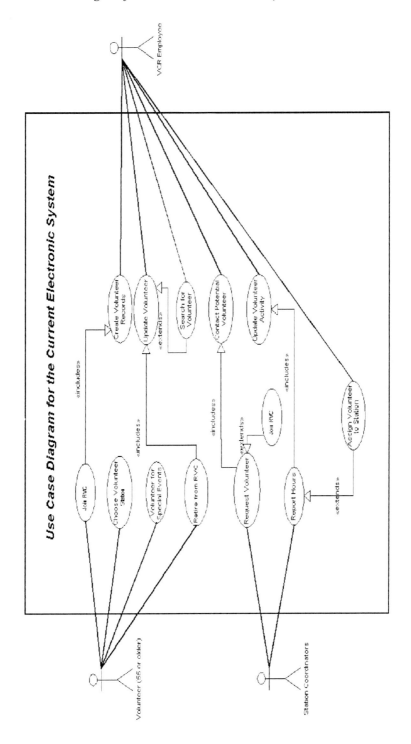

Figure 4. Use-case diagram for the current manual/paper processes (not integrated with the current electronic system)

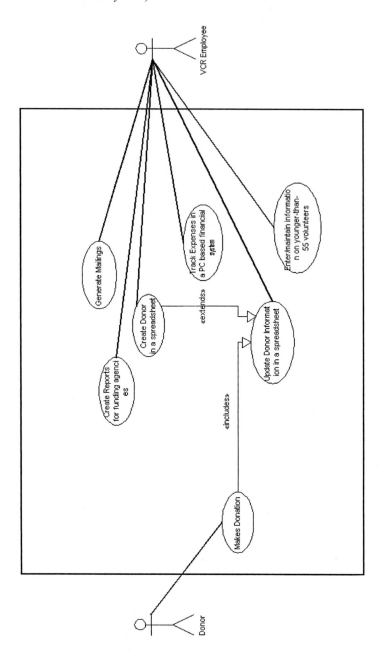

Figure 5. Volunteer Center of Racine — Use-case diagram

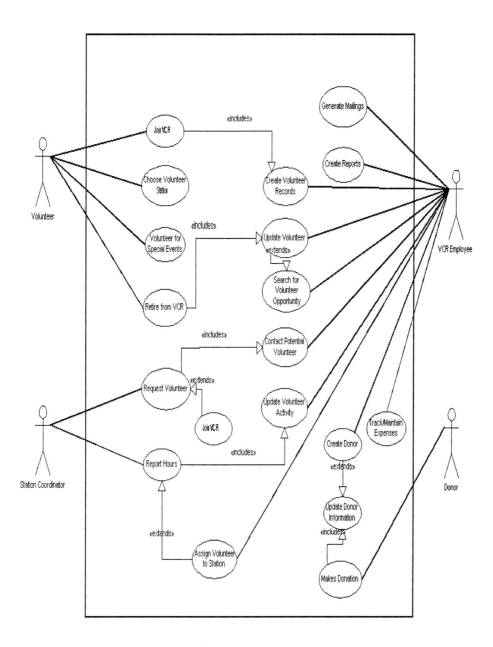

by volunteers on the electronic system, and type these hours on a report form that the funding agency provides. VCR employees track expenses in a PC-based financial system, while the donations to VCR and the donor information are maintained in a spreadsheet. Information on volunteers younger than 55 is also maintained in a spreadsheet.

Funding agencies are one source from which VCR gets its support, apart from donations by individual donors. Some of the funding agencies require reports on a regular basis. These reports should include the following pieces of information.

- Volunteer name
- Station name
- Station and job description
- Hours worked for the period

Some of the reports are indicated below.

- United Way Quarterly Report
- RSVP Homeland Security Report
- Wisconsin State Funding Report

From the above use-case diagram, it is clear that there is no comprehensive system at VCR that keeps track of the expenses, donations, and donors. In addition, volunteers who are younger than 55 are maintained in a spreadsheet.

Analysis of the Current System: Problems and Opportunities

Based on their analysis of the current system, Jeff and Lindsay developed a list of the following problems and opportunities for improvement.

- **Problem:** The Volunteer Center is using a hybrid paper and electronic system. *Opportunity:* Combine into one unified electronic system.
- **Problem:** The current electronic system is on one personal computer that holds data only on retired and senior volunteers (those who are 55 and over). Any remaining volunteer categories, such as youth and adult (under 55), are handwritten and entered on an Excel spreadsheet on a separate personal computer. *Opportunity:* Bring all volunteer data into one integrated system.
- **Problem:** The data is entered manually which can lead to input errors and data-integrity issues. For example, the same station names are entered differently at different times. *Opportunity:* Maintain consistent names and categories in the system, and minimize the user-input in the form of free text in the system.
- **Problem:** There is no support offered on the current electronic system. Questions about the operation of the RSVP system go unanswered. *Opportunity:* For the new system, provide support by creating user manuals.
- **Problem:** Reports are manually compiled. *Opportunity:* Improve the productivity of the VCR employees by generating reports required by different funding agencies electronically from the system.

- **Problem:** There are many fields of data required for reports that are currently not included in the system. Some of the fields that are not currently available in the existing system include person's ethnicity, driver's license number, actual number of hours for each volunteer, etc. A discussion with Marilynn revealed that there are at least 50 pieces of data not currently maintained by the system.
  Opportunity: Deliver a system so that it includes all the data needed by VCR.
- **Problem:** Security on the system seems to be non-existent.
  Opportunity: In the new system, provide security at the user level.
- **Problem:** The information cannot be shared with other users.
  Opportunity: Design the new system so that it is at least a client-server system so that users get their data from a centralized location (see Allamraju, 2001; Chalasani & Baldwin, 2003).
- **Problem:** There is no automatic backing-up of data in the current system. In addition, data could be typed over or errors made without proper verification at the time of entry.
  Opportunity: In the new system, arrive at procedures for backing up of data, and minimize the entry of free text by the users.

With these current processes in place, the Volunteer Center has struggled to perform two of its critical business functions. First, the Center has experienced difficulty in finding "best fit" volunteer candidates for stations requesting volunteer resources. As a result, a station requesting a volunteer may encounter situations where a volunteer's skills do not fully meet their needs. Secondly, the Center has encountered difficulty in accurately managing, tracking, and reporting volunteer resources using multiple systems. Because the Center relies on the volunteer resource reports to procure government funds, a consequence of inaccurate reporting is insufficient funding to the Center.

CASE DESCRIPTION

Jeff and the project team spent a considerable amount of time in the analysis and early design phases of the system development life cycle (SDLC). During this process several standard documents were produced, including use cases, a data model, and a project schedule. In addition, the project team noted other requirements, such as budget requirements, that would impact the choice of alternatives and the ultimate success of the project (Barki, Rivard, & Talbot, 2001). The various tasks required to complete the analysis and early design phases were divided among group members. Once an initial draft of a document was created, Jeff and Lindsay reviewed and integrated the work.

System Requirements

Early on, all parties agreed that the standard way to document the requirements was via use-case diagrams, and by providing details of each use case (Hoffer, 2002; Prowell & Poore, 2003). After numerous meetings with the VCR team, led by Marilynn, Jeff McCoy, with the help of the IS team, arrived at the following use-case diagram.

All processes, regardless of how they will be implemented, were documented as part of the use-case diagram (McConnell, 1998). There are four primary actors in this use-case diagram: Volunteer, VCR Employee, Station Coordinator, and the Donor. This use-case diagram shows the <<includes>> and <<extends>> relationships. For example, when a station coordinator reports hours, it triggers the "Update Volunteer Activity," and hence there is an <<includes>> relationship between the two activities. Similarly, updating information on a volunteer may cause a VCR employee to search for volunteer opportunities. Hence, there is an <<extends>> relationship between the "Update Volunteer" and "Search for Volunteer Opportunity" use cases.

Different members of the IS team documented the details of each use case (Booch, 1999; Krushten, 1999). For example, the "Join VCR" use case, developed by Lindsay, is detailed in Table 1. It includes key aspects such as the stakeholders, relationships to other use cases, normal flow of events, and alternate flows. This use case has three different alternate flows which model three different business scenarios in which a volunteer may join VCR (including enrolling by telephone, finding an enrollment form on the Web, and enrolling at an external recruiting event).

Table 2 indicates the details of the use case "Create Volunteer Records."

In addition to the use cases, the project team documented the following high-level requirements for the VCR information system.

(R1)   Need to maintain volunteers and their information.
(R2)   Need to maintain stations at which volunteers volunteer their time and the activities of the volunteers.
(R3)   Need to maintain information on the donors to the RVC and the donations.
(R4)   Need to generate reports for volunteer center management, and donors, which may include government agencies, private foundations.
(R5)   Need to maintain and track expenses and budget.
(R6)   Need to convert/transform current data into the new system, once the new system is built.

In addition to the use cases, the IS team developed a data model to highlight the data requirements of the system. The initial data model was developed by Judy. Part of the ER model (Baldwin & Paradice, 2000) is shown on the next page. The main entity in the ER model is the Person entity. Person has many attributes such as name and ethnicity. A person can be of multiple types — "Volunteer," "Donor," "Station Coordinator," and so forth. The type of a person is captured using the PersonType lookup table and PersonPersonType cross-reference table. This model is capable of maintaining multiple addresses, e-mail addresses, and phone numbers for a person. PersonPhone, PersonEmail, PersonAddress are separate entities that capture this data. Since most volunteers are retired and senior volunteers, it is possible that volunteers have some disability that restricts them from certain types of volunteer activities. PersonDisability captures this data, while PersonInterest captures the activities that a volunteer may be interested in (Figure 6).

The entities and the data fields contained in a few example entities are described in Table 3. Judy developed the initial version of the data dictionary (Hoffer, 2002). Jeff modified various entries to correspond to his view of the data requirements.

Special Requirements

Not-for-profit organizations frequently face challenges that may not be faced by for-profit organizations. These challenges most often stem from budgetary and time

Table 1.

Use-case name: Join VCR	ID: 1	Importance level: High
Primary actor: Volunteer	Use case type: Detailed, Essential	
Stakeholders and interests: Volunteer - Want to volunteer to provide a community service. VCR - Want many volunteers to join VCR.		
Brief description: Volunteer joins VCR and has the ability to volunteer.		
Trigger: Volunteer decides to volunteer at VCR.		
Type: External (event driven)		

Relationships:
    Association: Volunteer, VCR, Enrollment Form
    Include: Use Case: Create Volunteer Records
    Extend:
    Generalization:		

Prerequisites: Volunteer desire to perform volunteer services in the community through the VCR.		

Normal flow of events:
  1. Volunteer arrives at VCR.
  2. Volunteer inquires about volunteer work.
  3. VCR provides enrollment form.
  4. Volunteer completes enrollment form.
  5. VCR employee accepts enrollment from.
  6. Execute: Create Volunteer Records.		

Subflows: (Groups of Subflows should start with a caption that describes the subflow group. The caption should be identified with a label in the following format: S-# (e.g., S-1, S-2))		
Alternate/exceptional flows: 1a-1. Volunteer contacts VCR by telephone. 1a-2. VCR employee invites volunteer to VCR. 1a-3. Proceed to Step 3. 1b-1. Volunteer connects to VCR Web site. 1b-2. Volunteer complete online enrollment form. 1b-3. Volunteer prints copy of enrollment form. 1b-4. Volunteer delivers enrollment form to VCR. 1b-5. Proceed to Step 5. 1c-1. Volunteer completes enrollment form through an external recruiting event. 1c-2. VCR employee delivers enrollment form to VCR. 1c-2. Proceed to Step 5.		

constraints. For the Volunteer Center of Racine, even though Marilynn and Cheryl were completely committed to the project, they are unable to secure even limited funding to implement the project. For example, purchasing high-end PCs that implement new software is not an option; instead, they depend on local companies to donate equipment such as PCs. In addition, due to budgetary constraints, their current server and PCs are connected by a wireless network. The wireless network itself is supported by Mike Daniels, another volunteer. However, the wireless network is very unreliable with the client PCs losing their connections to the server very often during the day. Thus far, Mike has not been able to spend enough time to come up with a solution to the network

Table 2.

Use-case name: Create Volunteer Records	ID: 2	Importance level: High
Primary actor: VCR		Use-case type: Detailed, Essential

Stakeholders and interests: VCR - Wants to have a record of all volunteers.		
Brief description: VCR employee enters the new volunteer information into the system.		
Trigger: New volunteer completes enrollment form. **Type:** External (event driven)		

Relationships:
       Association: VCR
       Include:
       Extend:
       Generalization:		

Prerequisites: Must complete Use-Case: Join Volunteer Center.		

Normal flow of events:
   1.   VCR employee obtains enrollment form.
   2.   VCR employee gives enrollment form to Program Manager.
   3.   VCR Program Manager reviews enrollment from.
   4.   VCR Program Manager gives enrollment form to VCR employee for entry.
   5.   VCR employee enters information in the system.
   6. VCR employee files hard copy into file cabinet.		

Subflows: (Groups of Subflows should start with a caption that describes the subflow group. The caption should be identified with a label in the following format: S-# (e.g., S-1, S-2))		

Alternate/exceptional flows:
  3a-1. Program Manager finds error or incomplete form.
  3a-2. Program Manager or VCR employee contact volunteer for accurate information.
  3a-3. Proceed to Step 4.		

problem. Jeff and the project team are confident that they can implement a wired network for the VCR under a budget of $500. However, funding for this has not yet been secured. Such problems are routine in a non-profit organization, and cause dependencies that may affect the project schedules and project timelines significantly.

Another requirement for the project is that it should be completed by August so that Cheryl and others at the volunteer center can start using the system for numerous fall volunteer activities. In addition, implementing the new system in August will also facilitate creation of the year-end reports needed by the funding agencies using this new system.

Proposed Designs

Jeff and Rick arrived at four alternative solutions for the Volunteer Center Project. They presented these alternatives to the IS team, which conducted an analysis of the alternatives. Alternatives range from complete off-the-shelf packages to total custom developed system approaches. The identified alternatives and their analyses are presented below.

Figure 6. A partial ER model for the VCR database system

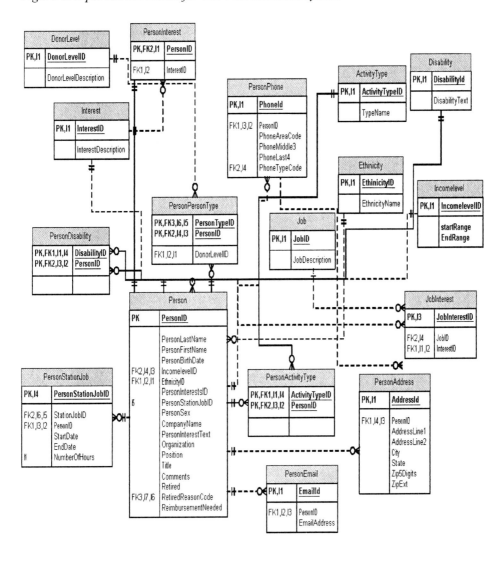

Alternative #1. Purchase Off-the-Shelf

This alternative would entail the purchase of commercially available off-the-shelf software that meets all the documented requirements. The product would then be used "as-is" with no additional configuring or modifications to meet the special needs of the business.

- **Benefits:** Complete system, reliable/proven system, customer support available.
- **Weaknesses:** High cost, proprietary code that cannot be modified easily for future customization or modifications, inability to configure to meet users' needs.

Table 3.

	Name:	Person
	Type:	Structure
	Alias:	
	Description:	Person is used to model a Volunteer, a Donor, a VCR employee or a Station coordinator
I	Fields:	PersonID, PersonLastName, PersonFirstName, PersonBirthDate, IncomeLevelID, EthnicityID, PersonInterestID, PersonStationJobID, PersonSex, CompanyName, PersonInterestText, Organization, Position, Title, Comments, Retired, RetiredReasonCode, ReimbursementNeeded

	Name:	PersonType
	Type:	Structure
II	Alias:	
	Description:	Lookup table containing values for person types (volunteer, donor etc.)
	Fields:	PersonTypeID, TypeName

	Name:	DonorLevel
	Type:	Structure
III	Alias:	
	Description:	Lookup table containing different donor levels depending on their contribution (Gold/Silver/Bronze).
	Fields:	DonorLevelID, DonorLevelDescription

	Name:	StationContacts
	Type:	Structure
IV	Alias:	
	Description:	Information on contact persons for each station is maintained in this entity
	Fields:	StationID, PersonID, PersonTypeID

	Name:	StationJob
	Type:	Structure
V	Alias:	
	Description:	Jobs at any station are maintained here
	Fields:	StationJobID, StationID, JobID, StatoinJobStartDate, StationEndDate, Impact

	Name:	Station
	Type:	Structure
VI	Alias:	
	Description:	Maintains information on a station
	Fields:	StationID, StationName, StationTypeID, GroupAffiliationID, Contract Date

Alternative #2. Purchase Configurable

This alternative would entail the purchase of commercially available off-the-shelf software that could be further configured by the user/developer. The product would be modified to meet the special needs of the business.

- **Benefits:** Ability to configure as per requirements, large selection of vendors, availability of customer support.

- **Weaknesses:** High cost, special skills needed to configure, limited customer support once configured.

Alternative #3. Custom Develop

This alternative would entail the purchasing of no software by the Volunteer Center. All software will be built by the project team to meet the special needs of the business.

- **Benefits:** Low cost, ability to build to meet users' exact needs, standard programming languages can be used (Visual Basic, Java, etc.).
- **Weaknesses:** Special skills needed to build, special skills needed to support, undefined maintenance responsibilities.

Alternative #4. Reengineer Existing System

This alternative would entail the reengineering of the existing system in place at the Volunteer Center. This alternative *cannot* be considered, as the existing system is a hybrid comprised of electronic and paper business processes. In addition, the existing electronic system uses proprietary code that is not accessible to the project team. A best attempt at reengineering would be to contact the software supplier and review current off-the-shelf offerings (the use of Alternative #1). This alternative was not considered further.

As the project team managed by Jeff pondered on the above alternatives, they needed to choose one of the above alternatives in a logical way (Goseva-Popstojanova, 2003). It appeared to Jeff that purchasing an off-the-shelf component (Alternative #1) will require at least $5,000, and may be as high as $15,000. Alternative #2 has similar costs for purchasing the software. In addition, some of these products require customers to sign a multi-year maintenance deal that can run into hundreds of dollars per year. On the other hand, a custom-developed solution (Alternative #3) will require a significant amount of time to be spent in system design and development. The VCR will not have to pay for this alternative, since this will be done by the IS project team on a pro bono basis.

Project Schedule and Remaining Tasks

In order to help determine the viability of the custom-development approach, Jeff and Lindsay decided to sketch a schedule for this alternative. Their high-level schedule is indicated in Table 4.

Even though the Waterfall method has been followed until the design phase, Jeff and the project team decided to use a phased approach that will implement the system in three different phases at the VCR site. The reason to use such a phased approach is to reduce the risk of implementation facing too many implementation problems, and also to incorporate user feedback into the system before the end of the project (Jorgensen 2004).

Approximately 50 screens need to be developed for the VCR information system. In addition, Microsoft SQL server software will be installed and used to maintain the data. The approximate division of effort among team members to accomplish these tasks is shown in Table 5.

Table 4.

Phase	Start Date	End Date	Completed?
Planning	09/16/03	10/31/03	Yes
Analysis	11/01/03	03/31/04	Yes
Design	04/01/04	05/15/04	In progress
Implementation (including Development)	05/15/04	07/31/04 Phase #1 - 05/31/04 Phase #2 - 06/30/04 Phase #3 - 07/31/04	Yet to begin
Post Implementation Support		08/2004	Yet to begin

Table 5.

Item	Task	Approximate Hours	Person Assigned	Start Date	End Date
1	Development, testing, and implementation of 10 screens	100	Bob Ferguson	5/15/2004	6/30/2004
2	Development, testing, and implementation of 20 screens	200	Zoya Alvi	5/15/2004	7/15/2004
4	Development, testing, and implementation of 20 screens	200	Rick Harrington	5/15/2004	7/15/2004
5	Development of Database in MS SQL Server and Installation of MS SQL Server and Troubleshooting	100	Lyndsay Nahf	4/1/2004	5/15/2004
6	Data Conversion from the current System to the New System	50	Lyndsay Nash	5/1/2004	6/30/2004
7	Creation of Test Plans	75	Lyndsay Nash	4/1/2004	5/15/2004
8	Project Coordination and Management	250	Jeff McCoy	1/10/2004	7/31/2004
9	Post-Implementation Support	75	Yet to be determined	8/1/2004	9/30/2004
	TOTAL	1,050			

CURRENT CHALLENGES/PROBLEMS FACING THE ORGANIZATION

The ITPC offices were quiet by the time Jeff began to fill in the project status report. The tone of the most recent meeting interfered with his ability to think. Jeff's drive for perfection created friction between him and some of his team members who felt belittled by his criticism of their work (Barki & Harwick, 2001). As an instance, when the data model and the data dictionary completed by Judy were substandard, Jeff spent a large amount of time modifying the models. Jeff felt that he needed to provide feedback and, if necessary, complete the task himself in order to obtain satisfactory results. He could not figure out why members of his team had problems with this approach (Radosevich, 1998).

In addition to the personnel issues, several other issues needed to be considered. Should the team recommend purchasing software or custom developing a solution? What risks face the project and how can the risks be mitigated (Ward & Chapman, 2003; Goseva-Popstojanova, 2003)? How might the risks affect the project schedule? Will the project be completed on time? Are there any omissions in the requirements specification? How should the team manage the project scope?

Jeff glanced at this watch, which now read 6:55. "Late movies are always good, fewer people in the theater," he thought.

REFERENCES

Allamaraju, S. et al. (2001). *Professional Java server programming J2EE 1.3 Edition.* Birmingham, UK: WROX Press.

Arrington, C. T. (2001). *Enterprise Java with UML.* Indianapolis, IN: OMG Press, John Wiley & Sons.

Baldwin, D., & Paradice, D. (2000). *Application development in Microsoft Access 2000.* Cambridge, MA: Course Technology.

Barki, H., & Hartwick, J. (2001). Interpersonal conflict and its management in information systems development. *MIS Quarterly, 25*(2), 195-228.

Barki, H., Rivard, S., & Talbot, J. (2001). An integrative contingency model of software project risk management. *Journal of Management Information Systems, 17*(4), 37-39.

Booch, G., Rumbaugh, J., & Jacobson, I. (1999). *The Unified Modeling Language user guide.* Reading, MA: Addison-Wesley-Longman.

Chalasani, S., & Baldwin, D. (2003). Software architectures for an extensible Web-based survey system. *Proceedings of the 2003 IASTED International Conference on Software Engineering and Applications,* Marina del Rey, CA.

Dennis, A. et al. (2002). *Systems analysis and design: An object oriented approach with UML.* Indianapolis, IN: OMG Press, John Wiley & Sons.

Goseva-Popstojanova, K. et al. (2003). Architectural-level risk analysis using UML. *IEEE Transactions on Software Engineering, 29*(10), 946-960.

Hoffer, J. A. et al. (2002). *Modern systems analysis & design.* Upper Saddle River, NJ: Prentice-Hall.

Hoffer, J. A. et al. (2002). *Modern database management.* Upper Saddle River, NJ: Prentice-Hall.

Jorgensen, M. (2004). Realism in assessment of effort estimation uncertainty: It matters how you ask. *IEEE Transactions on Software Engineering, 30*(4), 209-217.

Krushten, P. (1999). *The rational unified process: An introduction.* Reading, MA: Addison-Wesley-Longman.

McConnell, S. (1998). *Software project survival guide.* Redmond, WA: Microsoft Press.

Prowell, S. J., & Poore, J. H. (2003). Foundations of sequence-based software specification. *IEEE Transactions on Software Engineering, 29*(5), 417-429.

Radosevich, L. (1998, October 1). Smells like team spirit. *CIO Magazine*.

Ward, S., & Chapman, C. (2003). Transforming project risk management into project uncertainty management. *International Journal of Project Management, 21*(2).

Whitten, J. L. et al. (2004). *Systems analysis and design methods*. New York: McGraw-Hill-Irwin.

APPENDIX A

A Brief Introduction to UML

This section is written by the authors from the information gathered from the references indicated in the references section. Unified Modeling Language (UML) is a language for specifying, visualizing, constructing, and documenting the artifacts of a software system. UML provides a precise notation needed to model software systems. It enables the creation and communication of ideas.

- **Abstraction.** Abstraction means simplification or model of a real-world object or a process or a complex concept. A good abstraction highlights the relevant characteristics and behavior of something that is too complex to understand in its entirety. Abstraction helps us understand how different parts of a larger model interact together. Different interacting parts of a model are referred to as *objects*.
- **Encapsulation.** Encapsulation means that data and behavioral logic are hidden within the object. Abstraction highlights the important aspects of an object, while encapsulation hides the cumbersome internal details of the object. A well-encapsulated object allows other objects to use it without depending on any internal details.
- **Object.** A particular and finite element of a larger model. Examples of an object are indicated below.

  O   A specific car in a car dealer's inventory system (very concrete object)
  O   Individual's savings account in a banking system (invisible object)
  O   A transaction in a banking system (object with a short life)

  Objects have *state*, which describes their current condition and characteristics. For example, the car object has some characteristics such as make/model that never change, and other characteristics such as mileage that change over time.
  Objects have *behavior*, which describes the actions other objects may perform on an object.
  For example, the customer object may withdraw/deposit money from/into the bank account object. Logic corresponding to this behavior resides within the object. Similarly, this behavior depends on the state. Each object in the system must be *uniquely identifiable*. There must be one or more characteristics that set each object apart from the other objects. For example, the Vehicle ID Number uniquely distinguishes one car object from another.
  Class. A class is a group of objects that have something in common. A class provides an abstraction for the object and a *template* for object creation. It specifies

the type of data that the object can hold. It also specifies the type and number of objects that it knows about. For example, a car object may maintain information on one or more previous owners.

An object may have an association with a single object, with a certain number of objects, or with an unlimited number of objects. *Multiplicity* indicates the number of other objects to which a given object is related. There are several different types of relationships between objects. Some of these relationship types are described as follows.

- **Dependency relationship.** Dependency is the weakest relationship between objects. An object depends on an object if it has a short-term relationship with the object. A dependent object calls the methods of the other object to obtain services. In the object-oriented world, dependency means that an object may create an object as part of a method, configure it, and pass the object to the calling method as a return value. Or, an object may receive an object as a parameter to a method, use it or modify it, then forget about it when the method ends. For example the cashier object may interact with the customer object to ring up grocery items, a relationship that is inherently short term.

- **Association relationship.** Association is a long-term relationship between objects. Under association, an object can keep a reference to another object and call the other object's methods, as it needs them. An object may instantiate another object and keep it for future use. In addition, an object may receive an object as a parameter to a configuration method and keep a reference to the object.

- **Aggregation relationship.** An aggregation relationship indicates that an object is part of a greater whole. The contained object may participate in more than one aggregate relationship, and exists independently of the whole. For example, a developer object may exist on its own, but a project object may consist of multiple developer objects in addition to other objects.

- **Composition relationship.** An object is owned by a greater whole. The contained object may not participate in more than one composition relationship, and cannot exist independently of the whole. The part is created as part of the creation of the whole and is destroyed when the whole is destroyed. For example, a small gear object may not exist on its own, but should be completely contained as part of the engine object.

- **Interface.** Each interface completely specifies the signature of one or more methods, complete with parameters and return type. An interface captures abstraction, without addressing any implementation details. A class realizes an interface by implementing each method in the interface. Interfaces provide flexibility.

- **Polymorphism.** Polymorphism through inheritance means that more than one class inherits from a base class (extends). Polymorphism through realization means that more than one class can implement an interface (implements). An advantage of polymorphism is the unlimited flexibility it provides. That is, different implementations can be mixed and matched to achieve interesting effects. Another advantage is long-term extensibility. That is, new implementations can be introduced without affecting the code that depends on an interface.

  UML enables developers to build a single coherent model that describes a software system from several perspectives. A variety of participants can use the same model and speak the same language throughout the development process. Some of the diagrams that are developed as part of UML are indicated below.

- **Use-case diagrams.** A use-case diagram models all interactions between the user and a system in a single high-level diagram. A use-case diagram allows developers and customers to understand/capture the intent and scope of the system. Use-case diagrams are constructed by finding actors, finding use cases and the interactions between the actors and the use cases. In addition to the use-case diagram, often detailed descriptions of each use are constructed.
- **Class diagram.** A class diagram defines and constrains a group of objects in detail. It shows the state, behavior, and relationships with other objects that are mandated for each object that is instantiated from the class.
- **Sequence diagram.** A sequence diagram depicts how objects interact with one another to provide functionality corresponding to a single use case. A sequence diagram indicates the order of the interaction and the order of messages between objects. Sequence diagrams are often constructed based on the following steps:

  1. Add the objects that participate in accomplishing the use case to the sequence diagram.
  2. Work forward from the actor, finding behavior and messages between the objects as the use-case functionality is developed.
  3. Validate the sequence from the end.

For the purpose of object-oriented analysis, objects are classified into four categories: Entity, LifeCycle, Control, and Boundary objects. These four types of objects are described below. A sequence diagram often depicts the sequence of messages that flow between boundary, control, lifecycle, and entity objects.

- **Boundary objects.** Boundary objects are useful for presenting information to the actors (users). Boundary objects are identified by examining the relationship between the actors and the use cases. Each actor/use-case pair forms a boundary object.
- **Control objects.** Control objects provide workflow and session services to other objects.
  A high-level message from the boundary object to the control object is converted into a series of messages from the control object to the lifecycle and entity objects. Each use case translates into one control object. Control objects do not encapsulate any business logic; most business logic is delegated to the lifecycle and entity objects.
- **Entity objects.** Entity objects encapsulate the business data and part of the business logic of the system. Entity objects often have the attributes and the get/set methods that read/modify these attributes. For example, an account is an entity object, and similarly customer is an entity object.
- **Lifecycle objects.** Often, there is only one lifecycle object for each entity class. The lifecycle object is useful for accumulating and finding different instances of an entity class. Common functions of a lifecycle object include create, destroy and locate entity objects. Sometimes, lifecycle objects are also referred to as *factory*, *home*, and *container* objects.

APPENDIX B

Sample Project Status Report

PROJECT STATUS REPORT
Reporting Period: 12/02/03
PROJECT: Volunteer Center of Racine
PROJECT SPONSORS: Marilynn Pelky (VCR), Suresh Chalasani, and Dirk Baldwin (UW-Parkside)
PROJECT MANAGER: Jeffery McCoy
PROJECT TEAM: Jeffery McCoy, Rick Harrington, Judy Taft, Lyndsay Nash
SUBJECT MATTER EXPERTS: Marilynn Pelky (VCR), Suresh Chalasani, and Dirk Baldwin (Project Advisors)
PROJECT OVERVIEW: The project is to create a new system for the Racine Volunteer Center. The system should allow for better overall management of past, present, and future volunteers, donors, and businesses/organizations with volunteer needs ("stations"). The system will allow for new volunteers to be entered into the system and their progress to be documented and monitored. The system will also allow for donor information to be stored and updated to be used for miscellaneous purposes, including the reporting of state taxes. Thirdly, the system will allow for a higher quality of management of the stations to better track the needs of the business/organization, providing a higher level of volunteer service. Finally, the system will provide several reports that encompass the above listed processes for better overall documentation and control.

Project Current Status Summary

On Time	On Budget	People	Process	Technology	Confidence
Yellow	Green	Green	Green	Green	10

FOR ANY YELLOW, RED, or CONFIDENCE less than a 5 status identify:

ISSUE	*ACTION PLAN*
Currently there is only one programmer assigned to complete this project. The project requires a project manager and one additional programmer, at minimum.	We have a commitment from one student to join the team as a programmer for next semester. We also have a second potential student looking into joining next semester as well.
We have had a few additional requirements given to us by VCR. We do not anticipate much set-back, however our diagrams, data dictionary, etc. will require updating.	Update the diagrams, use cases, data dictionary ASAP.

Project Summary KEY:

On Task	Concerns	Danger
Green	Yellow	Red

Note: Include words Green, Yellow and Red in appropriate cells for B/W printers

Confidence Scale:
1= Project is beyond salvage, cannot to be completed with satisfactory deliverables
3= May be able to complete portions of the project with overruns likely
5= Project still has many unknowns but average risk for completion
7= Project moving well towards completion, adequate resources available
10= Project is virtually a certainty to complete on time, on budget, and to scope

Suresh Chalasani is an associate professor of management information systems at the University of Wisconsin - Parkside. Professor Chalasani specializes in supply chain management systems, e-commerce systems, technologies for e-commerce systems, parallel computing, and bioinformatics applications. He is a member of IEEE and IASTED, and has published extensively in IEEE *and journals and conferences in the area of information systems. Dr. Chalasani was a recipient of multiple research and instructional grants from the National Science Foundation and the University of Wisconsin System.*

Dirk Baldwin is an associate professor of management information systems and department chair of business at the University of Wisconsin - Parkside. Professor Baldwin conducts research related to multiple view systems, decision support systems, and document management. He has published in journals such as the Journal of MIS *and* IEEE Transactions on System, Man, and Cybernetics. *He has coauthored books on MS Access. Professor Baldwin is chair of the Information Technology Practice Center and was named Wisconsin Idea Fellow by the University of Wisconsin Board of Regents.*

Jayavel Sounderpandian is professor of quantitative methods at the University of Wisconsin - Parkside. He teaches project management, operations management, business statistics, and a few elective subjects. He has published in Operations Research, Interfaces, Abacus, Journal of Risk and Uncertainty, International Journal of Production Economics, *and several others. He coauthored the book* Complete Business Statistics *(McGraw-Hill/Irwin). He has won several awards for excellence in research and in teaching. He has 24 years of academic experience and seven years of industry experience. He is a consultant to many businesses in the region, and guides many students to do projects in those businesses.*

This case was previously published in the *Journal of Cases on Information Technology*, 7(4), pp. 79-104, © 2005.

Chapter II

Big-Bang ERP Implementation at a Global Company

Nava Pliskin, Ben-Gurion University of the Negev, Israel

Marta Zarotski, Ben-Gurion University of the Negev, Israel

EXECUTIVE SUMMARY

Dead Sea Works is an international multi-firm producer of Potash and other chemicals whose sales for 1998 were about $500 million. In 1996, the Information Systems group convinced top management to pursue a big-bang ERP implementation of SAP R/3. To reduce project risk, risk management was practiced. First, only modules that matched the functionality of the then-existing systems were targeted, avoiding as much as possible software modifications and process reengineering. Second, a steering committee was set up to handle conflict resolution and set priorities throughout the project and top users were given responsibility with implementing modules within their respective functions. R/3 went into production on July 1, 1998, six months ahead of schedule and without exceeding the $4.95 million budget.

BACKGROUND

Dead Sea Works Ltd., one of 15 member companies of Israel Chemicals LTD, is a producer of Potash and other chemical products from the mineral-rich Dead Sea, Israel's greatest natural resource. Situated at the lowest place on earth, it lies in a valley whose southern part is suitable for evaporation pans and enjoys ample sunlight for most of the year. This combination of chemical riches and topography that is amenable to practical use fired the imagination of Theodore Herzl, the father of modern Zionism. After hearing of a plan to extract minerals from the Dead Sea, during his 1896 visit to Palestine, Herzl described in his book *Alt Neuland*, a Jewish State whose economic strength would be derived from the treasures of the Dead Sea.

Moshe Novomeisky, chemical engineer, came from Siberia to Palestine at the beginning of the century inspired by *Alt Neuland* to turn this vision into a reality. In 1930, he obtained from the British Mandatory authorities a concession to extract minerals from the Dead Sea, established the Palestine Potash Company LTD, and constructed a plant in the northern part of the Dead Sea. In 1934 evaporation pans and a chemical plant were constructed in Sodom as well. This became the foundation for today's Dead Sea Works (DSW) which, since it was reestablished in the 1950s, has increased production steadily to its current level of close to three million tons of Potash per year. In addition to Potash, DSW produces Magnesium Chloride Flakes and Pellets, Salt, Bath Salts, Magnesium Metal, Chlorine and Bromine.

Instead of mining, as do most of its competitors, DSW extracts Potash from the Dead Sea. The production process begins with the pumping of Dead Sea water to 105 square-kilometer salt pans, where the solution is concentrated. An additional 40 square-kilometer pans are then used to crystallize materials, which after settling on the pan floor, are pumped by harvesters directly into refineries. In this process, DSW takes advantage of the energy of the sun, another important natural resource in the region. Artificially, these drying processes would require 10 million tons of oil per year.

Wherever Potash is produced, transportation is a major expense, as was the case for DSW because of the 900-meter altitude difference between the factory at Sodom, the lowest point on earth, and the nearest railway terminal. Since this gradient rules out the possibility of a direct rail link and the remote location makes road transportation expensive, DSW chose to build from Sodom to the railway an 18-km conveyor belt, whose incline at some points reaches 18 degrees. Since its completion in April 1987, DSW's transportation costs have declined substantially.

Currently, the multi-firm DSW Group (see Figure 1) is distributed internationally (e.g., Europe, and China) and within Israel (e.g., Sodom, Beer-Sheva, and Eilat). In Europe, DSW has been involved in several joint ventures. In 1996, DSW established Dead Sea Magnesium LTD., investing with Volkswagen (65%, 35%) close to $500 million. Yearly production capacity at the new plant has already reached 25,000 tons and, by the end of 1999, is expected to grow by 50%. In 1998, DSW has partnered with Eurobrom B.V. in Clearon Holding Corporation and acquired from the Spanish-Companies Authority, jointly with two Spanish partners, Grupo Potash, a producer of one million tons of Potash per year sold mainly to the Spanish and French markets. In late 1998, DSW joined the Chinese government in building a Potash production plant that will eventually produce 860 thousand tons every year. This joint venture is expected to increase DSW's sales to China, a market whose Potash consumption per year grows at a rate that exceeds the world's rate.

Figure 1. DSW mult-firm structure

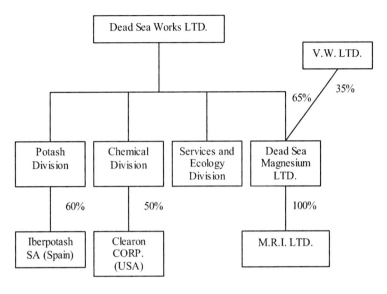

Figure 2. World-wide Potash sales; Total: 2,850 thousand tons

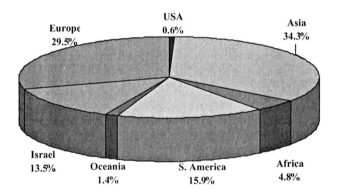

Due to these expansion activities, the number of DSW employees almost doubled over the last two years, reaching 2,458 at the end of 1998. Potash sales worldwide, which reached about 42 million tons in 1998, are growing at a rate of 3% each year (see Figure 2). The American and Asian markets are the biggest Potash consumers and importers, since their own production does not meet the demand. DSW sells to 50 countries on every continent, protecting itself from local market fluctuations, and is expected to increase its share in world Potash production from six to nine percent. Even though 10% of its sales are directed to one of its clients, DSW is not dependent on any one customer. It is also

Figure 3. DSW performance highlights

FINANCIAL FIGURES (in thousands of U.S. dollars)	1993	1994	1995	1996	1997	1998
Revenues	245,342	295,910	362,280	357,567	453,185	493,710
Net Income	17,852	28,013	35,171	39,840	39,645	49,901
Total Assets	526,462	628,092	742,182	934,450	983,598	1,245,460
Shareholders' Equity	305,703	320,109	333,005	351,372	368,415	418,468
Dividend Paid	21,792	13,907	13,917	21,220	36,808	9,680
Capital Expenditures	134,400	156,400	216,400	306,321	126,460	57,816
Earnings $ Per Share of NIS 1 par value (in $ U.S.)	0.06	0.10	0.12	0.13	0.13	0.17

QUANTITY FIGURES (in thousands of Metric Tons)	1993	1994	1995	1996	1997	1998
Potash Production	2,182	2,099	2,207	2,492	2,481	2,860
Potash Sales	1,968	2,317	2,451	2,178	2,861	2,916
Casted Magnesium Production	-	-	-	-	7.2	24.5
Casted Magnesium Sales	-	-	-	-	5.4	15.1
Table Salt Sales	58	63	80	86	104	99
Magnesium Chloride Flaked and Pellets Sales	51	74	81	90	68	63
Bath Salts Sales	1.3	2.2	1.9	1.9	2.2	2.1
Pan Salts Sales	268	235	178	191	261	219
Number of Employees	1,629	1,654	1,670	2,030	2,245	2,103

free from dependence on any supplier and any material that is not included in its license from the Israeli government.

Because DSW is a global company, its financial performance depends on trends in the world economy, including the economic conditions in South East Asia, Russia, and changing attitudes toward the environment. Despite periods when world Potash prices reached record low levels, DSW recorded a profit every year since 1970, while many of its competitors have faced difficulties (see Figure 3).

Strategically, DSW is focused on persistent growth by taking the following measures. First, DSW is constantly expanding Potash production in Sodom and else-where, while lowering costs. Second, DSW is accelerating business development around the world (e.g., in China and in Spain), including joint ventures in Salt and Chloride Aluminum. Third, DSW is investing in development of power and water resources. Finally, in the marketing arena, DSW is paying attention to widespread distribution of sales, sensing customer needs and responding to them.

SETTING THE STAGE

Information Systems (IS) at DSW were custom-developed specifically for DSW since the early 1970s, when the IS unit consisted of an IS manager, six data-entry clerks, three operators, and four programmers. The first functions to be automated, in batch mode, were accounting, costing, and budgeting. The number of users in those early days was 20. When hardware was upgraded in 1978 to IBM's System 3 Model 15, each functional IS was operating in isolation, using its own removable disk.

A technological turnaround took place in the 1980s in terms of both hardware and software. The IBM 4331 mainframe computer running the VSE operating system was acquired, setting the stage for later upgrading to an IBM 4341 and a 4341-31 that operated in parallel respectively for IS production/operations and for development/testing. In the software arena, the purchase from Cincom of Total, a hierarchical Data Base Management System (DBMS), and Mantis, the associated development tool, set the stage for upgrading to the Supra DBMS a few years later. With a DBMS in place, DSW recruited a number of systems analysts and expanded its IS group to include ten programmers, adopting a systems approach and building integrated systems that replaced fragmented ones.

Microcomputers also made their way into DSW during that time. Except for the first stand-alone system, all operated in terminal-emulation mode. By the nineties, microcomputers ran applications developed by the IS group, as well as user-developed applications.

Until the early 1990s, the following process was in place for IS renewal and maintenance: The IS group took the initiative by conceiving an idea, and then approached top management for a budget to turn the initiative to reality. This changed considerably when a new manager took charge of the IS group in 1992. Under his leadership, users were encouraged to take IS initiatives and to convince top management to allocate the needed resources. This approach allowed better budgeting, in advance, according to user requests. Consistent with this approach, the mission of the IS group was redefined as service provision and workshops for IS personnel were conducted to teach how to become high-quality service providers.

Additional changes, which had a major effect on IS management at DSW, occurred after a new CEO, who perceived the information resource as instrumental to business success, took office in 1993 and restructured DSW (see Figure 4). The IS group turned into a division, instead of a department, and its head was promoted to Vice President of Information Systems (VPIS), reporting to the Senior VP and CFO, instead of the VP of Accountancy and Control. A consulting company hired around that time helped DSW in its IS planning processes. For the long term, the consultants helped put together a five-year IS investment plan. For the shorter term, they recommended that users be allowed to seek IS services outside DSW and, at the same time, be charged for IS services that they opt to acquire internally from the IS group.

In 1993 the mainframe hardware was upgraded to ES/9000 with the VSE/VM operating system. In the communication arena, LAN and WAN infrastructures were installed, using Novell and TCP/IP. By 1995, the IS environment at DSW was serving 700 satisfied users (100 used dumb terminals and 600 used microcomputers). Despite the fact that the functional information systems at DSW were consistent with major business processes, it became clear that major IS changes were called for due to technological and

Figure 4. DSW Structure

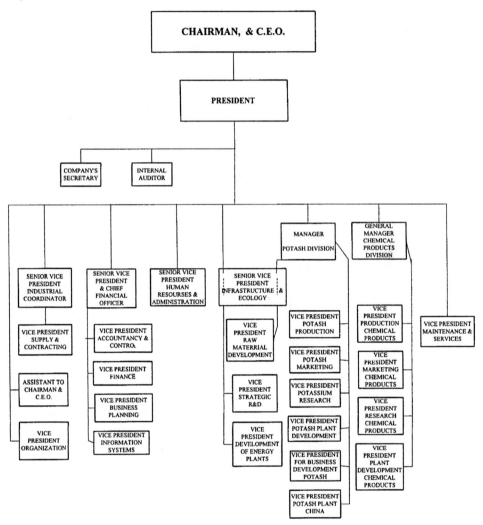

organizational reasons. Technologically, the Supra DMBS was no longer being supported and the systems at DSW were not state-of-the-art. Organizationally, the functional systems, which were developed to support the functioning of a single firm, could no longer support a multi-firm enterprise.

By 1995 the CEO and VPIS were well aware of the seriousness of the Year 2000 (Y2K) problem and concluded that for DSW, as for many other firms, resolution of the Y2K problem was critical to survival (Kappleman, 1997; Violino, 1997). Acknowledging that Y2K compliance was more of an organizational than a technical concern, the CEO charged the VPIS and the VP of Strategic R&D with planning how best to invest DSW financial and other resources to meet this challenge.

Like many organizations, DSW sent letters to all its suppliers in order to find out what their response to the Y2K problem was. In parallel, outside consulting services were recruited to help deliver Y2K solutions for embedded systems at a cost of about $0.5M. Both these activities are beyond the scope of this case study, which is focused as a main issue on a big-bang implementation of an Enterprise Resource Planning (ERP) system at DSW. The ERP implementation resulted from the Pandora's box that was opened following the realization that the information infrastructure and the IS applications at DSW were not Y2K compliant.

CASE DESCRIPTION

Decision Making Leading to ERP Implementation

To assess resource implications of converting all IS applications to comply with Y2K, the IS group prototyped Y2K conversion of one functional application. Based on this prototype, they concluded that Y2K conversion of all existing applications would cost more than $1.5M and would still leave DSW with legacy systems that revolve around a legacy DBMS.

The VPIS thus began to seriously consider avoiding Y2K conversion altogether and, at the same time, shifting from a "make" strategy to a "buy" strategy (Applegate et al., 1999.) As a subscriber of reports from META Group and GartnerGroup (1994-1996), he had already been exposed for a number of years to the growing popularity of the "buy" strategy, in general, and ERP, in particular. He was well aware that a number of software vendors offer ERP systems that integrate, on the basis modern database-management technology, a collection of modules for managing such functions as production, inventory, procurement, accounting, sales, marketing, and personnel. Although some vendors have originally developed their ERP products for mainframes, most made the transition to state-of-the-art client-server architectures.

The VPIS was also aware that some DSW competitors had already implemented ERP versions adapted to the chemical industry a few years earlier. Yet, until faced with the Y2K problem, he thought that ERP was intended either for larger and more global organizations than DSW was at the time, and/or for organizations whose IS applications, unlike DSW's, were fragmented islands of automation. Although module fragmentation was not one of DSW's problems, DSW could use an ERP package since it grew and became a multi-firm global firm.

Technologically, since none of DSW's existing applications were state-of-the-art, the VPIS expected ERP systems to be significantly superior in terms of speed and reliability. He also was aware that the core database, which was already stretched to the limit in terms of size and response time and was no longer being upgraded or even supported, was not suitable for handling globally distributed databases. Moreover, unlike ERP systems, each of the existing applications at DSW had its own user interface, making it inconvenient for users to move between applications and difficult for IS professionals to maintain data security as the number of users increased.

After becoming aware of ERP technical benefits, including speed, reliability, database distribution, convenience, and data security, the VPIS, VP of Strategic R&D, and their team began to consider the organizational implications of ERP. They soon learned that since ERP encompasses the whole organization at all sites, an ERP implementation can provide an opportunity for reengineering major organizational process and for achieving better business outcomes over time as a result of more informed managerial decision making processes.

Because of the perceived technical and organizational benefits of ERP, the VPIS and the VP of Strategic R&D began to view the turn of the millennium as an opportunity rather than a threat. They thus proposed to top management of DSW and its parent company, Israel Chemicals LTD, to avoid a Y2K conversion altogether and implement instead a Y2K-compliant ERP system that would facilitate:

1.   Renewing the hardware at DSW, from host-centric to network-centric and the software infrastructure at DSW, from outdated to modern;
2.   Supporting the transition of DSW from single-firm to multi-firm structure and from local to global operations; and
3.   Using the ERP implementation project at DSW as a pilot from which other members in the Israel Chemicals LTD group can learn.

Once top management approved the ERP implementation, a decision was made to abandon all upgrading of existing systems and to put on hold plans for developing new applications. For example, although the need for plant-maintenance automation was already acknowledged prior to the decision to move into an ERP environment, and even though it was already budgeted at $1M, actual analysis, design, and development were suspended.

The search process that followed, for software and hardware, ended in choosing the R/3 ERP software package from SAP, the Oracle DMBS software from Oracle, and the server hardware from HP. The fit between R/3 and DSW's needs was excellent for the following reasons: (a) SAP met the main functional requirements of DSW because its chemical-industry version of R/3 had already quite a number of installations worldwide. (b) According to reports from META Group and GartnerGroup (1994-1996) that the VPIS has read, the larger and more financially robust SAP was more likely to survive than its competitors. (c) SAP was holding the biggest market share in the world, in general, and in Israel, in particular. (d) SAP gained considerable experience with and has been considered especially suitable for international multi-firm enterprises. (e) SAP was investing more in R&D than competitors. (f) R/3 was localized in terms of language, currency, and regulations of many countries, including Israel, where SAP partnered with the ATL LTD, an experienced Israeli vendor with whom DSW has had good relations.

Toward the end of 1996, the resolutions made by top management at DSW guided the implementation project so as to increase the prospects of reaching successful completion of the R/3 implementation by January 1, 1999. Oriented towards thorough project and risk management, these resolutions aimed at carefully controlling project size, technology, and structure (Applegate et al., 1999).

In order to put an upper lid on project size, DSW chose to concentrate on implementing the functions which were already automated at DSW (financial accounting, material management (inventory, purchasing and MRP), controlling, treasury and human resources, rather than implement all R/3 modules. The only exception was plant maintenance, whose long-overdue automation was already budgeted for $1M and then suspended following the decision to implement ERP. About half way into the R/3 implementation project, management decided to implement the R/3 plant-maintenance module as well, having received assurances that this could be done within the deadline for an additional $70,000.

Another critical decision was to avoid parallel implementation and its associated interfacing efforts, opting instead for the more risky "big-bang" transition to R/3. Since IS professionals within DSW were unfamiliar with R/3 technology, management realized that outsourcing the big-bang implementation project could reduce project risk (McFarlan & Nolan, 1995.) By contracting IBM as the implementing vendor, DSW was able to overcome the pressing need for unique R/3 skills and knowledge.

Given the wide organizational scope of the R/3 implementation, including the need to deal with recent mergers and acquisitions, top management was determined to increase the structure of the implementation project and to facilitate smooth upgrades to new R/3 releases in the future (Bancroft et al., 1998.) To achieve these goals, DSW resolved to avoid as much as possible both customization of R/3 to DSW needs, on the one hand, and process reengineering, on the other. As a rule, management was more willing to abandon old DSW processes and regulations, which could not be supported by R/3 without customization, than to permit modifying R/3 to these processes. Only under such circumstances, even though project policy discouraged process reengineering, there was willingness on the part of management to reengineer new R/3-supported processes and replace the old unsupportable ones.

The SAP/R3 Implementation at DSW

The outsourcing contract with IBM was signed on the last day of 1996 and the implementation project started on April 1, 1997. Since then, the VPIS reported once a month to the board of directors about progress made. The CEO was committed to the implementation project and regularly briefed managers at all levels about his vision and expectations. Members of top management became very involved in the implementation project and each was asked to assume responsibility, as a top user, for implementing modules within their functional area. To make sure that implementation ended on time and within budget, the project was broken up into milestones. Since meeting milestone goals and target dates was deemed critical, any delay needed top management approval.

Measures were taken to facilitate prompt decisive action. A steering committee was formed to set priorities, to handle conflict resolution throughout the project, and to promptly respond to problems. For each functional area, a joint team of three, composed of the respective top user (Pliskin & Shoval, 1989), an R/3 expert from IBM, and a systems analyst from DSW, was created. The team, assigned with responsibility for part of the implementation project, was put in charge of choosing among R/3 processes and reports and setting priorities. Since a significant portion of top-user time was allotted to the implementation, they developed familiarity with the new environment and, later on, became very effective in providing the initial response to problems that emerged. IS professionals were constantly briefed with respect to progress as well as with respect to difficulties and ways to get around them. They were encouraged to report any concern to the respective top manager to insure a fast solution.

As planned, R/3 modifications were limited to the absolute minimum and permitted under exceptional conditions and only with formal CEO approval. The formal procedure, instituted to discourage R/3 modifications, was practiced throughout the project, despite

a number of unsuccessful attempts to eliminate it, especially during transition between CEOs.

Consistent with the initial intention to limit reengineering to a minimum, only a few processes were reengineered. The reengineered service entry process, for example, was perceived by users to be "the right thing to do" because it was dictated by R/3. They thus willingly adopted it before noticing that, because the new more reliable service entry process was 50% to 60% faster, a few jobs had to be eliminated. In any case, none of the employees whose jobs were eliminated was asked to leave DSW. Instead, they were transferred to other departments that were hiring at the time.

It is noteworthy that DSW, which prior to the ERP implementation opted to custom-make IS applications, wished to gain as much as possible from its decision to buy software and, at the same time, increase prospects for success. In other words, DSW was willing to abandon customization as much as it could, putting a lid on modifications and willing to force modification avoidance except under special circumstances. In an organizational culture that values labor relations, a threat of labor unrest in the form of a strike presents such special circumstances. The union was therefore consulted whenever avoiding R/3 modifications impacted compensation. In at least one case, the union's disapproval of modification avoidance forced an R/3 modification and labor relations were not hurt. It is noteworthy however that the union was willing, in most cases, to go along with and accept the implications of modification avoidance.

Additional initiatives paralleled the ERP conversion. Personal computers and terminals were upgraded. The network was stabilized to prevent down times. Data quality was addressed (through conversion, improvement, and creation). Even though time was short, specially-hired trainers joined top users and systems analysts, who participated in the implementation project intensively (Pliskin, 1989), to train, in four parallel classrooms, 400 trainees, including end users, systems programmers, operators, systems analysts, and programmers. Each trainer was put in charge of specific modules. Trainees were encouraged to come to the classroom for extra practice. A flexible and responsive computerized help-desk was staffed with individuals trained to either respond promptly or to refer swiftly to another person.

R/3 went into production at DSW on July 1, 1998, six months ahead of schedule and without exceeding the $4.95 million budget. In the beginning, the VPIS met with the IS professionals on a daily basis to air out problems. As the need to do so diminished, meeting frequency went down. As of January 1, 1999, all planned modules are working. The number of users, low- and mid-level managers, is 600 and growing.

It is noteworthy that both IS professionals and users cooperated with the ERP implementation and no resistance was observed. Although nobody in the company is willing to bet on the reasons for the lack of resistance, some speculations have been brought up. IS professionals were assured by the VPIS that their skills would be upgraded to state-of-the-art technologies through massive training and none would be fired. Users were led to believe that the R/3 implementation provided an opportunity for DSW to have modern information systems and provided with enough training to alleviate any fears about working with the new software.

As anticipated, the ERP implementation provided DSW with the opportunity to renew the hardware, from host-centric to network-centric, and to modernize its software infrastructure. Gradually, R/3 will be implemented at branches of DSW worldwide, helping DSW with the transition from single-firm to multi-firm structure and from local to global operations. The ERP implementation project at DSW served as a pilot, and the same ERP infrastructure is expected to make its way to other sister companies of DSW in the Israel Chemicals LTD. Implementation of R/3 by another Israel-Chemicals member is already approaching completion faster and cheaper than at DSW, under the leadership of an IS professional from DSW.

In retrospect, SAP R/3 has also provided DSW with some tangible savings: the number of pages printed per month was reduced by 80% from about 25000 to about 5000, because of the better ability to query online instead of printing reports. The number of shifts for server operations has gone down from 3 to 1.5 per day. With all batch processes substituted by online ones, information provision has improved in the sense that the raw data is now more up to date. Thus, for example, it is now possible to know in real time (as opposed to twice a week before ERP) what the real inventory levels are and, therefore, DSW is saving money on inventory without hurting production in any way. Because of the uniformity of screens for different modules, it is now possible to easily carry a transaction from one module to another (e.g., from a costing screen to a contractor screen). Another improvement has to do with the way materials are ordered from the warehouse. Until the ERP implementation, precious time was wasted when workers came to pick up materials without verifying availability beforehand. Under SAP R/3, pickup from the warehouse is permitted only after availability is verified through remote inquiry. DSW's employees accepted the R/3 process without resistance, despite failure to introduce a similar ordering process under the legacy systems in the early 1990s.

On the down size, there has also been some deterioration in information provision, especially for top managers who were accustomed to using the Commander Executive Information System. In some respects, they now have less access to information than before because Information-Center tools are not yet effectively integrated with SAP R/3. Even for lower levels of management, information provision is in some cases poorer than before because the design of several processes and procedures has been proven inappropriate. Some information provision processes now take longer and require navigation among a series of several screens whereas beforehand each of the same processes took only a single screen to complete.

In sum, DSW has already reaped substantial benefits from the strategic move to ERP. The hardware has been renewed. The IS applications and DBMS have been upgraded to Y2K-compliant and fully integrated functional modules, with uniform and smooth transitions among them. The highly needed yet missing plant-maintenance module has been implemented. DSW processes have improved and become more efficient. Having implemented a multi-company solution, organizational learning can now take place at other DSW and Israel Chemicals LTD locations. IS professionals at DSW, whose skills have been upgraded significantly, can rely upon complete documentation and apply the same set of standards and tools, including ad hoc drill-down capability and advanced quality-assurance tools.

CURRENT CHALLENGES/PROBLEMS FACING THE ORGANIZATION

The long list of benefits and the current perception of ERP success within DSW stand in sharp contrast to the growing number of horror stories about failed or out-of-control ERP projects (Davenport, 1998.) Against this contrast, it is of interest to consider the starting conditions, goals, plans, and management practices that may have increased the chances of success at DSW.

Changes in the competitive environment in the 1990s pushed top management at DSW to approve funding for the ERP implementation in order to support company growth and restructuring from single-firm to multi-firm. The ERP implementation served strategic DSW goals such as improvement of business results, technology replacement, and reduction in the total cost of technology ownership. The ERP implementation has also created a platform for reengineering business processes in the future and for integrating the supply chain. ERP plans were well thought of, arguing a general business case in addition to a technical case. The fact that benefits have been reaped despite the limited scope and minimal modifications suggests that there was, to start with, a good fit between R/3 and the needs of DSW.

Management practices contributed to success as well. Contractual arrangements with vendors worked well and good working relationships were maintained within the implementation teams. Project management adhered to the following principles: the partial scope of the implementation was not changed during the project, except for adding the maintenance module, software modifications were avoided as much as possible; and sufficient investment was made in testing, data conversion, and user training. Even though a change of guard took place in the IS organization a few years prior to the ERP implementation, the fact that the new VPIS was not a newcomer to DSW contributed to the stability of the IS governance and experience. In retrospect, if given the opportunity to rethink management practices, the only thing DSW might have done differently is to let the IS professionals and top users in development teams work full time on the project away from DSW's premises.

It is important to acknowledge that no external events and changing conditions beyond DSW's control worked against the implementation either: financial conditions were good, there was no turnover of key personnel, and vendors neither overstated their expertise nor went out of business.

The IS group is dealing with problems and challenges by working on continuous improvement to the R/3 environment. One problem is that, probably due to the decision to opt for a big-bang implementation with only minimal reengineering and software modifications, some cumbersome and unfriendly work processes exist following the R/3 implementation. To correct this and allow DSW to better take advantage of what the R/3 environment can offer, DSW processes will be gradually reengineered and R/3 software modifications will be permitted. Thus, many efficient and effective processes that R/3 can support, but were not implemented so far, will eventually be introduced to DSW.

Another problem, which has resulted out of the decision to limit the volume of routine reporting, concerns poor design of some routine R/3 reports and user demands for additional reports. Work is ongoing to alleviate this problem — and poorly designed reports, especially those consumed by outside parties, are being redesigned. In addition, new additional reports are being planned, including control reports that are needed to support newly introduced procedural changes.

Finally, some DSW functions are not yet supported by R/3. To meet this challenge, implementation of additional R/3 modules is being planned, including project management, marketing, and production-planning. Also in the planning are systems to support senior-level decisions, such as a data warehouse and an executive information systems.

REFERENCES

Applegate, McFalan, & McKenney. (1999). *Corporate information systems management*. Boston: Irwin McGraw-Hill.

Bancroft, N. H., Seip, H., & Sprengel, A. (1998). *Implementing SAP R/3: How to introduce a large system into a large organization*. Greenwich, CT: Manning.

Davenport, T. H. (1998, July/August) Putting the enterprise into the enterprise system. *Harvard Business Review,* 112-131.

GartnerGroup Reports. (1994-1996).

Kappleman, L. (Ed.). (1997). *Year 2000 problems: Strategies and solutions from the Fortune 100*. London: International Thompson Publishers.

McFaralan, F. W., & Nolan, R. L. (1995, Winter). How to manage an IT outsourcing alliance. *Sloan Management Review*, 9-23.

META Group Reports. (1994-1996).

Pliskin, N. (1989). Human resource management: Guidelines for effective introduction of microcomputer technology. *Journal of Information Systems Management, 6*(2), 51-58.

Pliskin, N., & Shoval P. (1989). Responsibility sharing between sophisticated users and professionals in structured prototyping. *Information and Software Technology, 31*(8), 438-448.

Violino, R. (1997, February 10). Year 2000 getting down to the wire. *Information Week*, 14-15.

FURTHER READING

Allen, B. (1998). Year 2000: Impact on the healthcare industry. *IS Audit and Control Journal*, (1), 11-13.

Ang, S., & Straub, D. W. (1999). Production and transaction economics in IS outsourcing: A study of the US banking industry. *MIS Quarterly, 22*(4), 535-554.

Benjamin, R. I., & Levinson, E. (1993, Summer). A framework for managing IT-enabled change. *Sloan Management Review*, 23-33.

Henderson, J. C., & Venkatraman, N. (1993). Strategic alignment: Leveraging IT for transforming organizations. *IBM Systems Journal, 32*(1), 4-16.

Jenkins, H. W. (1997, May 6). Turns out the year 2000 problem is just beginning. *Wall Street Journal*, p. A23.

Mensching, J. R., & Adams, D. A. (1991) *Managing an information system*. New York: Prentice Hall.

Pliskin, N., & Shoval P. (1987). End user prototyping: Sophisticated users supporting systems development. *DATABASE, 18*(4), 7-17.

Rockart, J., Earl, M. J., & Ross, J. W. (1996, Fall). Eight imperatives for the NEW IT organization. *Sloan Management Review*, 43-55.

Nava Pliskin is an associate professor at the Department of Industrial Engineering and Management of Ben-Gurion University in Beer-Sheva, Israel. Previously, she was a Thomas Henry Carroll Ford Foundation visiting associate professor at the Harvard Business School and visiting faculty member at Suffolk University, Babson College, and Boston University. Her research has focused on longitudinal analysis of Information-Technology impacts at the global, national, organizational, and individual levels.

Marta Zarotski is a graduate student at the Department of Industrial Engineering and Management of Ben-Gurion University in Beer-Sheva, Israel. Since she received her BSc degree in computer science, from Ben-Gurion University, she has been employed as a systems analyst in charge of implementing new systems and upgrading existing ones.

This case was previously published in F. B. Tan (Ed.), *Global Perspective of Information Technology Management*, pp. 107-122, © 2002.

Chapter III

Challenges of Complex Information Technology Projects:
The MAC Initiative

Teta Stamati, University of Athens, Greece

Panagiotis Kanellis, University of Athens, Greece

Drakoulis Martakos, University of Athens, Greece

EXECUTIVE SUMMARY

Although painstaking planning usually precedes all large IT development efforts, 80% of new systems are delivered late (if ever) and over budget, frequently with functionality falling short of contract. This case study provides a detailed account of an ill-fated initiative to centrally plan and procure, with the aim to homogenize requirements, an integrated applications suite for a number of British higher education institutions. It is argued that because systems are so deeply embedded in operations and organization and, as you cannot possibly foresee and therefore plan for environmental discontinuities, high-risk, 'big-bang' approaches to information systems planning and development must be avoided. In this context the case illustrates the level of complexity that unpredictable change can bring to an information technology project that aims to establish the 'organizationally generic' and the destabilizing effects it has on the network of the project's stakeholders.

ORGANIZATIONAL BACKGROUND

Located on the western edge of London, Isambard University received its Royal Charter[1] in 1966 and since then enjoys a considerable reputation for research and teaching in the science and technology fields in which it specializes. Close connections with the public sector, industry and commerce characterize Isambard University. These links were built through a commitment to the thin sandwich[2] undergraduate degrees which made the University's graduates among the most employable in the country and, by its distinctive competence in applied and strategic research. As a direct result, Isambard University is popular with undergraduates, while its earnings from contract research per member of academic staff are significantly above the national average in most of the cost centers in which it is active.

In the beginning of the 1990s the Higher Education (HE) sector in the UK started to experience dramatic changes. The Secretary of State invited comment on the scale, purpose and structure of HE, and the Government made its views clear through the introduction of numerous policy changes affecting universities' funding, teaching and research. Those were followed by the merger of the Ministries of Education and Employment, and the move of the Office of Science and Technology to the Ministry of Trade and Industry, signifying an increased requirement for public spending on HE to have a demonstrable effect on employment and national economic growth. For example, in November 1995, a 7% overall reduction in universities funding for 1996 was announced, including a 31% fall in capital funding, meaning that over a six-year period the unit of funding for teaching each student would have had to be reduced by 28%. Direct financial support for students was also reduced. The previous students' allowance scheme was terminated, with the balance between student grants and loans moving even more deterministically towards the latter, with the Government signaling its adamant intention to fundamentally review the funding mechanisms.

It was against this background of environmental turbulence that Isambard University, as indeed every other academic institution of HE, operated. Another one of the key environmental changes was the Government's plan to double the number of undergraduate students, from one million to two million, over a 25-year period beginning from 1989. In the medium term this was to be achieved through a strategy of 'expansion with greater efficiency.' Hence, a major challenge for Isambard University was to determine a plan and assure that the necessary infrastructure was in place for participating in this program of expansion in a way that would build upon and strengthen its distinctive characteristics. Associated with this change was the Government's decision to abolish the Council for National Academic Awards (CNAA[3]). Institutions with degrees validated by this body were now required to seek alternative means of validation, either through the acquisition of chartered status, or through association with an existing chartered institution. Opportunities to validate the awards of other institutions were therefore available for Isambard University.

Isambard University's strategy of actively seeking growth and diversity, by merging and fostering links with other institutions, came into fruition in February 1995, when the West London Institute of Higher Education was incorporated into the University as Isambard University College. This amalgamation marked the beginning of significant restructuring as the College departments had to be molded into a unified faculty structure. By the end of 1995, the Departments of Education from the two institutions were brought together into a single School of Education, and the Department of Design joined the Faculty of Technology. Furthermore, there were plans involving the splitting of the College Department of Human and Environmental Sciences into a Department of Sports Sciences and a separate Department of Geography and Earth Sciences. In addition, Isambard was for the first time planning to establish an Arts Faculty. This re-organization was the cause of considerable instability.

Adding to these was the intensification of the competition for research funding. Changes in the Funding Council's allocation model were directed towards greater selectivity in the use of research funding and an increased emphasis on research quality and proven research success. For these reasons, Isambard was experiencing a shift in its funding arrangements and had to obtain external funding to compensate for a reduction in central funds through the Higher Education Funding Council for England (HEFCE). Whereas in the past there were one or two revenue streams to be maximized, now there were at least five. These included:

- Central funding from the HEFCE based on a series of assessments (for example, Research Assessment Exercise)
- Project-driven funding from UK research councils and from the European Community
- Collaborative and contract research for industry and commerce
- Overseas student fee income
- Conference accommodation and catering income

Hence it was towards the end of the '80s and the beginning of the '90s that Isambard University found itself exposed to an operating environment that in many respects was borrowing the business — like characteristics of the commercial sector. In the Vice Chancellor's own words:

> *The only cloud on our horizon as we start the new year is the uncertainty of the environment in which we will be seeking to put those values [to continue to be a mixed teaching and research university which is financially sound; and to be characterized by teaching and research which is of relevance to its user community] into practice. 1995 entered with less clarity about the future of the UK Higher Education system than most of us working in it have ever known.* (Sterling, 1995, p. 16)

SETTING THE STAGE

Information systems played a critical role at Isambard University. Its orientation towards engineering and sciences dictated a high level of interest in, and use of such systems, among other high technology facilities. Since the mid-eighties its systems infrastructure developed from a central multi-user mainframe with islands of computation in the various departments, to a distributed computing system linking central and departmental resources and providing user access at required locations, via terminals, PCs, and workstations. Teaching and research staff, partnering with their close links to industry and commerce, demanded 'state-of-the-art' computing at industry standards.

The following elements constituted the framework for the University's computing infrastructure:

- UNIX for main service operating systems
- Networks based on X.25 and Ethernet
- IBM compatibility for PCs
- Adoption of UNIX-based workstations
- Application software of industry standards
- Centralized file service

It was also recognized that all administrative work ought to be underpinned with effective information and management systems. Historically, the administrative computing capability had been developed to service the central administrative functions. As management and administrative tasks and activities by departments and faculties increased, so did the need for support in those areas. This change in responsibility brought about the development, within some departments and faculties, of local systems to support their management and administrative activities and needs. In parallel with this, there was an increasing demand from departments and faculties for management information from central administration and support, in terms of access to system facilities. In 1988, it was observed that in terms of hardware, the host machine supported about the maximum number of peripherals it could, and was utilized beyond the normal expected level. This meant that any further expansion of support was not feasible without increasing computing power and capacity. In addition, the terminal access of administrative systems for individual departments provided via the University's network did not provide an adequate response to those remote users, and the service level did not always fulfill their needs. It was not necessarily the case that the information held within the systems was inadequate, but barriers existed which prevented or hindered its use by the departmentally base staff that needed it. There were also issues associated with the data itself, and it was felt that they could probably be resolved by developing new hardware and software architectures to support the differing needs of the users. In summary, the main issues were:

- **Format and structuring:** Data was not formatted and structured so that it could be presented to the user in a useful and meaningful way.
- **Access:** There was limited access to the data caused primarily by technical constraints.
- **Currency:** Data was found to be current for one set of users but out of date for others, due to differences in need and timescale.
- **Ownership:** There were areas where lack of ownership definition and responsibility had resulted in a lapse in maintenance of the data. Where ownership was at the center, but data was derived from other sources, there were problems in maintaining it. An example was customer records where ongoing information was provided from many sources, but there was no area responsible for collecting the data and no means of distributed input. Any breakdown of communication resulted in central and departmental information being different.
- **Completeness:** There was a wealth of information in all subject areas held by individual departments and within the faculties, which was not captured effec-

tively. The necessary mechanisms (i.e., coordinated and integrated systems) did not exist to enable this to happen.

The software applications processing this data had been developed over the last 12 years. Their development had been tailored to the specific needs of the users that applied at the time of development or subsequent amendment. As management and administrative roles and responsibilities were undergoing change, new users were bringing in a new set of needs to be satisfied. Similarly, changing circumstances — unpredictable demands from the Universities Funding Council (UFC)[4] and changing rules for allocating funds — and pressures were bringing about different needs. During the period of 1988-1990 it became clear that while the existing systems satisfied many of the central administrative requirements, new needs in both the management and administration of the university arose.

CASE DESCRIPTION: MANAGEMENT AND ADMINISTRATIVE COMPUTING INITIATIVE

The UFC's Management and Administrative Computing (MAC) initiative was announced in September 1988. The aim of the initiative was to promote the introduction of more effective and sophisticated systems to support the increasingly complex decisions that faced universities and colleges (Kyle, 1992). In addition, the systems were to provide the UFC with the information needed for allocating funds more effectively across the pool of universities. The cost of institutions 'doing it alone' was estimated at £ 0.5 million or more for each. To avoid this, the Universities Grants Committee (UGC[5] — precursor to the UFC) commissioned a study to develop an information/data specification or 'Blueprint,' which aimed to cover 80-90% of the needs of any single institution. A Managing Team was formed, and an initial study based on direct input from five universities and contributions from 20 more was completed. The team, comprising senior computing staff and university administrators, was chaired by the Vice Chancellor of the University of Nottingham.

The UFC decided that they would only fund information technology developments for MAC that were organized to suit 'families' of universities. The objective was to group institutions into five or six families with similar computing requirements. Whilst geographic proximity was helpful in promoting frequent contact between the family members, it was not to be the only consideration. Others included similarity in size, structure, type of institution, existing collaboration (for example on purchasing), and computing development needs.

The Initial Phases

The Blueprint undertaken by Price Waterhouse (now PriceWaterhouseCoopers) delivered at the end of 1988. The five main participants were Manchester University, Strathclyde University, Newcastle University, University College London and Isambard University.

In March 1989 the blueprint was sent to all universities, together with a request that each university prepare a 'migration strategy' report. This would have to include each university's present administrative computing situation, both in terms of its computing hardware and its existing applications, and of its development priorities and requirements for the future and additionally:

- A comparison of the information needs of the University with the generalized blueprint and an identification of gaps between the two
- The identification of the characteristics of the institution in order for the Managing Team to classify it
- The development of an outline strategy for migration from the University's existing systems to the outline architecture in the blueprint

Isambard's migration strategy was prepared with the assistance of two consultants from Ernst & Young and emphasized the importance placed by the University on the provision of management as well as operational information. There were also two additional features that were highlighted: one was the need to conform to the University's own information technology strategy[6]; the other was the fact that a new development platform had to be selected for any future systems, as the existing systems were coming to the end of their useful life. The preparation of Isambard's migration strategy for MAC took place at about the same time and led to a decision to integrate management and administrative computing systems. This decision for integration was one of the principal factors that led to a commitment to the Oracle database platform as it was the one supported by the University's computing services. This migration strategy was sent to the UFC in July 1989.

The Formation of Families

The MAC Managing Team used the migration strategies submitted by all universities as the basis for the formation of different 'families.' A consultant from the National Computing Center (NCC) assisted in analyzing the strategies. As a result of his analysis and at a meeting held in September 1989, it was proposed that the families should be formed around the four main relational database products available at that time and in use in universities, as the universities believed it to be the most important factor regarding their future systems development. In addition it was thought that this would enable them to achieve the objective of developing a common code to run on their hardware. The products were *Oracle*, *Ingres*, *Powerhouse* and *Secqus*. Each university was then asked to choose which family it wished to join, with the UGC hoping "that, in time, all members of any one family will be using the same administrative computing software which they will develop and maintain jointly." The process of forming the families took place during October 1989 and Isambard joined the largest one — the Oracle Family — which represented a wide variety of universities. Other reasons for this were the size of the family itself — the bigger the family, the smaller the contribution Isambard believed it would have to make — and the viability of the supplier; in terms of sales, Oracle was by far the largest of the four as well as the most 'open.'

In October 1989, the Family was simply a collection of universities that agreed to cooperate on systems development using a particular product. A constitution and *modus operandi* had to be drawn up for the Family in addition to a plan of its activities. This was necessary in order to obtain funding from the UFC. The constitution established a

Management Board in which each university had one representative and one vote. A Chairman was elected from among those representatives, and the Family incorporated as a limited company known as Delphic Ltd.

The Board also decided to form a number of what they called *Application Groups*, one for each area of the management and administrative systems identified in the Price Waterhouse's Blueprint. This did not mean that the groups had to undertake the development of the systems themselves, but that they were to be responsible for working directly with the commercial contractors employed by the Family. Each member of the Family had to be a member of at least one group, and Isambard took the decision to join the Management Information Application Group.

The Analysis, Design & Delivery Phases

In February 1990, it was decided to contract Mantis UK to undertake the analysis stage of the Family's systems development program. This involved the production of the functional analysis and data dictionary of the members' requirements, under the sections covered by the six Applications Groups set up by the Management Board: Students, Staff, Finance, Research and Consultancy, Physical Resources, and Management Information. The work on this contract commenced in February and ended in June 1990. It involved several consultants from Mantis UK plus many staff from all the member universities of the Family and was supervised by a Project Manager employed on a consultancy basis, together with a small group[7] chaired by the administrative computing manager of Bristol University.

The result of all the work — a huge coordinated effort between Mantis UK and the Family members — culminated in an enormous document running into several hundreds of pages which contained everything one ever wanted to know about management and administrative computing requirements in UK universities. It was made up of two main parts. The first was the analysis of all the management and administrative functions that universities needed the systems to help them carry out (the *Function Hierarchy*). The second identified all the data items required by these functions and the relationships between them (the *Entity Relationship Model*). These were followed by proposals concerning the development of the required systems. The document therefore comprised the deliverables from the analysis stage on the basis of which the system was to be designed and built.

The next stage was to commission someone to design and build the systems software on the basis of this analysis and data dictionary. An initial description of the work to be tendered was issued by the NCC on behalf of the Family at the end of April 1990, and expressions of interest in receiving a full tender document were invited. The formal invitation to tender was issued in June to three companies expressing interest. These were Mantis UK, Hoskyns and Price Waterhouse. The Family received the three tenders on August 7, 1990, and spent the rest of the month assessing them. A detailed scoring system was used to evaluate the three tenders against a whole range of factors. This evaluation process was followed by a period of intense negotiation over the costs with each of the suppliers and significant reductions over the original tender price were eventually achieved.

The outcome was that Mantis UK was offered the contract to develop the full set of management and administrative systems. The recommendation was formally accepted by a meeting of the Management Board in September 1990, and a contract was subsequently drawn up with Mantis UK with the assistance of specialist legal advice. The complexities of the negotiations over the contract were such that it was not formally signed until May 1991, although the work itself started and continued during the negotiation period.

Although the MAC system was designed as one closely integrated system, its software was to be made available in phases (see Appendix). All applications, with the exception of payroll, would use *SQL Forms V.3* with pop-up windows etc. as part of the user interface. The Finance application was based on Mantis's own accounting package that was to be enhanced to cater for the additional functionality requested by the Family. Whenever the Mantis development team finished writing and testing a release of software, this was to be passed over to the appropriate Application Group for them to run their own acceptance tests on it. It is important to note that the '80/20' rule applied here. A small part of the system was left to the discretion of the programmers working at each of the universities, who after an Mantis software release and in close cooperation with Mantis developers, would attempt to 'tailor' the system to the specifics of the sites (Pollock, 2001). If an institution was encountering problems in running the software, the 'Delphic Support Desk' had to be contacted. This would assess the problem and then pass the solution back to the institution responsible for the particular application. If the problem could not be resolved, it was forwarded back to Mantis which had to redesign and rebuild the application.

Management and Administrative Computing Initiative Outcome for the Delphic Family

Towards the end of 1994 and with the funding for the MAC Initiative nearing its termination date of March 31, 1995, the Delphic members were experiencing severe delays concerning the delivery of the main application packages. The Anticipated Availability Schedule (see Appendix) shows the time slippages. Kyle (1994) summarized some of the main causes for the delays as follows:

1.   The design of the Student Structure was found to be flawed, and had to be redone.
2.   Mantis's decision to merge its development team responsible for its own Finance package with the one responsible for the MAC's Finance module.
3.   The loss of senior Mantis development staff, particularly during critical design stages.
4.   The introduction of a new stage: implementation by a test (lead) institute between the end of acceptance testing and the release of an application in its supported state.
5.   The decision of Delphic to make modules available in 'baskets.' This meant that the first module accepted had to wait until the acceptance of the last module in the basket before it could be implemented.

Complementary to the above a number of observations can be made regarding this state of affairs concerning the initiative.

Price Waterhouse's approach for conducting the initial feasibility study (i.e., the Blueprint) was considered hardly appropriate for as complex a system as MAC was. On the basis of the knowledge they had acquired about university administration from developing information systems for Durham and Leeds Universities, and because time was of essence, they adopted a 'drive the user base instead of letting the user base drive you' approach. This meant that Price Waterhouse as in effect designing the Blueprint based on its assumptions of what was needed, and then presenting it to the representatives from a cross-sample of universities, inviting them to comment.

However, the representatives did not have the blueprints in advance to study and to comment interactively with the consultants — they were given to them at the meetings, where at the end a decision had to be made. This, coupled with the large size of the project and its 'open' structure, resulted in some areas being overlooked and others not being looked at in sufficient detail. The final Blueprint was a huge and complicated technical document, and by large the universities did not check it out as they ought to have done. It was of a hierarchical structure cut down to functions described in little detail, which made it difficult for systems personnel to understand, let alone explain it to their line managers and get the much-needed feedback. The fact that this approach was problematic became evident when the families started their own individual developments. They found out that the result was not as much of the Blueprint as they had thought it to be.

The application of the '80/20' rule mentioned in the preceding section meant that the finalization and successful implementation of the various modules was heavily reliant on the skills and efforts of the programmers who were working the code so as to make it compatible to the specifics of each site. But they were tasked to work with the system only in certain ways, as Mantis wanted to ensure that the code would only be modified in the ways they deemed appropriate. In a sense they were "...attempting to configure the local programmers as their users..." (Pollock, 2001, p. 7) and this gave rise to a lot of friction. The following excerpt from a final report to the Delphic Support Desk regarding an issue illustrates this:

> ...As you may know, [the University] migrated from [MAC] 1.3 to 1.4 last week and encountered some problems which we helped with. We also advised them to migrate to 1.5, as 1.4 was no longer supported. This they did over the weekend and again had some problems, which I have mentioned in the log. They contacted me on Monday morning and I have been looking at the problem(s) over the last day and a half. We have carried out a few checks and offered some advice on overcoming some of the problems, but it would appear that the problem lies in the data that they are working with and not a problem in any of our code...Quite simply, I cannot justify any more time on this problem as it does not appear to be a problem with our software, rather a problem on site which may well require a great deal of time to identify...Their current work-around is to use the basket 4 forms against the basket 5 database. I have expressed my concern over this and warned them that this is unsupported but they appear to be confident that they have an adequate work-around. (Pollock, 2001, p. 14)

Arguably, the causes for the delays mentioned above can be experienced in any project of MAC's scope, scale and complexity. However, the first one on Kyle's list draws one's attention, as it was the result of an environmental discontinuity that could have not been anticipated — that of semesterization8. It was felt as something that was clearly overdue, a departure from a rigid and inflexible academic structure that originated in the beginning of the last century to a more open and clearly cost-effective scheme. As a result of semesterization, Isambard, for example, was able to increase considerably its student numbers by offering a wider range of choice regarding the structure of its courses, rather than only the four-year thin sandwich course option. This change affected mainly the Student Module. The fact that in 1994 parts of it had not been contracted (see Appendix), although the initial delivery date for the completed module was July 1992, shows clearly the magnitude of the effect that this change had.

The Student Module was driven by what was called "*Program Structures*" — schemes of study. "Program Structures" was designed in such a way that in an attempt to provide for integration, every single module was required to know what the structure was when dealing with student administration. For example, the Student Registration, Student Finance, and the Assessment and Degree Conferment modules related first of all to the Program Structure and its maintenance, and in effect were totally dependent on it. This module's development had to start virtually from scratch again because of semesterization, and it was estimated that its delivery had to be put back by a year to 18 months.

Twenty-six months later and there was still no definite delivery date, although an estimation was that a 'formal' deliverable had to wait for another two years. Needless to say, no member of the Family could afford to bear the cost of a product that had not been proven to work, and in which acceptance tests had to take place throughout a whole academic year and be evaluated against the annual cycle of activities. The metaphor of the old lady who is trying to cross the road and waits for someone else to do it first, in order to see if he gets run over, illustrates the case. Angela Crum Ewing, Deputy Registrar at Reading University (a member of the Delphic Family), said after they decided to hold onto their in-house applications, rather than implement a MAC solution: "MAC is in a position of transition. We did not want to commit to a new, untried system, when we had our own in-house systems which worked well" (Haney, 1994).

A 'sneak preview' of the modules by Family members resulted in a lot of skepticism about the future, stemming from the fact that continuous disappointment would mean dissatisfied stakeholders who will not stop placing pressure in favor of project abandonment. The effect of semesterization had major repercussions not only on Mantis UK as the system developer, but on all members in the Family who were counting on the deliverables and had already made their migration plans. For Isambard University, only the quantifiable costs amounted to the region of more than £50,000 — two extra man-years of further systems development work that no one had anticipated.

CURRENT CHALLENGES/PROBLEMS FACING THE ORGANIZATION

In September 1994, after almost six years of systems development and six months before the termination of the funding, only one of the Delphic modules that were to be made available was finally adopted by Isambard University (Figure 1).

The state of affairs regarding the seven main areas was as follows:

Figure 1. MAC modules adopted by Isambard University after almost six years of systems development

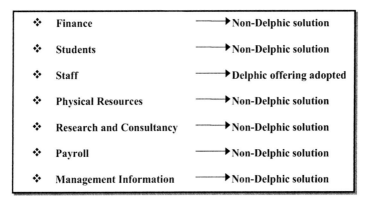

- **Students:** Although at the time Isambard's existing system infrastructure could hardly accommodate semesterization, the administration of the University, tired of waiting for Delphic to come up with a deliverable, was pushing persistently for a new system. In November 1993, after 'shopping around' for any Mantis-based student system in use that could be able to satisfy Isambard's own requirements, a decision was made to consider the system of the University of Liverpool. After some time it was found out that for a number of reasons, this was not the solution either. Firstly the system was designed to meet Liverpool's own requirements in a very specific way and it was never developed as a package for other universities to use. Isambard's own requirements were completely different to theirs. Secondly, it was developed on an older version of Mantis. This meant that its blind adoption would pose problems in the future concerning its integration with any Delphic deliverables. On the other hand, an attempt to modify it would mean major overhead. Finally, from a technical point of view, the system was not documented — a 'black box' in the systems team's own words. Isambard had no alternative but to develop and design its own in-house student system whose first phase went live in the first week of October 1994 to coincide with the beginning of the new academic year. The system covered the Registration process, but no project was under way regarding the two other main areas — Student Finance and Student Accommodation.
- **Finance:** The development of the Finance module which was a base offering from Mantis UK and which had been enhanced to meet the extra requirements, was also off schedule. As a result, an Mantis quasi-commercial accounting package was adopted and implemented. The package had nothing specific to offer to universities, and if there were a choice, it would have not been taken on board by Isambard. It was developed by Mantis UK (in much the same way as Price Waterhouse delivered its MAC Blueprint) in an attempt to quickly capture a slice of the off-the-

shelf software market when it had decided to enter it a couple of years ago. This meant that several enhancements were necessary and it took more that 200 person hours alone to determine whether or not it could replace the existing system. Subsystems to deal with the maintenance of research contracts, and to allow for the issuing of monthly statements of accounts to heads of departments and senior researchers, were designed, and eventually the system went 'live' in August 1994 — the beginning of the new financial year.

- **Staff:** Following the installation and assessment of the pre-release version of the first module from Delphic (Posts, People, Appointments and Organization), the implementation team agreed and the old system was subsequently discontinued in September 1993. It was replaced by this and the second module (Skills, Recruitment and USR Return). However, at that time (September 1993) Delphic still had not provided any documentation for the system.

- **Physical resources:** The initial Delphic offering proved to be an 'overkill' for Isambard's requirements. It provided more than was actually needed, and two key areas had already been covered by in-house-developed Mantis systems. One area was the administration of the University's own housing facilities and the people who occupied them, and the other was an inventory system for mobile equipment. The Delphic offering still held some level of attraction to Isambard's Management Services team, but only when used in conjunction with the Delphic Finance Module, as it offered the facility the option to debit directly a departmental account at a store as soon as an item was issued out. The Stock Control Module was at the time running at test mode, but as these two packages were designed to be highly integrated, there was a deadlock situation as the Finance module had not been delivered. Moreover, as mentioned above, a commitment had been made to the in-house-developed finance system, which was unlikely to be replaced for at least two years.

- **Research and consultancy:** No view had been formed about this module as there had not been a delivery. Supposedly it provided the ability to maintain profiles of staff and possible customers who could require applied research to be undertaken by the University on their behalf. An in-house-developed Mantis system was then in operation centered around publications of Isambard staff and information on customers. The accounting side (e.g., the recording of costs against research projects) was partly accommodated by the core finance system. Again, it was rather like Physical Resources — nothing particularly attractive given the overhead in implementing either of the Delphic modules that tended to be reasonably sophisticated for Isambard requirements.

- **Payroll:** A bureau service from a leading UK bank catered for the payroll function at Isambard. The consensus of the Director of Financial Services was that it was adequate, and therefore he was cautious and opposed any change. What were however lost by this decision were the integration and the economies, such as saving in paperwork and clerical time that came with the Delphic module, and that were associated with raising the cost of various processes between the two interconnected functions — payroll and personnel. However, the high level of integration offered between Delphic's Payroll (not delivered at that time) and Staff modules were attractive to Isambard, as it had implemented the latter. After some careful consideration it became clear that its adoption was very unlikely to happen, as at the outset it seemed a very general package; again, many enhancements would have been necessary. This was a significant requirement considering the size of Isambard's Management Systems Team and its constrained time scales.

- **Management information:** Similarly, no 'final' view was formed. There had been a development where Management Information was considered to be the 'Cinderella' module — the sort of one where by residing within the other modules, management information requirements at a strategic level could be easily accommodated. In September 1994, only statistics of various sorts could be generated for Government use, and those with considerable difficulty. In order to cure the problem, Delphic bought the rights for individual universities to acquire *Holis* — a powerful expert system, as there was general consent that Mantis UK was delivering 'textbook' systems. This meant that they had gone too far in terms of splitting down to tables for the database, without considering that most legacy systems already in place at universities were hierarchical, thus operating with one table. This transition posed a considerable challenge. It required a lot of effort and man-hours for the Management Services team that had to undergo the process, as *Holis* was not available when the initial design decisions were made. *Holis* was generally looked upon as the solution in gluing and running the whole of the independent databases together as it could accommodate any set of computerized data-like spreadsheets and flat files which did not necessarily have to follow Delphic's database format.

The MAC Initiative was funded from 1988 to 1995 and a total of 11 million were invested in those seven years. "Universities snub software policy," read a headline in *Computing* (September 22, 1994) — a professional trade magazine. "UK universities are going their own way to buy core administrative software after finding a government-sponsored scheme out of touch with their business needs," the article continued. Birmingham and Reading Universities both confirmed in September of that year that they were moving outside the MAC initiative for their latest developments, and the University of Sussex being dissatisfied with the delivered software for undergraduate student admissions eventually chose a separate system. With the funding for MAC running out in July 1995, similar moves from other institutions were being planned, as there was no other viable alternative.

The outcome was that although Families continued to exist in a rather informal way, MAC-related activity slowly came to an end after the central funding terminated. The Delphic and Mantis UK Management Boards agreed and concluded their contract at the end of April 1996. The agreement was to deliver all remaining software in an 'as-is' state at the end of January in order to be tested at the University of Liverpool. The software was to be accepted at the end of February, with any 'bugs' to be remedied under the warranty agreement. Delphic was to make no further development demands on Mantis (Philips, 1996). It is without doubt that many interpretations can be given regarding the final outcome, and in retrospect each Family managed to achieve the objective of producing software to cover a number of the Data Blueprint areas. Some of these systems did run quite successfully in a number of institutions (Hillicks, 2002). What must be noted, however, is the fact *that no university managed to achieve the initial objective of using only the MAC modules exclusively.*

The ending of the contract meant that Delphic was in total control of the situation rather than having to work through Mantis, and in 1996 MAC was a far cry from the initial objective for an integrated information system where all the functional subsystems could be seamlessly linked so that one would not end up with a collection of disjointed and ineffective systems (Kanellis & Paul, 1995; Kanellis, 1996). For Isambard University in particular, the main attraction in joining the Delphic Family was the integrated solution that they were offering. Graham Kyle, manager of the Management Services team, summarized eloquently the situation: "…as you can observe, the way we are staggering here at Isambard, there is no sign of integration as far as we are concerned." One feature of Delphic that did not apply to any of the other families was that from day one the deliverable was designed as one system. It caused Mantis UK problems because, when the first major slippage occurred (the Students Module), Mantis had to respond to pressure from the Delphic representatives who demanded some deliverables." This meant that Mantis had to unbundle the system by separating and redesigning the links, a major cause for MAC's failure to meet deadlines. Almost all deliverables were at least two years late, according to the dates quoted by Mantis UK in the original specification, and this caused considerable stress and frustration to Isambard, which had to decide which route to follow regarding its infrastructure: to wait and see how Delphic would handle the situation after the termination of the contract with Mantis, to see how to integrate the various probable solutions described in the beginning of this section or to make a fresh beginning abandoning all previous investments? Difficult choices indeed and hardly the type one expects to be faced with at the end of an information technology development project that started with the best of expectations.

REFERENCES

Haney, C. (1994, September 22). Universities snub software policy. *Computing,* 14.

Hillicks, J. (2002). *Development partnerships between HE and vendors: Marriage made in heaven or recipe for disaster?* Retrieved from http://www.jiscinfonet.ac.uk/Resources/external-resources/development-partnerships/view

Kanellis, P. (1996). *Information systems and business fit in dynamic environments.* Unpublished PhD dissertation, Brunel University, UK.

Kanellis, P., & Paul, R. J. (1995, August 2-5). Unpredictable change and the effects on information systems development: A case study. In W. A. Hamel (Ed.), *Proceedings of the 13th Annual International Conference of the Association of Management* (pp. 90-98). Vancouver, BC: Maximilian Press Publishers.

Kyle, G. W. (1992). *Report on the UFC MAC initiative.* London: Brunel University.

Kyle, G. W. (1994). *MAC situation report.* Brunel University, UK.

Philips, T. (1996). *MAC progress report.* Retrieved from http://www.bris.ac.uk/WorkingGroups/ISAC/13-2-96/i-95-10.htm

Pollock, N. (2001). The tension of work-arounds: How computer programmers. [Paper submitted to *Science, Technology & Human Values*]

Sterling, M. (1995). *Vice-chancellor's report to court.* Brunel University, UK.

ENDNOTES

[1]   Royal Charters have a history dating back to the 13th century. The original purpose was to create public or private corporations and to define their privileges and purpose. Nowadays, Charters are normally reserved for bodies that work in the public interest and can demonstrate pre-eminence, stability and permanence in their particular field. Many older universities in England, Wales and Northern Ireland are also chartered bodies.

[2]   Sandwich courses involve a period of work in industry or a commercial organization. On a 'thick' sandwich course, the student spends the third year working away from university. The 'thin' sandwich course has placements lasting six months each calendar year.

[3]   The CNAA was founded by Royal Charter in 1964, with the object of advancing education, learning, knowledge, and the arts by means of the grant of academic awards and distinctions.

[4]   UFC became the Higher Education Funding Council for England (HEFCE) which was established following the Further and Higher Education Act 1992. A principal feature of the legislation was to create one unified higher education sector by abolishing the division between universities and polytechnics.

[5]   Under the education Reform Act of 1988, the University Grants Committee (UGC) was replaced with the Universities Funding Council (UFC) which in turn was replaced by the Higher Education Funding Council for England (HEFCE) to conform to the Further and Higher Education Act 1992 which made provision for a single system of higher education, with a unified funding structure and separate funding councils for England, Scotland and Wales.

[6]   It was during 1989 that Isambard University was required to prepare a renewed internal information technology strategy to support its bid to the UFC's Computer Board for funds related to academic computing from 1990 onwards. The principal objective of the strategy was to make available a range of integrated computing facilities to staff and students throughout the University using an infrastructure of distributed computing based on campus networking.

[7]   Members comprised of the chairmen of the six Applications Groups, plus a couple of other members nominated by the management.

[8]   A standard of measurement in higher education used to group weeks of instructional time in the academic calendar. An academic year contains a minimum of 30 weeks of instructional time. An individual semester provides about 15 weeks of instruction, and full-time enrollment is defined as at least 12 semester hours per term. The academic calendar includes a fall and spring term, and often a summer term.

APPENDIX

Delphic Family Schedule of Deliverables

(a) DELPHIC family initial schedule of deliverables

1990/1991	1991/1992	MARCH 1993
STUDENT REGISTRATION, FEES, EXAMINATIONS	FULL STUDENT SYSTEM	MANAGEMENT INFORMATION & ALL SYSTEMS
FINANCE PHASE 1	FINANCE PHASE 2	
PAYROLL PACKAGE	PERSONNEL PHASE 2	
INTERIM PERSONNEL PACKAGE	RESEARCH AND CONSULTANCY 1	
	PHYSICAL RESOURCES PHASES 1,2,3	

(b) DELPHIC family schedule of deliverables (as at 30.09.1994). Note: (1) Denotes specific dates agreed by Mantis; (2) denotes acceptance test failed; (3) denotes awaited; (4) denotes not yet contracted

Module	Applications	Design	System Test	Acceptance Test Signed- Off
FINANCE	Sales Document Input	11/91	2/92	10/92
	Purchase Document Input, Budgets & Commitments	11/91	2/92	10/92
	Sales & Purchase Ledgers	4/92	3/93 (1)	4/93
	Nominal Ledger	2/93	5/93 (1)	(3)
	Payroll Integration	1/93	3/93	(2)
STUDENTS	Program Structures	5/92	8/92	1/93 (3)
	Registrations	11/92	12/92	(3)
	Student Finance	10/92	3/93	(3)
	Admissions	10/92	3/93	7/94
	Assessments	10/92	8/93	(3)

(b) DELPHIC family schedule of deliverables (cont.)

Module	Applications	Design	System Test	Acceptance Test Signed-Off
PERSONNEL	Degree Conferment	3/93	8/93	(3)
	Timetabling	(4)	(4)	(4)
	Accommodation	(4)	(4)	(4)
	Alumni	(4)	(4)	(4)
	Posts, People, Appointments & Organisations	11/91	3/92	6/92
PAYROLL RESEARCH PHYSICAL RESOURCES	Skills & Recruitment	12/91	7/92	1/93
	Absences & Occupational Health, Committees, Reviews	15/1/93	12/3/93	7/93
	Superannuation	11/92	3/93	6/94
	Integration			
	Stand Alone	-	10/92	(3)
	Integrated	6/92	3/93	(3)
	Project Application	2/93	3/93 (1)	(3)
	Research Projects	2/93	3/93 (1)	(3)
	Asset Register & Allocation	10/91	4/92	6/92
	Stores Control & Management	10/91	10/92	2/93
	Job Progress & Costing	6/92	1/93	3/94

Teta Stamati is currently a sales manager in Delta Singular S.A. in Athens, Greece. She holds a degree in computing from the Informatics and Telecommunications Department at National and Kapodistrian University of Athens, an MPhil in computing and information systems at UMIST in UK, and an MBA in Lancaster Business School at Lancaster University. She is a research fellow in the Department of Informatics and Telecommunications at the National and Kapodistrian University of Athens.

Panagiotis Kanellis is currently a program manager with Information Society S.A. in Athens, Greece. He was educated at Western International University in business administration (BSc), at the University of Ulster in computing and information systems (Post-Graduate Diploma), and at Brunel University in data communication systems

(MSc) and information systems (PhD). He is a research fellow in the Department of Informatics and Telecommunications at the National and Kapodistrian University of Athens and an adjunct faculty member at the Athens University of Economics and Business.

Drakoulis Martakos is an associate professor at the Department of Informatics and Telecommunications, National and Kapodistrian University of Athens. He received his BSc in physics, MSc in electronics and radio communications, and PhD in real-time computing from the same university. Professor Martakos is a consultant to public and private organizations and a project leader in numerous national and international projects. He is author or co-author of more than 50 scientific publications and a number of technical reports and studies.

This case was previously published in the *Journal of Cases on Information Technology*, 7(4), pp. 46-62, © 2005.

Chapter IV

Designing and Implementing a Learning Organization- Oriented Information Technology Planning and Management Process

James I. Penrod, University of Memphis, USA

Ann F. Harbor, University of Memphis, USA

EXECUTIVE SUMMARY

Higher education is changing. Driven by the need to increase productivity, quality, and access while meeting the challenges of competition, universities, especially state-assisted institutions, are seeking ways to do more with less governmental support. Information technology (IT) is perhaps the enabling tool that will bring transformative change (Oblinger & Rush, 1997). The organizations that have had primary managerial responsibility for IT implementation on many campuses need to change and be restructured if the technology is to live up to its potential. This case study provides an overview of the process utilized in implementing a broad-based strategy to address the information technology needs of a large public university, the University of Memphis. It deals at length with the planning and creation of an IT governance structure and a strategic planning and management model. In this case, modern theories of organizational change and strategic planning were applied to the creation and improvement of the University's IT structure.

CASE QUESTIONS

- What IT changes are needed to significantly improve a large state-assisted urban campus?
- What organizational structures are necessary to enable meaningful IT decision making?
- What types of "people" changes need to occur and in what time frame?
- What are the major barriers in making planned IT change happen?

INTRODUCTION

Background

The University of Memphis (UoM) is the flagship institution of four-year universities within the Tennessee Board of Regents system of higher education. The campus of approximately 20,000 students, with its primary location in the geographic center of the city, is ethnically, socially, and economically diverse. This regional, urban, doctoral granting institution is within a relatively short commute of 1.5 million residents of the mid-South. The institution has two campuses and a growing number of other locations offering courses. It consists of nine schools and colleges and five centers of excellence. The University employs about 2,400 faculty and staff members. An annual state and non-state budget of approximately $220 million meets educational and service needs.

The University of Memphis is a state-assisted institution governed by a state-regulated system office. As an urban university, it strives to provide a stimulating academic environment consisting of innovative undergraduate education and excellence in selected research areas and graduate programs. Exposure to diversity in the composition of the student body, faculty, staff, and administrators enhances educational experiences. The University responds to the challenging responsibility of being located in a culturally diverse region by developing a unique blend of teaching, research, and service that contributes to the general welfare and growth of the region.

Historical Context

Shortly after assuming the leadership of The University of Memphis in 1991, President V. Lane Rawlins recognized that the existing IT unit could not provide the vision and ongoing assistance needed to support the institution as it began a significant change process. Initially, he instituted self-studies and brought in an outside consultant to define the magnitude of needed change. This led to a decision to create a chief information officer (CIO) position and to combine various IT-related units into one.

Thus in the fall of 1995, the president established a new division of Information Systems (IS) and created the position of Vice President for Information Systems & CIO (VP/CIO). The new unit had responsibility for networking, academic and administrative computing, and telecommunications. As chief information officer, the new vice president also had responsibility for developing an IT strategic planning process, an associated governance structure, and a much-needed information policy for the institution.

The new IS organization was formed from units that had previously reported to either the Vice President for Business & Finance or the provost, who each had IT staff with mid-manager or below levels of authority. The need to restructure and redirect the organization was evident. Experienced senior-level administrators were required, and several existing positions within the organization needed to be redefined. The need for different management principles, a renewed service orientation, team-based activities, and a planning focus would lead to a commitment to begin an organizational cultural change toward that of a learning organization.

A learning organization is one that continually expands its capacity to create its future. For such an organization, "adaptive learning" must be joined by "generative learning" — learning that enhances the capacity to create. Characteristics include shared visions, personal mastery, systems thinking, and team learning. Such organizations can also be defined as:

> *[...] organizations where people continually expand their capacity to create the results they truly desire, where new and expansive patterns of thinking are nurtured, where collective aspiration is set free, and where people are continually learning how to learn together.* (Senge, 1990, p. 3)

Shortly after appointment, the new VP/CIO initiated three major multi-year projects relating to information technology. The first involved completion of the basic network infrastructure for the University by connecting all offices and a proportion of classrooms and dormitories to the campus network and selected locations to Internet2. The second project was to develop an integrated, standardized academic system (including support roles) consisting of computing laboratories, classrooms, and faculty offices. The third initiative was to significantly decrease maintenance of the University administrative system by enhancing it with World Wide Web (WWW)-based access and eventually moving to a next-generation administrative system in an object-oriented and relational database environment.

During his tenure, the president appointed several new executive officers and senior administrators to work together with remaining long-term senior administrators and executives in a collegial and collaborative style for the betterment of the organization. The addition of strong executive support and leadership, along with experienced new academic leaders and staff, is allowing needed changes to occur at a more rapid pace than would otherwise be realized (Penrod, 1998).

Restructuring the IT Unit

The requirement to move ahead with significant system upgrades while restructuring the IT unit necessitated an IT strategic planning and management process closely coupled with a well-understood IT decision-making structure. It was equally important to link the IT planning and management model to existing institutional processes such as planning, budgeting, and personnel administration. Additionally, a learning organization component was critical to ensure that adaptive change would occur within the staff.

When the CIO arrived, the institution lagged behind its regional and national peers in IT infrastructure and, consequently, in usage. There was a lack of direct state funding to support institutional IT requirements, in addition to a need for internal restructuring of IT financial support. The first action was the development of both an operational and linked capital budget. Initially, a reserve account and year-end funds addressed major IT-related administrative costs and upgrades. Now the capital budget is directly linked to the operational budget, and meaningful ongoing planning for administrative and infrastructure needs may be conducted.

Students historically paid a very modest technology access fee (TAF) of up to $15 per semester. In the fall of 1997, this fee increased to $50 per semester; then in 1998, it was raised to $100. This enhanced fee provides a steady source of revenue allowing ongoing modernization of academic computing and instructional networking.

The University Strategic Plan called for a concerted effort to enhance the overall image and regional stature of the institution. Because of historical issues — a commuter campus environment and statewide reduction of higher education funding over the last decade — the university often suffered from an image that does not match the quality of existing programs and offerings that are available in certain disciplines. Strategies were devised to address this and to continue to increase overall quality — especially in five designated areas that included information technology, health sciences, international programs, performing arts, and undergraduate academic achievement.

Introducing any significant change in organizational culture is always difficult. An attempt to aggressively move a university forward requires the creation of a plan of action. One of the first exercises in such an endeavor is to define the barriers that exist. Establishing appropriately enhanced ongoing operational and capital budgets in a state university with severe budget constraints is difficult, even when there is presidential support. A major infusion of budget money for academic needs comes from increased fees, and student support was necessary to convince board members of that need.

Money, however, is not the only resource necessary. Initiating a formal IT planning process linked to the institutional planning process was a place to begin. Furthermore, linking IT planning directly to individual behavioral change, management style and practice, and unit and personnel evaluation set the stage for productive use of existing and additional budget allocations. Moving from a traditional data processing-oriented structure to one aimed toward 21st century management processes requires a change in organizational culture. Senge's (1990) learning organization theory provides an appropriate methodology to bring such change. Adaptive change in people requires the individual to determine that he/she wishes to change. If change is truly to occur, it is imperative for organizational changes to be apparent as well. Personal empowerment, professional development opportunities, team-based activities, involvement in decision making, and the linking of personal and organizational values are examples of unit changes that provide a stimulus to motivate individuals.

Against this backdrop, the president authorized creation of the new IS unit and supports its development to help position the University for the future. The need for such action is crucial:

We are entering a second era of information technology in which the...applications of computers, the nature of technology itself, and the leadership for use of technology are all going through profound change. Organizations that cannot understand the new era and navigate a path through the transition are vulnerable and will be bypassed. (Tapscott & Caston, 1993, p. 13)

The initial IS organization consisted of disparate units that had functioned as a divisional group for several months led by an outside consultant. Many had not engaged in any substantial professional development for some time and were not adequately equipped with desktop computing capabilities. Additionally, many individuals were long-term staff members of the university with little or no experience elsewhere. Almost without exception, they did not know what to expect from a new CIO or what the institution expected of them.

The University publication, *The Strategic Plan: Defining Excellence 1995-2000*, called for major IT advancements in both academic and administrative areas. It defined the need for a concerted effort to enhance the overall image and regional stature of the institution. For a variety of reasons, the University's image did not match the quality of programs and offerings that are available in certain disciplines. Responses devised by senior administrators to address this included the advancement of an information strategy. Near-unanimous agreement by senior executives and within the Information Systems Division indicated the need for change that was planned, bold, supported, and nurtured.

The president recognized the need for urgent change in sustaining institutional quality, and the CIO recognized that building a learning organization and implementing a strategic planning and management process were critical components to attaining that shared vision. It was neither necessary nor prudent to spend a lot of time analyzing that situation. Instead, the IT governance structure, enabling quick decision making, was established within the first three months of the CIO's appointment. The governance process immediately embraced and involved up to 100 key institutional players in a new direction for IT across the University.

The formal structure consists of a senior policy level council (a group with presidential designated decision-making authority) and advisory committees representing academic (primarily faculty), administrative, and student interests. In addition, various role-defined groups also have the opportunity to provide input into decisions that affect them (technical support providers, college-level committees, other administrative groups, etc.). Movement away from a fairly rigid bureaucratic structure within the central IS unit toward a coordinated but distributed organization was called for as rapidly as feasible. Finally, it was essential to define an appropriate role relationship between the central IT organization and other IT units located in academic and administrative departments.

The obvious need for a structural overhaul coupled with an expectation for developing future excellence called for a process of organizational alignment. Alignment takes place when a group of individuals works as one with a deeply shared sense of vision and purpose. Alignment of individuals can be powerful, but it is not enough. The organizational processes, systems, and structures must also be in alignment. When there is reasonable alignment in an organization, learning — individual learning, team learning, and organizational learning — results. It is a powerful energy source (Smith & Yanowitz, 1996). The president and CIO immediately developed, defined, and instituted this IT governance structure with overlapping membership, which began making institutional decisions and defining IT direction. To steer the effort, the president instituted a policy-level body, supported by three advisory committees — academic, administrative and student. The new structure called for the creation of a number of new councils and committees:

Information Technology Policy & Planning Council

This council is entrusted with the primary decision-making authority regarding IT issues. It provides a forum for discussion and approval of all institutional IT policies, IT-related standards, the *IT Strategic Plan* for the University, and IT issues that require policy-level deliberation. The Council works in conjunction with, and coordinates the activities of, student, academic, and administrative IT advisory committees. This body is also charged with responsibilities to help ensure good cross-functional communication and to ensure that agreed-upon IT plans are carried out. The Council consists of the campus executive officers, deans, the president of the Student Government Association, Faculty and Staff Senate representatives, internal auditor, chairs of advisory committees, the University librarian, and the CIO. The president appoints the chairperson.

Information Technology Academic Advisory Committee

This group advises the CIO on IT matters related to academic issues; provides input to and reviews the academic sections of the *IT Strategic Plan*; establishes priorities of all IT academic projects brought before the committee; participates in the development of IT standards, guidelines, and procedures related to academic information technology; and helps facilitate communication across the campus on all IT-related matters. Membership includes students, representatives of each college, the library, research institutes, the provost, and the Faculty Senate.

Information Technology Student Advisory Committee

The students advise the CIO on matters related to information technology access for students, matters related to certain academic or administrative issues, and use of student technology fees. The committee helps facilitate communication to student groups across the campus on IT-related matters. Members include student leaders, both graduate and undergraduate.

Information Technology Administrative Advisory Committee

The committee advises the CIO on IT matters related to administrative issues; provides input to and reviews the administrative sections of the *IT Strategic Plan*; establishes priorities of all IT administrative projects brought before the committee; participates in the development of IT standards, guidelines, and procedures related to administrative information technology; and helps facilitate communication across the campus on all IT-related matters. This committee consists of representatives from the provost's office, each vice presidential unit, the schools and colleges, a representative from the Staff Senate, and representatives from Information Systems.

IT Strategic Planning and Management Model

The IT strategic planning and management model also stressed the necessity of a shared vision for the internal IS staff. From this staff of approximately 100, about 65% voluntarily met throughout the fall of 1995 to collectively begin the process of aligning their services and skills with the aggressive initiatives that faced them and to begin building a shared sense of vision, understanding, and buy-in.

The first alignment process was to assess individual core values and then to derive a values statement for the new organization for which there was a consensus commitment. A number of exercises from *The Fifth Discipline Fieldbook* (Senge et al., 1994, pp. 193-234, 297-350), including "Personal Mastery" and "Shared Vision," were used. This resulted in a list of 13 values for the IS organization, which are now posted in each unit office. The fundamental purpose of IS, a broad-based extended mission statement, and a three- to five-year futures scenario were also derived for the new division. The outcome of this initial planning stage was the development of six institutional strategies designed to provide guidelines for moving to the envisioned future. Each of these "pieces" was initially developed by the IS staff in draft form then discussed, modified, and approved by the governance structure. The exercise and rapid defining of institutional strategies, while not without some controversy, serve as the linchpin to future efforts and provide focus to initiatives that have institutional ramifications and require a great degree of collaboration and leadership at all levels.

Planned and bold steps by the institution were required to contend with its peer competitors. Because major shifts in education are being realized by all institutions of learning — older, nontraditional students, virtual classrooms, more learning by discovery, instructors as facilitators of learning, and distributed campuses— it was critical that changes be strategically planned. It was necessary to recognize the relationship between the institution and its IT environment, to make difficult decisions concerning the institution's desired IT future, and to realize the ultimate purpose of IT planning — which is decision making to support the good of the institution (Shirley, 1988).

During the fall of 1995, meetings were held with all college deans and administrative unit heads to understand the current environment and discuss future needs and initiatives. Input was sought during these visits on perceived institutional and IS divisional strengths and weaknesses that influence information technology implementation and support.

Within the IS Division, planning centered on making a thorough self-examination and then exhibiting a willingness to make the sometimes difficult decisions to act upon identified changes. Examinations focused upon: how the unit was staffed; how the unit was budgeted and how those resources were utilized; what the physical facilities lacked and how existing facilities could best be utilized; what technologies were in place and what were necessary; what the competencies of the IT staff were and what were the needed competencies; what image was projected to clientele; what was the cultural climate in which the unit operated; and what were the services provided. Strengths and weaknesses in each of these areas and in the internal and external environment in which the unit operated were carefully analyzed.

In examining service offerings, the IS unit first reviewed new service concepts internally, then submitted them for review to the advisory committees, compared recommendations, and came to meaningful agreement. The examination of existing services helped determine which services to eliminate, how the staff felt about those decisions, and how clients felt about the decisions. Some services simply needed modification and some services were unchanged. Having completed that exercise, it was necessary to get the resources properly assigned and aligned to ensure delivery.

An aggressive decision to serve as a beta site for a new administrative systems support platform and outsourcing of University systems development personnel to provide training and leadership occurred during year two of the new administration. Elsewhere within the IS division, alignment of positions and incumbents was taking place. Certain individuals retooled their skills and transitioned successfully, others less so, and a few, not at all — who ended up leaving University employment.

Fiscal Support

External factors required addressing fiscal resource support. The University was suffering severe budgetary constraints, and the forecast for future state assistance continued to be bleak. However, this did not prevent significant IT progress. The University president actively sought funding through traditional avenues but was also very proactive in developing influential constituencies at local and regional levels.

One example of fiscal support and the decision-making process is the campus allocation of student technology access fees (TAFs) that now generate approximately $4 million annually. These fees, closely monitored at the system level, may only be used for purposes that directly benefit the instructional component. Fund usage is endorsed at the IT Policy & Planning Council level, but the real use determinations are made at an operational level. The associate vice president for IS, who has budgetary responsibility for TAF, works with IS staff and an infrastructure support group to develop a campus-wide "footprint" for infrastructure and academic computing resources. This proposal is discussed among the deans from not only a campus-wide perspective, but also how it affects individual colleges. Final recommendations are submitted to the IT Policy & Planning Council for endorsement and to the University Budget Committee for approval. This illustrates a process that pushes decision making to the lowest and most practical level, and has allowed significant and meaningful change to occur.

Human Resource Support

Human resource support is also a major concern. Developing and acquiring IT staff to support the new learning organization and the associated planning and management process entails a concerted and coordinated institutional approach. A process of staff self-examination identifies skills necessary for successful IS operation. Once the IT governance structure and the Information Systems staff agree upon desired outcomes and services, designated training and professional development exercises became points of focus. Units that have project responsibility define needs and identify individual training and development plans. The VP/CIO office carves out a significant allocation of the existing budget to support the retraining efforts. Distributed IT support at the college and administrative unit levels is also critical. The Policy & Planning Council collectively identified an institutional strategy that redefined more than 50 existing positions for localized IT support. These Local Support Providers (LSPs) are an important ad hoc working group that meet on a regular basis to discuss tactical roll-out issues such as scheduling, interdepartmental coordination, training, public relations (which must be coordinated), as well as common support concerns.

IS personnel are trained by the VP/CIO office and professional consultants in what it means to be a learning organization and how that alters the way they work and make decisions — both individually and collectively. This requires them to work in different ways with clientele and builds levels of trust and confidence that had not existed before. This strengthens the IT planning process between constituencies by supporting a shared vision and common goals (DiBella & Nevis, 1998).

The idea of individual adaptive change, previously mentioned, pertains to both management and staff, and encompasses every IS employee. Managers must move from the stance of traditional bureaucrats and technical managers to that of managerial mentors and facilitators (with staff) and relationship managers (across the university). This means that individuals need to commit themselves to an unending path of learning. It also means that individuals must grow accustomed to rapid and ongoing personal change. Neither is easy to do for people who have worked many years in a bureaucratic environment. A change in organizational culture does not come quickly; full realization of a learning organization environment takes a minimum of five years and perhaps much longer (Schein, 1997). Perceptible changes in many individuals, however, are visible three years into the process.

Process Support

Process support is crucial to any change effort. A learning organization model can be successfully implemented only if processes are in place to support it. This can often prove to be one of the more challenging components to meaningful change. It may very well threaten existing internal structures, power, and influence. The IS staff is encouraged to think independently, let common sense be their guide, "communicate-communicate-communicate," "focus-focus-focus," and "just do it" when it makes sense. Query is fundamental and, in a culture where that had not been encouraged to any great degree, change comes slowly (Watkins & Marsick, 1993). Nevertheless, illogical bureaucratic chains-of-command are beginning to dissolve when confronted. Rules, regulations, and perceived constraints are continually analyzed within the decision-making context to make new and better corporate decisions (Mankin, Cohen, & Bikson, 1996). Time does not allow consensus on some issues, so when a critical mass of support is secured, action is taken.

Recognition is an invaluable process support mechanism. Lead by a grassroots volunteer committee, the IS staff designed a rewards program that incorporated both contemporary and traditional methods of recognition. It allows recognition to occur at the time it is earned, encourages team values, supports innovation and risk-taking, and respects diversity. This highly successful program (which has very few "rules" associated with it and virtually eliminates collegial competition for competition's sake) helps bring together a staff that celebrates one another's successes (Hesselbein & Cohen, 1999). Another form of recognition is deriving more competitive compensation levels for IT staff through a rigorous exercise of benchmarking and using industry standards to define job roles and responsibilities. The IS organization works closely with Human Resources (HR) to assure equity and parity, and gives exhaustive attention to recruitment and retention mechanisms that work. All IT positions across the institution are linked to the area market.

Few processes can be as supportive as leadership-by-example. There can be little discontinuity between corporate lip service and daily practices, leaders must "walk the talk." Leaders cannot ignore the need for the skills required for managing change, and they can encourage creativity while they take the sting out of failure (Bennis & Beiderman, 1997). To help develop such abilities, the IS unit again works with the HR training department to provide professional development especially in "soft skill" areas. Areas such as conflict resolution, project, time, and stress management require continuous support.

Ongoing attention and focus create nurtured perceptions. "The primary function of culture management during a process of change is to implement and sustain changes" (Galpin, 1996, p. 54). The infusion of new planning and management practices and the associated behaviors expected of the IS staff are carefully and continuously supported from their introduction, thus allowing them to begin the embedding process into the organizational culture. Achieving and sustaining organizational change mandates that the culture of the organization be affected. Changes in organizational culture are supported by tangible reinforcements such as pay-for-performance in selected cases, reassignment of work to better align skill sets with tasks at hand, providing people with meaningful work, and continually communicating the big picture (Floyd & Wooldridge, 1996).

The old performance evaluation process within the Information Systems Division has been significantly revised. Evaluations now include self-appraisals, supervisory reviews by line staff, and peer reviews at the management team level (Reddy, 1994). These reflective exercises promote meaningful dialogue between raters and individual staff on issues such as training and development. This allows a planning focus as well as an evaluative process to take place. Merit salary adjustments, when available, directly correlate to staff appraisal scores, and the organization takes great care to ensure equity across the division.

An ombudsperson program exists to provide an avenue for problem resolution when regular organizational channels do not meet an individual's needs or are not appropriate. After nomination by their peers, two individuals appointed by the CIO serve on a rotational two-year term as IS ombudspersons. Internal staff as well as clients are encouraged to utilize the services of the ombudspersons, and the program is publicized in each edition of the campus technology newsletter and on the IS Web site.

Every level within the organization needs leadership. The behaviors of those leaders (whether at the executive, management, or supervisory level) prove to have a tremendous impact on the success of managing change to support the IT strategic planning and management model (Hesselbein, Goldsmith, & Beckhard, 1997).

ANALYSIS

Outcomes

The IT strategic planning and management model has met with early success. The fifth IT strategic plan is now in effect, and critical masses of decision makers across the institution have bought into the process. Meetings conducted twice annually with each major academic and administrative unit to determine IT need and solicit feedback work well. The academic deans meet regularly with the associate vice president for IS to specify academic IT needs and to make recommendations to the IT Policy and Planning Council for prioritization. The IS staff is also comfortable with the process and has met stated goals for completing objectives in each of the four prior plans (completing in excess of 90% of the initially stated objectives each year). Metrics for ongoing assessments of what constitutes satisfactory service are established and published on the Web monthly and discussed with client groups periodically. The overall IS productivity, as measured by the size of the IT infrastructure in relation to the number of full-time equivalent staff positions, has increased by a factor of five, and there is demonstrable progress on all three of the major IT initiatives that were initially set forth in 1995.

The initiative to move toward a learning organization culture is slow, as expected, but exhibits steady progress. A number of meaningful organizational adjustments are now in place including: providing at least three professional development opportunities for each staff member annually; establishing two ombudsperson roles; initiating ongoing focus groups; selecting, training, and implementing work teams; and creating a process to recognize and celebrate individual and team-based achievement. Regular ongoing workshops on learning organization principles and skills exist for staff members, and a mentoring process for managers is being introduced during this fiscal year. Both formal and informal assessment indicates that the staff is gaining skills and using them in providing service to the client community.

The governance process has been modified somewhat and defined in greater detail over the years (see below) and is functioning effectively and efficiently. The IT Policy and Planning Council meets approximately every six weeks during the regular academic year where it approves IT-related decisions of consequence to the entire University and establishes IT policy. The advisory committees meet monthly, review progress toward objectives, and make recommendations on selected issues. As previously noted, a year ago the institution was selected to participate in the "Institution-Wide Information Strategies" project sponsored by the Coalition for Networked Information.

The Budget Committee for the campus has steadily increased the proportion of institutional budget (augmented by the TAF) allocated for IT-related expenditures. Over a four-year period, that ratio has increased from approximately 3.5% to about 6%, enabling the University to be fully competitive with its designated peers. The University has moved from near the bottom of its 10 designated peers to near the top in this ratio and other benchmark ratings.

The IT organization is judged to be considerably stronger from both the addition of well-qualified professionals and by the elimination of some who were not performing up to their potential. A number of existing positions were upgraded and/or redefined to better fit the current needs of the institution. Of particular note in this regard is the shift of some half-dozen positions from primarily administrative functions to primarily academic support positions. A strategy for the IS unit to provide the main support for the IT infrastructure and for distributed IT positions to be the primary routine desktop support was approved by the IT Policy and Planning Council in 1997. Since then, approximately 55 LSP positions have been created across the campus. This has enabled reasonably clear roles to be established for IS personnel and for the LSPs, which together provide an improved service level to the campus community.

Successes/Failures and Adjustments

In addition to the major successes noted above, one other should be stressed — support from the executive officers of the university. Without their broad-based level of support, the necessary involvement of faculty and staff would not have been so forthcoming. The failures have come from decisions related to implementation procedures rather than from the more global strategies. It was determined that participating as a beta test site would provide a way to move aggressively to a new administrative system. Once that decision was made, it became obvious that the existing staff needed to be upgraded and augmented to accomplish the goal. It was thought that outsourcing a portion of the staff to the vendor with whom the beta test was to be done would best accomplish this. Due to time constraints and certain legal reasons, the outsourcing decision could not be discussed with the staff until it was to be implemented. This proved to have been an unfortunate circumstance. As one might expect, the staff was initially shocked, then disturbed by the move. After several months, it became evident that the product scheduled for installation would not be the "next generation" system that was desired, and the beta involvement was ended. Shortly after that, by mutual agreement, the outsourced staff returned to the employment of the university. A great deal of time and energy has been exerted to repair the damage, and progress has been considerable, but lingering feelings are still evident at times. Fortunately, a new beta test is underway with a true next generation system, and staff training in new technologies is underway. This staff was also part of the first work teams formed.

Although the governance structure has become a major success, it got off to a rocky start. Appropriate care was not taken to define in enough detail the role of Policy and Planning Council members. It soon became obvious that some members were not carrying out their duties as expected and some were unhappy because they were not as involved in operational decisions as they had anticipated. This occurred simultaneously with the increased TAF, and some deans asked that the increased funds be directly allocated to academic units according to a formula. First, the Policy and Planning Council held a retreat with a facilitator to get all of the concerns from all parties out in the open for discussion. Secondly, the provost and the CIO came to an agreement to set up a process that would involve all of the deans in helping to put forth recommendations for TAF usage, with the stipulation that it would focus on overall university priorities. Finally, based on the retreat results, the CIO drafted and the president approved a more detailed role definition for the Policy and Planning Council; at the same time, they reconstituted the Council membership to include all of the deans and vice presidents. This created a group that makes IT decisions — one that has the charge and the authority to see that decisions are carried out.

CONCLUSION

Several factors contributed to the renewal of the IS unit and the success of institutional IT strategies. Consistent support and the articulation of that support by the executive officers were essential. Implementing a flexible IT strategic planning and management model purposefully linked to previously existing institutional processes set the stage for initial change and continues to define ongoing, progressive change. Another key component is the definition and evolution of an IT governance structure empowered to make decisions and charged to implement them. The reallocation of existing resources and the development of new funds to support IT initiatives is crucial to current and future success. The adaptation of learning organization principles to routine organizational operation and the infusion of them into the planning and management model seem to have begun a progression toward a new culture. Finally, the involvement of a broad array of people across the institution in governance, decision making, and team-based activities is leading to the "buy-in" so essential to long-term success.

After approximately four years, the IS Division is more than halfway through the timeframe required to acquire the characteristics of a learning organization. If the rate of progress to date can be sustained, the unit should be prepared to provide the quality of service needed by the university to meet goals of the early 21st century.

DISCUSSION QUESTIONS

1. What types of organizational changes have been brought about by information technology in your organization?
2. What are some of the barriers that make it difficult to effect information technology change? How is this different for administration, faculty, students, and support staff?
3. How important is governance structure in information technology strategic planning?

REFERENCES

Bennis, W., & Biederman, P. W. (1997). *Organizing genius: The secrets of creative collaboration*. Reading, MA: Addison-Wesley.

DiBella, A. J., & Nevis, E. C. (1998). *How organizations learn*. San Francisco: Jossey-Bass.

Floyd, S. W., & Wooldridge, B. (1996). *The strategic middle manager*. San Francisco: Jossey-Bass.

Galpin, T. (1996). *The human side of change*. San Francisco: Jossey-Bass.

Hesselbein, F., & Cohen, P. M. (1999). *Leader to leader*. San Francisco: Jossey-Bass.

Hesselbein, F., Goldsmith, M., & Beckhard, R. (Eds.). (1997). *The organization of the future*. San Francisco: Jossey-Bass.

Mankin, D., Cohen, S. G., & Bikson, T. K. (1996). *Teams and technology: Fulfilling the promise of the new organization*. Boston: Harvard Business School Press.

Oblinger, D. G., & Rush, S. C. (1997). *The learning revolution: The challenge of information technology in the academy*. Bolton, MA: Anker Publishing Company.

Penrod, J. I. (1998). Information technology governance and strategic planning. *CNI-Institution-Wide Information Strategies*. Retrieved April 24, 1998, from http://www.cni.org/project/iwis97rep/iwis97.html.

Reddy, W. B. (1994). *Intervention skills: Process consultation for small groups and teams*. San Diego: Pfeiffer & Company.

Schein, E. H. (1997). *Organizational culture and leadership*. San Francisco: Jossey-Bass.

Senge, P. M. (1990). *The fifth discipline*. New York: Doubleday.

Senge, P. M., Kleiner, A., Roberts, C., Ross, R., Roth, G., & Smith, B. (1999). *The dance of change*. New York: Doubleday.

Shirley, R. C. (1988). Strategic planning: An overview. In M. Kramer (Series Ed.), & D. W. Steeples (Vol. Ed.), *New directions for higher education, Vol. 64. Successful Strategic Planning: Case Studies* (pp. 5-15). San Francisco: Jossey-Bass.

Smith, B., & Yanowitz, J. (1996, Third Quarter). The role of leadership in a learning organization. *Prism: Leadership and the Accelerating Organization*, 58-59.

Tapscott, D., & Caston, A. (1993). *Paradigm shift: The new promise of information technology.* New York: McGraw-Hill.

Watkins, K. E., & Marsick, V. J. (1993). *Sculpting the learning organization: Lessons in the art and science of systemic change.* San Francisco: Jossey-Bass.

This case was previously published in L. A. Petrides (Ed.), *Case Studies on Information Technology in Higher Education: Implications for Policy and Practice*, pp. 280-296, © 2000.

Chapter V

Development of an Information Kiosk for a Large Transport Company:
Lessons Learned

Pieter Blignaut, University of the Free State, South Africa

Iann Cruywagen, Interstate Bus Lines (Pty.) Ltd., Bloemfontein, South Africa

EXECUTIVE SUMMARY

An information kiosk system is a computer-based information system in a publicly accessible place. Such a system was developed for a large public transport company to provide African commuters with limited educational background with up-to-date information on schedules and ticket prices while also presenting general company information in a graphically attractive way. The challenges regarding liaison with passengers are highlighted and the use of a touchscreen kiosk to supplement current liaison media is justified. System architecture is motivated and special services offered by the system are discussed. Several lessons were learned regarding the implementation of such a system in general, as well as in this environment specifically. An online survey indicated that the system fulfils its role of providing useful information in an accessible medium to commuters in a reasonable time.

ORGANIZATIONAL BACKGROUND

The transport of workers between their place of residence and workplace is a worldwide phenomenon, which has been given a unique twist in the Republic of South Africa due to the policy of Apartheid imposed by the previous government. This policy has given rise to cities such as Botshabelo in the central Free State, 47 kilometers from Bloemfontein, the industrial center of the region. Even though Apartheid has been abolished and citizens are free to stay where they choose, practical necessity dictates that Botshabelo, as a legacy of the Apartheid policy, will remain viable and populated for a long time to come.

The workers of the central Free State, settled far from their workplace and unable to afford private means of motorized transport, use public passenger transport. In the absence of commuter trains in this region, this need is addressed by 16-seater minibus taxis and buses.

Interstate Bus Lines (Pty.) Ltd. as a Major Transporting Company

The public transport service provider in the central Free State, Interstate Bus Lines (Pty.) Ltd. (IBL), was founded in 1975 as Thaba 'Nchu Transport, and has since grown to a major company with 508 full-time employees. IBL operates a fleet of 62 train and 134 standard buses from the cities of Botshabelo, Thaba 'Nchu, and Mangaung to the terminal building at Central Park in Bloemfontein. A train bus pivots around a center point and may carry 110 seated passengers, whereas a standard bus is rigid and is designed to transport 65 seated passengers. IBL operates 702 trips daily in this area and transports 70,500 to 80,000 passengers weekly between their homes and workplaces (see the map of the operational area in Figure 1).

Figure 1. Operational area of IBL

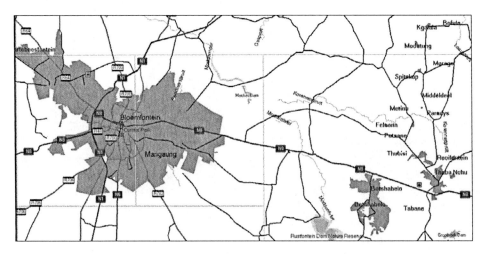

Depending on the exact area where a person lives or works, it may happen that he or she will have to take more than one bus for a one-way trip. At Central Park, commuters may transfer to other buses heading for various businesses and factories, as well as the traditionally white suburbs. Central Park also serves as the main ticket selling point.

IBL also provides other services to its community, for example, unsubsidized feeder services in Botshabelo, as well as between Botshabelo and Thaba 'Nchu, and the transport of students to and from schools. Passengers living to the north and south of Thaba 'Nchu are also provided with transport services (Figure 1).

Interstate Bus Lines has a fleet of buses fully committed to peak demand, with allowances made for workshop allocation. IBL is equipped to render a service, along with the minibus taxi industry, to satisfy the public demand. IBL itself services and maintains its fleet of buses. The bus fleet is of the most modern in the Republic of South Africa, with an average age of 4.8 years per bus. IBL trains its own drivers during an intensive six-week course. Drivers receive annual retraining and evaluation, lasting a further two weeks.

IBL's income is based on ticket sales along with a government subsidy and a small special trip market, and averages around USD 2 million per month, which amounts to an annual turnover of around USD 24.2 million. IBL's fleet of buses travels approximately 14.5 million kilometers per year while consuming 5.6 million liters of fuel.

Services run from 4:15 to 22:30 daily. The peak requirement is from 6:00 to 07:45 in the mornings and from 15:30 to 18:00 in the afternoons — peak being defined as the time when the total bus fleet is fully committed to the transport of commuters. Figure 2 indicates the times when the largest concentration of commuters passes through Central

Figure 2. Average number of passengers passing through central park per half hour interval during week days

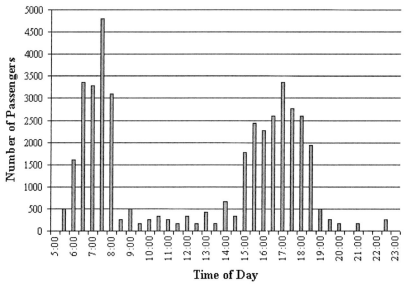

Figure 3. Graphical representation of IBL's clientele base

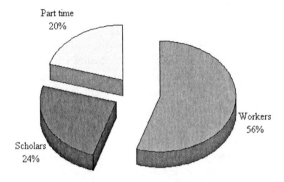

Park. All commuters must be in possession of a valid ticket, purchased from the Central Park ticket kiosk. These tickets are daily, one-way, weekly or monthly tickets.

Passenger Profile

Interstate Bus Lines conducts frequent surveys in order to determine the profile of its passengers. According to the most recent survey (Breytenbach, 2003), passengers are mostly African (89.1%), Sotho-speaking (51.0%), female (52.3%), and are predominantly domestic workers (20.8%). According to the living standards index, 95.8% have electricity in their homes, and 63.2% earn between $135.00 and $275.00 per month. The average educational level of commuters is grade six, although 27.3% of passengers are enrolled for a post-school qualification. Less than 10% of IBL's passengers have access to computers and less than 5% have access to the Internet, either at home or at work.

IBL transports predominantly domestic workers, although students, part-time workers and shoppers constitute almost half of the company's clientele base (Figure 3). Many passengers are younger than 30 years of age and are studying or have just completed some form of education.

IT Infrastructure

Business processes are fully supported by information technology. IBL uses a system of electronic ticket machines (ETMs) and all ticket sales are recorded in a database. Tickets bear a magnetic strip and when a passenger boards a bus, the ticket is swiped and the passenger recorded for the specific route and trip. Special electronic equipment is installed in the gearbox of every bus that records movement times and speed. The raw data from these devices is processed and used to prepare statistics on passenger numbers and kilometers traveled on a monthly basis. These statistics are then used as proof for the monthly government subsidy claim.

On the passenger liaison side, however, IT applications are non-existent. One would think that potential for a Web page exists but the lack of access to computer technology and the limited computer literacy of commuters would make this a futile exercise.

SETTING THE STAGE

Need for Communication

Dora Ramakoatse works as housekeeper in the home of a wealthy Bloemfontein business man. She is 46 years of age and her native tongue is Sesotho. She also speaks some Afrikaans and English. She has formal school education up to grade 5 and has a limited reading capability.

Dora lives in Botshabelo and every morning at 5:00, she boards a bus for a trip of some 50 kilometers to Central Park. There she transfers to another bus for the suburb of Hospital Park where her employer and his family live. At about 6:30 she is just in time to wake the kids, prepare breakfast and start her daily duties of washing, cleaning and ironing. At 15:30, she once again takes a bus to Central Park and from there to Botshabelo. At around 17:00, she arrives at her own home, exhausted but still with the responsibility of seeing to the basic needs of her own family, such as preparing meals for the evening and the day to come.

Dora is entirely dependent on the commuter service to get to and from her workplace. She used to complain about buses being late or not even turning up for scheduled trips. In the winter, she has a problem with buses being extremely cold in the early mornings. Sometimes she complains of buses being overloaded or having reckless or impatient drivers. Being dependent on a basic minimum wage, annual tariff increases hit hard and she does not always understand why these increases are necessary.

What Dora needs is to be able to express her complaints in a medium that will allow her to comment immediately when the problem occurs. Also, Dora needs the assurance that her complaints will reach those who can do something about it. This medium should not only allow commuters to give feedback on IBL's services, but should also present commuters with information on schedules and ticket prices.

Communicating with Commuters: The Traditional Approach

Upon taking up this matter with IBL's management, Dora's employer was told, as part of their customer care drive, IBL has implemented a toll-free hotline, where complaints, questions, and suggestions are handled and processed. Also, George Mokgothu, public relations officer of IBL, holds regular focus group discussions where community leaders can raise their concerns and express their needs on a monthly basis. George takes note of specific complaints, and provides information on relevant items such as route changes, tariff increases, and feedback on previous enquiries. George also hosts a weekly, hour-long radio talk show on Lesedi FM, the radio station patronized by 86.3% of IBL's passengers. As a part of this show, listeners are invited to phone in and question him, live on air, about IBL's service.

Infrequently, IBL also runs advertisements in local newspapers, advertising mostly for the special trip market. Annual tariff increases are communicated via major advertisements in the local media. Need-to-know passenger information, for example, tariffs for specific routes are available for perusal in each bus. Brochures with timetables, routes and stops are available on request at Central Park. These may also be faxed or e-mailed to passengers on request.

Figure 4. Touchscreen information kiosk at IBL ticket office in Central Park

But Dora was still not happy. She does not have the confidence to phone in to the radio talk show and raise her concerns in public. She also does not have personal contact with the community leaders who represent her in the focus groups. She wants a medium of communication through which she can complain about IBL's services, knowing that her complaints will reach the right ears and will be attended to. She wants access to schedules and tariffs without having to wait for an initiative from IBL. She also complains that the brochures are often outdated before they hit the streets. People also remove the brochures from the buses and notice boards.

George confirms that it is difficult to replace brochures on just about 200 buses with updated ones at short notice. He also confirms that he cannot keep up with answering all the queries to the satisfaction of both IBL and its clientele on a regular basis. He needs a way to disseminate information regarding route and schedule changes, tariff increases, and so forth at short notice.

Communicating with Commuters: Alternative Approach

After consulting with George, passenger representatives and local authorities, Interstate Bus Lines approached the Department of Computer Science and Informatics (DCSI) at the University of the Free State (UFS) early in 2003 to assist in a search for a solution. A touchscreen information kiosk (Figure 4) was identified as a way of supplementing the communication techniques mentioned previously while at the same time overcoming some of the disadvantages of these techniques. Additionally, it could also serve the purpose of improving the company's corporate image among commuters and could expose previously deprived people to technology. The idea was that the system should present commuters with the opportunity to query a database regarding routes, schedules and ticket prices. During periods of inactivity, the system should present general company information on a continuous basis. As an added bonus, advertisements from shops in the center could be displayed. Passers-by or people queuing in front of a ticket box should then be able to follow the presentations which are accompanied by attractive graphic animations and sound or video clips.

It was imperative that the system be updatable on a regular basis as ticket prices increase, timetables change, shops change their special promotions, and so forth. Furthermore, it should be possible for George and other staff members of IBL to do these updates themselves after the developers of the system have handed over the completed system. In an attempt to conform to these requirements, a user-friendly switchboard application was integrated with a set of presentations and a single-user database package to set up a comprehensive information kiosk while allowing maintenance by people with end-user skills only.

Because of the centralized location of the ticket office, it was not necessary to connect the system to other information kiosks. Also, because of the non-existence of a Web page, no need existed to connect the system to the Internet. Since the complete timetable is in any case maintained in an Access database for scheduling purposes and driver instructions as part of the business process, it was worthwhile exploring the possibility of connecting the kiosk system to this database by means of a local area network.

This case study outlines the impediments, design issues and pitfalls that were encountered during the implementation of the system.

CASE DESCRIPTION

Information kiosk systems are computer-based information systems in publicly accessible places, offering access to information or transactions for an anonymous, constantly varying group of users with typically short dialogue times and a simple user interface (Holfelder & Hehmann, 1994). Depending on the nature of the business, the presence of an information kiosk could be a necessity, but most probably is a supplement to existing means of communication. The success of such systems depends largely on the attractiveness of their user interfaces, how easily they allow access to information and how clearly the information is presented (Borchers, Deussen, & Knörzer, 1995). It is no use having the technology with all the latest information if Dora and others like her cannot access it or do not understand how to use it.

Classification of Information Kiosks

Borchers, Deussen, and Knörzer (1995) propose a classification of kiosk systems according to their major tasks:

- Information kiosks have the primary goal of providing information in a limited subject field, for example, at a railway station where users can find information on a connection to a chosen destination. Users of such systems use the system because they need the information — they do not have to be extrinsically motivated to use the system.
- Advertising kiosks are installed by companies to present themselves or their products to the public in an attractive and innovative way. The missing initial motivation of potential users has to be compensated for by a visually attractive

design. The contents should be interesting and entertaining and should motivate the user to explore the system further.

- Service kiosks are similar to information kiosks with the added functionality of information entry by the user, for example, hotel reservation systems where data such as names and addresses have to be entered to make a booking.
- Entertainment kiosks usually do not have a specific task apart from entertaining the user.

Borchers, Deussen, and Knörzer (1995) acknowledge that most information kiosk systems will belong to two or more of the previously mentioned classes. The system that was developed for the IBL ticket office can typically be regarded as both an information kiosk and an advertising kiosk with the potential to include the functionality of a service kiosk at a later stage.

System Architecture

Development Tools

Several possibilities regarding the development tools were considered in order to develop a system that would fulfill in the needs as expressed previously. A presentation package such as Microsoft PowerPoint® provides for easy end-user updates while allowing attractive graphical animations and multimedia effects. The preparation of an individual slide for every trip makes this, however, an impractical solution.

A user-friendly front-end system to query the database for the relevant information or a fully-fledged object-oriented database environment to store graphic images, video clips, and so forth as well as the route and timetable information, could have been developed by professional programmers. Another possibility that was considered was a series of HTML and ASP files to be viewed in a browser. Such an environment would have allowed the combination of graphic attractiveness, the use of multimedia and database querying. Although these tools might have done the job, they would have been difficult to maintain for people with end-user skills only.

Finally, it was decided to develop the IBL system by integrating a dedicated end-user application (developed in Delphi®) with a presentation package (Microsoft PowerPoint®) and a single-user database package (Microsoft Access®) inside Microsoft Windows® as operating system. Together with the fact that the complete timetable was already available in Microsoft Access, both PowerPoint and Access were reasonably well known by the staff members of IBL who would be responsible for system mainte-nance. The integration was done in such a way that commuters would not be aware of transitions between the environments. A diagrammatic representation of the system is shown in Figure 5.

A form at the bottom of the screen acts as a switchboard (Figure 6). Buttons on the switchboard allow users to navigate through the system. Some of the options activate MS PowerPoint presentations in the upper part of the display. These presentations convey general company information, ticket office hours, contact telephone numbers, advertisements from shops in the center, and so on. Other options enable users to query the MS Access database for route information, ticket prices, schedules, and so forth.

Figure 5. Diagrammatic representation of the IBL system

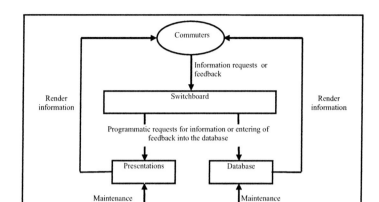

Figure 6. Switchboard and MS PowerPoint presentation

Figure 7. On-screen keyboard to allow free text input with touch typing

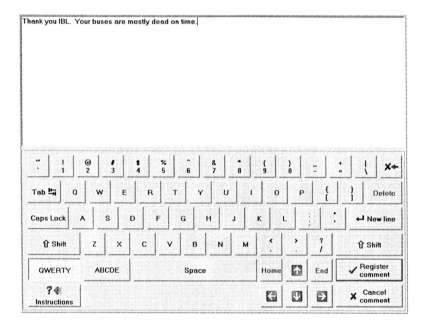

The use of a dedicated end-user application as switchboard also allows the programmatic capturing of research data such as frequencies of usage, commuters' preferences regarding language, typing speed, as well as a limited user profile. These values are saved into the underlying database and are analyzed periodically by the researchers.

Services Offered

One of the most important needs that Dora expressed was to be able to lodge complaints as they arose. Also, in order for George to be able to communicate passenger needs to management, he has to know what they think and how they experience the services that IBL renders.

The information kiosk allows commuters to register comments, complaints, requests, and so forth by means of an on-screen keyboard (Figure 7). The idea for this technique is accredited to researchers at the Human Computer Interface Laboratory at the University of Maryland (Plaisant & Sears, 1992; Sears, 1991; Sears, Kochavy, & Shneiderman, 1990; Sears, Revis, Swatski, Crittendon, & Shneiderman, 1993). Valuable feedback for IBL has been generated in this way. Although many passerbys use this facility just for the sake of playing around and to get the feel of using a touchscreen, some 800 valid and useful comments were registered in the period May to December 2003. Since the information kiosk is available night and day, Dora is now happy that she has a way to express her concerns the moment that she gets off a bus. Also, George has expressed his satisfaction for getting honest and unbiased feedback on a daily basis.

Figure 8. Form to query database for trip details

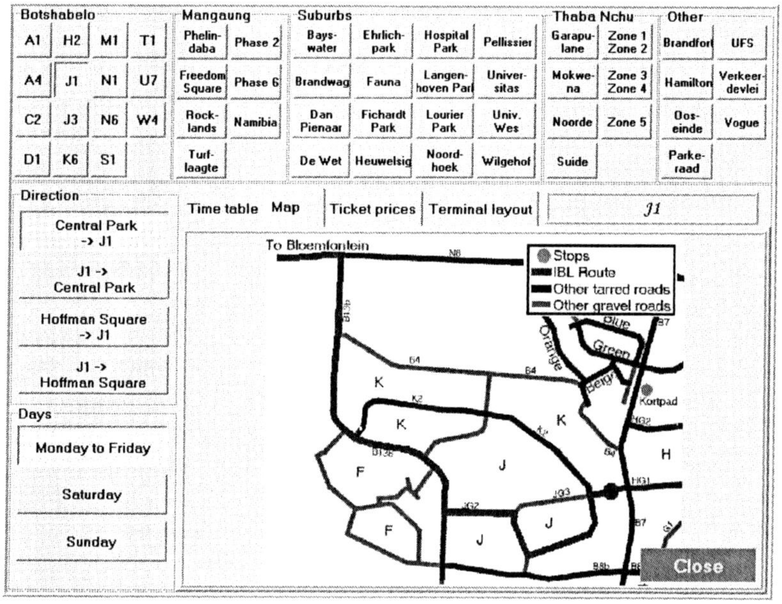

Route and timetable information is kept in an MS Access database. Commuters are able to query the database by means of a form that is displayed full-screen, covering the running presentation windows. Figure 8 shows a screen print of this form.

Lessons Learned During Development

Several sources are available that provides guidelines for the design of touchscreen-based information kiosks (Borchers, Deussen, & Knörzer, 1995; ELO Touch Systems, 2002; ELO Touch Systems, 2003; MicroTouch Systems, Inc., 2000). These guidelines are mostly generic of nature and not specific to a particular package or an integrated approach as is proposed here. During the development of this system, several lessons were learned that proved to be critical in an integrated development approach.

Physical Mounting of the Screen

According to ELO Touch Systems (2002), the cabinet in which the touchscreen is installed should be in the company colors, have proper ventilation and should be mounted at a viewing angle that minimizes differences in user height. The design of the cabinet should be attractive and sturdy. In the current study, the system was installed in a metal casing just below average eye-level and mounted against the wall between two cubicles of the ticket office at a slight angle (Figure 4). The screen was placed inside the metal casing in such a way that only the glass part was accessible in order to avoid users tampering with the screen's adjustment controls. The screen could be closed by a lockable lid after hours. This has worked well and to date no incidences of tampering or vandalism have occurred. The continuous presentations attract the attention of passerbys and are visible to people queuing at the ticket offices. This near-vertical mounting also prevents people from putting objects, for example, food, parcels, and so forth, on the screen.

Touch Modes

Potter, Weldon, and Shneiderman (1988) describe a lift-off strategy for touchscreens that implies that the selection is not made when the user touches the screen but when he lifts his finger from the screen. This allows the user to put his finger on the screen and then make a correction to adjust the position of the pointer. 3M Touch Systems (2002) indicates that the so-called desktop mode is most useful for general-purpose desktop applications. In this mode, a touch positions the cursor in much the same way as a mouse does. Holding the touch steady is equivalent to pressing and holding the mouse button. Lifting off is equivalent to releasing the mouse button.

In the current study, it was found that both these strategies seem to be unnatural to the average user from the IBL commuter community. These users expect a reaction from the system as soon as they press a button. If nothing happens, they tend to press harder without lifting the finger. It was found that the button-mode was the most appropriate strategy for this user group. In this mode, touching the screen is equivalent to pressing and releasing the mouse button. The action occurs as soon as you touch the screen.

System Cursor

The lift-off strategy proposed by Shneiderman (1991) implies that a cursor should be visible on the screen that is not obscured by the finger. The concept of a visible cursor is contradictory, however to the idea of ELO Touch Systems (2003) that there should be no cursor because the user should focus on the entire screen instead of the arrow.

The normal pointing cursor for button-aware applications is the northwest pointer, but for PowerPoint presentations, the default cursor for links is the pointing finger. In order not to confuse commuters, it was essential to change the cursor to a consistent graphic throughout the system. A top-down arrow has its hot spot on the bottom tip of the arrow and presents good feedback with regard to the exact item selected since the cursor is not entirely obscured by the finger. To replace the top-down arrow with a hand with finger pointing downward would, however, suggest an awkward physical position. In the end it was decided that the visual clue of a hand with a pointing finger outweighs the disadvantage of occasional obscuring.

Use of Sound

The effect of sound to attract attention and for purposes of feedback is well known (Preece, Rogers, Sharp, Benyon, Holland, & Carey, 1994). The value added with regard to information conveyed is somewhat less, however. Speech has a transient nature. If you did not catch the message then you did not catch it, while written text has the advantage that it can be read over and over again at the reader's own tempo until he/she understands what is said.

At the IBL kiosk, each one of the running presentations had accompanying sound effects and narration. The facilities that expected user input had short written as well as spoken instructions. Users could at any time press a button to listen to the instructions again.

Touchscreens have no tactile feedback like a button on a soft microwave oven keypad that gives when pressed or a button on an elevator's keypad that can physically be depressed. Sound effects (e.g., an audible click with every valid press) and display changes (e.g., a button that is displayed differently when selected) are important to inform the user that the input was accepted.

The placement of the loudspeakers presented a problem. The speakers were placed inside the metal casing, facing the ventilation holes at the sides of the unit. The kiosk was placed in a public foyer with very bad acoustics, noise from nearby stores, and even a night club. Users complained that they could not hear properly, even with the volume setting at its highest. It would have been better had the casing been made a little wider so that the speakers could fit in next to the screen, facing towards the users behind a grid similar to the ventilation holes. A sound amplifier would also have been an improvement.

One Window with Many Inputs or Many Windows with One Input Each?

Due to users' limited previous exposure to technology and limited educational background, the need to keep the user interface simple and easy to use was identified from the start. For example, it was thought that, whenever a series of user inputs was required, a single screen capturing all the inputs would provide the simplest user interface. It was found, however, that such a screen confused and frustrated the users. The error messages they got due to incomplete inputs caused them to walk away. This approach was then replaced with one where the user inputs were obtained through a series of modal dialog boxes, appearing one after the other (Figure 9). Each dialog box had only one set of mutually exclusive buttons. This was accepted much more easily as users were guided to answer one question after the other.

Navigating Through a Series of Dialog Boxes

Initially, the series of dialog boxes was provided with a set of *Previous/Next* buttons similar to the typical setup wizards for many software applications. It was found,

Figure 9. Series of dialog boxes to determine user profile

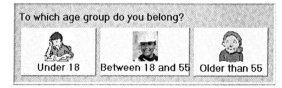

however, that users at the IBL ticket office did not understand the concept of going back to edit a previous input, became frustrated, and walked away leaving the system halfway through a sequence. The *Previous* buttons were then replaced with *Restart* to allow users to start with the query all over again. The *Next* buttons were taken away — when the user made a selection the next box in the sequence was automatically displayed. This approach was much better accepted. This might be another confirmation of the findings of Blake, Stevenson, Edge, and Foster (2001), as well as Walton and Vukovic (2003), that African people have a different view of hierarchies and sequences than Western people have.

Control Types: Buttons, Scroll Bars, Sliders, Radio Buttons, etc.

According to Shneiderman (1991), it is possible to use actions other than clicking a button on a touchscreen, for instance, sliding, dragging, rubbing, etc. He asserts that many actions that are unnatural with a mouse are more intuitive with a touchscreen, for example, dragging the arms of an alarm clock to set the time. Shneiderman (1991) discusses evidence that most users succeed immediately in using a touchscreen information kiosk that utilizes these kinds of interactions.

Our experience with the current study, however, was that users find the single tap on the screen easier than a slide. It was easier for them to adjust the sound volume if the control consisted of a set of discrete values implemented with radio buttons (Figure 6) than when they had to drag a slider along a continuous scale. It must always be kept in mind that users of the IBL system are casual users who are unlikely to use the system time and time again and will, therefore, never have the opportunity to practice the action of dragging.

Do Away with the Windows Task Bar

ELO Touch Systems (2002) recommends that the system should not have a "Windows look." There should be no indication of the operating system and users should not even think of the system as a computer system. In the current system, this lesson was learned the hard way. Initially, the Windows task bar was always available at the bottom of the screen, even though it was set to "auto-hide". Some of the users would press on a specific button and then read the information presented on the screen while dropping their hands off the screen at the bottom edge; this sometimes caused accidental touching of the screen again, which caused the task bar to jump up. For computer literate users, especially teenagers, this presented a challenge to fiddle around with the system, edit the PowerPoint presentations, search for evidence of Internet availability, and even close down the system. For computer illiterate users, the sudden appearance of a bar at the bottom of the screen distracted their attention and even made them uncertain about whether some reaction on their part was expected. When the task bar was removed altogether, these problems were largely solved.

Cater for User Ignorance

One of the general design guidelines for information kiosks states that system reaction must be immediate to prevent users from walking away (ELO Touch Systems, 2003). Any presentation must at any time be immediately available on request of a commuter. In this case study, all presentations were activated to run in the memory simultaneously, one behind the other. On request, the appropriate presentation can only be brought forward on the screen with no time delay due to loading.

It was also observed that some of the commuters, especially teenagers, just played around with the system, pressing one button after the other in quick succession. Commuters can press the buttons on the screen much faster than they can click a mouse, thereby expecting the system to switch between the various presentations or query the database and display results in a matter of milliseconds. To cater for these scenarios, it was important to ensure ample resources for the computer system. In this case study a PIII 866MHz CPU with 256 MB memory proved to be stable and efficient enough.

In a typical information kiosk environment, it is always possible that a specific user may leave the system halfway through a process or query. The next user might then be confused and even unable to get to the information he or she requires. It was, therefore, essential to add functionality for the system to reset itself and to return to the main screen after a period of inactivity.

Commuters' Comments

An online questionnaire allows commuters to select their answers from a set of possibilities (Figure 10). Norman, Friedman, Norman, and Stevenson (2001) provides guidelines regarding the layout of such online questionnaires.

Results obtained from this survey revealed that 71.1% of first-time users and 83.8% of follow-up users found the system easy or moderately easy to use. Also, 68.6% of first-time users and 70.6% of follow-up users indicated that they experienced a positive emotion, e.g., satisfaction or enjoyment, while using the system.

A rather low percentage of 40.2% first-time users indicated that they had found what they had been looking for. This was probably because the commuters expected the system to allow them to buy tickets from the machine rather than having to queue for them; something that had not, from the outset, been the intention of the system. The fact

Figure 10. On-screen survey form (extract only)

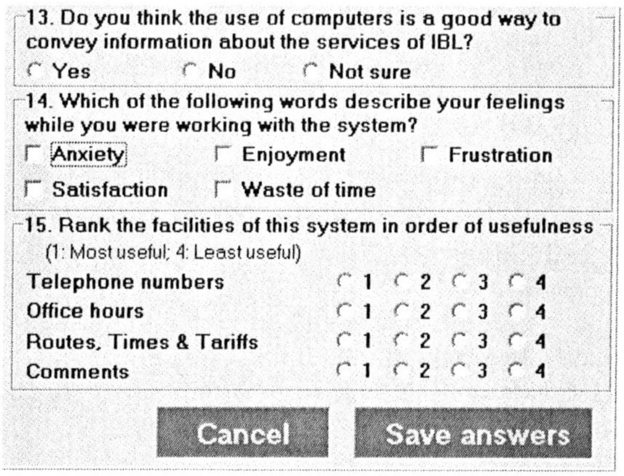

that 71.8% of follow-up users indicated that they had found what they had been looking for, confirms that the commuters realize the intention of the system after some exposure.

The fact that 70% of first-time users and 88% of follow-up users indicated that they found the information useful was regarded as an indication of commuters' rating of the value of the system.

In a usability study, selected users were asked to search for information on six specific items that were representative of the available information. On average, first-time users found 90.1% of the requested items correctly while follow-up users found 97% of the items correctly. The fact that follow-up users could obtain these items in about 4½ minutes can qualitatively be considered as acceptable to good in comparison with the two minutes that an expert user took to complete the tasks.

CURRENT CHALLENGES/PROBLEMS FACING THE ORGANIZATION

When a new IT installation is on the cards, one can always ask the question: Is this a "nice-to-have" or a critical necessity for business survival? How often does one see potential for implementation of an IT solution that promises to work better than the existing manual system with a concomitant saving in time, money and manpower and a positive impact on annual turnaround, but due to the skepticism of management and reluctance of employees to use it, the system is either not implemented or not utilized to the full?

This was and still is one of the biggest stumbling blocks that needed to be overcome with this kiosk system. Despite the fact that management and the PR, George, are convinced that the system adds value to the company, despite the fact that the usability results reported favorably to a large extent, and despite positive feedback from individuals such as Dora Ramakoatse, there are still those who are skeptical about the system. This was especially evident from employees at the ticket office who were assigned the task of ensuring that the system runs smoothly on a day-to-day basis. They were trained to restart the system in cases of power failures or system crashes. Those employees are, however, not enthusiastic about the system. It was found that, if one of the researchers or George or another member of management does not visit the installation at least once per week to prove interest in and the importance of the system, the employees do not consider the effort to keep the system up and running worthwhile. They view the system as an extra (unnecessary) burden that is nice to have but not essential.

Because of this lack of interest on the part of IBL employees, it was extremely difficult to find an individual who was willing to take responsibility for the system on a continuous basis. This meant that the researchers could not easily withdraw from the system once their job was done.

Because of the fact that ticket salespeople work with huge amounts of cash, and because of the high crime rate in the area where the ticket office complex is located, intensive security measures are in place. Among other things the whole environment, inside and out, is under constant surveillance of closed circuit television (CCTV). Because of the risk of insiders working together with criminals to deactivate the CCTV prior to a robbery attempt, the computer for the CCTV system is behind a security door where not even the sales people can enter. For reasons of limited space and power outlets, as well as the existence of a heat extracting fan, the computer for the information kiosk is also behind this security door. This isolation of the information kiosk computer causes a certain amount of inconvenience. It happens quite often that a power failure or, especially in the early days, a malfunctioning system causes the system to shut down. The salespeople cannot solve the problem or restart the computer and the researcher has to be called out time and again.

The public environment in which the system is functioning implies a high risk for potential vandalism and even theft of equipment. Currently the touchscreen is installed in a metal cabinet in such a way that only the glass part is accessible. Furthermore, the touchscreen is also undercover by CCTV. The risk still exists, however, that a person with a vandalistic inclination could hit the screen with a hammer during quiet hours and then disappear. Due to the high crime rate in South Africa, the police would probably not have the time nor the manpower to follow up the TV recording.

Much research has previously been done on user interfaces for touchscreen kiosks (Borchers, Deussen, & Knörzer, 1995; ELO Touch Systems, 2002; ELO Touch Systems, 2003; MicroTouch Systems, Inc., 2000; Sears & Shneiderman, 1991; Shneiderman, 1991). This research was, however, always focused on users with average computer literacy skills and exposure to technology according to Western standards. For an interface to be developed for users from the IBL passenger community, special considerations should be taken into account. As previously indicated, these people are mostly from an African community with very limited educational background. One of the initial research aims for this project was to investigate the ways in which a computer interface must be adapted to accommodate users of this profile. To date, no clear-cut set of guidelines could be formulated and it remains an open question as to how much users of this user community gain from a Westernized interface in a non-native tongue that is not always well understood.

Commuters who travel the same route every day do not have to consult the system time and again to determine departure times or ticket prices. This means that they would not have any motivation to consult the system on a regular basis, thereby probably missing out on important notices that IBL communicates from time to time. It is, therefore, essential to determine effective ways to motivate commuters to use the system on a regular basis.

With reference to the techniques of liaison and obtaining feedback that were in place prior to the implementation of the information kiosk, the ultimate question is whether or not the information kiosk adds value. It is accepted that the existing techniques should not be replaced by the information kiosk and that the kiosk should act as a supplementary source of information, but would the old ways not suffice without the information kiosk? In other words, does the information kiosk system really fulfill the needs of Dora Ramakoatse and others like her?

REFERENCES

3M Touch Systems. (2002). *Online help of the TouchWare software driver for TouchScreen monitors.* Version 5.63 SR3.

Blake, E., Steventon, L., Edge, J., & Foster, A. (2001). *A field computer with animal trackers*. Paper presented at the Second South African Conference on Human-Computer Interaction [CHI-SA 2001], Pretoria, South Africa. Retrieved from http://www.chi-sa.org.za/chi-sa2001/chisa2001new.htm

Borchers, J., Deussen, O., & Knörzer, C. (1995). Getting it across: Layout issues for Kiosk Systems. *SIGCHI Bulletin, 27*(4), 68-74.

Breytenbach, H. J. (2003). *Interstate Bus Lines passenger survey: Executive summary*. Passenger survey conducted by independent consultant.

ELO Touch Systems. (2002). *Keys to a successful Kiosk application*. Retrieved January 5, 2003, from http://www.elotouch.com

ELO Touch Systems. (2003). *Touchscreen application tips*. Retrieved January 5, 2003, from http://www.elotouch.com/support/10tips.asp

Holfelder, W., & Hehmann, D. (1994). A networked multimedia retrieval management system for distributed kiosk applications. *Proceedings of the 1994 IEEE International Conference on Multimedia Computing and Systems*.

MicroTouch Systems, Inc. (2000). *Kiosk planning & design guide* (Document number 19-251, Version 2.0).

Norman, K. L., Friedman, Z., Norman, K., & Stevenson, R. (2001). Navigational issues in the design of online self-administered questionnaires. *Behaviour & Information Technology, 20*(1), 37-45.

Plaisant, C., & Sears, A. (1992). Touchscreen interfaces for alphanumeric data entry. *Proceedings of the Human Factors Society: The 36th Annual Meeting*, Atlanta, Georgia (Vol. 1, pp. 293-297).

Potter, R. L., Weldon, L. J., & Shneiderman, B. (1988). Improving the accuracy of touchscreens: An experimental evaluation of three strategies. *Proceedings of the Conference on Human Factors in Computing Systems*, Washington, DC (pp. 27-32).

Preece, J., Rogers, Y., Sharp, H., Benyon, D., Holland, S., & Carey, T. (1994). *Human-computer interaction*. Addison-Wesley.

Sears, A. (1991). Improving touchscreen keyboards: Design issues and a comparison with other devices. *Interacting with Computers, 3*(3), 253-269.

Sears, A., Kochavy, Y., & Shneiderman, B. (1990). Touchscreen field specification for public access database queries: Let your fingers do the walking. *Proceedings of the ACM Computer Science Conference '90* (pp. 1-7).

Sears, A., Revis, D., Swatski, J., Crittendon, R., & Shneiderman, B. (1993). Investigating touchscreen typing: The effect of keyboard size on typing speed. *Behaviour & Information Technology, 12*(1), 17-22.

Sears, A., & Shneiderman, B. (1991). High precision touchscreens: Design strategies and comparisons with a mouse. *International Journal of Man-Machine Studies, 34*(4), 593-613.

Shneiderman, B. (1991). Touchscreens now offer compelling uses. *IEEE Software, 8*(2), 93-94, 107.

Walton, M., & Vukovic, W. (2003). Cultures, literacy, and the Web: Dimensions of information 'scent'. *Interactions, 2*, 64-71.

Pieter Blignaut is an associate professor at the Department of Computer Science and Informatics at the University of the Free State, South Africa. He is also head of the Centre of Excellence at the university that focuses on ICT related research. He teaches programming in high level languages as well as software engineering to senior students. His research interests are focused on adapting user interfaces for users with limited reading skills and the cognitive aspects that characterize successful computer users.

As traffic admin manager, Iann Cruywagen supervises the control room of Interstate Bus Lines. He has his pulse on the daily operational activities of the company and is also in close contact with passengers. He holds two MSc degrees and has also completed a diploma in transport economics. Having been a bus driver himself for eight years, he is well-acquainted with a wide variety of aspects in the passenger transport industry.

This case was previously published in the *Journal of Cases on Information Technology*, 7(4), pp. 27-45, © 2005.

Chapter VI

Fostering a Technology Cultural Change:
The Changing Paradigms at the University of Minnesota Crookston

Dan Lim, University of Minnesota Crookston, USA

EXECUTIVE SUMMARY

Many people in higher education wonder where the rapid changes in information technology are going to take them. Many more fear that the ongoing information technology explosion may eventually leave them behind. Due to entrenched mindsets and bureaucracy in higher education, fostering a technology cultural change requires paradigm shifts in all areas of administration, teaching, and research. A fundamental paradigm shift must happen in four areas before a technology cultural change can be set on a forward path. This chapter focuses on four essential components of a paradigm shift in technology and higher education at the University of Minnesota Crookston (UMC). This case describes how a paradigm shift model can help to promote a long-term technology cultural change in a higher education institution. The model consists of technology commitment, technology philosophy, investment priority, and development focus. It has been used at UMC to bring about a reengineering of the entire institution to support a ubiquitous laptop environment throughout the curriculum and campus. The model has helped UMC achieve an overwhelming success in utilizing laptop computing and other technology to enhance learning.

CASE QUESTIONS

- Who is ultimately responsible for a technology cultural change in an institution of higher education?
- How does the institutional technology climate support or discourage the use of technology to enhance learning?
- What are the difficulties in integrating computer technology into curriculum?
- What types of strategies can be used to help faculty become more comfortable with computer technology?

CASE NARRATIVE

Background

Located in the fertile Red River Valley in Northwestern Minnesota, the University of Minnesota Crookston (UMC) is the fourth and youngest campus in the University of Minnesota System. UMC became a four-year college in 1993. Surrounded by rich farmlands, UMC provides technology resources to enhance the regional economy and labor force. It produces technology-oriented graduates sought after by regional, state, and national businesses and corporations. UMC's location in the farming region of the Red River Valley has played a vital role in supporting the use of technology to create alternate delivery of courses and degree programs.

The University of Minnesota Crookston has numerous degree programs in Agriculture and Natural Resources, Arts and Sciences, and Business and Technology. Its technology implementation is supported by the Computing Services, Media Resources, Computer Help Desk, Instructional Technology Center, and Web Team units. In general, faculty at UMC have accepted that technology will become an inseparable part of teaching and learning in the classroom, and have responded well to computing and courseware training. Administrators and other staff at UMC have adopted the Web environment for daily communication and operation. In short, the organizational climate at UMC is structured to be supportive around issues of technology that can be used to enhance learning.

From the start, the UMC administration moved toward a technology-based position. In 1993, when it first became a four-year college, it immediately determined to have a ubiquitous laptop computing environment. The University requires and issues laptop computers to all its students. As the first laptop university in the nation, UMC has become a national showcase in ubiquitous laptop computing. Hundreds of delegations from across the nation and around the world came to learn about ubiquitous laptop implementation.

UMC also did away with middle layer bureaucracy and empowered working groups and committees to make decisions and execute various operations without further consultation. The total commitment to technology from the very top was the major step of embarking on a sweeping technology cultural change at UMC. Since the changes happened so quickly, faculty support and training was quite haphazard. The early adopters among the faculty did use the laptop environment for some limited learning applications. Most faculty, though, felt that the technology initiative was an added burden. The challenge of motivating and training the rest of the faculty to incorporate laptop technology into classroom teaching took center stage.

The challenge faced by the University of Minnesota Crookston was how to take full advantage of the ubiquitous computing infrastructure and have 100 percent of the faculty using the technology to enhance learning. A technology cultural change needed to take place among top management, technology personnel, faculty, and staff.

Technology Culture: A Model for Change

The technology cultural change model has embedded within in it four distinct paradigms that must shift simultaneously in order to enhance learning. The four changing paradigms are technology commitment, philosophy of technology, investment prioritization, and development focus. The four paradigms must shift together dynamically, meaning that stagnation in any one paradigm shift may affect the other three, potentially crippling the positive impact on learning.

Paradigm 1: Technology Commitment

If technology is going to change education the way it has changed workplace and lifestyle, it is imperative that a total commitment is made to involve and infuse technology into the curriculum. Educational technology as an add-on to the university budget is not enough. It has to be a significant part of the recurring budgetary process. The add-on paradigm in technology funding and implementation does not originate with the university mission. Technology is funded whenever there is extra money available. It does not matter how much money has been made available, nonrecurring funds cannot sustain a long-time wish list in technology implementation and integration. In fact, the larger a one-time funding is, the harder it is to continue and maintain any technology initiative, let alone keep up with the rapid changes that occur in the computer industry.

The funding of educational technology needs to be committed to a long-term recurring process so that technology implementation will not experience budget reduction or budget cuts. The "add-on" mentality must be replaced by an absolute commitment to technology before any serious plan that will impact learning can be implemented.

If technology is important to a university, it should be reflected in the university's mission. The budgetary process should allocate financial and personnel resources to reinforce technology as mission-critical to the university. Even if there is some nonrecurring funding, both the nonrecurring funds and their stipulating conditions should be worked into the university's mission and budgetary process.

A total commitment to technology and its integration into the curriculum was made at the University of Minnesota Crookston in 1993. The UMC administration's commitment to educational technology was reflected in the amount of resources allocated for it. The university Chancellor and his administration restructured the entire university organizational, financial, and human resources setup to make the bold technology venture work. Since funding was the most crucial factor, a significant reallocation of financial resources to fund campus-wide laptop use and technology integration sent a strong message to the entire university faculty and staff that the technology initiative was not a temporary fix but a long-range mission-critical component for the university.

Staff restructuring and hiring of new technology staff to implement and support the laptop initiative was the next crucial step. The entire campus quickly understood the administration's unwavering commitment to technology. In view of more instructional technology support, faculty were more willing to commit themselves in terms of time and resources to integrate technology into classroom learning. The presence of more technology staff in important committees continued to reinforce the administration's commitment to total technology integration at all levels within the university.

Ongoing organizational restructuring to support technology was vital to counter any doubt about the university's commitment. The sweeping changes in technology and the explosion of the Internet required the university organizational structure to "reinvent" itself as often as possible. Organization structure is as good as the administrators who form it. At the University of Minnesota Crookston, the administrators were a community of learners of sound administrative support and technology skills. The top management, consisting of the Chancellor, Vice-Chancellors, and Center Directors, were constantly attending technology workshops and utilizing cutting-edge technology at work. They not only set a contagious example, but also formed a tremendous driving force through their technology-enriched office.

Paradigm 2: Technology Philosophy

Another paradigm shift required for technology cultural change in schools is that education should "drive" technology rather than vice versa. Technology is a tool that should be built around how teachers teach. Teachers should not have to adjust their lesson plans to suit some computer software. Wherever possible, technology should be implemented to help make the work of teaching easier, or at least, more enjoyable. Administration and computing staff must not implement technology without consulting teachers. The learning outcomes and teachers' instructional agenda should play the central role in determining what software to procure and how it will be implemented. The question is not if a university has the necessary technology but if the technology is meeting the needs of teachers and students. Technology should not dictate how teachers teach, but teachers should determine what technology is best suited for achieving specific learning outcomes.

Although technology is the main driving force at the University of Minnesota Crookston, the administration recognizes that technology must be driven by learning outcomes and by the faculty. The emphasis is to improve or strengthen the learning design. Unless faculty know what they want students to learn, they will not know what is the most appropriate technology tools to use or how to assess whether technology indeed makes a difference in learning. After all, faculty are hired to teach and help students learn. If teaching is what they have committed to, it is only logical to help them focus on their content area before any matching technology tools can further enhance their work.

Since UMC required and issued laptop computers to all students with the objective to enhance learning, the administration has realized that integration of technology into curriculum is crucial to keep the entire laptop initiative on track. The technology "operational" feasibility among faculty can only be improved if the concerns of faculty are addressed and needs met. The decisions on hardware, infrastructure, software, and training must have strong faculty input. The most "intelligent" software does not do any good if no one uses it. The ultimate goal is not to "sell" a particular brand of technology to the faculty, but to use the most appropriate technology to "sell" learning to the students.

The administration at UMC found that an individual technology plan for each faculty member works best. Technology staff conducts ongoing needs assessment of faculty technology needs. Instead of viewing faculty as groups, the staff take time to work with individual faculty to work out an individual technology plan over a certain period of time in terms of meeting their needs, customizing training, and providing timely instructional and technical support. In essence, the technology personnel bring technology to faculty and build it around the way they teach and the way they expect their students to learn.

Paradigm 3: Investment Priority

The next paradigm shift is toward investing heavily in teacher training and development instead of leaving little funds available for training after buying hardware and software. It is better to spend more on training teachers to fully utilize available software than purchasing additional software whose packages teachers may not even have time to open. It is common that teachers hardly use a technology application for the simple reason they do not know how to use it. Training and development should not be an afterthought. It should be a vital part of any successful implementation plan for technology in education.

The major obstacle most higher education institutions face in technology integration is general faculty resistance toward using computers to teach. Comprehensive planning and implementation of aggressive training programs are crucial to overcome faculty resistance toward computers. Training must become the central component in strategic technology planning and its budgetary process. Resistance toward the use of computers can be attributed to the lack of time, anxiety toward computers, or lack of training.

Training needs should also play a part in software selection. At the University of Minnesota Crookston, the choice of authoring platform was based on educational principles used in software interface, customization flexibility, and built-in functionality that makes training and development easier for general faculty. Appropriate technology incentives help faculty get started and maintain momentum in courseware development. Timely recognition rewards also reinforce continual commitment toward technology integration among faculty. Technology staff must recognize that the faculty plays the key role in technology integration. They must do whatever it takes to make software transition and integration as transparent as possible for the faculty.

Paradigm 4: Development Focus

Since technology is more conspicuous than teaching and learning, it is easy to focus solely on technology as if it alone can lead to success. It is education that provides the concept, content, and design for developing a sound educational technology. Administration and instructional technology staff should concentrate their efforts in promoting the need to improve teaching and learning. The need for technology will take central stage as soon as teachers become excited about improving instructional design. As long as extensive access to technology is provided, teachers who are motivated to improve teaching and learning will take full advantage of using appropriate technologies to enhance learning. Promoting technology without relating it to teaching and learning may increase resistance or anxieties among teachers because they feel learning and using technology is an added burden.

At the University of Minnesota Crookston, technology has taken center stage since the 1993 campus-wide implementation of laptop computer use. Students got into the habit of using the laptops almost immediately while faculty needed some gentle "pressure." After three years, when most of the faculty finally embraced the use of laptop computers in the classroom, many faculty were torn between technology and teaching. They found themselves spending too much time on technology issues at the expense of teaching. It became a vicious cycle that the more technology was promoted, the less likely faculty were going to increase using it to enhance learning.

In 1997, the UMC administration realized that the focus of technology-enhanced instructional development should not be centered on technology. Instead, the focus should be on learning innovation. Faculty should spend most of their time designing learning and developing content. Training workshops in instructional systems design were conducted to help faculty plan learning and identify the right technologies. One-on-one consultations were held with faculty to identify their teaching needs and development areas. Faculty could visualize the need for technology when they became excited about using matching technologies to implement their new learning design and content.

One approach that helped change this paradigm was using interactive authoring templates. In order to help faculty to concentrate most of their time on designing and developing content rather than worrying about learning or troubleshooting technology, a set of specific interactive authoring templates was created for the faculty to develop interactive online learning applications. These templates were designed to save faculty time and frustration from authoring interactive learning activities from scratch. Some templates were derived from interactive modules already developed by some faculty. They were made into templates for other faculty to reuse over and over again. The templates were placed in catalogs built into an authoring software package. Faculty only had to select the desired authoring template, enter the content, and post it on the Local Area Network or the Web for students to self-learn, practice, or review for exams. Generally, faculty spent between 15-30 minutes to generate an interactive exercise posted on the Web.

ANALYSIS

The changing technology culture, represented by a paradigm shift from a technology focus to a learning focus, at the University of Minnesota Crookston has changed the attitudes of faculty members toward technology training workshops. Three four-day interactive courseware camps held in the past summer were quickly filled up by faculty, many of whom would not attend even a short workshop. Using the technology cultural change model, the interactive courseware camps were focused on determining what and how faculty wanted to teach and building a set of interactive technologies that would deliver their design. Faculty were allowed to select designs and technologies that fit their content and the way they wanted to deliver, as well as using resources with which they would feel comfortable.

The downside to the above approach is twofold: it takes longer for some faculty to adapt to using more advanced technologies, and it is more difficult to support their development because of diverse technology packages. Although it may take longer and more effort to support faculty technology development, it is important to encourage faculty to trust the process of letting learning "drive" the implementation and integration of technology into curriculum. This new technology culture among the faculty is fragile, though. It will quickly revert back to the old paradigms if administration and technology staff are only concerned with quick results or more streamlined courseware development.

Universities and colleges that do not have a high level of technology and staff support may need to find a scalable model of fostering technology cultural change. The scenario described in this chapter is applicable to traditional campuses if the central administration, departmental administration, faculty, and technology staff share the same vision of promoting a technology cultural change in the four areas described in the model. A shared vision will help in the design and implementation of a scalable model that will foster the necessary paradigm shifts.

CONCLUSION

The technology culture at any institution of higher learning is shaped and formed whether or not a conscious effort has been made to steer it toward enhancing learning. If a conscious effort is made, it should be conducted strategically, effectively, and holistically. The four-component model of fostering a technology cultural change has been used with success at the University of Minnesota Crookston. It was an innovative approach that helped to bring about a ubiquitous mobile computing environment at UMC in 1993. It became even more innovative and revolutionary by setting teaching initiatives as the driving force behind technology integration in higher education at UMC. Other institutions of higher learning may want to consider using or adapting the UMC model to reengineer technology implementation and integration at their campuses. However, it is important to keep in mind that this model is not static. It must continue to evolve, renew, or eventually reinvent itself in other forms.

DISCUSSION QUESTIONS

1. How can administration move from an add-on paradigm to a total commitment paradigm in technology resource planning?
2. What are the pros and cons of requiring and empowering teachers to develop their own learning applications?
3. Why is technology training usually not given adequate funding?
4. What kinds of incentives might be used to help motivate faculty to use technology to enhance teaching and learning?

ADDITIONAL RESOURCES

Oblinger, D. G. (Ed.), & Rush, S. C. (1997). *The learning revolution: The challenge of information technology in the academy.* Bolton, Mass: Anker Pub.

Benchley, R. S. (1999, Spring). The results are in: ThinkPad universities assess their first 'connected' years. *Multiversity.*

This case was previously published in L. A. Petrides (Ed.), *Case Studies on Information Technology in Higher Education: Implications for Policy and Practice*, pp. 240-246, © 2000.

Chapter VII

Experiences from Using the CORAS Methodology to Analyze a Web Application

Folker den Braber, Norway

Arne Bjørn Mildal, NetCom, Norway

Jone Nes, NetCom, Norway

Ketil Stølen, SINTEF, Norway

Fredrik Vraalsen, SINTEF, Norway

EXECUTIVE SUMMARY

During a field trial performed at the Norwegian telecom company NetCom from May 2003 to July 2003, a methodology for model-based risk analysis was assessed. The chosen methodology was the CORAS methodology (CORAS, 2000), which has been developed in a European research project carried out by 11 European companies and research institutes partly funded by the European Union. The risk analysis and assessment were carried out by the Norwegian research institute SINTEF in cooperation with NetCom. NetCom (www.netcom.no) is one of the main mobile phone network providers in Norway. Their 'MinSide' application offers their customers access to their personal account information via the Internet, enabling them to view and change the properties of their mobile phone subscription. 'MinSide' deals with a lot of sensitive customer information that needs to be secure, while at the same time being easily available to the customer in order for the service to remain usable and competitive. The goal of the analysis was to identify risks in relation to the use of the 'MinSide' application and, where possible, suggest treatments for these risks. This was achieved through two model-driven brainstorming sessions based on system documentation in the form of UML sequence diagrams and data flow diagrams.

ORGANIZATIONAL BACKGROUND

NetCom

NetCom is the second largest mobile phone network provider in Norway, providing solutions for mobile communication. NetCom is an innovative company that uses new technology and knowledge to meet its customers' demands and aims to be a leading company in Norway within the market of mobile communication. A main goal for NetCom is that their products shall be competitive on price and quality, while at the same time remaining easy to use and understand for all its customers. With offices in Trondheim, Bergen, Stavanger, Kristiansand and Tønsberg, and its main office located in Oslo, NetCom has 740 employees in Norway.

NetCom is owned by the Swedish-Finnish company TeliaSonera, the leading telecom company in the Nordic and the Baltic regions. Based on the number of customers, the company is the largest mobile provider in Sweden and Finland, the second largest in Norway (NetCom) and the fourth largest in Denmark. TeliaSonera is also the largest fixed voice and data provider in the region, with leading positions in Sweden and Finland. Furthermore, TeliaSonera is the largest operator in the Baltic region, with consolidated mobile and fixed line operations in Lithuania and consolidated mobile operations in Latvia. The TeliaSonera share is traded in Stockholm, Helsinki and on the NASDAQ Stock Market in the United States.

Table 1. NetCom's key figures

	2002	2001	2000	1999	1998
Customers					
Number of customers	1,178,466	1,082,850	900,282	745,089	535,892
NetCom's market share (of total amount of mobile phone customers)	29%	26%	28%	30%	30%
Total share of mobile subscriptions in Norway	86%	81%	75%	62%	48%
Finance					
Turnover/Sales (million NOK[1])	4,591	3,752	2,914	2,494	2,032
(million USD[2])	670	547	425	364	296
Result/Profit (million NOK)	1,101	725	421	331	103
(million USD)	160	106	61	48	15
Calling minutes per customer per month					
Subscription	255	227	214	179	-
Prepaid	63	58	64	79	-
Text messages (SMS[3])					
Total amount (in millions)	-	502	310	157	36

[1]NOK Norwegian Kroner
[2]USD United States Dollars
[3]SMS Short Message Service

SINTEF

SINTEF is a Norwegian research institute with 1,700 employees. SINTEF performs research for the industry and the public sector in a number of different fields, ranging from oil and process industry to IT and medical research.

The group involved in this case study is the group for Quality and Security Technology (QST), which consists of seven people. This group was also strongly involved in the CORAS project during which the used methodology was developed. QST is part of SINTEF Information and Communication Technology (ICT) with about 300 employees.

SETTING THE STAGE

Communication is a key aspect for NetCom's products; naturally, the quality of the communication with its customers is an important part of the services offered by NetCom. NetCom offers its customers roughly three possibilities for interaction:

- a 24-hour telephone-based helpdesk and customer service center;
- e-mail and regular mail can be used to get answers about various topics; and
- a Web application which lets customers log on to their own mobile phone account Web site to view billing information, usage history information, and more.

Focus during the risk analysis was on the last of these three alternatives, the Web application called 'MinSide' (Norwegian for 'MyPage'). MinSide makes it possible for each customer to get a complete overview of his or her mobile phone account, at any time of the day and from any place. The helpdesk/customer service was also slightly addressed but only where it was influenced by the MinSide application.

Giving customers the ability to interact with NetCom's databases and view their personal and sensitive information through the Internet requires a high level of security. With the help of the MinSide application, users are able to get information about their calling history and their calling cost status. MinSide also opens up for more interactive functionality, allowing the customer to send SMS and change their personal information and preferences.

In addition to security, this kind of service leads to requirements on availability. Serving more than a million users, the system needs to be able to handle all customers at any time, satisfying their wants and needs with respect to the use of their personal Web site.

A helpdesk where telephone operators are answering requests from customers related to their mobile phone account on a 24-hour basis is very costly. As a sub-goal, the MinSide application is meant to save money by relieving the helpdesk. Even though extra traffic will be generated from people with questions or problems related to MinSide, it is still believed that the MinSide application contributes to a reduction of the total helpdesk traffic.

Security

Having personal Web sites and login functionality is nothing new. However, the fact that all users are mobile phone owners opens for some extra possibilities, both for users such as people having a NetCom mobile phone account, and misusers such as people illegally exploiting MinSide. NetCom uses a combination of a password and a PIN code for the login process. The password needs to be remembered by the customer while the PIN code is sent to the customer's mobile phone in a text message (SMS).

NetCom's situation related to serving its customers with a Web application giving them direct access to their mobile phone account means that there is a need to identify both the security status and the security requirements related to the MinSide application. This case study describes the process used to analyze risks related to the MinSide application and to identify possible treatments to eliminate or reduce these risks.

CASE DESCRIPTION

The main goal of the analysis was to identify possibilities for misusing the MinSide application by violating one of the four security requirements: confidentiality, integrity, availability or non-repudiation, as defined in a number of standards related to IT security (ISO/IEC TR 13335, 2001; ISO/IEC 17799, 2000). This was achieved by carrying out a risk analysis based on the CORAS methodology. CORAS is specifically designed to address risk analysis of security-critical IT systems and offers a tool supported methodology for model-based risk analysis (MBRA). During a model-based risk analysis, models, in particular UML models, are used for specification and documentation of both the system (target of evaluation) and the risks. Also these models are the main medium for communication among the participants.

We will not explain the complete methodology here, but provide a short outline of the process in order to illustrate the main steps of a risk analysis based on the CORAS methodology.

Activities of the Risk Management Process

The CORAS risk management process is based on the Australian/New Zealand Standard 4360 (1999) and provides a sequencing of the risk management process into the five sub-processes illustrated in Table 2.

Table 2. CORAS risk management process

Sub process	Description
1 Context Identification:	Identify the context of the analysis. Describe the system and its environment; identify usage scenarios, the assets of the system and its security requirements.
2 Risk Identification:	Identify the potential threats to assets, the vulnerabilities of these assets and document the unwanted incidents.
3 Risk Analysis:	Evaluate the frequencies and consequences of the unwanted incidents.
4 Risk Evaluation:	Identify the level of risk associated with the unwanted incidents and decide whether the level is acceptable. Prioritize the identified risks and categorize risks into risk themes.
5 Risk Treatment:	Address the treatment of the identified risks and how to prevent the unacceptable risks.

Each of these five sub-processes comprises a number of activities, and the CORAS methodology for model-based risk analysis proposes different methods and models for use in the different sub-processes and activities.

The CORAS methodology is developed to address systems of all kinds and sizes. For this field trial, one of the goals was to perform a lightweight risk analysis; therefore, several activities in the standard full CORAS methodology were skipped or modified. A description of the techniques and activities used is given below where the different sub-processes are described in more detail. Another goal was to test the CORAS tool that supports the risk analysis methodology.

Hypotheses for the NetCom MinSide Risk Analysis Field Trial

Prior to the field trial, a list of hypotheses concerning the use of the CORAS methodology and tool was produced. One of the goals of the field trial was to test whether these hypotheses were valid. The hypotheses were:

- A lightweight model-based risk analysis (CORAS light) produces results whose value corresponds to the investment.
- The CORAS light methodology leads to risk analysis results at the "correct" level of abstraction.
- The CORAS Web-based risk analysis tool supports the risk analysis process and makes it more efficient.
- The CORAS Web-based risk analysis tool provides the functionality that is required to perform a (lightweight) risk analysis.

Model-Based Risk Analysis

The CORAS methodology defines its own UML stereotypes and methods for describing UML models related to security analysis. These specific security-related UML aspects are caught in the CORAS UML profile (OMG, 2003b). This UML profile for security modeling defines an abstract language for supporting model-based security analysis. The asset, threat and treatment diagrams in Figure 2, Figure 5, Figure 7 and Figure 8 are examples of how this profile is used, and shows where the term "model-based" comes from.

Organization of the Trial

The field trial described in this case study was carried out over a period of three months, lasting from May 2003 to July 2003. It consisted of two brainstorming sessions that took place on the 21st and 27th of May, in which people from both NetCom and SINTEF participated. The preparations and analysis work before and after these sessions were mainly carried out by the risk analysis experts at SINTEF. Table 3 shows how many people from the two organizations were involved in the analysis and what roles they had.

Three Phases

The field trial was split into three main phases.

Table 3. Roles

Role	Description	Organization
System owner 1	Project leader for the MinSide application	NetCom
System owner 2	Project leader for the security part of the MinSide application	NetCom
System developer 1	A developer working on the MinSide application	NetCom
System developer 2	A developer working on the MinSide application	NetCom
Network expert	A network system administrator	NetCom
Security expert	A system administrator responsible for security in different NetCom applications	NetCom
Risk analysis (RA) leader	Leader of the risk analysis	SINTEF
RA secretary	The risk analysis secretary	SINTEF
Observer 1	Observing the risk analysis process	SINTEF
Observer 2	Observing the risk analysis process	SINTEF

- The first phase consisted of context identification and high-level risk analysis. This was performed by the risk analysis experts (SINTEF) with input from NetCom.
- The second phase was the risk identification and analysis. This consisted of two half-day meetings at NetCom, as well as preparatory work performed prior to each meeting by the risk analysis experts.
- The third phase consisted of continued analysis, treatment identification and structuring of the results gathered during the brainstorming sessions.

Context Identification

The goal of the first sub-process is to identify the context of the analysis, in other words: what are we going to analyze? This includes describing the system, its environment and the target of evaluation, and identifying usage scenarios, the assets of the system and its security requirements. The process steps that were followed for the context identification are illustrated in Figure 1.

With assets we mean those parts of the system that contain a value that can possibly be lost. This can be anything from information to hardware. The identified assets are documented in an asset diagram, which is a UML class diagram. The asset diagram for this case is shown in Figure 2.

Every context identification process ends with an approval meeting where all stakeholders involved in the coming risk analysis agree on the chosen target of evaluation and the describing documentation.

It was decided that NetCom's MinSide application was a suitable target of evaluation for the field trial. Prior to the context identification activity, NetCom provided system documentation in the form of UML (OMG, 2003a) use case (Cockburn, 1997) and class diagrams, use-case descriptions and other textual descriptions.

The risk analysis experts produced UML sequence diagrams based on the use-case descriptions provided by NetCom, which were sent to NetCom for review and approval. Following is a selection of risk analysis documentation in the form of tables and diagrams that specify the target of evaluation and provide the main input to the risk identification sub-process.

Figure 1. Context identification

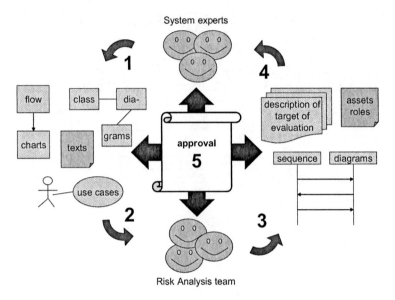

Figure 2. Asset diagram

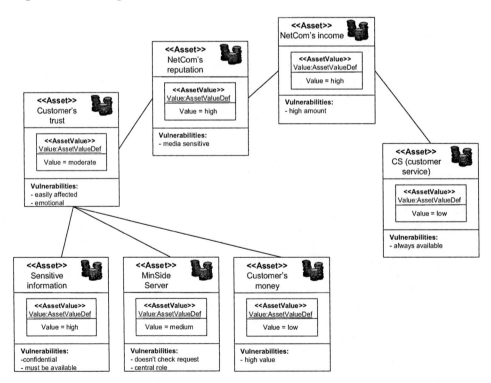

Table 4. Target of evaluation table

Target:	MinSide – Web application to give customers access to view and change the properties of their mobile account
Objective:	Provide customers with information and self-service solution
Service/Function:	- Send SMS - Retrieve New Password - Create Web Account - Manage Web Account
Security Aspects:	- Data Confidentiality - Data Integrity

Table 5 contains a use-case description made by NetCom. This is shown to illustrate how such a description looks and to show the source for the sequence diagram in Figure 3. The description contains some terms that are specific to NetCom; they are irrelevant for the understanding of the case and will therefore not be further explained.

Based on this use case, a sequence diagram was created, as shown in Figure 3. The sequence diagram shall specify the same behavior as the use-case description. However, we believe that the sequence diagram is much easier to read and therefore more suitable as a starting point for a risk analysis. This sequence diagram was one of the diagrams used during the first risk analysis session.

The data flow diagram shown in Figure 4 was one of five diagrams provided by NetCom as system documentation to be used during the second risk analysis session.

Risk Identification

The risk identification process was performed during two meetings at NetCom on May 21 and May 27. These two risk identification sessions were the key activities in the analysis. They not only served to generate risk analysis results, but also gave valuable feedback on the CORAS process. Following is a description of these meetings.

21st May — First HazOp Analysis

The meeting started with an approval session where the risk analysis leader performed a walkthrough of the context identification results and sequence diagrams that would be used as a basis for the risk identification. This was done as part of the first risk analysis meeting instead of conducting a separate approval meeting.

Based on the results of this approval meeting, some information was added to the asset and risk evaluation criteria tables, but no other significant changes were made. Later it became clear that the importance of this approval was underestimated by both the system experts and the risk analysis team, as described.

HazOp Analysis

After the approval session, the risk analysis leader gave a brief introduction to HazOp (Hazard and Operability) analysis (Redmill, 1999), a risk analysis method to be used during the risk identification session. A HazOp analysis can be described as a

Table 5. Use case description — Retrieve new password

High-level description		
	A NetCom Personal Customer has lost the password and requests a new one. Can be used to change the password. The function is used by other NetCom Web-portal.	
Actors		
	- NetCom Personal Customer starts the use case, called user in the use case. - Profile server, the data storage of profile data. - NetCom Web-portal, the originating system for the request, e.g., MinSide, Mother or mms.netcom.no. - SMSC (SMS center)	
Pre-conditions		
	P1.	The user has accessed this system from other Web-based self-service and information systems at NetCom.
Post-conditions		
	Undefined	
Flow of events		
	1.	The use-case starts when the user requests to retrieve a new password. If msisdn is not given in the URL, the user is asked for msisdn.
	2.	The system gets the secret question and answer from the profile server. The system displays the question to the user. (A1)
	3.	The user enters the secret answer. (A4, A5)
	4.	The system validates that the entered answer matches the answer in the profile server, the system asks the user for a new password. (A2)
	5.	The user enters the new password and confirmation of the password. (A4, A5)
	6.	The system verifies the new password. The password should be a minimum of five characters, not only numbers or letters. (R1)
	7.	The system generates a one-time password and asks the SMSC to send this in an SMS to the user's GSM number. The system then asks the user to enter this one-time password. The one-time password is only valid within five minutes from generation.
	8.	The user enters the one-time pin code received in the SMS. (A4, A5)
	9.	The system verifies that the one-time password is entered within the time limit and is the same as the generated one-time password sent. (A3)
	10.	The system updates the profile server with updated profile data.
	11.	The user is displayed a feedback message.

Table 5. Use case description — Retrieve new password (cont.)

Use Case description – Retrieve New Password		
Alternative events		

	A1.	If the user doesn't have a personal secret question and answer the user should enter both question and answer and password on the same page.
		  1. The system asks the user for question, answer and password.
		  2. The user enters information. (A4, A5)
		  3. The system validates the information. If the information is not valid, the next event is event 1 in A1. (R1)
		  4. The flow of events continues at event 7.

	A2.	If the user is unable to answer the secret question, the flow of events returns to event 3. The user has max 5 attempts to answer the secret question.
	A3.	The user fails to enter the pin code; the system displays an error message to the user. This use case ends.
	A4.	The user requests to cancel registration process. The system sends the user back to the originating NetCom Web-portal. This use case ends.
	A5.	The user leaves the registration process for more than 30 minutes. The system does necessary cleanup and displays an error message to the user. This use case ends.
Special requirements		
	R1.	The user has max 5 attempts to answer the secret question and enter the pin code.

'structured brainstorming.' The idea is to focus on certain items in the system documentation that are part of the target of evaluation, and try to identify risks connected to failure or incompleteness of these items. In this case, the use cases and especially their corresponding sequence diagrams were used. In order to find threats to the scenarios described in the use cases, one can ask the following questions for every message in a sequence diagram.

What happens if this message...

*   ...is not sent?
*   ...is not received?
*   ...is delayed?
*   ...is changed?

During a HazOp session, the knowledge, expertise and intellect of all the members in the group is exploited, in order to find as many relevant risks as possible. The session is led by the risk analysis leader while the risk analysis secretary is responsible for writing down the results of the analysis itself. The results are stored in a HazOp table. Table 6 shows a part of the HazOp table produced during this risk analysis session. The CORAS tool was used to store the results from the HazOp analysis.

Figure 3. Sequence diagram — Retrieve new password

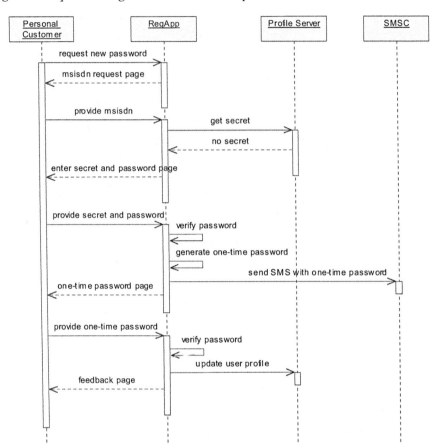

The threats identified during the HazOp analysis are drawn in a threat diagram. An example of such a diagram from this analysis is given in Figure 5. The threat diagram shows the security scenarios that initiate the unwanted incidents that affect the assets.

This case showed the importance of displaying the system documentation, which is the source for the analysis. The system documentation diagrams are the main input to HazOp, and it is therefore important for the people involved in the analysis to be able to look at them during the whole session.

While analyzing the different steps of the sequence diagrams, it became clear that the diagrams did not describe the system correctly, for example, they were not complete or showed wrong behavior. In an ideal situation this would have been recognized and corrected during a separate approval phase. The fact that this was not the case here indicates that the approval session deserves more attention.

An important organizational detail for this type of analysis is the physical separation of analysis objects and recording results. Only one laptop was used for showing the

Figure 4. Data flow diagram — Password forgotten

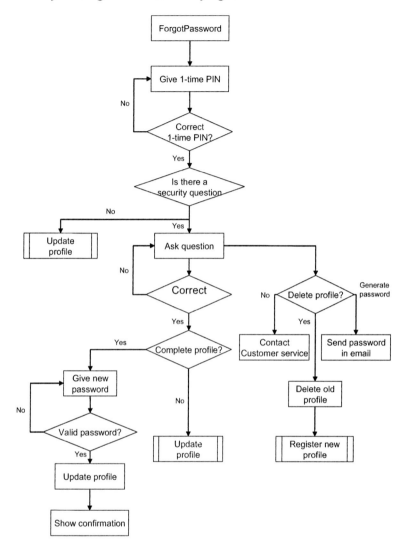

diagrams to be analyzed and for recording the analysis results, which led to confusing situations. A better solution would have been to use one laptop for showing the diagrams to be analyzed and one laptop for gathering the analysis results. The second analysis session proved this was indeed a right conclusion.

A comment from the system experts was that the information in the sequence diagrams was at too low a level of abstraction and that they were not very suitable to identifying threats. A bigger picture was suggested that could include more of the surrounding environment (users, mobile phones, customer service, social hacking, etc.). As mentioned above, this also motivates using a reasonable amount of time on approval

Table 6. HazOp table template

Risk ID	Every identified risk gets its own unique ID. One row contains one identified risk and
Asset ID	Every asset identified during the context identification phase gets its own unique ID
Item	Here is the name of the diagram used when this risk was identified
Guideword/Attribute	The guideword that was used to find this risk
Security Scenario	The security scenario initiating the unwanted incident
Unwanted Incident	Description of the unwanted incident for this risk
Consequence/Frequency	Specification of consequence and frequency values
Treatment	Description of treatment measures

of system documentation, not only to ensure that the documentation is correct, but also that it is addressing the right level of abstraction.

It was decided to update the target of evaluation and to use data flow diagrams supplied by NetCom as the basis for the analysis during the second meeting. This meant that focus was shifted to a subcomponent of the MinSide application responsible for the login and authentication process. The system specification used during the second session consisted of data flow diagrams. One of these diagrams is shown in Figure 4.

27th May — Second HazOp Analysis

This time, the data flow diagrams were used as an input to the risk analysis process. The risk analysis leader led the brainstorming session, using one laptop to show the diagrams that were being analyzed to all the participants. Another laptop was used by the risk analysis secretary to record the results on the fly. This activity was hidden from the other participants, allowing them to focus completely on the brainstorming session and coming up with new threats and risks. The risk identification process is illustrated in Figure 6.

A selection of the results of this second HazOp analysis session is given in Table 7.

Again the results of the HazOp analysis were translated into threat diagrams. Figure 7 shows one of them.

After the risk analysis leader had gone through all the data flow diagrams, the HazOp table was shown to everyone, and the remaining time (about one hour) was spent cleaning up the table and filling in the missing information such as frequencies and consequences.

Figure 5. Threat diagram — first session

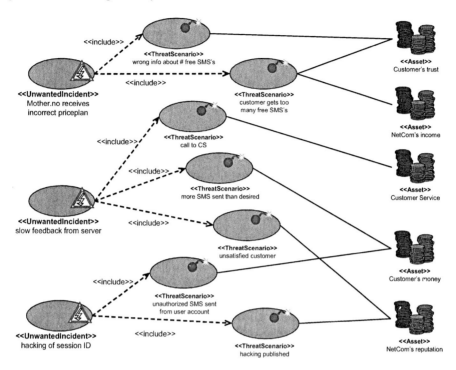

Figure 6. Risk identification

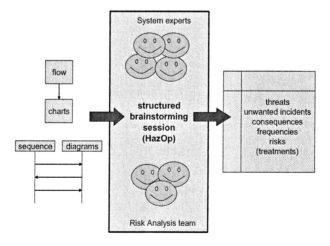

Figure 7. Threat diagram — Second session

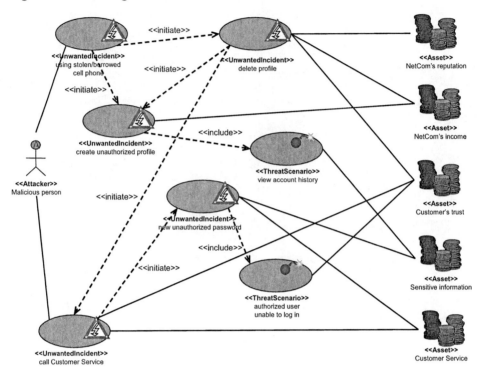

Risk Analysis

As described above, during the risk analysis sub-process, the consequences and frequencies for the identified unwanted incidents are determined. Unwanted incidents become risks as soon as they are assigned a consequence and frequency value. Doing this requires a thorough knowledge of the analyzed system and is therefore also performed in cooperation with the system experts. When this is done the risk matrix can be drawn. Table 8 shows such a risk matrix.

The qualitative values for both consequence and frequency scales where already indicated in the context identification phase, and are given in Table 9 and Table 10.

During a complete risk analysis, a technique called Fault Tree Analysis (FTA) (IEC 1025, 1990) is used in order to calculate consequences of complicated unwanted incidents.

Because of resource restrictions during this analysis, it was decided to combine the risk analysis sub-process with the risk identification process that was carried out at the two NetCom meetings. Instead of using FTA, consequence and frequency values were estimated with the help of the system experts, and these values were recorded together with the other risk information in the HazOp table.

Table 7. Fragment of filled in HazOp table

Id	G2.4	G2.3	G2.2	G2.1
Asset	NetCom's Reputation	Customer Service	Customer's Trust	Sensitive Information
Item	Password	Password	Password	Password
Guideword	Other than	Other than	Other than	Other than
Security Incident	Customer Service resets *unauthorized* password	Customer Service resets *unauthorized* password	Customer Service resets *unauthorized* password	Customer Service resets *unauthorized* password
Unwanted incident	Published in media	Customer calls Customer Service	Authorized user unable to log in	Tells unauthorized user new password
Consequence *Very low* *Low* *Medium* *High* *Very high*	High	Medium	Very high	Medium
Frequency *Very low* *Low* *Medium* *High* *Very high*	Send new password as SMS	Send new password as SMS	Send new password as SMS	Send new password as SMS

Table 8. Risk matrix

Frequency / Consequence	Very low	Low	Medium	High	Very high
Very low	Negligible	Negligible	Low	Low	Moderate
Low	Negligible	Low	Low	Moderate	High
Medium	Low	Low	Moderate	High	Extreme
High	Moderate	Moderate	High	Extreme	Extreme
Very high	Moderate	High	Extreme	Extreme	Extreme

Table 9. Consequence values

Consequence value	Description
Very low	Less than 1.000 NOK direct or indirect costs
Low	1.000 – 10.000 NOK direct or indirect costs
Medium	10.000 – 100.000 NOK direct or indirect costs
High	100.000 – 1.000.000 NOK direct or indirect costs
Very high	More than 1.000.000 NOK direct or indirect costs

Table 10. Frequency values

Qualitative frequencies	Definitions	
	- for threats related to specific use of the service	- for persistent threats
Very low	Incidents that occur less often than 0.01% of the times the service is used.	Incidents that occur less often than once every 20th year.
Low	Incidents that occur between 0.01% and 0.1% of the times the service is used.	Incidents that occur more often than once every 20th year, but less than once every second year.
Medium	Incidents that occur between 0.1% and 1% of the times the service is used.	Incidents that occur more often than once every second year, but less than three times every year.
High	Incidents that occur between 1% and 5% of the times the service is used.	Incidents that occur more often than three times every year, but less than once every month.
Very high	Incidents that occur between 5% and 100% of the times the service is used.	Incidents that occur more often than once every month.

Table 11. A selection of ranked risks

Risk value	Id	Security incident	Unwanted incident
High	G2.2	Customer Service resets *unauthorized* password	Authorized user unable to log in
Moderate	G2.4	Customer Service resets *unauthorized* password	Published in media
Low	G2.3	Customer Service resets *unauthorized* password	Customer calls CS
Low	G2.1	Customer Service resets *unauthorized* password	Tells unauthorized user new password

Risk Evaluation and Risk Treatment

The NetCom meetings were the only two sessions where the system experts and risk analysis experts physically met. The results of these sessions were structured and summarized by the risk analysis experts. As a result of this, sub-process 4 — risk evaluation and sub process 5 — risk treatment were combined, and these were performed mainly by the risk analysis experts at SINTEF. The risk treatment sub-process was however to a certain degree also combined with the risk identification process, by recording treatments that were suggested during the HazOp session.

Using the information of Table 8, Table 9 and Table 10 for the identified risks mentioned in the HazOp Table 7, we can range the risks after their risk value. This is done in Table 11.

Following is a selection of the indicated treatments for the risks with risk ID G2.1, G2.2, G2.3 and G2.4, here identified by G2.*. The treatment for these risks is specified in a treatment diagram and a treatment activity diagram.

CURRENT CHALLENGES/PROBLEMS FACING THE ORGANIZATION

The field trial produced valuable results in the form of identified threats and risks as well as possible treatments. One challenge for NetCom is to adjust these results of the analysis to its own organizational structure. Even though the analysis was restricted to address the MinSide application, the results of this analysis will affect other parts outside the scope of MinSide but inside NetCom's organization.

In fact, since the termination of the field trial, it has already been shown that the effect of this trial on new projects at NetCom has been considerable. The methods used during this field trial have been adopted in several new projects in order to indicate risks and possible treatments at an early stage in the development or maintenance process.

An individual project or case study with restrictions on both time and resources, carried out in a relatively large organization, will naturally have a corresponding limit on the ability to affect the organization. However, the choice of addressing only a small part of the organization implies a limit in itself. The expectations of such a project should reflect the amount of time and effort that is put into the case.

The scope of the risk analysis described in this case was restricted to the MinSide application. Even though the results of such a risk analysis cannot be expected to have a major impact on how NetCom handles its customers, it certainly gives a good overview on the functionality of this specific service.

The main problem connected to the use of the MinSide application that NetCom faces on a 24-hour basis is offering the customers the service they pay for, while protecting them at the same time. Through carrying out this risk analysis, this ability has increased. Since systems are continually updated, these analyses will also need to be updated. NetCom will always strive to be one step ahead of the people looking for the security holes in order to protect its customers. Hence a major challenge for NetCom is to obtain a correct picture of relevant risks and their risk values, and maintain the validity of this picture as the application, its context and NetCom's business objectives evolve.

Another issue related to this field trial is the relation between a system and its risk analysis over time. Is it enough to carry out a single risk analysis for a system like MinSide? Should a risk analysis of MinSide be carried out every other year? Every year? Are there systems that can safely be put into production without a preceding risk analysis?

These are topics that span far wider than the scope of this teaching case. We refer to the list of additional sources of reading to find references to books and articles about risk analysis in general and model-based risk analysis in particular.

Figure 8. Treatment diagram for the risks G2*

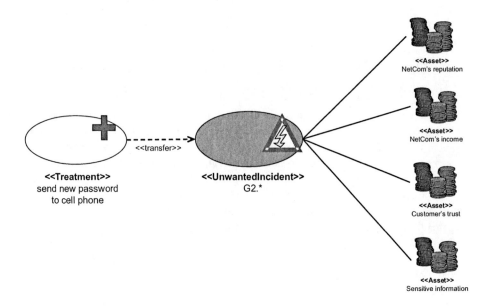

Figure 9. Treatment activity diagram for the risks G2*

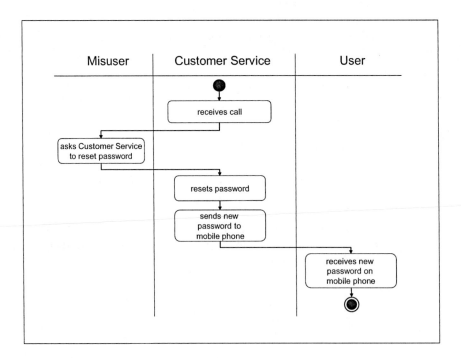

REFERENCES

Australian/New Zealand Standard AS/NZS 4360. (1999). *Risk management.*

Cockburn, A. (1997). Structuring use cases with goals. *Journal of Object-oriented Programming*, (September/October), 35-40; (November/December), 56-62.

CORAS. (2003). *A platform for risk analysis of security critical systems.* IST-2000-25031. Retrieved from http://coras.sourceforge.net/

IEC 1025. (1990). *Fault tree analysis (FTA).*

IEC 61508. (2000). *Functional safety of electrical/electronic/programmable safety related systems.*

ISO/IEC. (1999). *Information technology — Security techniques — Evaluation Criteria for IT Security ISO/IEC, 15408-1.*

ISO/IEC 10746. (1995). *Basic reference model of open distributed processing.*

ISO/IEC TR 13335. (2001). *Information technology — Guidelines for the management of IT security.*

ISO/IEC 17799. (2000). *Information technology — Code of practice for information security management.*

OMG. (2003a). *Unified Modeling Language specification.* Version 2.0 (OMG Document No. ptc/03-09-15).

OMG. (2003b). *UML profile for modeling quality of service and fault tolerance characteristics and mechanisms, OMG draft adopted specification* (OMG Document No. ptc/ 2004-06-01).

Raptis, D., Dimitrakos, T., Gran, B. A., & Stølen, K. (2002). The CORAS approach for model-based risk analysis applied to the e-commerce domain. *Proceedings of Communication and Multimedia Security, CMS-2002* (pp. 169-181). Kluwer.

Redmill, F., Chudleigh, M., & Catmur, J. (1999). *Hazop and software Hazop.* Wiley.

Sindre, G., & Opdahl, A. L. (2000). Eliciting security requirements by misuse cases. *Proceedings of TOOLS_PACIFIC 2000* (pp. 120-131). IEEE Computer Society Press.

APPENDIX

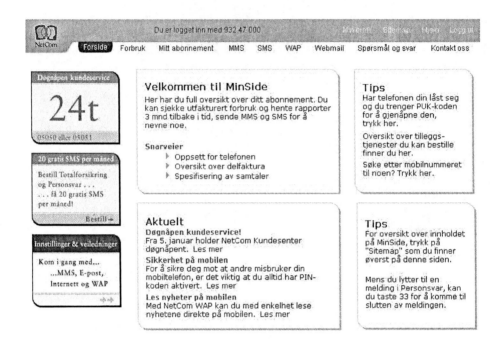

Folker den Braber holds an MSc in Computer Science from the University in Leiden, The Netherlands. He has been employed as a research scientist in the Cooperative and Trusted Systems group of SINTEF Information and Communication Technology since 2001. Through his work on several projects around model-based risk analysis, he has been able to apply and increase his knowledge about specification, design and modeling. Other fields of interest are formal methods, Petri Nets and genetic algorithms.

Arne Bjørn Mildal has worked for NetCom since 1996 and has held various positions within the IT organization. His present position is development manager of IT & Internet with responsibility for all IT development activities within NetCom. This includes internal IT systems for billing and customer care, ERP systems, portals and self-service applications for customers and partners. Before joining NetCom he worked in several large projects, building offshore constructions for the North Sea with responsibility for instrumentation and telecom engineering and testing. He holds an MSc in electrical and computer science from the Norwegian University of Science and Technology (1988).

Jone Nes holds a master's degree from the Norwegian School of Management. After working as a consultant for Avenir (now Ementor), where he worked with system development and project management, he is now project leader for NetCom. He works mainly on development projects with a focus on customer aspects, both internal and external. The past year he has been the driving force behind the establishment of a data management group within NetCom, with the task of designing a logistic data model for the entire organization in order to facilitate internal business communication.

Ketil Stølen is senior scientist and leader for the Quality and Security Technologies group at the Department for Cooperative and Trusted Systems at SINTEF Information and Communication Technology. He is also a professor in computer science at the University of Oslo. Dr. Stølen has broad experience from basic research (four years at Manchester University; five years at Munich University of Technology) as well as applied research (one year at the Norwegian Defense Research Establishment; three years at the OECD Halden Reactor Project; and four years at SINTEF Telecom and Informatics). He completed his PhD, "Development of Parallel Programs on Shared Data-structures," at Manchester University on a personal fellowship granted by the Norwegian Research Council for Science and the Humanities.

Fredrik Vraalsen received his MSc in Computer Science from the University of Illinois at Urbana - Champaign (2001). Since 2001 he has been employed as research scientist in the Cooperative and Trusted Systems group of SINTEF Information and Communication Technology.

This case was previously published in the *Journal of Cases on Information Technology,* 7(3), pp. 110-130, © 2005.

Chapter VIII

Systems Requirements and Prototyping

Vincent C. Yen, Wright State University, USA

EXECUTIVE SUMMARY

This case study is based on a multi-year information systems plan for a marketing firm. Initially, the investigation was enterprise-wide. We describe the critical components of the enterprise system, including the software and hardware architectures. For the application systems, the accounting system and the job scheduling system receive top priority. Since the accounting system was a commercial off-the-shelf product, our focus was on the development of the job scheduling system. We explain the manual job scheduling process and how the automated system might be developed. The justification for adopting Microsoft's Access, SQL server, Exchange, and Project as the development tools is presented. Microsoft Access was used just for the prototyping. Eventually, the job scheduling system will be implemented on the Project software with some rewriting of Visual Basic codes. To date, a prototype using Access had been developed and demonstrated. It received favorable comments and has been approved for the next development phase. The case study concludes with remarks on the advantages, issues and lessons learned from the project.

BACKGROUND

The subject of our study is a reputable market research firm that spans more than sixty years. The firm is employee owned. Clients of the firm include well-known names in business and Fortune 500 companies. The firm maintains sales offices in Atlanta, Boston, Cincinnati, Dallas, Detroit, Los Angeles, New York, Philadelphia, and San Francisco. The company had a mission "to help clients measure and monitor customer needed and requirements in order to provide a fact-based foundation for continuous quality improvement efforts focused on enhanced customer satisfaction and retention." Currently, the firm offers a variety of services; including:

1. Assessment of internal and/or external client profile.
2. Analysis of performance goals at managerial and operational levels, products and services, and customer satisfaction.
3. Assistance in design, implementation, and training of program evaluation processes.

All of these services involve data collection and analysis. For data collection, the company offers:

- Telephone and mail surveys
- Personal in-depth interviews and group sessions
- Comment cards in-room, point-of-transaction or with product
- Traditional in-person focus group discussions
- Teleconference focus group discussions
- Benchmarking visits to best in class companies
- Mystery shopper and quality audits of performance
- On-site visits to customer locations to facilitate client/customer team meetings

Usually the data needed by a project requires a combination of the above activities. The design and analysis of data were managed by the statisticians of the company, many of whom hold advanced degrees. The company strives to produce quality services for its clients corresponding to the mission statement.

The Organizational Structure

The organization of the company was straight forward. Units of the organization were setup by functions. The president of the company directly manages: administrative division (human services, accounting, computer operations, etc.), marketing division, consulting/analytical service division (data analysis), research service division (managing project and report production), customer satisfaction division, and the customer research division. A number of departments may exist within each division. For example, the human services department was a branch of the administrative division.

Current Information Systems

The company had a small systems department responsible for maintaining hardware and software operations. It did not have staff to support information systems develop-

ment. Installed hardware included Windows-based personal computers, Sun workstations, and Macintoshes. Local area networks were installed, and remote connections
were available between the sales office and the corporate office. They use four different
operating systems: DOS, WINDOWS, UNIX, and Apple's SYSTEM 7.

The various commercial software used were routinely dedicated to a single purpose
or function. For example, SAS was used as the statistical analysis system, and ACE was
an automated cost estimating system developed by end users with Foxpro. With the
exception of the accounting department (whose systems and its support were out-
sourced), all other applications were either purchased or developed by in-house end
users. Because the company did not have a software procurement policy, different word
processors, spreadsheet programs, and database software co-exist. For example, Sybase,
Foxbase+, Foxpro2, and Paradox were databases used by the company. Due to differences between the files' data format, it was frequently difficult to exchange data between
applications. The applications developed by end users were created to provide a solution
to a particular operational problem. For example, end users have used Foxpro in
developing a cost estimating program, a weekly activity report program, and a job order
information database. These applications were ad-hoc in nature and generally were both
ill-designed and isolated.

The Management Initiatives

The firm's arena of market research had been booming in the last few years. Very
often, the company receives more than ten job orders a day. Managing these projects
becomes more demanding both in accountability and timing. Recognizing the rapid
advancement of information technology and its potential impact to the service industry,
the firm decided to investigate opportunities in IT that may improve its competitiveness.
Because of limited in-house IT capabilities, in the spring of 1993, the firm issued a request
for proposal with the following stated objectives.

1.   Improve the efficiency of the project management and financial accounting pro-
     cesses.
2.   Improve the data transportability and the applications integration across the
     diverse platforms and operating systems.
3.   Maximize the efficiency of existing data networks.
4.   Explore new information technologies for long-term productivity improvements.

In short, the management of the firm was interested in improving its productivity
and efficiency through streamlining the existing information system, while selecting an
information systems architecture for long-term growth. After a lengthy search process,
a consulting company was given the contract. The contractor assembled a team of
investigators consisting of a systems analyst, a computer engineer, and a programmer
to work with the project. On the company side, a project coordinator was assigned to work
with the team. The coordinator was a knowledgeable staff member who was familiar with
the company operations and capable of answering many questions. The appointment of
a coordinator had benefited the company and the project team immensely. Following the
systems development life cycle methodology, the project team's first major task was the
requirements analysis.

DEFINING REQUIREMENTS

Methodologies

The first phase of systems development was requirement analysis. The team needed to understand how the existing system works. The data and knowledge gained through the analysis will serve as the basis for defining system boundaries, project scope, and the new system features and functions. However, in order to obtain the right kind of information, it must be carefully planned. The team proceeded with several information collection techniques, such as structured interviews, critical success factors (CSF) analysis, joint application development (Wetherbe, 1991), and document reviews.

To facilitate the data/information gathering, the company established a cross-function advisory committee comprised of departmental chiefs, division heads, or their representatives. The team had several meetings with the committee, including a brain storming session about the company's business operations and procedures. These meetings provided the team members with an overall conceptual business model and information of how the existing "system" works.

More detailed information about the existing system was pursued by: (1) interviewing the members of the advisory committee, (2) studying the employee job specification handbook, and (3) reviewing current information systems. During this process, the team collects sample forms, reports, business procedures, information systems documents, etc.

To find out the information requirements at the managerial level, the team conducted a structured survey according to the concepts of business systems planning, critical success factors, and end/means analysis. The survey had about 45 participants including members of the advisory committee. Participants were given two weeks to respond the questionnaires. The questionnaire consists of questions each with a maximum of five open-ended sub-questions. As a result, a wealth of information was collected. The data set reveals the information systems requirements of the company and serves as the basis for the design of the firm's information system architecture.

Techniques used so far for information gathering or requirements identification may still leave out certain activities/interfaces between functional areas. For this reason, the team conducted two joint application development (JAD) meetings with the members of the cross-function advisory committee. JAD meetings were not only capable of eliciting information of importance to two or more functional areas but also capable of producing the desired new system functions or characteristics (e.g., scheduling/job tracking systems).

Survey Results

The survey participants were very cooperative, they responded to each question whenever they could. The enthusiasm was probably due to the common desire to achieve a higher level of productivity while simplifying the operational process. Upon analysis of the survey, it was clear that the company needed a comprehensive information system, including but not limited to, job tracking, accounting, scheduling, experience database, time keeping, and data networks. The questions based on the CSF concept were given to middle level managers and staff. The following list highlights some salient information systems requirements perceived by the management:

1.   Up-to-date information on the progress and the cost of an active project
2.   Accessing schedules of all persons working on a particular project
3.   Consistent estimated results from ACE (automated cost estimating software)
4.   Complete information on the client requirements and expectations
5.   Internal communication

In addition to the survey results, separate findings on accounting, data networks, job tracking, scheduling, experience database, and time keeping were documented, along with an enterprise-wide data flow diagram in the Phase I report. The report points out many information systems worthy for development, including: sales and marketing support, cost estimating, financial accounting, job costing, job order, job tracking, time reporting, job scheduling, and progress reporting. Upon evaluations by the company staff, the firm gave the accounting system the first priority. This was because the company wants to be in full control of the accounting data as opposed to the current out-sourced service that did not permit easy access of required data. In addition, there were many accounting packages which were immediately available, reasonably priced and meeting their needs. After a detailed comparison of features and costs among several major accounting packages, the company purchased the Windows-based Platinum Accounting Systems (compatible with many popular databases like Foxpro and Access). The compatibility feature was important because otherwise, accounting data could not be easily shared with other users of the company.

After the purchase of the accounting system, work on data conversion, the system installation, the system testing, and end user training took an extended length of time. Since Platinum provided all the services needed by the company, the consulting team did not involve in the implementation of the system. When the new accounting system was successfully completed, in the spring of 1995, the company wants to proceed with the computerized job scheduling system because of its practical and strategic value.

CURRENT JOB SCHEDULING SYSTEM

The current job scheduling system relies, for the most part, on paper, pencil, telephone or e-mail coordinations, and schedulers' judgment. There were several databases supporting the job scheduling, for example, the job order database, and the experience database. The job order database consists of a client file and a job file. The client file had all pertinent data about the client, while the job file contains records about the job's survey research methods, field survey dates, contract price, etc. Scheduling was entirely manual. Since these databases were not properly designed and normalized they subject to data redundancy and anomaly problems. In this section, we describe the current job scheduling system.

Marketing

The company's account executives (AE) were responsible for the sales or marketing efforts of the company's services. Account executives were expected to contact all prospective clients and provide them with assistance in determining and refining research objectives, designing appropriate research plans, and presenting research results and recommendations. In addition, AEs were responsible for providing a full-range of research expertise and to manage client relationships while meeting specific sales and profitability goals. Normally, after several meetings with his/her client, the AEs have determined critical requirements of the client's potential research project, such as objectives of the project, types of sampling method (e.g., mailing, telephone, interview), sample sizes, tabulation of survey results, statistical analysis, project start date, project ending date, and graphical representation. Requirements of the project were used to generate an estimate of the cost and time for the project. The project's cost and time estimates were then sent to the client for approval. Once the project was sold a unique job number for the project was created by the research services division and this number was also used by the accounting department to keep track of the project payments and costs of company resources.

Estimating Cost and Completion Time

Before the closing of a job AE must provide the client with an estimate of the cost and completion date of the job. A prompt response of the cost and completion date will generally lead to an earlier client decision on the job. These estimates were currently given by the experienced staff and the ACE (automated cost estimating) system. The present ACE system was inadequate in that (1) it only provided estimates for a small subset of tasks, (2) estimates were not within the reasonable range of accuracy, and (3) it did not update automatically when the new project data were entered.

The ACE system demonstrates that the company was aware of the value of the past project experience. Apparently, they hope one day ACE would be capable of generating the estimates for the cost, labor, and time of a project automatically. This was a difficult, if not impossible, task. But, there was no disagreement that the present ACE system could be potentially upgraded to a much useful operational and competitive information system. Consequently, ACE was recommended as one of the high priority projects.

The Experience Database

The database used by the ACE system was called the experience database because it was a database of past projects. The experience database provided historic data for the costs, labor time, duration, and research design of the past projects. Since similar projects share many common characteristics the experience database was valuable for developing standards for them. The development of standards requires the use of statistical techniques. The standard time and cost for each task not only could be used for the price quotes of new projects but also could be used for scheduling new projects. Unfortunately, the experience database was not computerized at this time. The existing automated cost estimating (ACE) program uses a limited number of past case data as the basis of estimation. Thus, the estimates provided by the experience database may be quite inaccurate. This explains why staff must use their judgment to manually make adjustments and modifications for the job schedules.

Senior Account Managers (SAM)

Once a new project was sold, senior account managers (SAMs) assume project management responsibility to oversee all facets of a research study from questionnaire design, cross-tab planning, report compilation to analysis and interpretation of research data. Thus, following the job number creation, SAM will produce an initial project schedule with several critical due dates assigned, e.g., project starting date, project finish date. The critical due dates were referred to as milestones of a project, they also include the field survey start date, and the field survey ending date. This was because the survey was the heart of the project, it carries much information about their products or services in the market place. Clients were eager to see the raw survey results before the sophisticated statistical analysis because the raw results could provide the initial confirmation about the survey objectives.

The completed preliminary job schedule was sent to various departments by e-mail. Departments assign its staff to the job schedule on a task by task basis. In the event that departments cannot scheduled tasks without impacting timely completion of milestones, then the departmental scheduler (normally the head of the department) will have to work out a revised job schedule with a SAM. Obviously, such a job scheduling system was quite labor intensive and chaotic when the number of daily job orders were large.

THE CASE OF THE NEW SCHEDULING SYSTEM

The new job scheduling system was considered as a competitive information system by the management. The decision to develop the scheduling system had led to several meetings between the development team and the firm's sponsors. These meetings have produced the following set of objectives for the new scheduling system:

1. Provide for standard job inputs
2. All schedules should be available online and real time. Changes will be restricted to those that have permission to do so
3. Automatically adjust the time elements of all related tasks due to changes of task durations, or resource utilization and availability
4. Monitor costs and resource utilization
5. Produce job status reports
6. Provide links with the accounting system

Before proceeding, it was made clear that the new scheduling system will seek for maximizing the automation of routine scheduling operations, not for optimizing the resource allocation purpose. The reason was that the latter problem did not have easy solutions for large scheduling projects.

An Overview of the System

There were many options capable of achieving the above objectives, for example, reengineering the current system. However, after a number of interviews, it was clear that users would like to preserve the essential scheduling process as described in section 3. The reason for preserving the current process might be due to the comprehension of the existing system and the unwillingness of taking risks.

Before developing the system the manual process must be clearly defined. Studies of the current process suggest that a structured three-level cooperative model was the underlying system framework. At level one, the top level, for each job proposal the main project scheduler (PD or SAM) will use data from the estimates of ACE, the judgments of AEs and SAMs, clients requests, etc., to determine the major milestones and the associated due dates of the job. The output of this level was the initial job schedule. Then, through e-mail (Microsoft Exchange), the initial job schedule was sent to the respective departments, which was level two. The department managers allocate their resources to the initial job schedule from the department's resource schedule (that was a combined individual staff schedule and time sheets of actual time worked). The output of the second level was either a completed schedule meeting all critical due dates or an incomplete schedule. In the latter case, they were resolved by juggling resources and due dates until all parties will agree. So resolving a scheduling conflict was an iterative process between the department managers and the main project scheduler. It should be pointed out that the conflict was inevitable because the main project scheduler tends to go along with the customer demands in closing a sale. Finally, the level three was the individual staff schedule including the time sheet processing. However, the individual at the third level may not be an internal employee, because he/she could be a contractor responsible for telephone surveys, mall surveys, and mail surveys. The scheduling at the survey centers or at the contractors level did not belong to the scope of this project.

Evaluation of Alternatives

How should the system be developed? The team considered three typical alternatives: (1) developing from scratch using the system development life cycle methodology, (2) purchased package, and (3) prototyping. The first alternative was quickly ruled out because it was not feasible with the given time and budget constraints.

The second alternative calls for an evaluation of all commercial applicable packages. Fortunately, a timely review article (King, 1995) had detail information and critique on the following project scheduling packages: CA-SuperProject 3.0 for Windows, Microsoft Project 4.0 for Windows, Project Scheduler 6 for Windows, SureTrack Project Manager for Windows, Texim Project for Windows 2.0, and Time Line for Windows 6.1. The team requested product literature, and obtained copies of the scheduling system (some companies provide a free 30-day evaluation copy, e.g., Microsoft). The packages were evaluated on the basis of cost, ease of use, data compatibility, networking capability, PC Windows/Windows NT environment, and modification flexibility. In the end, Microsoft's Project 4.0 emerges as best meeting the criteria except the flexibility in program modification and the number of simultaneously adjustable resources of the related projects (limited to 80). Incidentally, project 4.0 is modifiable with the Microsoft Visual Basic programming language.

The third alternative "prototyping" (Jenkins & Naumann, 1982) is a well understood and practiced methodology today. It could be used to build a model of the proposed system and using it to test our understanding of the real requirements. The prototyping process is iterative, evolutionary, and with an emphasis of fast delivery. So, prototyping requires some levels of support by the computer aided software engineering (CASE) tools. A minimum set of components in the CASE is a strong fourth generation language, graphical user interface tools for input and report generation, end-user query language, and database facility. Today, there are plenty of low-cost and PC-based software available for prototyping. Examples are Microsoft's Access, Foxpro, and Visual Basic,

Borland's dBase for Windows, Borland's Delphi, and Sybase's PowerBuilder, and many others. These software have strong relational database support, semi-object-oriented programming styles, and a rich set of tools for input forms creation and output report generation.

The evaluation of the three alternatives was also based on time, budget, and company's technology architecture grounds. The final development strategy calls for the use of Microsoft's Access as the prototyping tool and Microsoft's Project as the implementation system. This was because Project was not a prototyping tool. By using Access, the analyst and end users could build a job scheduling system prototype with databases supporting customized input forms and report features. The prototype will be used as a basis to customize the Project for the final target system. Another reason for choosing Access and Project was that they fit in the company's application development architecture. The architecture will be based on Windows NT, SQL Server, and Exchange (a groupware similar to Lotus Notes.) One of the advantages of these software was the built-in OLE (object linking and embedding), OLE automation, ODBC (open database connectivity), and MAPI (massaging application programming interface) tools allowing "seamless" integration between application systems.

The Project Scope

As the detail of the system requirements unfolds, the company management and the team learn that a job scheduling system (JSS) could be extremely complex. For example, a JSS had many interfaces with subsystems/functions ranging from the client and proposal management to the billing and reports production. Updating a schedule change and optimizing the resource utilization were even more difficult. With this understanding, the firm's management decided to take an evolutionary approach by starting development of a small set of core components of the project. The core components were the job order system, the job tracking system, the resource scheduling system, the job costing system, the experience database management system, and the report generation system. Figure 1 depicts these core components and their related sub-systems.

The Data Model

The forms, reports and computer systems documents collected earlier contain valuable information for data modeling. Using the entity-relationship (E/R) approach, the analysis of data results in a conceptual database model (Figure 2). The model will be used to establish the database files. A brief explanation of the E/R diagram follows. An account executive could have many clients. A client could order many market research jobs. A job could be performed or researched in several ways; thus a job may have many sub-jobs (or job versions). Each sub-job must have one study design. Of course, a study/research design may be used by many sub-jobs. A sub-job consists of many tasks and a task could belong to many sub-jobs, thus we have a many-to-many relationship between the sub-job entity and the task entity. Hence, we create an intersection entity: task-subjob schedule, containing scheduling data of the tasks of a sub-job. Since tasks have precedence relationships, the set of all task-precedent pairs forms the task-structure entity. One task had many task-structures but a task-structure could only be

Figure 1. Sub-systems of the job scheduling system

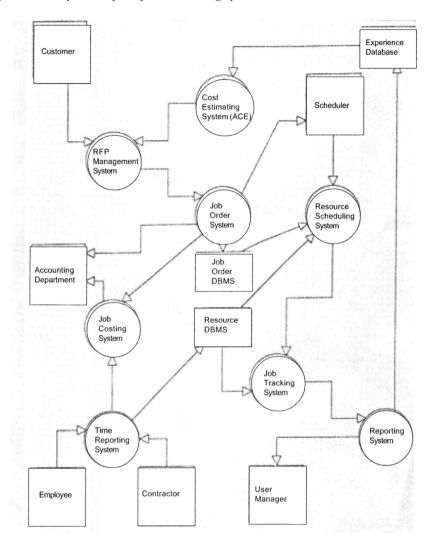

related to one task. A "task-subjob schedule" could be assigned to many employees and an employee could work on many task-subjob schedules, here was another many-to-many relationship. An entity assignment schedule was created to break up the many-to-many relationship. An employee files many weekly time sheets a year, and of course a time sheet could only belong to one employee. A department had many employees and one of the employees was the head of a department.

Figure 2. The E/R diagram for the job scheduling system

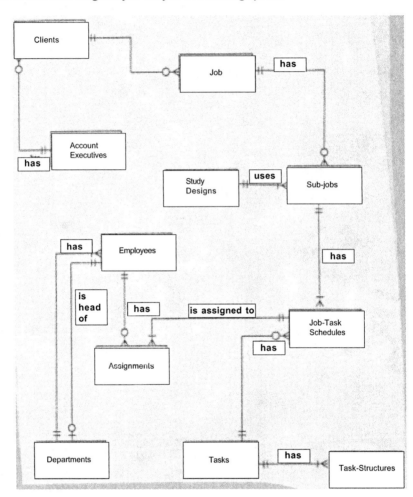

CURRENT STATUS: A PROTOTYPE

Based on the structured three-level cooperative model and the data model, the team built a job scheduling system prototype in the fall of 1995. The prototyping began with the input forms of the scheduling system.

Input Screens

For each table of the database, an input screen was built for data maintenance functions. User interface forms were established on the top of the database according to the user operational requirements. Formal approaches to the design of user interface screens should begin with analyzing users, and tasks they perform (Lee, 1993).

Next, the main screen of the job scheduling was created. The main screen acts like a switchboard that provided the navigation path between screens of data and operations. The menu bar of the main screen had the following options:

- **Job:** for the job level operations like: New, Open, Close, Save, Mail to, options, etc.
- **View:** for displaying the job order related screens like Client, Research Team, and Job Master Schedule, ACE, etc.
- **Reports:** for generating job progress reports, status reports, etc.
- **Database:** for maintenance of tables of the job scheduling database
- **Resource:** for resource allocation/assignment at the departmental level
- **Time:** for maintenance of time sheets

Following the three level scheduling system concept, an input form "job master schedule" for each job was created in level one. This form was in the View menu of the main screen described above. The job's master schedule defines tasks that must be performed and the starting and the ending date of the "critical" tasks. The ending dates of the critical tasks were referred to as milestones. The milestone dates were entered by the master scheduler (SAM/AE) with/without consultation with department managers. In the job master schedule screen, the scheduler could invoke the ACE program and show its output in the same screen. Upon completion of the due date assignment, the schedule was then distributed to all departments via e-mail.

In level two, each department manager had access to his/her staff schedule showing the job assignments and its percentage of completion, by each staff and job. The staff schedule was used for tracking job progress, for determining the feasibility of the job master schedule, and for staff task assignments. The department manager could open the staff schedule as a subscreen of the job master schedule. The assignment of staff to tasks was manually done by the department managers with occasional reference of ACE estimates. If the milestones could be supported at this level, the manager completes and sends back the initial job schedule to the level 1, and, notifies the staff for the assignments.

In level three, each staff had a time sheet input screen that contains task assignments, scheduled completion dates, and the regular time or overtime entries, etc. Staff executes his/her assignments according to the staff schedule, and enters the amount of time worked, and posts sick and vacation days, etc. to the time sheets. Obviously, the time sheet data were interrelated with the departmental staff schedule.

Since data entered at each level were stored in the Access database end users could now retrieve the job related information more flexibly and timely. The prototype did not have a "resource leveling" component at this time, but it will have once it was converted to the Microsoft Project.

Output Screens

The output screens were mainly reports for users and managers; some examples were:

1. Client and job profile report. It contains the client and the job contract information.
2. Job progress report. It provided the status of each task and the percentage of completion of a job.

3. Job cost/estimate report. It provided the up-to-date actual job cost data. It could also be used as for estimating the cost of a proposed project.
4. Time report. It was a weekly employee hours worked report for accounting, payroll and staff schedule updates.
5. Job summary report. It was a summery of all job progress and cost status over a specified time by each client.

SUCCESSES AND FAILURES

The prototype was demonstrated and scored well, but did not confirm that the entire development process was error-free. The following is some successes and failures observed.

Successes

1. The design of the software and hardware architecture.
2. The objectives of the new scheduling system as stated in section 4 were realized; except that it did not allow for the update of due dates when changes were made.
3. The data model was correctly specified this allows end users retrieve the information they want more easily.
4. The new system will greatly reduce the effort and time spent in updating the schedule when resource and due dates change.
5. The experience database was established as a by-product of the scheduling system (with some modifications).

Failures

1. The computerized scheduling system did not completely substitute the manual system because (a) it could be inflexible if tasks required were not in the database, (b) it was difficult to reach an agreement when more than two parties have scheduling conflicts (no conference call facility), and (c) above all, impersonal.
2. The scheduling was not user friendly because the prototype did not have a graphical scheduling facility such as the Gantt chart.
3. The response time of *Access* and *Project* was below expectations.
4. The lack of detail process description in the functional analysis had led to the (three months) delay of the prototype development. An example was the precedence relationship between tasks, a critical feature in any scheduling system, but a written master precedence relationship table did not exist.
5. The program (in ACCESS Basic) for the automatic adjustment of time due to changes in due dates and/or resource availability still had bugs. This prevents a lively demonstration of the prototype.
6. The inability of dealing with the "resource leveling" function.

EPILOGUE AND LESSONS LEARNED

The project presented here had well defined objectives. The manual job scheduling system, although developed internally, had been working for many years and was relatively stable. However the manual system was not a sophisticated scheduling system; it was labor intensive and prone to errors. So replacing the current system by a computerized scheduling system, the company could potentially improve operational efficiency and gain a competitive advantage.

In this project, we have created a prototype. Following the development strategy, the next phase was to migrate the database to the Microsoft SQL Server, and to customize the Microsoft Project according to the prototype model. A proficient Visual Basic programmer was indispensable in this phase.

The following were some of the important lessons learned from this project:

1. **Defining the project scope:** The project had many interfaces with other systems (e.g., accounting system; See Figure 1). This increased the complexity of the project and the development risk. One way to contain the complexity and the risk would be to start small by limiting the project scope to a few functions and interfaces.

2. **Document the process procedure:** Although a lot of forms, manuals, reports, and program listings were received, these were bits and pieces about the job scheduling system in question. How these bits and pieces work together to support various functions of a company should be clearly spelled out. The process documentation was important in that (a) it could lead to the early discovery of inadequate procedures, and (b) it could augment comprehensive support for latter stages of system development.

3. **Avoid project interruption:** The scheduling project should not be interrupted by the accounting system implementation (which took about nine months) because the team must relearn the system and the business when they resume their work. This was particularly true when there were two turnovers in the development team.

4. **Select the right technology:** Knowing the state and the trend of information technology (hardware and software) is vital in the design of the hardware and software architecture.

QUESTIONS FOR DISCUSSION

1. Why were the experience database and the automated cost estimating system so important to the company?
2. What were the possible applications of the experience database (besides serving as a source of data for estimating the task time and the cost)?
3. What were the reasons for the top management to launch this project?
4. What were the reasons for selecting Microsoft products in this project?
5. Had the company worked out the detailed procedures of the job scheduling system? Explain.

REFERENCES

Bischofberger, W., & Keller, R. (1989). Enhancing the software life cycle by prototyping. *Structured Programming, 1*, 47-59.

Geoff, L. (1993). *Object-oriented GUI application development*. PTR-Prentice Hall, Inc.

King, N. H. (1995, April 11). On time and on budget. *PC Magazine,* 165-199.

March, S. T., & Kim, Y-Gm. (1992, Summer). Information resource management: Integrating the pieces. *DATABASE,* 27-37.

Milton, J. A., & Naumann, J. D. (1982). Prototyping: The new paradigm for systems development. *MIS Quarterly, 6* , 29-44.

Wetherbe, J. C. (1991, March). Executive information requirements: Getting it right. *MIS Quarterly,* 51-65.

Vincent C. Yen is associate professor of management science and information systems at Wright State University College of Business Administration. He received his PhD from the Ohio State University in operations research. His research interests include strategic information systems planning, determination of systems requirements, systems development processes, decision support systems, fuzzy control, and fuzzy decision making. He and Prof. H. Li co-published a book in 1995 entitled Fuzzy Sets and Fuzzy Decision-Making *by CRC Press.*

This case was previously published in J. Liebowitz & M. Khosrowpour (Eds.), *Cases on Information Technology in Modern Organizations*, pp. 107-120, © 1997.

Chapter IX

ERP Implementation for Production Planning at EA Cakes Ltd.

Victor Portougal, The University of Auckland, New Zealand

EXECUTIVE SUMMARY

This case details the implementation of the Systems Applications & Products (SAP) Production Planning module at EA Cakes Ltd. The market forced the company to change its sales and production strategy from "make-to-order" to "make-to-stock." The decision to change the strategy involved not only the company's decision to invest much more money in accumulation and keeping stocks of finished goods, it required a complete redesign of its production planning system, which was an integral part of an ERP system that used SAP software. A team of IT specialists and production planning personnel was formed for designing computer support for the new production planning system business processes. There was no consensus in the design group. IT specialists were sure that existing SAP software could provide adequate computer support. The production planning staff had doubts that SAP modules are relevant to their business processes. They argued that poor fit between the business processes implicit in the software and the business processes of EA Cakes will result in failure. To resolve the problem, the management invited a consulting company. The consultants suggested quickly designing a rough prototype system. Analyzing this system would help the working group to reach a consensus. Apart from giving adequate computer support to the new production planning system, the SAP implementation had to solve several implementation problems identified by consultants. The question is: can a standard software system like SAP give adequate computer support to an individually designed business management system?

ORGANIZATIONAL BACKGROUND

EA Cakes Ltd., New Zealand, is a successful food manufacturing company with a major share of the market in New Zealand and the Asia-Pacific region. It produces more than 400 different kinds of fresh and frozen food products.

From a shelf-life point of view, the company manufactures three types of products:

1.   Shelf-stable and frozen food with practically infinite shelf life (up to one year)
2.   Chilled products with a medium shelf life (from three to six months)
3.   Short shelf life products (from one week to six weeks)

The demand for many products is uneven. Christmas cakes and puddings, for example, are mainly sold during November and December. Generally, the demand for cakes is lower during summer than during winter. Sales are also volatile because they are conducted through numerous channels, including major supermarket chains, route outlets (such as groceries stores), and food service for hospitals, hotels, and restaurants. Sales to Australia, the major export market, add uncertainty to demand.

For years EA Cakes Ltd. built a reputable brand name and had enjoyed a stable market. As a result, the dominant production strategy of the company was make-to-order, MTO (see for example, Vollmann, Berry, & Whybark, 1997). Permanent customers, such as supermarkets, shops, and restaurants, placed orders either for the next week, or for longer intervals with a regular delivery, and the company provided good customer service both in terms of quality and of on-time delivery.

In the late 1990s EA Cakes Ltd. began to observe a decline of its market share in many of the traditional markets. Marketing analysis showed that the main reason for the drop in sales was price increase due to the company's high production costs, and as a result competitors offered lower prices on similar products. The famous brand name did not attract customers enough to support the higher prices. An attempt was made to compete on low retail prices, with the results of slightly increased sales volumes, but significantly decreased profit.

Soon the company was forced to reconsider its sales and production strategy. Two major faults were identified:

1.   To support its MTO strategy, the company was forced to have a significant capacity cushion both in labor and equipment. It was necessary for providing stable customer service while the demand was uneven, sometimes with huge lumps. During Christmas, for example, the company usually tripled their average sales

volumes. EA Cakes Ltd. was accustomed to seasonal variations and Christmas sales lumps, and coped with them by accumulating stock. Daily and weekly variations, however, led to losses in production time in low periods and to excessive use of overtime during peak periods. High labor cost variances (as compared to the standards) and low machine capacity utilization were prevalent.

2.   The MTO strategy implied that the company always quoted lead times to customers; for example, an order placed this week would be promised to deliver next week, or the week after, if there were too many orders. Old traditional customers agreed with this system, and the company was mostly successful in keeping its promises. The market, however, had become much more dynamic. Increased competition from NZ and overseas and a heavy promotional activity required improved "speed to market." Many customers wanted the product on demand, not next week. The company was unable to exploit such opportunities and lost this significant part of the market.

As a result EA Cakes Ltd. had decided to change its production and sales strategy (as recommended by operations management literature; see for example, Vollmann, Berry, & Whybark, 1997) for long and medium shelf-life products from "make-to-order" (MTO) to "make-to-stock" (MTS). The MTS strategy costs more in inventory than MTO, but it has two benefits:

1.   Increased "speed to market" allows expanding the market share by attracting new customers and by catching unexpected opportunities.
2.   Capacity may be utilized more efficiently using the inventory "cushions" instead of capacity cushions (see McNair & Vangermeersch, 1998).

MTS companies hold stocks of all advertised products. The stocks usually are managed by a "min-max" rule: stocks below or close to minimum trigger production until they reach or approach the maximum level. The difference between minimum and maximum is defined by the demand forecast during a planning period. The production process is driven by the current levels of stocks rather than by customers' orders.

The decision to change the strategy from MTO to MTS involves not only the company's decision to invest much more money in accumulation and keeping stocks of finished goods, it requires a complete redesign of its production planning system. There are several major reasons for making significant changes in production planning:

•   MTO is driven by customers' orders, MTS is triggered by forecasts; a forecasting system had to be designed and implemented.
•   There are no significant stocks of finished goods under MTO, so there is no need for stock management; for MTS, an inventory management system for finished goods had to be developed.
•   Under MTO there are no significant information links between the company planning and shop floor production planning; under MTS it is vital that the planning system preserves continuity. It has to be continuity in planning. That means the plans produced by each level are detailed plans of the top level. Also

there must be feedback continuity: feedback of the top levels is an aggregation of bottom level feedback — for more detail see McNair and Vangermeersch (1998).

The production planning system was an integral part of an ERP system that used SAP software. Its redesign was a part of a major project of the ERP system development, carried out by Ernest Edams Ltd. for two years.

SETTING THE STAGE

The new production planning system consists of three levels (Figure 1).

Aggregate Capacity Planning (ACP)

The first (top-level) procedure is part of the general budgeting procedure, which starts from sales budget development. Sales budget is not a simple forecast of the amount of products that could be sold in the future. The budget not only predicts, but also directs the sales and marketing efforts of the company. Thus it is more a sales plan than a forecast. This defines the dual nature of the budget: on the one hand it should be realistic and should define what could be sold; on the other hand it should meet the business and financial goals of the company.

The sales budget is a management tool for control of company performance by the Board of Directors. The Board provides the inputs to this budget in the form of key performance indicators. The marketing department provides other inputs (launch of new products and other marketing initiatives). The sales budget is developed for the fiscal year, and it is redeveloped every quarter with a one-year time horizon (a rollover procedure). All the budgets and rollovers are stored in the information system for reference and subsequent statistical processing. At any time two versions are available for analysis and use in the sales and production planning: a full budget for the current fiscal year, approved by the board of directors, and a current rollover budget.

ACP has all the features of a capacity planning procedure. Starting from the sales budget, it produces an aggregate production plan for the following planning periods up to the planning horizon. The plan is balanced against the agreed target capacity, and at the same time meets the production and sales goals of the company. The demand forecast, the financial goals of the company, the target stock levels and actual stock levels are kept in the budget database.

The planning starts from defining an optimum production strategy. The production strategy that follows the demand pattern month by month ("chase" strategy) is not sustainable here because of high seasonality of some products. Figure 2 shows that the "level" strategy with even production levels is not sustainable as well, because there is not enough time for stock accumulation from the beginning of the year until the start of the peak season. If production starts earlier, then the level of stocks becomes excessive.

The optimum "mixed" strategy that combines stock accumulation with overtime use is shown in Figure 3. It plans some overtime at the peak season, and decreased resources utilization at the beginning of the year to compensate for the effect of increased production.

The optimum mixed strategy, expressed in sales dollars, then is converted to an aggregate production plan. The planner uses:

Figure 1. Three-level production planning system supporting MTS strategy

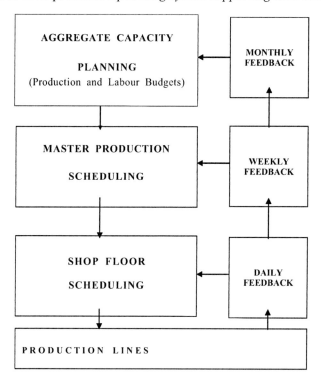

Figure 2. The "level" strategy is not sustainable — Negative stocks show this

Month	Apr	May	Jun	Jul	Aug	Sep	Oct	Nov	Dec	Jan	Feb	Mar	Total
Stock	1.65	3.17	3.82	5.48	6.89	3.56	0.85	-3.5	-5.9	-2.9	-0.7	-0	
Sales	3.87	3.99	4.87	3.86	4.1	8.85	8.22	9.85	7.94	2.51	3.36	4.77	66.2
Indicis	0.83	0.85	1.05	0.82	0.88	1.17	1.03	1.39	1.72	0.53	0.71	1.02	12

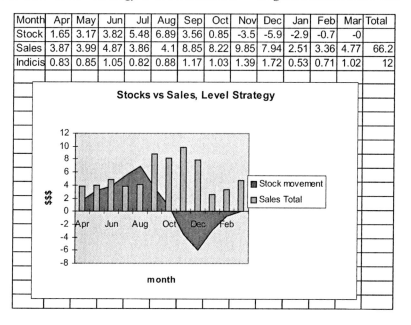

Figure 3. Optimum "mixed" strategy

Month	Jan	Feb	Mar	Apr	May	Jun	Jul	Aug	Sep	Oct	Nov	Dec
Stock	1.51	2.66	2.91	4.56	6.08	6.73	8.39	9.80	6.47	4.26	0.92	0.00
Production	4.02	4.52	5.02	5.52	5.52	5.52	5.52	5.52	5.52	6.02	6.52	7.02
Overtime	-1.5	-1.0	-0.5	0.00	0.00	0.00	0.00	0.00	0.00	0.50	1.00	1.50

- conversion tables, containing unit prices;
- capacity tables, which show the lines' capacity (units/hours); and
- labor content tables (labor hours/machine hours) — these are necessary because different lines have crews of different sizes.

Here the planner shifts shelf-stable seasonal products to an earlier month, targeting the optimum stock levels and loading the lines up to their capacity. The development of an aggregate plan based on the optimum strategy is necessary because:

- The strategy gives total sales dollars and cannot be used for production planning while the plan is expressed in units of each products.
- There is no direct relationship between the selling price and production hours, therefore the strategy is not balanced against capacity.

Thus, the strategy serves as a goal for ACP. The aggregate capacity plan is developed initially for the fiscal year, and it is redeveloped every quarter with a one-year time horizon (a rollover procedure).

Master Production Scheduling

The master production scheduling system is the most important managerial tool for the operations manager of an MTS company. Master Production Schedule (MPS) gives

Figure 4. Make-to-stock production

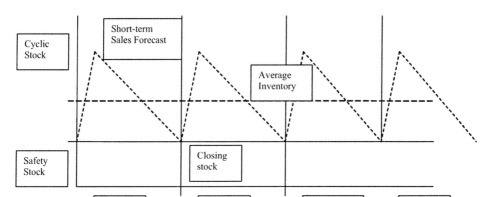

the ability to ensure that available capacity is allocated with a customer service focus. The main MPS inputs are:

- aggregate capacity plan for the following two months,
- actual stock levels, and
- short-term demand forecast.

The sales team prepares a short-term demand forecast by-product for the next five weeks, each week (a rollover forecast). The sales managers of particular products modify the monthly sales forecasts from the current budget, taking into account changes in demand, planned promotions, and so on.

Starting from the demand forecast for the following planning period, the Master Scheduler produces a weekly production plan for the next five weeks, which is balanced against capacity, and at the same time meets production and sales goals of the company.

As shown in Figure 4, the MPS Process uses the following logic:

Opening Stock + Production – Sales Forecast = Closing Stock

The MPS is calculated using several planning runs and is being balanced with the capacity. This can highlight where the capacity is insufficient for meeting the schedule or where the capacity utilization is insufficient within the schedule.

The procedure is performed initially at the beginning of the planned month (the main run) in order to work out the MPS for the month. Only the first week of the plan is valid (and frozen). The rest of the plan is necessary for keeping the continuity of planning during the month. At the end of each week, when feedback on actual production and updated demand forecast become available, the procedure is run for the rest of the planning period (a control run). During this run the updated MPS for the following weeks will be produced. Also, instant changes in demand can initiate a control run in order to react quickly to the market demand.

The primary function of the MPS is to produce feasible assignments for all product lines, which ensure their performance according to ACP with minimum cost.

The other functions of this level are:

1. To keep desirable stock levels
2. To implement a "speed-to-market" principle: react quickly to significant changes in market demand

Shop Floor Scheduling

This level performs actual scheduling for the next week (with a daily subdivision), specified by production lines and products.

The scheduling constraints (for both men and machines scheduling) have been worked out as fixed recommended schedules for different proportions of the output. Set-up times, planned downtime and average capacity losses due to unplanned downtime are known and used for realistic scheduling. This required a downtime reporting procedure and a schedule for major planned maintenance. The scheduling is performed initially at the beginning of the planned week (the main run) in order to work out an optimal weekly schedule. At the end of each day, when feedback on actual production becomes available, the procedure is run for the rest of the planning period (a control run). During this run the updated plan for the following days, subject to the same planning constraints, is produced.

It was assumed that this level would be supported by a whole set of shop floor control procedures recognized in literature (Sherer, 1998).

Similar to most organizations, EA Cakes Ltd. operates on a hierarchical basis.

All activities and documents are organized through the Production Planning hierarchy. The hierarchy is organized so that the aggregate capacity planning (ACP) process is at the highest level of aggregation, while the shop floor scheduling process is at the lowest level. These levels can be presented using different parameters. Thus it includes a product hierarchy, time hierarchy, and organizational hierarchy. Each level varies in purpose, time span, and amount of detail (Figure 5).

CASE DESCRIPTION

The implementation of the Systems Applications & Products (SAP) Production Planning module at EA Cakes Ltd. in order to provide computer support to the MTS production planning system started from the detailed analysis of the problems.

The production planning system described above carries specific features of production planning of EA Cakes. Standard software (and SAP by definition is standard software), on the other hand, comprises programs developed for an anonymous market. The question is: can a standard software system like SAP give adequate computer support to an individually designed business management system?

This class of problems is widely discussed in literature (e.g., Robey, Ross, & Boudreau, 2002; Jacobs & Bendoly, 2003), with rather uncertain results, always pointing at the specific features of the enterprise. Because of this, a team from IT specialists and

Figure 5. Breakdown of product, time, and production planning system hierarchies at EA Cakes Ltd.

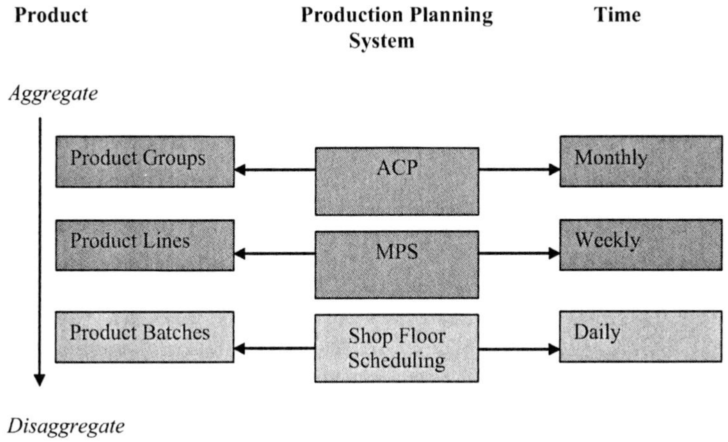

production planning personnel was formed for designing computer support for the new production planning system business processes.

The concept of a business process is central to many areas of business systems design, specifically to business systems based on modern information technology (see Scholz-Reiter & Stickel, 1996). In the new era of computer-based business management, the design of business process has substituted the previous functional design. There are many definitions of a business process (see Davenport, 1993; Sharp & McDermott, 2001; Rosemann, 2001). According to Sharp and McDermott (2001), a business process is a collection of interrelated tasks initiated in response to an event that achieves a specific result for the customer of the process. Thinking in terms of business processes helps managers to look at their organization from the customer's perspective. Usually a business process involves several functional areas and functions within those areas. Thus, a business process is cross-functional.

Definitely, this is the case of the production planning at EA Cakes.

The aggregate capacity planning uses sales budget, stock feedback, and available capacity (manpower and machinery). The master scheduling involves forecasting, feedback on stocks. The shop-floor scheduling and control absorbs a huge variety of activities from other functional areas such as material control, human resource management, inventory management, and so on.

Quite to the contrary, standard software was initially developed only for certain functions that could easily be standardized. Modern standard software such as SAP is said to be object oriented or process oriented (see Kirchmer, 2002). However, it is still mostly functional, and the necessary orientation can only be achieved by adjusting the appropriate parameters. Even after the adjustments, the functionality of SAP may not be completely relevant to the business processes of a particular company. Then the implementation team will have only two options (Sawy, 2001):

1.   To substitute the business processes of the company for the business processes implemented in SAP.
2.   To create additional special software for providing computer support to production planning.

There was no consensus in the design group.

When the production planning staff got acquainted with the business processes suggested for production planning by SAP, they had doubts that these modules are relevant to their business processes. They argued that SAP, like most ERP systems, still focuses on the function such as inventory, production, accounting, finance, and so forth. The functional view poorly represents the interaction with other functional views. Many companies have to modify their current business activity in order to use the ERP system. The members of production planning staff were the authors of the new production planning system, and they had a rather firm position that their planning processes were the most efficient for EA Cakes. No changes would be accepted.

On the other hand, IT specialists were sure that existing SAP software could provide adequate computer support. They argued that SAP software mostly represents the "best-of-breed" solutions, thus producing a system that better fits each process in the company. While the best-of-breed solution would not fit precisely, it may be an investment that provides greater long-term flexibility and better solutions to the company's problems.

So, the management of EA Cakes was presented with the following dilemma:

1.   Believing the IT specialists and continuing to implement the existing SAP modules on comparatively low cost, but facing all the risks of losses due to planning inefficiency.
2.   Believing the planning staff and ordering high cost computer support in addition to existing SAP system.

The management invited a consulting company. The consultants suggested quickly designing a rough prototype system (Hoffer, George, & Valasich, 1998), using ARIS (Sheer, 1999). Analysing this system would help the working group to reach a consensus.

Apart from giving adequate computer support to the new production planning system, the SAP implementation was intended to solve several implementation problems (Hong & Kim, 2002) identified by consultants.

Problem 1

The manufacturing process requires an updated short-term forecast each week. Sales managers must produce the forecast, and then it is automatically processed within the Master Production Scheduling. Sales figures for individual products have to be provided on a weekly basis for the current month and the next month. Actual sales made each week are captured and available for reporting on the following morning (after actual sales completion). Sales staff compare actual sales with long-term forecasts and using judgement make necessary adjustments. Currently, forecasts are prepared manually and then put into the database. It needs computer support to relieve sales personnel and to eliminate data entry.

Problem 2

The Master Scheduler has to check the capacity requirements and to change the production volumes according to available capacity. Then he must present the changes to the Sales Department and the Production Department for acceptance.

Problem 3

Presently at EA Cakes Ltd., scheduling is only done on finished items. It is desirable to schedule some components production as well.

Problem 4

It is necessary to provide a reliable method for checking inventory availability. The question is: Can the SAP implementation solve all these problems?

CURRENT CHALLENGES

One of the biggest problems for EA Cakes Ltd. is low capacity utilization. The company has sufficient regular work force. Nevertheless, the Master Scheduler sometimes has to schedule overtime production, paying for overtime labor, which results in higher production costs for products. This can also cause shortages or stock-out of some materials for production, further increasing the cost of production. Managers are especially frustrated when an instant need for overtime follows a period of low demand, when inventory could have been built up; for example, in anticipation of an increase in sales following production promotions by marketing.

Another problem was identified in inventory management. Stock control of raw material and finished items needs double-checking. Initially, the line manager records the data about actual production and actual use of raw materials. However, due to possible conflict of interests, this data is not absolutely reliable. The actual amounts of goods produced should be verified regularly. Any variances must be investigated; hence the necessary data must be kept for a longer time. More thought is required on the handling of rejects/seconds, as some are almost planned by-products. This will also have ramifications with stock control and sales analysis.

There are hopes that these problems could be fixed after the ERP implementation by existing SAP tools. Of course, the company must modify its current business activity in order to fully use the functionality of SAP. If the planning staff will accept modest trade-offs, then the IT specialists are still sure that existing SAP software could provide adequate computer support.

REFERENCES

Davenport, T. H. (1993). *Process innovation.* Boston: Harvard Business School Press.

Hoffer, J. A., George, J. F., & Valacich J. S. (2002). *Modern systems analysis and design* (3rd ed.). Upper Saddle River, NJ: Prentice Hall.

Hong, H. K., & Kim, Y. J. (2002). The critical success factors for ERP implementation: An organisational fit perspective. *Journal of Information and Management, 40*(1), 25-40.

Jacobs, F. R., & Bendoly, E. (2003). Enterprise resource planning: Developments and directions for operations management research. *European Journal of Operational Research, 146,* 233-240.

Keller, G., & Teufel, T. (1998). *SAP R/3 process oriented implementation.* Harlow: Pearson Education Ltd.

Kirchmer, M. (2002). *Business process oriented implementation of standard software* (2nd ed.). Springer.

McNair, C. J., & Vangermeersch, R. (1998). *Total capacity management: Optimizing at the operational, tactical, and strategic levels.* Boca Raton, FL: St. Lucie Press.

Robey, D., Ross, J. W., & Boudreau, M. (2002). Learning to implement enterprise systems: An exploratory study of the dialectics of change. *Journal of Management Information Systems*, 17-46.

Roscmann, M. (2001, March). *Business process lifecycle management.* Queensland University of Technology.

Sawy, O. A. (2001). *Redesigning enterprise processes for e-business.* Boston: McGraw Hill, Irwin.

Scholz-Reiter, B., & Stickel, S. (1996). *Business process modelling.* Berlin & New York: Springer.

Sharp, A., & McDermott, P. (2001). Just what are processes anyway? *Workflow modeling: Tools for process improvement and application development*, pp. 53-69.

Sheer, A.-W. (1999). *ARIS: Business process frameworks* (3rd ed.). Berlin: Springer-Verlag.

Sherer, E. (1998). *Shop floor control: A systems perspective.* Berlin: Springer-Verlag.

Vollmann, T. E., Berry, W. L., & Whybark, D. C. (1997). *Manufacturing planning and control systems* (4th ed.). Chicago: Irwin.

Victor Portougal is associate professor in the Department of Information Systems and Operations Management, Business School, The University of Auckland. His research interests are in quantitative methods both in management science and information systems. In information systems his research specializes in security, information systems design and development, and ERP. Dr. Portougal's practical and consulting experience includes information and ERP systems design and implementation for companies in Russia and New Zealand. He is the author of many articles in scholarly journals, practitioner magazines, and books. He holds degrees from the University of Gorki, Russia (BSc, MSc, computer science), Academy of Sciences, Moscow (PhD, operations research), and the Ukrainian Academy of Sciences, Kiev (Doctor of Economics).

This case was previously published in the *Journal of Cases on Information Technology,* 7(3), pp. 98-109, © 2005.

Chapter X

Developing Effective Computer Systems Supporting Knowledge-Intensive Work:
Situated Design in a Large Paper Mill

Martin Müller, University of Zurich, Switzerland

Rolf Pfeifer, University of Zurich, Switzerland

EXECUTIVE SUMMARY

The case to be discussed is a joint project between the university of Zurich and "Swiss Paper,"[1] a large paper mill in Switzerland. The paper mill had recently undergone deep structural changes after an investigation of by of the world's leading management consulting companies. Our project is mainly concerned with support of energy management by means of computer technology. There were essentially three goals. The first one was to minimize energy consumption while keeping it at a constant level. The second goal was the exploration of a scientific hypothesis, namely that expert behavior cannot be adequately explained in terms of "information processing," but is more adequately seen as "situated action." The latter emphasizes the actual organizational and social circumstances. The objective of Situated Design — a particular project methodology that we have been developing in our group at the university over the last few years — is to support "situated action" by means of computer technology, rather than to formalize human expertise. Applying and refining this methodology is the third major goal of the project. In this paper we will discuss our experiences with Situated Design at Swiss Paper. The software industry's biggest problems are well known — projects arriving late, over budget or not delivering what is needed. We will argue that one of the main problems is a misconception of human cognition and behavior. We claim that this misconception is at the source of the problems of software development in general. We suggest an alternative approach which has grown out of our experience with many projects in the area of "work place design by means of computer technology."[2] One of the underlying assumptions that we will discuss in the paper is that the goal of software engineering is support rather than automation. Thus, we do not intend to develop software packages that will take all the design decisions for the software engineer. This position can be contrasted with, e.g., the conviction underlying CASE systems, where the design process and the whole software life cycle can be formalized. All the designer has to do is apply the detailed recipes prescribed by the CASE software. What we have in mind contrasts sharply with this view. It is our belief that an answer to the so-called "software crisis" is to optimally exploit human expertise, not automating it. Furthermore, design involves a lot of communication. The software designer has to listen and observe carefully, in order to better understand the latent user's needs. The aim of Situated Design is to stimulate the designer's awareness of the issues involved in the design process, such as the expertise used in daily work. It should encourage the discussion and confrontation of these issues from different perspectives among all members of a project team, designers as well as the people concerned. The goal is not to provide "canned" solutions, but to optimally bring to bear the user's as well as the designer's knowledge. The success of the project depends on the human designer's experience in perceiving related issues which are not optimally exploited. In order to test and refine the methodology of Situated Design we have defined a project with Swiss Paper. The investigation of one of the world's leading management consulting companies has been the first consequence of a preceding declaratory capital reduction. Though the company's interest in the project is energy management, our approach will rather emphasize the communication between all workers about energy issues than to understand the energy process itself. Therefore, the objective is to improve or, respectively, to enhance the existing computer infrastructure in a way that the communication process about the energy issue will be improved. Finally, we expect that an improved communication will enhance the paper mill workers' understanding and mastery of the energy management.

BACKGROUND

The Holding

Swiss Paper specializes in high-quality paper production with a total annual production of 300'000 tons. Swiss Paper is one of two paper mills belonging to the "Swiss Paper Holding"[3] with a total production of 450'000 tons. The second paper mill produces newsprint. In 1994, the business volume of the holding was roughly US$600 million with a loss of US$50 million. This has to be contrasted with the mid 1980s, where Swiss Paper Holding made large profits (in 1989 they still had a surplus of 13 millions) and accounted a very high liquidity (60 %).

During the period of 1994/95 two subsidiary companies engaged in paper manufacturing and paper trading were sold as a result of restructuring. With the attempt to increase productivity the work force of the holding was reduced from former 3295 to 1675 persons. At Swiss Paper itself there was a reduction from 1300 to 900 employees. Both paper mills have a function-oriented, hierarchical organizational structure (see Figure 1).

Our Partner: "Swiss Paper"

The main activity of Swiss Paper is the production of high-quality paper. In addition to the paper production itself, it manufactures high-quality paper into semi-finished levels (cut-size sheeting and packaging). A total amount of 300'000 tons is produced by three independent paper production lines with different production capacities (49%, 29%, and 22%). However, the primary raw material, the pulp, is not produced by Swiss Paper itself, but bought from independent deliverers.

Until 1988 there was a shortage of high-quality paper on the European market. In 1991, after a market analysis of future developments, Swiss Paper invested US$400 million into a paper production line of the newest generation. Nowadays, this production line is producing nearly half of the total amount of paper. At about the same time, strong German and Scandinavian competitors were making similar investments which lead to a significant over-capacity of the whole European paper industry around 1992/93 (there was a previous over-capacity of 25% in 1991). As a consequence, the price for paper dropped. However, European paper production capacity was still rising, which was probably the reason why the pulp price increased also. This market development caused difficulties for Swiss Paper.

There were a number of additional, specific factors contributing to the already difficult situation of the company. First, the European market within the European Union had become well established, making it more difficult for a company in a non-member country like Switzerland to compete. As a side effect of the European alliance, there were large fusions going on. During 1994 the ten biggest European paper mills were producing two-thirds of the total amount of European paper. Second, there had been some unfortunate investments. For example, Swiss Paper decided to assign the contract for the development of the control system of the new paper production line to a new-comer in paper industry. This decision lead to a lot of system crashes during the first two years. These frequent crashes had an immediate negative impact on the production capacity and on the quality of the paper. 1993 was a bad year for the company: the holding's losses totaled US$100 million. Also, there is the general phenomenon that the market has become more dynamic. For example the price of the pulp increased from October 1994 to October 1995 from US$380 to US$1000 per ton. This was another unfortunate development for Swiss Paper, because there was a practice of making contracts with their customers for a period of one whole year in advance, based on the current pulp price.

In this kind of new market situation companies not only have to be able to produce efficiently, but they must react dynamically to unforeseen changes. Last but not least,

Figure 1. Organizational structure of Swiss Paper

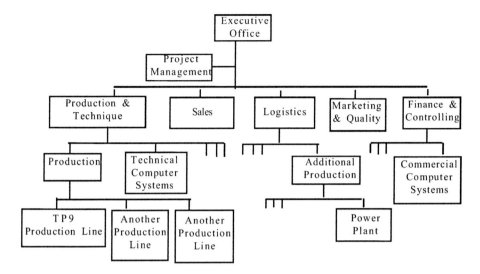

there was also the great danger that the company would have to file bankruptcy. It was obvious that something had to be done to get the company back on track.

At the end of 1994 Swiss Paper had to write down the capital. Additionally, in early 1995 a consortium of banks launched a far-reaching restructuring operation — just before our project had been approved by the CEO. While the management consulting company was focusing on the overall organization, our project was focusing on a more operative level.

SETTING THE STAGE

The Operative Level

Our efforts are centered around the complex issue of energy management. This focus was chosen for several reasons:

(a)   Energy costs for paper production amount to approximately 10% of the total production costs. Energy is a strategic factor for the paper industry, first because of the high energy costs, which can be expected to increase in the future. Moreover, currently the average cost for electricity in Switzerland is extremely low as compared to the surrounding countries. It can be expected that this situation will change in the near future. Second because of ecological considerations that will become even more relevant in the future.

(b)   According to one of our hypothesis, energy consumption is linked with paper quality. Thus, if we get the energy situation under control, the paper quality will also be improved.

In 1994, for example, Swiss Paper expended about 228 GWh of electrical energy (68% were produced by Swiss Paper's own power plant), and about 495 GWh of thermal energy. The total cost of the company's energy consumption amounted to US$21 million, including the cost for additionally purchased energy. The cost for the 72 GWh bought from an external electricity provider totaled US$7 million. Energy required for the production of one sheet of paper is equal to the amount of energy expended if you leave a bulb of 60 W on for 12 minutes (see Figure 2).

To convey a flavor of the situation of the company at the operational level, we will emphasize some characteristic "cultural" points. Now we present a short overview of some managerial, organizational and technical concerns, which are important for understanding our project partner's situation.

Fields of Investigation

Because of our focus on energy, the investigation could be constrained to the company's own power plant as the energy supplier and the three paper production lines as the main energy consumers. 84% of the company's total electricity production, and 81 % of the company's total steam production is consumed by the paper production lines. Our research capacities were too low to handle all three production lines, so we decided

Figure 2. Top: Total consumption of electricity in 1994 subdivided into the three main consumers (the paper production lines TP9, TP8 and TP6) and various others; TP9 is subdivided into the paper machine (PM9), the grinding system (MA9) and various (Rest TP9). Bottom: Energy costs for a sheet of paper (for explanations see text)

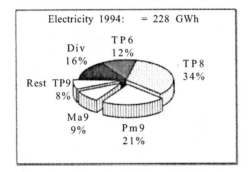

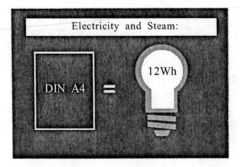

to concentrate on the most advanced and most energy consuming one, called TP9. TP9 is Swiss Paper's ninth paper production line since its foundation in 1862. Geographically, the power plant and TP9 are at a distance of one kilometer from each other with several buildings in between them.

The Power Plant

As mentioned before, Swiss Paper runs its own power plant which produces most of the paper mill's energy demand (e.g., 68% of the total electricity consumption). Both gas and liquid fuel are used for producing electricity and steam (see Figure 3).

An advanced gas turbine produces electricity and heats a boiler. The boiler in turn produces high pressure steam. In addition there are four older boilers running by gas and liquid fuel which also produce high pressure steam. The high pressure steam from all the boilers is used to drive two steam turbines producing electricity. The resulting low pressure steam is subsequently used to dry paper.

A large part of the electricity is produced by means of the steam turbines. A second part is produced by the advanced gas turbine. A third part, however, is bought from an external electricity company (see Figures 3 and 4).

The Staff and the Paper Machine

The production of paper, and consequently the energy production as well, run 24 hours a day and 7 days a week. In the control room of the *power plant* there are two operators working in each shift of eight hours. During the day, the manager of the power plant is present as well.

In order to run the *paper production line* TP9, there are 30 workers present in each shift. The production line is divided into three consecutive production parts, namely the *paper production* itself in the paper machine, the *processing of the paper for improving its quality* (surface and whiteness), and the slitting system for producing smaller reels. Unlike the operators at the power plant, each worker at the production line has a certain specialization:

Jobs	Task
paper makers	mainly being responsible for fulfilling the production planning guidelines and monitoring paper quality.
1st engineers	controlling the machine process and enforcing quality norms
2nd engineers	supporting the '1st engineer'
handymen	doing the work assigned to them by the engineers
shift manager	maintaining the communication between the three parts of the production line; belongs to a shift.
line manager	responsible manager of the whole paper production line, only present during the day.
two additional persons	at the production quality laboratory, also belonging to a shift.

The main part of the paper production process takes place in the first third of the paper production lines, in the paper machine. The paper machine itself has two main sections. In the first one, paper pulp, a quite liquid substance, is poured on a large plane, 30 meters long and 5.68 meters wide. This plane is in fact a sieve which slides with a

Figure 3. Energy flow at Swiss Paper (for explanations see text); also indicated is the maximal load of steam flow (55 t/h) and electricity (25 MW)

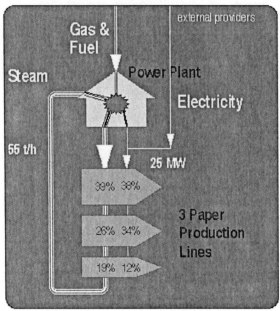

Figure 4. Technical situation at the power plant of Swiss Paper (for explanations see text)

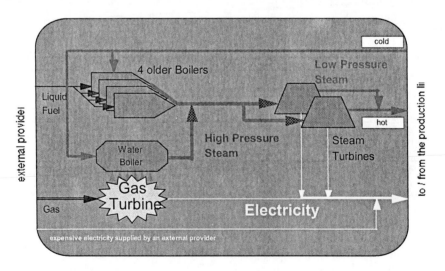

velocity up to 1000 meters per minute over tens of bars, extracting the most part of water from the pulp. That means that after less than two seconds the 5.68 meters wide paper strip is already strong enough to withstand tension without the support of a carrying plane, which facilitates movement around 39 cylinders. These cylinders are heated with the low pressure, but hot steam originating in the power plant. The function of this second section of the paper machine is, of course, to dry down the paper strip to the expected value. At the end of the paper machine the paper strip is rolled up on a huge reel of final weight about 20 tons. Now the main paper production process is finished. The paper on the reel is now ready for further manufacturing, mainly concerned with quality improvement and cutting into customizable sizes.

The Dynamic Interrelation Between Steam Consumption and Electricity Production

There is a mutual dependency of steam consumption and the production of electricity, which is caused by the steam turbines: the higher the rate of paper production, the higher the rate of steam consumption, the higher the plant's electricity production.

There is a paradoxical phenomenon that occurs here where the paper strip inside the paper machine is torn for any reason (thus interrupting the flow of paper production), the machines of the paper production line continue to run (thus still requiring current). However, steam is no longer required because there is no paper to dry. As most of the electricity is produced by steam turbines and as steam is no longer needed, the power plant's steam production is consequently reduced which implies that its electricity production will also go down. As a result, electricity may have to be purchased from the external electricity company. Due to specific contract issues in which the electricity company *guarantees* to supply any amount of electricity to Swiss Paper at any moment, this additional electricity can be very expensive, even if the actual amount of electricity consumed is relatively small. The account Swiss Paper has to pay for the purchased electricity is two-fold. Besides the cost for the total amount of electricity consumed during a month (counted in MWh), Swiss Paper is likewise charged with respect to the highest peak they reached during the same time (counted in MW), independent of how low the next lower peak is. That means that two months with the same total consumption of electricity (MWh), in one case with a stable consumption over time (hardly any peaks), and in the other case with a dynamic, unstable consumption (high peaks), can result in vastly differing amounts. For example, if the company is able to bring its monthly highest electricity peak down by 3 MW, given the same total consumption, it will save four hundred thousand dollars a month. The development of some of the key variables is shown in Figure 5.

The understanding of the interrelationships between the various processes are so far understood by Swiss Paper's experts as they are displayed in Figure 5. Most of the workers aren't even aware of these facts. Further considerations about this financially crucial process, such as how electricity cost could be reduced by appropriate reactions at the three paper machines, have not been regarded by Swiss Paper's engineers. It was assumed that the interrelationships are too complex to be handled appropriately. Furthermore, it was stated by managers that any possible alternatives — should any exist, would probably have unwanted, negative consequences on the logistics of the whole production process.

Figure 5. Interdependency of electricity production and steam consumption at the moment when the paper strip is torn

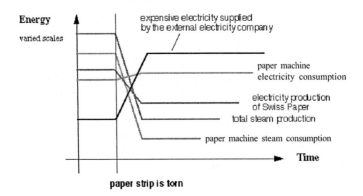

Other Dynamic Aspects

There are two other dynamic aspects worth mentioning. Firstly, because pulp is a natural product, it is very hard to predict how actual pulp suits the requested paper quality standards. Pulp contains various types of wood fibers and other components. For example, there can be remarkable differences between fibers of Canadian and Australian pine resulting in a different paper production process, even if the trees have the same age. Moreover, the quality of the pulp is strongly influenced by hardly accountable measurements, for example, by the amount of sunshine the trees were exposed to. The paper maker uses his experience to decide on the pulp mixture, which has a strong influence on the quality of the paper.

Secondly, the paper quality cannot be objectively defined. It also depends on the customers' subjective impression. For example, although the paper may fulfill defined standards, some customers will complain. This is so, because, for example, during an economic recession customers are less liable to accept the average paper quality. Or take the example, that if the picture printed on the paper has a blue area in it, e.g., a part of the sky, paper imperfections will be detected more easily and become a source of complaints. If the picture does not have any blue in it, the paper can be sold even though it does not fulfill the defined quality standards. In this case, the customers accept or do not even notice the imperfections, which still exist from an objective point of view. Consequently, the quality standards are designed in a way to meet an average of the customers' expectations. In fact, the crucial decision whether a reel of paper is qualitatively acceptable even though the paper does not meet defined quality guidelines, lies in the hands of the workers at the production lines.

The Current Standard of Computer Systems

Swiss Paper's computer infrastructure is two-fold. On the one side, there is a computer infrastructure for the support of commercial and financial tasks. These systems constitute a kind of MIS (Management Information System) consisting of financial programs, data bases, production planning utilities, and general managerial support tools. On the other side, there is a huge and highly complex real-time system which is needed for monitoring and controlling the sophisticated paper production lines and the power plant machinery. It is, in essence, based on signal processing systems technology.

Many of the computer systems are insufficiently supported by the technical staff of Swiss Paper, in particular the exchange and interrelation of the two kinds of computer system infrastructures. The staff supporting the real-time system, the 'Technical Information Systems Department,' consists of four persons. They are responsible for maintaining the four independently running process control systems of all three paper production lines and the power plant. This number should be compared to the 20 people which are available for the maintenance of the MIS, the so-called 'Financial Information Systems Department.' Five years ago, the 'Technical Information Systems Department' consisted of 14 employees. Probably because of the massive investments in advanced machinery, the technology had become too complex for the average systems engineer to handle. The company had to hire external expertise. Then for financial reasons it had to reduce its own staff. Today, there is a serious lack of know-how in building and maintaining the complex process control systems by the 'Technical Information Systems Department' (cf. Figure 1).

The real-time computer systems at Swiss Paper are more or less independent of each other. There is only one computer per production line connecting the company's real-time systems to the network of the MIS. The connection between the two computer systems is a known source of problems.

The Integration of the Computer Systems

There is a need for data exchange between the MIS and the process control computer systems. Some of the data required for running the process control system at TP9, is produced by the MIS. For example, data about planned production capacities which is generated on the commercial side, has to be transmitted to the process control system. Likewise, data collected by the process control system has to be transferred to commercial departments which monitor the progress of the paper production process and the extent to which the customer orders have been fulfilled.

This interface is realized by just a few computers. They have to handle the different technologies and protocols. The maintenance of these protocols is known to Swiss Paper's computer engineers as being very problematic. A known source for these problems are release updates with changes in data structures. Interestingly enough, neither the manager of the MIS, nor the head of the real-time systems are willing to assume the responsibility for the maintenance of this interface. Because the connecting software system has been developed by a third party, this interface is poorly understood and therefore not well maintained.

The Data Situation

At the power plant control room, a lot of data about boilers, turbines and other machines are displayed on two screens. This data represents the operational state of the power plant machinery. In their daily work the operators also have to monitor and adjust the controls located directly next to the boilers. Note that the boilers are a ten minute walk away from the control room.

No data about the energy consumers (i.e., the paper production lines) is available at the power plant. There is even no data about production planning and none about the current state of the production process available. For example, the actual electricity and steam consumption of the various production lines is not available at the power plant. Although, there is an optical fibre cable belonging to the data processing network (part of the MIS) going through the power plant, there is no computer attached to it. There are two alarms indicating when the paper strip is torn at one of the two older production lines. Interestingly, such an alarm is missing for TP9, the most advanced production line.

One of two screens at the control room of the power plant summarizes the data about steam production, the other displays an overview of the electricity production (MW) of the gas turbine and the two steam turbines. The rate of electricity consumption for the electricity supplied by an external provider, is also shown. All data of the process control system at the power plant is electronically stored for three days.

At TP9, the most highly computerized production line, the process control system continually collects thousands of data records: quality data, such as the whiteness or the thickness of the paper, production data, such as the number of tons of paper produced, and finally process control data, such as the current steam consumption or the flow of pulp and water. All data collected at TP9 is electronically stored for seven days. Although the US$7 million control system of TP9 is collecting and displaying data on the current electricity consumption of hundreds of single engines, pertinent summary data about electricity consumption is missing. It is not surprising then that there is a lack of awareness about electricity use among the production line workers, and that the electricity consumption does not influence their working activities.

The Distribution of Competence and Communication

The only communication device connecting the paper production lines and the power plant is a telephone. The workers at the production lines are instructed to inform the operators at the power plant about planned activities such as the start of the machinery, changes in the production plan, and incidents that interrupt the paper flow, such as when the paper strip is torn. Incidents of this sort require the full attention of the operators at the power plant. They have to readjust the controls of boilers and turbines to comply with the changed energy demands. Nevertheless, the line manager of TP9 has forbidden his line workers to do the requested phone call when the paper strip is torn, because the line workers have to do a lot of hurried work and have no time for other tasks such as calling the power plant. Of course, this is only justified as long as energy cost is ignored.

When the paper tears, it is also possible that the power plant is not able to produce enough steam which in turn may lead to a total system crash. Further detail about this matter are omitted here, because technical explanation is required. However, a reduction of the current steam consumption at the production lines could prevent such crashes, for example by reducing the speed of the paper machine.

Thus, it would be advantageous if the operators at the power plant could demand changes in the operation of the paper production lines and vice versa. However this would demand a better understanding of the interrelationships in order to define action alternatives applicable to daily work. That means that such instructions must be interpretable by the workers with respect to current problems. Yet, as we already outlined earlier, Swiss Paper's managers don't believe in the possibility to reach a better understanding than described above and are therefore not willing to invest in respective investments. Moreover, they force their workers to act in just the opposite way.

THE PROJECT DESCRIPTION

The Methodology

At the outset of Situated Design, a vision has to be created which is shared by all participants (by us as Situated Designers as well as by the involved management and the selected workers). The vision that has been implicit in what has been said so far is the overall improvement of the energy situation. The vision can be vague and overly general and should not specify concrete aspects of the project. Although the vision must be shared by all project members, it should leave open the operative details. It is reasonable to start with a general analysis about the current state of the art. Of particular interest are contradicting results and opinions. The second step consists of a complete analysis of the working place with respect to the defined vision (c.f. the "Setting the Stage" section). The collected data and observations have to be evaluated and discussed in order to define an operative starting-point (see "Conclusions of the First Analysis").

The third step is to define a small project that can be realized within a short time (a few weeks or months) and quickly yields payoffs. The "art" of Situated Design is to find small projects that are immediately of use, but at the same time do not compromise the original vision. Then the systems developed within the projects have to be introduced into the working situation. Finally the effect on the whole work place has to be evaluated and the cycle can be repeated starting with new projects. All developments have to be made together with the staff that will have to deal with the system. The idea is to get the staff interested and to bootstrap a process. Thus, the main task is the initialization of a process of continuous learning and change, rather than a product. To support learning is the key point here, not rationalization. This seemed to be the underlying problem of Swiss Paper: many insufficiently understood, relatively isolated phenomena. In Situated Design, the computer scientists in the project team have the function of a catalyst or a moderator. Eventually their function will be reduced to one of informing the company on new developments.

The general stages are: (1) Developing a vision of where you want to go, (2) Analysis of the complete working situation; Initialization of the process, (3) Designing the initial system, (4) Introduction of the system into the working environment, and (5) Evaluation (take into account new working environment; generate ideas about new system).

This procedure hardly differs from the current understanding in software engineering and organizational design. However, Situated Design emphasizes a quite different view on particular aspects of how to improve work places by means of computer technology. For example, the understanding of the dynamic characteristics of the "real world" (see Pfeifer & Rademarkers, 1991, and Pfeifer, 1996), the social nature of knowledge and communication (see Heath & Luff, 1996, and unpublished), and the situation of human expertise (see below) result in different understandings about (a) the necessary focus of analysis, (b) the possibilities of computer technology, (c) the nature and ability of human expertise, and (d) the situated character of the design process itself.

Further, these steps are formulated in a fairly abstract manner. The methodology of Situated Design is almost by definition a methodology that cannot be couched into very precise terms. Making things much more precise would defeat the whole purpose of situated development. Because adaptability, interactivity, and change are the main issues of concern, it is virtually impossible to precisely define all the details in advance. This is in contrast to traditional CASE-like approaches. CASE tries to formalize all the steps in a project development process. The underlying assumption of CASE is the controllability of the entire process. If your main concern is budget and deadlines, CASE seems like a good solution. However, the real world is different. Because during the project the ideas, goals, and attitudes change, it is clear that predictability is only limited. The introduction of a new computer application not only changes the way in which a particular task is performed, but it changes the whole work place. And over time, the computer systems are used in different ways and their results are interpreted differently. The methodology of Situated Design tries to take this into account.

The goal is not to develop a kind of an expert system. Rather, Situated Design can be seen as an instance of user-centered software engineering. But in addition to traditional, user-centered approaches, Situated Design intends to bootstrap a process of organizational learning and enhanced communication among the company's workers and mangers, rather than to develop fancy software. The goal is not to build a sophisticated 'Decision Support System' (DSS). The work of an expert is not sensibly characterized by a series of decisions. A better conceptualization is in terms of 'situated actions' (see below). In the context of DSS — as well as in the context of any traditional software engineering approaches — the experts (synonyms: users, workers) are treated as information-processing entities; as well as the computer itself. Consequently, there is, firstly, no substantial difference recognized between the nature of human cognition and the computer's computational power. Secondly, the situated nature of human behavior is totally neglected. And finally, social processes are reduced to a kind of cybernetic system.

To define a small project, we started by looking at the individual work place of the employees while keeping the company as a whole in mind. The design process is largely bottom-up. Having the employees at the very bottom of the ladder involved seemed very important. First, because we hoped to generate enough motivation for the project in this way, second, because we see the workers as main holders of knowledge — they are the real experts of the domain concerned. The real experts have to have a strong say in what the new system should look like — not only we as designers. They have to compare the trial results achieved with the new system with the previous situation, based on their professional experience.

Theoretical Considerations of Situated Design

On the one hand Situated Design implies a critique of the most widely held misconceptions of human expertise and the power of computers, and on the other — as a consequence — an alternative approach in designing work places. The fact that other methods are needed has been argued by many other authors (see, e.g., Landauer, 1995;

Winograd & Flores, 1988; Suchman, 1987; Dahlbom & Mathiassen, 1993; Ehn, 1988; Greenbaum & Kyng, 1991; Pfeifer & Rademarkers, 1991). We will first briefly summarize the theoretical foundations and then we will discuss the implications for a design methodology.

In order to understand the misconceptions let us start by looking at the concept of "knowledge." For the purpose of this case description, let us define knowledge as the experience that guides an expert's behavior as she or he interacts with the environment. This characterization has to be contrasted with the view of knowledge endorsed in the expert systems literature. There, the aim is to formalize knowledge, to make the knowledge explicit. Formalizing knowledge implies that knowledge has the same quality as data. By data, we mean entities that can be syntactically manipulated. Data differs from information in that the latter implies interpretation by an individual. A similar argument has been made by McDermott (cf. *Artificial intelligence meets natural stupidity*, 1976). In this paradigm — the one underlying expert systems -knowledge can be "extracted" from an expert like coal from a coal mine (cf. the 'knowledge mining' metaphor). There is a strong belief underlying this paradigm, namely that knowledge can be reduced to (possibly complex) representations (e.g., formulas, algorithms, plans, plain text etc.). However sometimes the term 'tacit knowledge' is used to indicate that knowledge cannot be reduced to representations (e.g., Polanyi, 1967). Dreyfus and Dreyfus (1986) characterize, in essence, knowledge as "tacit" and not amenable to rationalistic description.

Knowledge

Reducing knowledge to representations, however, neglects the fact that there has to be an individual, who is a member of a community and therefore able to interpret the meaning of the representation with respect to the community's agreements on and use of the representations. Formulas, algorithms, plans, and the like in and of themselves do not constitute knowledge — representations represent the knowledge only with respect to social agreements. The real knowledge — so to speak — is and can only be defined in terms of the particular situation in which an individual is behaving and with respect to community members.

Knowledge can be communicated without the need for explicit representation. For example, masters are able to teach their apprentices by referring directly to reality. They can use the world as its own best model (Brooks, 1991). Second, a group of people are able to cope with the real world in a more effective way than one person alone. Of course, a group will normally be faster on a particular task than one person alone. But this is not the point here. The point is that the motivation for group work is, among other things, that the product of the group will be qualitatively better.

Let us illustrate these rather abstract reflections by an example. The main concern of our project is "energy management." Obviously, both parties, the energy producer (power plant) and the energy consumers (production lines) are influencing the result, i.e., how much energy is finally consumed and how expensive it has become. Today, both parties have only limited knowledge of the task. The power plant operators know how to drive the boilers and turbines. But they do not know how to react to the specific circumstances at the production lines. They do not have the appropriate information at their disposal (except for information about the current steam and electricity consumption by the whole company). For example, they rarely know why one paper machine is currently using less steam than a short time before. At least a phone call would be necessary to find out.

Similarly, the paper machine workers do not really know anything about energy production. Neither do they know when the problematic situation of a lack of steam comes up, nor are they aware of the current electricity consumption of their machines. As mentioned earlier, there exists no data about the current energy consummations (e.g., which production line is producing what kind of paper quality and therefore is consuming how much energy for how long). The idea is now that if more data about energy are available to all the workers, energy will be used more effectively — if workers knew how to read (interpret) the data. In other words, they learn to communicate with each other about energy issues. This implies that the interpretation of the energy data (the task of defining the meaning of the representations pertaining to energy) cannot be performed by the members of one party alone — both the members of the power plant as well as the members of the production lines have to communicate their ideas about the meaning of the new data (with regard to the current situation and to the common and individual goals, etc.). Only when this kind of organizational learning is supported will there be a fair expectation of improving the company wide energy task.

Situated Actions, Situatedness

Suchman (1987) introduced the concept of 'situated actions' which brings us a step further towards a better understanding of human expertise.

One of the assumptions underlying all of our work on designing computer systems is that if we have a better understanding of what people do, we can design better systems. In our theory, we argue that the classical view of humans as 'information processing systems' (or, more accurately 'data processing systems') is inappropriate. An essential point of criticism is that the classical view does not explain how data becomes meaningful. We point out that meaning can only be understood in terms of — typically implicit — social conventions. In other words, we have to look at entire communities, not only individuals. We also introduce the term 'tacit knowledge,' meaning that knowledge is not an explicitly available "substance" that can be seen, formalized, stored, and manipulated in a computer system. Rather, it is whatever guides the individual's actions in a particular situation. 'Situated action' means that the agent brings to bear its own experience — in the form of (socially shared, tacit) knowledge in the present situation.

Note that the action the actor takes in a particular situation, e.g., increasing the speed of the paper machine, depends on the context (customer demands, general economic situation), on the operator's experience, and on the specific situation (paper quality, state of various machines, etc.). Because the real world is indefinitely rich, unanticipated situations can always occur. A complete description of all the potential situations is not possible. Coping with novel situations implies adaptability, which in turn implies taking the (novel) general context and the (novel) specifics of the situation into account. Humans are adaptive in the physical and social world because they have grown up in it, because their 'tacit knowledge' has been acquired in the continued interaction with it. This kind of adaptability is another essential factor of situated action. An additional aspect of situated action is the so-called "indexicality of language" (Suchman, 1987), which means that otherwise ambiguous expressions acquire unique meaning within a situation. The simplest example is the use of terms like "this one," which can only be disambiguated in a particular situation.

We mentioned that the action a human takes depends strongly on the particular situation. Humans very strongly interact with their environment: they are, in a sense, coupled to it. In case of an emergency, e.g., a torn paper strip, the operator will move into a position where he has a good view of the machine, where he can perform the required actions. These actions will be different on every occasion (even though they share some similarity). Rather than basing their actions on elaborate internal models, the current real-world situation is exploited in the decision process.

There is another central aspect of a situated actor. Situated action also implies that the actor perceives the situation locally. His actions are based on what is currently available to his sensory system. This aspect of locality is particularly important for systems design. It provides us with strong heuristics on where the human could be supported (see below).

The goal of Situated Design now, is to develop computer technology (or technology in general) in order to support a human, now conceived as a 'situated actor.' In the paradigm of Situated Design behavior is not sensibly conceived as process of abstract "decision making," as argued above. Note that this notion of human expertise sharply contrasts with the classical one. Behavior (and decision making) is no longer based on detailed plans, elaborate internal models, or sophisticated rules for logical inferences, but on "situated action." Needless to say, the nature of the support will be very different.

Implications for Systems Design

Given that systems must function in the real world, and given that human experts are situated actors, we can draw the following conclusions about the goals of the system to be designed, its technical characteristics, and about issues to take into account when designing systems. For further discussion, the interested reader may be referred to Pfeifer (1996) and Müller (in preparation).

The goals of system development that we pursue with computer technology support are: short-term practical utility, maintenance and improvement of expertise, support of exploration, support of creation of external representations, support of communication and cooperation, and support for adapting to change.

There are certain relatively obvious technical characteristics systems must meet if they are to support the above- mentioned goals. They are: transparency, easy manipulation, flexibility, "what-if" tools, graphical tools, and tools for communication and cooperation.

A good example of a type of system that incorporates many of the features mentioned is a spreadsheet. People use them in many different ways, they do a large variety of things with them from financial planning, to producing nice graphics, to normal statistics, to simple bookkeeping. The concepts of spreadsheets have been around since 'Visicalc' in the late seventies, early eighties. Essential success factors are the large variety of things people can do with them, and the powerful "what-if" facilities.

Tools and Techniques

Situated Design is a method for bringing computer technology into the real world, i.e., into companies. Situated Design projects are computer projects and therefore computer tools, as in any other project, will be an essential part. We have tried to characterize the sorts of tools we are looking for. The means for developing these tools are standard prototyping tools, code generators, or whatever. We will not go into them, they are well-known from standard software engineering practice. The book by Greenbaum and Kyng (1991) is a rich source of tools and techniques that can be applied to systems development. Some tools and techniques that are not so common are outlined in Pfeifer (1996). Some examples that a discussed there earlier originate from the field of 'knowledge acquisition,' like the user dialogue, or "expert-guided novice problem solving."

Other Approaches

There are a number of approaches in modern software engineering aiming in a similar direction. Examples are 'Cooperative design' (Kyng, 1991; Greenbaum & Kyng, 1991), 'Participatory design' (also called the "Scandinavian school," see Ehn, 1988; Floyd, Zullighoven, Budde, & Keil-Slawik, 1992; Schuler & Namioka, 1993), 'anthropological a roaches' (see, e.g., Zuboff 1988), 'Philosophical approaches' (see, e.g., Dahlbom & Mathiassen, 1993), 'Human-computer interaction' (HCI), and 'Computer supported cooperative work' in general. It comes as no big surprise that the first four are highly compatible with our own views. Their work, like ours, has been strongly influenced by Lucy Suchman's seminal book, "Plans and situated action" (Suchman, 1987). The "Scandinavian school" (e.g., Ehn, 1988) is based on the ideological assumption, motivated by the strong position of the trade unions in Scandinavian countries, that the people affected by a certain technology should have a say in it. We feel that this ideological assumption is not necessary, but the approach can be justified by considerations about the real world and situatedness.

The field of human computer interaction or HCI is focusing on developing computer systems with which humans can interact in natural and efficient ways. This perspective is important and should be given serious consideration in every project. However, HCI — in its traditional form — isolates the user-system dyad. Even the term "user" is somewhat inappropriate since it views the world through the perspective of the computer system. The "user" of a computer system has a job to do which implies many activities, some of which are supported through the computer. But it also requires making phone calls, interacting with a physical process, interacting with other employees, drinking coffee, going to meetings, talking to customers, etc. Viewing system development in this more global context brings new perspectives into the design process and defines new requirements for the systems to be developed. This is why the formerly rather narrow field of HCI has now, for the better part, adopted a more broad perspective, compatible with Situated Design.

Finally, CSCW has been a buzzword for quite some years now. The overall goals go in a similar direction. To our knowledge, the focus has been on providing tools. The best-known tool in this area is probably 'Lotus Notes.' We have been experimenting with 'Lotus Notes' in this project and we have come to realize that there is much more to cooperation than connecting workstation via a network. The chemistry within the project, and the entire work situation of the participants has to be taken into account. But it is very likely that within a Situated Design project, CSCW tools can be employed beneficially.

SITUATED DESIGN OF THE ENERGY SUPPORT SYSTEM

The Project Team

The project, we started with Swiss Paper, was funded for three years by the National Energy Research Foundation of Switzerland[4] (German abbreviation: NEFF). The scientific team, lined up by members of two independent research groups at the University of Zurich and the Federal Institute of Technology of Switzerland respectively, mainly consists of three graduate students. The academic research group is extended by two Ph.D. students acting as project managers and the two leaders of the involved research groups.

At Swiss Paper the project manager is a member of the executive board (cf. Figure 1). Five managers are reporting to him, namely the line manager of TP9, the manager of the power plant, the manager of the 'Financial Computer Systems Department,' the person responsible for ecological concerns of the paper mill, and an additional member of the executive board. After a year, the manager of the 'Technical Computer Systems Department' was also invited to participate in the project team meetings. Swiss Paper's CEO is not a member of the project team, but he was one of the initiators of the project.

Even though one of our main methodological concerns is to involve the end-user, i.e. the power plant operators and the workers at the production lines, none of them was a member of the project team. However, we strongly assume that the line workers are the real experts, because they decide "which button has to be pushed in which situation" — according to their knowledge and experience. They hold the operative (tacit!) knowledge we want to support with computer systems in order to enhance the quality and effectiveness of their work. So, they still remain to be the main target group of our intended process.

It is also one of our main methodological concerns to start a project by accepting the project partner's values. Unfortunately, this implied that the line workers have not been involved in the project team meetings (cf. the discussion in the section on 'successes and failures'). For the discussion of theoretical reasons why workers must be continuously involved in a project, the interested reader is referred to, for example, Greenbaum and Kyng (1991).

Conclusions of the First Analysis

Given this above background on the operative situation of the company (c.f. the section "Setting the Stage") we can identify some problems. For the next step of Situated Design, this first analysis has to be evaluated by all members of the project team in order to find a common, more focused project goal.

Five important issues have been identified. First, there is a general lack of understanding of the interdependencies of different processes. Second, there is a lack of communication between departments. Third, there is a lack of expertise concerning the different kinds of computer systems. Fourth, data resources are not coordinated and not explained. And last, but not least, the possibilities for change are underestimated by the staff of Swiss Paper. Let us briefly discuss these points in turn.

Lack of Understanding of Interdependencies and Understanding of Possibilities for Change

Although some managers are aware of the interdependence between steam consumption and electricity production, the details are not well understood. Moreover, this insight is not generally known. But there are additional reasons that prevent operators from taking measures to save energy. On the one hand, the managers and the operators doubt that there is any way in which the energy consumption can be influenced. On the other, because of the unsatisfactory economic situation, the focus is entirely on fulfilling the customer orders. One straightforward way to reduce the peak load would be to lower the velocity of the machines. But this option is not even considered. The situation is perceived as unchangeable.

Lack of Communication Between Departments

Because the 'Financial Computer Systems Department' and the 'Technical Computer Systems Department' do not communicate well, there is a lack of understanding of each other's problems. Managers even explicitly refuse to communicate. As we have seen, one of the results of this lack of communication is that nobody is willing to assume the responsibility for the interface between the MIS and the real-time systems.

There is also a lack of communication between the energy consumers (the production lines) and the energy producer (power plant). Let us illustrate this point with an example. There is an official guideline that emergency situations at the production lines have to be reported by phone to the power plant operators. As opposed to the official policy the TP9 line manager does not allow his workers to make this call. The explanation given by the manager is that at this very moment he needs all his workers to get the machine back to normal. There is no time to lose, least of all to make a phone call which is considered unnecessary, anyhow. This argument illustrates the general environment. Although the manager of TP9 and his colleague at the power plant often have lunch together, they do not really understand each other's reasoning. It seems that current function-oriented hierarchical organizational structure does not encourage the communication. At one of our project meetings the TP9 manager explained his motivation for the ban on phone calls to his managerial colleague — apparently for the first time. It is obvious that if the energy costs are to be reduced the knowledge about the actual energy situation has to be improved, which implies that the communication between the energy producer and the consumers has to be intensified.

Lack of Knowledge About Computer Systems

There is strong evidence that there is a lack of knowledge about the company's computer systems (hardware and software). There is a general reluctance to touch anything that might interfere with the real-time system. For example, even a simple operation like extracting data from the real-time system is considered a delicate matter. Let us again explain this point with an example. In order to learn more about the work of the TP9 workers, we observed them on several occasions during our investigation. We compared statistical data about the process with our own observations. This task was very tedious because the data was only available in printed form. Several reasons were given for this problem. First, the 'Technical Information Systems' staff justified this obviously unsatisfactory situation with the expected costs for reprogramming the complex signal processing systems to make electronic data available. Second the real-time systems do not have the capacity to store this mass of data. And because the real-time systems are principally isolated they cannot resort to the MIS for this purpose.

Uncoordinated Data Resources and a Lack of System Integration

An enormous amount of potentially useful data is generated continuously. Thousands of signals are produced by the control systems at TP9 every tenth of a second. However, they are not systematically recorded. Between the consumers and the supplier there is practically no exchange of data. An exception are the alarms indicating that the paper strip has been torn. But these data items do not indicate, e.g., the location at which the paper strip was torn in the production line. This location could be used for estimating the expected time of interruption. It would also be of interest to power plant operators to know about the so-called grade (gr./m2) of the paper under production. This would enable them to better approximate the expected reduction on steam consumption during an interruption. Most important of all would be data about the current steam and electricity consumption of every single production line. The current rate of steam consumption is available to workers at TP9 but not to the power plant operators. Moreover, the actual power consumption is totally unknown.

Unclear Ideas About "Autonomy" of Workers and Processes

An important topic at the project meetings was the question of how autonomous the workers at the paper production line are in their decisions. To what extent can they influence energy consumption? Some experts in the company maintain that there is hardly any "autonomy" for the workers at the production lines. They claim that technology is so dominant that the production processes have no independence, and that there is no room for individual decisions. Others claim that the opposite is true, arguing that there are, for example, clear differences in quality between shifts. The argument for limited autonomy was primarily made by leading managers who normally do not directly interact with machinery. The line manager of TP9 agreed with this opinion although he is concerned with instructing his workers day by day. He also made contradictory statements with respect to the "autonomy question." Actually, he was the one who made a proposal to improve the awareness of the TP9 workers about the actual power consumption. He suggested to install a kind of "light column". This "light column" should visualize the current electricity consumption of the entire production line, or of particular machines. A the moment of our first analysis the workers had no idea about the impact of their activities on energy costs.

Such contradictory situations are normally not intrinsically "bad." On the contrary, they can be fruitfully exploited. They provide an excellent starting-point for potential innovation.

The First Operative Steps

After a long period of discussions of the previous issues with the people at Swiss Paper, we decided to focus on the communication problem between the paper production lines and the power plant with the intermediate goal to produce a load management support system. In a first phase, the data about electricity and steam consumption should be made available and displayed in intuitively comprehensible form on a computer screen in the power plant. In this way, the energy producers should be able to handle situations of high load in the very short and intermediate term, by communicating their capacities to the energy consumers. An important aspect of load management is the assessment of the "autonomy" of the various processes: which processes can be delayed without problems (e.g., starting up a pulper, or the slitting machine). This should lead to a reduction of the peak load and thus of the electricity consumption from external providers.

The second phase then, should be a more complete energy information system. This should enable the company to perform some kind of more long-term planning, leading to a more stable energy consumption rate. Moreover, and that is an extremely important factor, it should lead to a better understanding of interrelated processes and variables, and, last but not least, of the needs of the other employees. From an organizational point of view, the hope is that this enhanced understanding will lead to a more adequate communication between the operative workers about the energy concerns of the paper mill, and finally will lead to process of continuous learning of the two working groups themselves. It is no coincidence that these objectives are quite similar with the ones which are well known in the context of 'Total Quality Management.'

CURRENT STATUS OF THE PROJECT

In order to define a small initial project, as required by the methodology, we engaged in a number of activities. We had a lot of discussion with Swiss Paper managers. We conducted many interviews and so-called participant observation sessions at the work places of the power plant operators and the paper machine workers. We also organized quite a few workshops with the people concerned. We produced many protocols summarizing our observations and conclusions.

Moreover, we did a lot of statistical analysis of collected data, etc. As a result we proposed two complementary projects:

- **Project "Power Plant":** The first is aimed at fulfilling the information requirement of the power plant operators by providing refined information about the company's energy situation. This requirement is to be satisfied by additional data transferred from the production lines to the power plant in order to enhance the "autonomy" of the operators when dealing with boilers and turbines.
- **Complementary Project:** The second project is to fulfill the complementary information requirement of the "*Production Line*" paper machine workers by further data about the current energy consumption rate in order to influence the paper machine workers with regard to current and expected energy costs.

At a project meeting it was decided to pursue the first proposal to begin with. The hypothesis that load management could be improved if more data about future energy demands were available, was considered to be plausible. The other hypothesis, namely that enhanced awareness of energy-related issues of the paper machine workers could improve the energy situation, was met with a certain amount of skepticism.

For us, it was clear from the start that both projects would have to be realized, otherwise the intended communication support between the two parties could not be fully successful. We were convinced that cultural changes would also be required. The intention was to promote and support this cultural change by means of computer technology, rather than by "preaching."

Project "Power Plant" in Progress

The goal of project "Power Plant" is to support the load management task at the power plant. The idea is to provide more data about expected demands of steam and electricity. Remember that currently, the power plant is only re-acting to production lines demands. It tries to satisfy every request. This means that the boilers and turbines have to be controlled in such a way that every demand can be satisfied in a short time. This control strategy is certainly not optimal with regard to energy consumption. Being ready for any kind of change implies having, e.g., two boilers running continuously although one boiler could supply the current energy demand. But two boilers running simulta-neously typically have lower efficiency coefficient characteristics than one boiler alone.

This situation is to be improved by providing three sorts of data:

1. **Energy data:** Data about the current steam and electricity consumption of each single production line and each single paper machine respectively.
2. **Process data:** Data about the current process situation, such as the velocity of the paper stream, the type of paper (i.e., the grade), an indicator signaling a torn paper strip, and the location where in the paper machine this has happened. The aim of this indicator is to forecast the time of interruption depending on, for example, the place where the paper strip was torn. In forecasting, it is always a difficult task to determine the relevant factors. The necessary data must, of course, be available for statistical analysis.
3. **Planning data:** Data about the production planning, such as "which grade of paper ("quality") should be produced when and by which paper machine?" Together with the second sort of data, statistical data can be calculated — once more — forecasting the consumption of steam and electricity depending on, for example, the paper grade and the velocity of the paper machine.

At the moment no algorithm or statistical procedure is known (yet) to make the predictions. As we have discussed, the interdependencies of the various subsystems and the dynamics are very complex. Even the weather, the quality of the pulp, and the staff can have an influence on energy consumption. And there may well be other unknown factors. But the operators have a lot of experience — there is a lot of distributed 'tacit knowledge' present. Giver the right kind of data, the operators will be able to optimally bring to bear their experience in the current situation. One crucial condition is that the workers do communicate with their colleagues about the particular circum-stances and potential future developments. Together, they have a higher chance of being successful because every individual taken for him or herself knows too little. Addition-ally, we could say that a lot of knowledge about the energy management task is only "alive" and reachable if it is actively communicated during and with respect to the current situation and therefore shared by all involved experts, power plant operators and paper makers, a clear case of 'socially shared knowledge.' And this is compatible with our original design goal, namely to optimally exploit human expertise.

In addition, on the basis of statistical data, we expect to better understand the relationship between velocity, paper quality, and steam consumption. With enough empirical data a more sophisticated paper production planning process could be realized. Given this additional information, the distribution over the three production lines could be carefully planned in order to minimize energy costs.

At the moment project "Power Plant" is in the implementation phase. Among other things, we are evaluating possible human-computer interfaces in collaboration with the power plant operators. In the discussions with the operators, there are already new ideas popping up which were not present before we started the project. We take this to be an indication that the methodology is beginning to work — even before the first small system has been installed.

COMPLEMENTARY PROJECT "PRODUCTION LINE"

The further analysis of project "Production Line" and its realization is deferred until after a first re-evaluation of the project "Power Plant." We are convinced that the full benefits of the project "Power Plant" will only become obvious if the project "Production Line" is also realized. We hope that through the implementation of the first system, the motivation to develop the second one will also increase. For example, the paper maker must be able to compare similar situations to each other, so he can test the influences on energy cost, e.g., when he changes the velocity of the paper machine, and learn for future times. The ultimate idea is to develop a so-called "expenses tracking system" (cf. Zuboff, 1988). The idea is not to totally automate a seemingly well-defined task, but rather to support the learning process of the individual workers and of working groups. This objective should be reached through the implementation of the "expenses tracking system," because it provides the necessary data and supports the communication between the workers involved. To us (the computer scientists, or better: work place designers by means of computer technology), the main goal is not to find the "right" data structures and their "correct" algorithmic relationships, but rather to learn and to experiment what implementation, what design has the highest value with respect to the organizational goal. Because this kind of work place design is understood with respect to its intrinsically social nature, it must start and regularly be re-evaluated on an empirical basis.

Presumably the production line workers would need data about the power plant and the other production lines. Moreover, they would need support from the experts at the power plant to interpret the data. Imagine that there is evidence of an impending expensive electricity peak. The normal reaction is to lower the velocity of the machinery. If the paper machine operator communicates with the power plant operator they might decide that, this single time, it would be unreasonable to slow down, because this would set off a highly complex dynamics that might make matters even worse. Of course, such a conclusion can only be made by the experts based on a analysis of the situated circumstances.

It is crucially important to involve those concerned into the design process in order to determine the information requirements. The adequacy of the data that is put at the operators' disposition is an empirical question. But note that the needs of the operators change over time because in the real world, there is always change. One important type of change is the introduction of a new artifact (here: new software or new computer system). As a result the situated interpretation of the data changes, too. These changes may in turn induce requirements for new or differently presented data.

In addition to the information requirements about the energy costs, we found that some emergencies at the power plant should be communicated to the energy consumers. For example, a serious emergency that rarely occurs is when the power plant is no longer able to produce enough steam. If the consumers do not reduce their steam consumption, they run the risk of a total power plant breakdown. A total breakdown would result in a loss of at least half a million dollars because of a production interruption for at least eight hours and high repair costs. Currently, the workers at TP9 do not fully understand the importance of such considerations.

SUCCESSES AND FAILURES

At the moment we are not able to report successes and failures of a finished project, because it is still in progress. We will simply report some of our experiences so far.

First of all there is the fact that the cost for project "Power Plant" is US$100 thousand compared to an estimated savings in energy cost of US$250 thousand per year. These figures are based only on an estimate of potential improvements due to a more optimal working point of the boilers and turbines. The estimate does not yet include returns, due to a reduction of the electricity peaks. Overall we predict that with the realization of project "Power Plant," 2.5 % of the actual energy consumption can be saved.

Another positive effect is that since our project was launched, the issue "energy" has become an important topic at Swiss Paper. Here is an episode that illustrates the point. Once we were interviewing operators at the power plant during their normal work. Accidentally the advanced gas turbine had a serious crash. The influence of this crash on the production lines was so strong, that the paper strips were torn. As pointed out, the power plant operators were not used to receiving phone calls from the paper machine workers. Of course, the paper machine workers did not know anything about the reason for this incident at the time. But this time the operator whom we were just interviewing, received calls from two of the paper production lines. Both callers were telling him about their own accident, as it had been demanded from them for a long time. After responding to the calls the operator showed us his honest surprise, assuring us, that these had been the first calls for months. This episode happened about one month after we had conducted regular interviews with employees at the production lines.

As is typical of user-centered methods, Situated Design is to involve those concerned from the very beginning. In this way, discussions about visions (like the energy topic) and about their concrete work situation can be initiated. These discussions should be continued when we, the university partners, leave the company. The new computers and the newly developed software will still be there and have to be maintained and enhanced. The process which has been initiated during the project has to "survive" our involvement in the cooperation.

Partly, this strategy has been successful. It has been successful because of the TP9 line manager. He was the person who created the idea of the "light column," an indicator of the electricity currently consumed by the paper machine. It was thought of as an actual "light column" because it should have a strong presence in the workers control room, indicating the importance of its message. Somehow it was the starting point of project "Production Line." This kind of involvement is necessary if our methodology is to work.

Partly, our strategy has not been successful. Our aim to involve the front line workers into the decision process has failed so far. Even though they participated in our interviews and the workshops, none of them were permanent members of the project team. Additionally, most members of the project team were asked by the management to participate. They had no choice. As a consequence, not all the participants were very motivated. Moreover, the unfavorable economic situation was not conducive to a positive mood. These are all reasons why progress was relatively slow. We hope that this situation will change in the future.

On the other hand there is the story of how the load management support system got off the ground. It was necessary to have the data about the different boilers and turbines in the power plant control room. Some of them were missing. This required a bit of hardware (some cables, a board), and a bit of programming. Originally this was seen as a real problem. Finally, it was done by one of the operators at the power plant in a few days on the side, i.e., during his normal working hours while performing his job as an operator. The fact that the relevant energy data could now be displayed, aroused the interest of others and demonstrated that with relatively little effort, a lot can be done.

Finally, as mentioned above, the ideas about the "autonomy" of individual processes and employees were contradictory. The project made them explicit and we found that there is much more room for individual decision making than the engineers — and sometimes the operators themselves — were aware of. For example, it could be demonstrated that steam consumption, which is considered as given by the technical requirements of the production line, could be increased by the operator by nearly 50%, at least for a short period of time.

In summary, we have been confirmed in our intuitions, that with Situated Design a lot can be achieved with relatively little effort, few resources, and only small financial commitments. Given the dramatic situation of the company, the achievements seem even more relevant. We plan to finish the first phase by the end of this year. We are convinced that this will lead to a process that is mostly driven by the employees of the company. At some point, our task will only be to keep the company up-to-date on recent developments in computer science, and the continuous learning and development process will have become autonomous and running on its own. But even now, we feel that we have succeeded in being the catalysts.

EPILOGUE AND LESSONS LEARNED: CHALLENGES FOR PROJECT MANAGEMENT

Situated Design represents a challenge for project management. The traditional view is focusing on a product: the goal of an computer technology project is the development and installation of a particular product. In recent years, computer technology has been used as an enabler, as a kind of vehicle to support the restructuring of companies. But even there, a goal state is defined as clearly as possible at the very beginning of the project. The experience with BPR ("Business Process Redesign") projects has shown that on the one hand the clear definition of the goal state is far from trivial and that it is entirely open how to achieve the goal state. The situated perspective suggests that typically the goal definition has to be adjusted as the project evolves.

Situated Design does not start with a clearly defined goal state or product specification. Rather, it starts with a vision and then tries to initialize a process. The focus of the methodology is on this process. The conviction is that innovation requires a process of continuous change and learning. This point has been made very nicely by Peter Senge in his book about the learning organization (Senge, 1990). Situated Design is compatible with this philosophy of the learning organization. One of its main goals is to support "learning" in its many forms.

But if we do not start by defining concrete goals, how should we measure progress in the project? Where are the milestones? How do we know how much the project is going to cost? How can we make a budget? How do we know how to allocate personnel to the project? If it is a process and if the goal is that the process evolves on its own, how do we ensure it is going in the right direction? How do we know what the right direction is? These questions are all justified and we must somehow find an answer for them. Otherwise, the methodology will have a hard time being accepted by companies.

At the moment we really do not have good answers to these questions. It will be particularly hard to provide quantitative measures for success. Partly we will have to rely on common sense, partly we can use tools from work psychology. If there are a few factors that are generally accepted as indicators for progress, this is a lucky coincidence. If they can be found that makes the approach much more convincing, even if improving this particular quantity may not be all that central to the overall vision. Cutting the costs through load management system is a case in point, the expenses tracking system will be another.

There is an additional difficulty. Because of the involvement of the people and because of the initial investigation of the working environment, the situation is already changed. Thus, it is hard to have an exact before-after evaluation. But our goal is inducing change.

Dialogues at all levels, intensive communication, carefully performing the evaluation step (step 4, above), will be extremely consequential for the project. Our experience has shown that this continued interaction of the management and the project developers with the user, quickly shows whether the project is going in a desirable direction. Moreover, during the process, very often many new ideas emerge. Again, measuring ideas quantitatively is very hard, but it is obvious when the atmosphere is conducive to creativity.

Coping with change and uncertainty is the main point. Perhaps the control and evaluation of a Situated Design project might require more time from both the participants in the project and the management responsible for it. But the hope is that this additional effort is more than compensated by the quality of the results: innovation does not come for free.

Computer technology, if applied wisely, might just provide the right tools for project management in rapidly changing, highly unpredictable environments. Imposing strict guidelines with the goal to make everything controllable seems to be defeating the point.

We are optimistic that courageous and innovative students and practitioners of management will take up these ideas and investigate more thoroughly the issues raised by such an approach. A prerequisite is, of course, that they accept the basic assumptions of Situated Design.

QUESTIONS FOR DISCUSSION

1. Characterize the term *knowledge*!
2. What are the main points distinguishing Situated Design from traditional software engineering methodologies?
3. Where do you see the main problems of Situated Design?
4. Given the background in this case description, why do you think so many expert systems failed?
5. In your opinion, what will be the effects of an 'expenses tracking system' once implemented?

REFERENCES

Brooks, R. A. (1991). Intelligence without representation. *Artificial Intelligence, 47,* 139-160.

Dahlbom, B., & Mathiassen, L. (1993). *Computers in context: The philosophy and practice of system design.* Cambridge, MA: Blackwell.

Dreyfus, H. L., & Dreyfus, S. E. (1986). *Mind over machine: The power of human intuition and expertise in the era of the computer.* New York: The Free Press.

Ehn, P. (1988). *Work-oriented design of computer artifacts.* Stockholm: Arbetslivscentrum.

Floyd, C., Züllighoven, H., Budde, R., & Keil-Slawik, R. (Eds.). (1992). *Software development and reality construction.* Berlin: Springer.

Greenbaum, J., & Kyng, M. (Eds.). (1991). *Design at work: Cooperative design of computer systems.* Hillsdale, NJ: Lawrence Erlbaum Assoc.

Heath, Ch., & Luff, P. (unpublished). *The social organisation of complex tasks: The naturalistic analysis of human conduct and computer system design.* Private collection.

Heath, C. C., & Luff, P. K. (1996). Convergent activities: Collaborative work and multimedia technology in London Underground Line Control Rooms. In D. Middleton, & Y. Engestrom (Eds.), *Cognition and communication at work: Distributed cognition in the workplace.* Cambridge: Cambridge University Press.

Kyng, M. (1991). Designing for cooperation: Cooperation in design. *Communications of the ACM, 34,* 65-73.

Lamberts, K., & Pfeifer, R. (1993). Computational models of expertise: Accounting for routine and adaptivity in skilled performance. In K. Gilhooly, & M. Keane (Eds.), *Advances in the psychology of thinking.* New York: Simon and Schuster.

Landauer, T. K. (1995). *The trouble with computers: Usefulness, usability and productivity.* Cambridge, MA: The MIT Press.

McDermott, D. (1976). Artificial intelligence meets natural stupidity. *SIGART Newsletter, 57,* p.4.

Müller, M. (1997). *Situated aspects of the software engineering process and the work place design* (AI-Lab Reports). University of Zurich, Department of Computer Science, AI-Lab, Switzerland.

Pfeifer, R. (1996). *Real world computing* (Unprinted Lecture Notes). University of Zurich, Department of Computer Science, Switzerland.

Pfeifer, R., & Rademarkers, P. (1991). *Situated adaptive design: Toward a new methodology for knowledge systems development.* Paper presented at the Verteilte Künstliche Intelligenz und Kooperatives Arbeiten, Proceedings des 4. Internationalen GI-Kongress Wissensbasierte Systeme, Munich, Germany.

Polanyi, M. (1967). *The tacit dimension.* London: Routledge & Kegan Paul.

Schuler, D., & Namioka, A. (Eds.). (1993). *Participatory design: Principles and practices.* Hillsdale, NJ: Lawrence Erlbaum Associates.

Senge, P. M. (1990). *The fifth disci line. The art & practice of the learning organization.* London: Century Business (Random House).

Suchman, L. A. (1987). *Plans and situated actions: The problem of human-machine communication.* Cambridge: Cambridge University Press.

Winograd, T., & Flores, F. (1988). *Understanding computers and cognition: A new foundation for design.* Norwood, NJ: Ablex.

Zuboff, S. (1988). *In the age of the smart machine: The future of work and power.* New York: Basic Books.

ENDNOTES

[1]   Name changed.

[2]   We prefer this term as opposed to 'software engineering' because of the too restricted meaning of the latter.

[3]   Name changed.

[4]   Grant-No. 356.

As a PhD student at the AI-Lab of the Department of Computer Science at the University of Zurich, Switzerland, Martin Müller's dissertational subject was "Situated Design," a software development methodology which takes the situational and social nature of human conduct into account.

Rolf Pfeifer is a full professor of computer science and heads the AI Lab at the Computer Science Department of the University of Zurich in Switzerland. His main research interests are foundations of AI and cognitive science, autonomous agents, adaptive behavior, and "situated design."

This case was previously published in J. Liebowitz & M. Khosrow-Pour (Eds.), *Cases on Information Technology Management in Modern Organizations*, pp. 225-249, © 1997.

Chapter XI

Power Conflict, Commitment and the Development of Sales and Marketing IS/IT Infrastructures at Digital Devices, Inc.

Tom Butler, University College Cork, Ireland

EXECUTIVE SUMMARY

This article explores the political relationships, power asymmetries, and conflicts surrounding the development, deployment, and governance of IT-enabled sales and marketing information systems (IS) at Digital Devices, Inc. The study reports on the web of individual, group and institutional commitments and influences on the IS development and implementation processes in an organizational culture that promoted and supported user-led development. In particular, the article highlights the problems the company's IS function encountered in implementing its ad-hoc strategies and governance policies. It will be seen that the majority of these problems occurred because of the high levels of autonomy and budgetary independence of the IT-literate, engineering-oriented business 'communities-of-practice' that constituted Digital Devices. The case therefore provides rare insights into the reality of IS development and IT infrastructure deployment in organizations through its in-depth description of the positive and negative influences on these processes and their outcomes.

ORGANIZATIONAL BACKGROUND

Digital Devices, Inc. was founded in 1965 in Cambridge, Massachusetts, by Ray Stata and Matt Lorber. In 2003, the company was acknowledged as one of the leading designers and manufacturers of high-performance linear, mixed-signal and digital integrated circuits (ICs), which addressed a wide range of signal-processing applications in the electronics and related industries. Digital Devices is headquartered in Norwood, Massachusetts, and has a significant global presence in all major markets in the electronics industry. The company has numerous design, manufacturing and direct sales offices in over 18 countries and employs more than 7,200 people worldwide (Figure 1). The company's stock is traded on the New York Stock Exchange and is included in the Standard & Poor's 500 Index. Many of Digital's largest customers buy directly from the company, placing orders with its sales force worldwide; the remainder obtain their products through distributors or over the Internet. Just fewer than 50% of Digital's revenues come from customers in North America, while the balance came from customers in Western Europe and the Far East.

Ray Stata, Digital's co-founder and longtime CEO, recognized the importance of fostering a culture of openness, where employees were empowered and encouraged to be innovative. This was reflected in the company's structure, which exhibited a high degree of process decentralization, especially in the allocation of capital and operational budgets, and, in particular, the locus of decision making. Figure 2 illustrates the company's structure: the core business functions are the 'product line' Computer Products Division, Communications Division, Standard Linear Products Division, Transportation and Industrial Products Division, and the Micromachined Products Division, which was taken over by Ray Stata when he stepped down as CEO. Shown directly beneath these are corporate business divisions that provided support for product line divisions. It is of significance that Human Resources and Finance Divisions aside, all support divisions were engineering oriented, even the World Wide Sales and Corporate

Figure 1. Digital Devices, Inc. worldwide design, manufacturing and sales functions

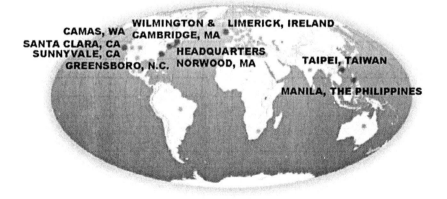

Figure 2. Digital Devices, Inc. organizational structure (as of 2000)

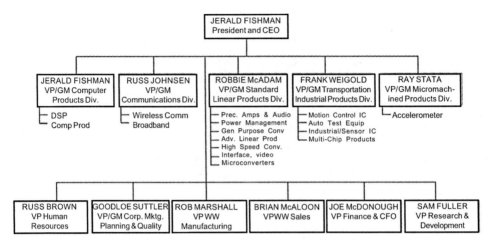

Marketing and Planning Divisions. This engineering-oriented culture was to have profound implications for IS development and governance in several areas of the company's operations, as will be seen.

Since its inception, Digital Devices gained a reputation as an excellent employer, where employees were respected, well remunerated and benefited from lucrative stock options. Individual commitment to the organization was manifested in the low level of staff turnover and the lifelong employment of many senior employees and engineers. The vast majority of employees remained loyal to the company despite the large salaries and attractive bonuses on offer from competitors. Significant too was the low level of turnover in employees from areas like sales and marketing, which was comparatively high in other companies in the sector. In December of 1997, *Fortune* magazine selected Digital Devices as one of the top 100 companies to work for in America and, later, in 2000, *Fortune* named the company as one of America's most admired companies.

SETTING THE STAGE

The process of information systems development is akin to Shakespearean drama, with its various acts, scenes, plots, counterplots, characters, tragedies and uncertain outcomes. This section of the article sets the stage for the drama described by introducing the major players: (a) design engineers in the marketing sub-functions of the Standard Linear Product Division; (b) marketing managers/engineers and communication professionals from the Corporate Marketing Division; (c) Central Applications support engineers, and sales and field engineers from the Sales Division; (d) IS professionals from the IS function, which is a sub-unit within the Finance Division; and (e) IT professionals from external consultancy firms. Customer design engineers from Digital's customer base constituted the ultimate end-user/stakeholder group. In order to better understand the issues discussed herein, a short overview of the major actors in the drama of the development of sales and marketing and governance of IT infrastructures at Digital Devices, Inc. is first offered. Following the major sections on theory and research method, the main section of this article then describes the origins of the political tensions surrounding IS development and associated issues of governance. These subsections are followed by three that describe how the various 'actors' and their 'communities-of-practice' participated in the development and implementation of: (1) the sales and marketing component of the company's Intranet and (2) the Corporate Web-presence. The evidence adduced in describing these complex IS development 'dramas' facilitates an understanding of the roles that power, political conflict and commitment play in shaping both the development process and its product — these are discussed in the penultimate section. The case therefore provides a real-world example of the 'reality' of systems development in innovative organizations.

The IS Function

The company's IS function was located at corporate HQ in Norwood. Unlike senior executives in the sales or marketing divisions, the senior IS executive, the CIO, reported to the VP of Finance, the CFO (Figure 2). This is important, as most large organizations in the US had established relatively autonomous IS functions by the mid-1990s. Product line and support divisions at Digital Devices had IS managers and IT professionals dedicated to take care of their particular IS needs and IT infrastructure support. For example, the Sales and Corporate Marketing divisions had one IS team to take care of their Sales and Marketing IS requirements: however, in all cases report relationships of IS staff were to the CIO and thence to the CFO. The following overview of IS operations at Digital indicates the outcome of this structural arrangement.

In the early 1990s, Digital's IS were centralized and based around an IBM mainframe. In this scheme of things, the role of IS was to gather corporate data. Subsequently, Digital's major business systems were based around SAP-packages. The first SAP module was implemented in 1994. In that year, the IS function also decided to standardize the desktop platforms in use across the organization, in order to provide all users with a common suite of applications and lower the total cost of ownership. Although many end-users preferred the Apple Macintosh platform, the decision to go with the PC hinged on the paucity of business applications for the MAC. So, while there was some opposition to this strategy within the organization, Digital opted for Microsoft Windows-based PC platforms worldwide and rolled out Banyan-Vines Network Operating System on the local area network. The one exception to this strategy of standardization was the engineering community in the product line and R&D divisions, who used Sun UNIX workstations. At the end of 1998, there were about 4,000 Windows-based desktop PCs and approximately 2,000 Sun Unix workstations in Digital's IT infrastructure. It was considered by many that Digital had a state-of-art IT infrastructure, although others were of the opinion that the same could not be said of IS support for areas like sales and marketing.

Central Applications: The Nexus of Sales and Marketing Product Knowledge at Digital Devices, Inc.

Digital's Sales and Corporate Marketing Divisions together served a wide range of customers in the US electronics industry and played a pivotal role in servicing customer needs worldwide. It must be noted that while Corporate Marketing was concerned with the formulation of Digital's worldwide marketing strategies, each of the product line divisions had their own marketing sub-functions. The company's IT infrastructure and related IS — that is, its Internet e-commerce and e-business application, corporate intranet systems, and emerging sales and marketing information systems — played a major role in helping the sales and marketing operations deal with the large number, and wide geographical dispersion, of Digital's products and customers.

Based in Wilmington, a suburb of Boston, the Sales Division's Central Applications function was the corporate nexus for all product-related knowledge at Digital Devices. It was through this function that sales and field engineers, in addition to product distributors, were trained and supported. It also had close functional relationships with the marketing engineers from the various product line divisions. This function also provided technical support via 1-800 toll-free lines direct to Digital's customers. Each day it accepted and processed about 200 technical support questions from customers, and recorded each and every call. Central Applications also advertised new products, mainly at technical seminars, and through this forum it reached about 10,000 design engineers every year. The function also provided a fax-back service to customers — here, customers faxed in a request for data sheets[1] and these were automatically dispatched by fax in a matter of hours. Application engineers also used the information contained in the data sheets of over 2,000 new and established products to compile the company's short-form product catalogue and the related CD-ROM. This product data was also published on the company's Internet Web site, and later became the preferred method of access, thus replacing Fax-Back. One of Central Applications' key roles was in providing product support and technical information over the corporate intranet with its own Lotus Notes-based product and technical support application. Because of the need to better manage customer-related call tracking, customer contact, and product application problem-solving, this system evolved from a client/server platform into a web-based solution. Since its inception as a client/server system, this application, which consists of several separate but related databases, has been extended and ported to the corporate intranet via Lotus Notes Domino Server.

Why Engineering-Oriented Business 'Communities-of-Practice' Generally Held the Balance of Power in Shaping IS/IT Infrastructures

The majority of senior, middle and line managers at Digital Devices came from engineering backgrounds; as such, they shared common educational and professional interests. This shaped the various 'communities-of-practice' that existed within and between 'business' divisions and their functional sub-units. This is in contrast to staff from the company's administrative and IS functions, the vast majority of whom were not engineers. This had a significant impact on the formation of Digital's social matrix and the manner in which IT architectures were deployed and in how IS development was conducted. Two comments highlight this point graphically. The first comes from Standard Linear Products Division's (SLPD) marketing manager, who was an engineer and who was with the company for 26 years:

Part of it is the corporate culture within Digital, it has always been an engineering-run and an engineering-driven company, seldom in a time of contraction has the research and development budget been cut...all the guys come from the same universities, from the same professors and they all have been taught the same things.

The common background in electrical and electronic engineering provided social actors with a shared language that facilitated communication and learning across functional areas within the organization — however, there were obvious differences in objectives between engineering and non-engineering 'communities-of-practice' that led to a degree of institutional tension around IS development and the deployment and operation of IT infrastructures. Such differences were reflected in the way IT resources were employed. For example, while engineers in the product line divisions used the corporate LAN and WAN infrastructure, they were relatively independent in terms of the computer platforms and applications they used. The IS manager described it thus:

This federated decentralized approach to building Digital's IT infrastructure resulted from the way in which the company operated since its foundation, where the product divisions and the product lines at the various sites maintained their own IT budgets and tended to provide for their own IT needs.

The important point here is that of ownership and control of non-corporate applications rested exclusively with the end-user community, with the IS function acting in support roles only. On one hand, this engendered a local sense of community that helped reinforce each engineering 'community-of-practice.' On the other, this independence of corporate IS extended beyond engineers in the product divisions, as is evidenced in the Sales Division's Central Applications function, which was staffed by applications engineers who developed and operated a key element of the corporate intranet, with the blessing, but not with the support of the corporate IS function.

THEORY AND PREVIOUS EMPIRICAL RESEARCH: COMMITMENT, POWER AND POLITICS

Three separate but related theoretical perspectives are now briefly explored to help understand the case and associated analysis.

Institutionalized Commitment and Organizational Purpose

The role of 'commitment' in the design, development and implementation of IS has been elaborated on in several studies. In computer science, Winograd and Flores (1986) highlight the role of commitment in shaping the design of computer-based information systems, while Abrahamsson (2001) illustrates the role of commitment in the success of software process improvement initiatives. Sabherwal et al. (2003) highlight the role of commitment in successful information system development; however, theirs was one of several that focused on the dysfunctional escalation of commitment and its consequences. All this is indicative of the vital role of individual and organizational commitments in shaping the trajectory of the development process and its outcomes. This study draws on Selznick (1949, 1957), who illustrates that the process of institutionalism gives rise to, and shapes, the commitments of organizational actors and groupings. Selznick (1957) argues it is through commitment, enforced as it is by a complex web of factors and circumstances, and operating at all levels within an organization, that social actors influence organizational strategies and outcomes. Here, 'commitment' refers to the binding of individuals to particular behavioral acts in the pursuit of organizational objectives. Selznick identified the sources of organizational commitment viz. (a) commitments enforced by uniquely organizational imperatives; (b) commitments enforced by the social character of the personnel; (c) commitments enforced by institutionalization; (d) commitments enforced by the social and cultural environment; (e) commitments enforced by the centers of interest generated in the course of action. However, these commitments do not evolve spontaneously through the process of institutionalization, they are shaped by 'critical decisions' that reflect or constitute management policy: as Selznick illustrates, the visible hand of leadership influences the social and technological character of organizations. Thus, Selznick (1957) maintains that organizational, group, and individual commitments determine whether organizational resources, such as IT, are employed with maximum efficiency and whether organizational capabilities are developed to leverage such resources to attain competitive advantage.

Power and Politics

Power is another concept that has been used to help explain different preferences among stakeholders in IS development; as such, it provides a useful complement to commitment theory. Jasperson, Saunders, Butler, Croes, and Zheng (2002) provide a comprehensive review of previous research on the subject which includes perspectives from the user participation literature (itself comprehensively reviewed by Cavaye, 1995). This short review therefore draws on this body of work as a convenient point of access to what is a comprehensive literature. The dominant view in the literature holds that participants in the development of IT infrastructures shape the socio-technical features of an IS through the exercise of power. User participation, for example, in systems development leads to the exercise of power by users to change development outcomes. So does the exercise of power by competing groups of managers. Thus, in line with the pluralist perspective, power may be defined in terms of users' abilities to influence the behavior of others to achieve specific objectives (Jasperson et al., 2002). Keen (1981) therefore argues that the development of an IS is a political process. In light of this, IS managers require organizational mechanisms to provide them with the necessary influence and resources to successfully develop an IS within the context of competition among political actors and groupings in an organization, who will possess divergent aims and commitments. While Markus (1983, p. 442) illustrates that "[w]hen the introduction of a computerized information system specifies a distribution of power which represents a loss to certain participants, these participants are likely to resist the system"; she also showed how the reverse also holds. Echoing Markus (1983), Kling and Iacono (1984) contend that in order to gain control over the development trajectory of an IS, key actors will engage in conflict-related activities such as domination, sabotage or compromise. The concepts of commitment and power therefore inform the readers' interpretations of the case in that they promote an understanding of the purposeful actions of actors in achieving IS development outcomes in terms of shaping process and influencing product.

RESEARCH METHOD

A qualitative, interpretive, case-based research strategy was adopted to conduct this study. This involved a *single instrumental case study* (Stake, 1995) that was undertaken to obtain an understanding of the circumstances surrounding the design, development and deployment IT-enabled information systems at Digital Devices Inc. Purposeful sampling was employed throughout (Patton, 1990). Research of Digital Devices, Inc. was conduced at three sites located in Limerick (Ireland), Wilmington (Boston, MA) and at the company's corporate headquarters in Norwood (MA) in mid-to-late 1998. Fourteen taped interviews were made with a cross-section of 'key informants' from business and IS 'communities-of-practice' — each interview was up to two hours in length. Additional data sources included documentary evidence and informal participant observation and discussion at the three sites. Elements of Selznick's (1949) theory of commitment and insights from the literature on 'power' were employed as 'seed categories' to interpret the interview transcripts and other documentary sources. Finally, the case report approach was used to write up the research findings.

CASE DESCRIPTION: DEVELOPMENT AND GOVERNANCE OF IS AND IT INFRASTRUCTURES AT DIGITAL DEVICES, INC.

The following case report is structured into four sections, each of which provides a different, but complementary, perspective on the issues surrounding the development of IS and governance of IT at Digital Devices, Inc. The first provides the context for the other three by describing the origins of the political tension between the IS function and some of the 'communities-of-practice' responsible for sales and marketing operations in the company. The second delineates the problems with IS governance, while the third and fourth sections then describe the factors that influenced the development, implementation and governance of two IS/IT architectures: the company intranet and the corporate Internet system. The events described in the case occurred between 1996 and 1999.

Political Tension Surrounding the Development of IT-Enabled IS

Previous sections have made reference to Digital's unique character and idiosyncratic business practices, which had a significant impact on the manner in which IS had been developed, operated and used in the company. The following comments provide insights into the kernel of the issues described in the case: the first comes from the IS manager for Sales and Marketing.

Traditionally the company has been based on a culture where autonomy has been promoted and creativeness of engineers encouraged in designing new products, getting into spaces where they need to be visionaries, an area that's where the real disconnection is, in the culture that's been built here. And also, if you think about the product line guys, they are all engineers — you know they are not known for their discipline. And most of the sales people are engineers, so you got a lot of these people running around and we have to instill some discipline, put some standards in here, so we say 'We need to slow you down because it's good for everyone.' I'm not sure that that's something that they would agree with it.

He was more specific when it came to describing the activities of one product support unit:

Take [the manager of Central Applications, he] has been very successful at developing systems to support what he needs to do. He and I joke about it all the time because we made a decision a couple of years ago not to use Lotus Notes, it just did not fit into our architecture, we went the Microsoft way, he's been very successful deploying small Lotus Notes applications for his group. I'm not going to come in with a hammer and say "You have got to get rid of that because it's against standards," it fits a niche. Fortunately, with the advent of the Internet, Lotus Notes and its Domino server is just another Internet server, as opposed to the whole infrastructure change, where we would have to deploy servers everywhere — it just plugs into the intranet. So we do have situations now where groups will go and implement their own technology for their own niche requirements as opposed to something for everybody.

Hence, business managers developed information systems out of their own budgets, and without IS input, through in-house development or by importing the required competencies from external consultants to aid in the development endeavor. This independence and autonomy, which enhanced creativity in product development, caused problems elsewhere in the organization, especially for the IS function, and it resulted in a certain degree of friction between IS and the business community. While there was ample evidence of amicable social interpersonal relationships between the respective 'communities-of-practice', that is, between those populated by engineers and IT professionals, professional relationships, on the other hand, appeared to be less than amicable. Take for example a comment made by the manager of the Central Applications function in the Sales Division:

In terms of IS...they introduced a SAP system for accounting and order processing, they maintain the system, but did not develop it; they are essentially system integrators and IT architects. One of the major issues with them is that our technical support needs are not being met. They have elaborate solutions for simple needs, and they impose restrictions on applications support. But because I have my own budget, I have instituted in own solution based around Lotus Notes: this is not a Corporate standard, so I am a mini-IS owner. An uneasy truce exists between myself, my department and the IS people in Norwood; essentially, what I have found is that their grand solutions are impractical.

That said, IS managers did not just ignore end-user development, as a formal protocol existed whereby independent units and sub-units could develop their own applications. If those applications complied with the corporate standards, and were of use to other organizational units, the IS function rolled them out across the organization, and subsequently supported them. This happened with an application developed by engineers in the Santa Clara facility — later, that system was rolled out by the IS function, as it had found favor with engineers in other divisions. The Central Applications Lotus Notes/Domino application, which could be accessed through an Internet browser over the intranet, gained acceptance at IS, as it did not interfere with corporate standards due to its use of a Web browser on the desktop: in any event, IS staff refused to support the underlying Lotus Notes Domino system.

Problems with IS Governance

In terms of IS governance and independence, engineering-oriented business managers across divisions at Digital were universally unhappy with the IS function being under the control of the Finance Division. For example, a senior marketing manager in the Standard Linear Products Division in Wilmington argued that:

There are no good reasons for having the IS function under finance, there are very good reasons for having it as a shared resource: because we are a decentralized company and because we have five different business units, and we can't have an IT function in every single business unit, and we do not want business units making decisions on expenditures that result in overlapping systems that don't talk to each other. It's the kind of [mess] that [the manager of Central Applications] is in right now, he is married to Lotus Notes — and Lotus Notes is a loser, I'm sorry. And is not supported in Digital at all, and any time something breaks and any time something hiccups in Lotus Notes, he has got to pay a contractor to fix it — and Lotus Notes doesn't talk to anything, and you cannot link it to the Internet, so you're screwed.

It is ironic that the marketing manager was in agreement with IS people in relation to Lotus Notes, while sharing the same opinion, more or less, as sales managers with regard to the IS function. IS managers were sensitive to such opinions, and in defense of the status quo one stated:

I know that reporting through to finance has always been an issue out there, but I think our CFO has a very good perspective and good vision on where IT fits in the whole organization, so I would say he's been a most positive force in driving us where we are today to the point where everyone has access to the same capabilities and functionality.

Notwithstanding this positive opinion, no formal IT strategy was ever articulated for the organization. Instead, this manager said:

I think we all walk around generally understanding what needs to be done. [The CFO] overcomes the problem of not having [a strategy] by communicating with a lot of people, he's very much in touch with all of the VPs, he communicates his plans and so forth.

Even so, the IS manager underlined the fact that Microsoft was the corporate desktop standard, although it was not written down anywhere, nor indeed was it codified that SAP was the first choice when it came to developing corporate applications. In addition, the IS managers interviewed considered the CFO to be really unique due to his passion for IT and his understanding of its benefits to the company. They also thought that few senior executives within Digital were as enthusiastic proponents or sponsors of IT as he. Nevertheless, the following statement from the IS manager for Sales and Marketing is revealing, in that it may indicate where the fundamental cause of the frustration with the IS function existed:

I think there would be good agreement that there are areas, especially in Sales and Marketing, that he just does not understand — the soft stuff, customer relationship management [etc.]…There is agreement that he is probably too removed from that side of the business, that he might say: "Well, wait a second, why are we spending money on that?" And well sometimes you know at the high level that many of the vice-presidents communicate when these initiatives are being discussed, but I think what he tends to fall back on is that if the vice president responsible is willing to fund it out of his own budget, and put his best people on it, then he would be willing to support [it].

While the IS function was not held in the highest regard by Sales and Marketing engineers, the reverse was also the case, as both Sales and Marketing (including the marketing sub-units in the product line divisions) tended to go it alone more often than other organizational units when it came to providing their own IT solutions. Nevertheless, IS was always the first port of call whenever new systems were planned in order to determine whether or not the IS function could deliver the desired solution. However, because of human resource limitations and skills shortages, the demand for corporate-wide systems, and attendant need to prioritize the systems to be developed, IS was not always in a position to deliver a particular solution.

The Other Side of the Governance Coin

The IS function ran into problems that were not of its own making in undertaking certain projects for business 'communities-of-practice.' For example, it had been badly burned in the past, with, for example, the original Opportunities, Strategies and Tactics (OST) System for Digital's sales team and, also, the organization's sales forecasting system — both of which were failures. Accordingly, the IS function tended to tread carefully so as not to get embroiled in change management problems and resultant system failures. Hence, they adopted a policy that required business areas to appoint a project leader who was highly competent in his field, and who would have top management support, as they did with the successful SAP Logistics and Order Fulfillment System. In this project, a senior manager from manufacturing acted as user project manager, and an IS project manager handled development. The problems that arose in the implementation of this system revolved around the significant change in the logistics process that would effectively eliminate all product distribution warehouses worldwide, save for those at the manufacturing site of origin. The new system allowed for a form of just-in-time manufacturing whereby products were to be shipped directly from the manufacturing site of origin direct to a customer once ordered. As the IS manager responsible outlined:

> *An IT guy could not make that type of business decision, and an IT guy could not get through political issues in Europe: like saying that we are going to close down that warehouse and make 30 people redundant. The business manager who did that had the support of the vice president of worldwide sales. And that is the struggle I alluded to before, but now we're in the space of systems where someone comes up with [a] great idea and says well I think we should do this, and I say fine, but who are you going to put into this to run it? And the response might be: "Well I don't really have any one that I am willing to give up at present." That is signal to me that the system is not that important.*

Whereas change management problems were resolved when the SAP system was implemented, the new sales forecasting system was more problematic however, as problems of a cross-functional nature between the manufacturing and marketing functions, and a lack of buy-in on the marketing side, caused the system's implementation to fail. One of the major problems here was that Manufacturing and Corporate Marketing had separate sales forecasting needs. Furthermore, their existing approaches to forecasting, although separate, were pretty much dependent on each other. In any event, managers from manufacturing locations and the marketing groups participating in the development redesigned the forecasting processes and developed the system around the new processes. However, the system was never used to its full potential because business managers not involved in the design and development were reluctant to change fundamental forecasting processes. Thus, while the new system was implemented, the basic business processes involved in forecasting were never changed. The IS manager responsible for this development project stated that it became "a pass the buck issue" with both marketing and manufacturing. As a result of these implementation problems, responsibility for forecasting was removed from the marketing function, and the relevant planning activities were transferred and integrated into manufacturing processes and then ported back into marketing. Hence, the new planners effectively spanned both functions. The IS manager for Sales and Marketing summed up the situation thus:

> *It seems to me that everyone is always fascinated with new systems, and they believe that a particular solution is going to solve all their problems; and [whether the systems work or not] it all comes down to whether or not the organization is lined up — that the right people, with the right incentives, are in place, and that business managers have thought through what this is going to mean, and so on.*

In response to the problems they were experiencing with the Sales and Marketing divisions, IS managers wanted to see a single vice president of Sales and Marketing so that there would be coherence, vision and leadership in the planning, development and implementation of Sales and Marketing Systems. The other side of this coin, however, was that such a move had the potential to reduce political infighting and, perhaps, act as a mechanism to impose corporate standards on highly innovative operations like Central Applications.

Building the Intranet the Digital Way

In 1996, the IS function put in place a strategy for the corporate intranet. Prior to this, islands of Web-based sites had appeared across the wide area network (WAN), and business and IS managers wished to tap into the potential for intra-organizational communication and learning that such systems offered. Essentially, business users were employing Web-based technologies to share their knowledge of products and customers with each other. In order to develop a strategy that would bring order to the chaos that then existed, the IS function benchmarked its proposed strategy with companies such as DEC, Hewlett Packard, Sun Microsystems and Silicon Graphics. The IS team observed two dominant approaches to implementing intranet technologies in these companies. First, they noted that Sun Microsystems and Silicon Graphics had adopted a *laissez faire* strategy and basically let staff do their own thing, whereby every workstation had the potential to become an intranet Web site. DEC and Hewlett Packard took a much more disciplined and rigorous approach by instituting a formal strategy that included the adoption of exacting standards, in conjunction with a corporate template that mandated a certain look and feel for each site. The IS function at Digital adopted a strategy that lay somewhere between the two reported.

In implementing this strategy, an umbrella intranet site was first established and the representatives of all the other sites were informed of the new policy. Essentially, this involved the observance of some basic guidelines that end-user developers had to follow — these guidelines merely set certain standards for the Web sites. No effort was made to tell users as to what they could or could not place on their sites, but nevertheless, certain policies had to be observed. The IS project manager responsible commented on this endeavor and maintained that it had "worked out pretty well, but there was some duplication of effort. For example, if I need a phone list of people, there are probably 10 of them out there now, and each one, apart from the corporate one, is maintained for people in a particular Web group." Nonetheless, in response to such issues, and to introduce more functionality and cross-site accessibility, a cross-functional intranet development steering group was established. This group was charged with two tasks — to develop standards and to develop generic tools like a search engine. The group had responsibility also for the formulation of a strategy to guide the direction of the Intranet and to determine what, if any, additional standards needed to be put in place. However, in keeping with the organizational culture, rigid structures were not put in place, nor were Web authors questioned in regards to what they were doing with their sites. Even so, some control was levied over the use of resources to prevent particular groups from monopolizing them and thereby preventing other voices from being heard.

Central Applications Leads the Way in Providing Intranet Support for Sales and Marketing

As indicated previously, Lotus Notes was not supported by the IS function, and because the Digital's CIO did not want Lotus Notes client software on corporate desktops, it seemed unlikely that the applications developed using Lotus Notes would be of general use to the people that needed them — the sales and field engineers. However, with the advent of the corporate intranet, and with the capability of Notes' Domino Web-server, the Central Applications product support system came into its own, and such was its success that the product divisions and the product lines looked to Central Applications to host new product information. The IT consultant at Central Applications described it thus:

> When Internet technology and Web servers first became available and popular, a lot of people went out and set up their own intranet servers, and it was fun and games for a while. But they soon realized how much work it was to maintain their own sites and keep their information fresh...So what we have done is make it easy for people [by hosting their intranet sites], and the [Central Applications manager] feels that if we keep it easy for people, they will come.

In addition to hosting new product data for the product divisions, something that was pivotal in helping sales and field engineers to promote Digital's diverse product range, Central Applications also hosted intranet Web sites for the product lines, as many of them had neither the time nor the inclination to maintain their own sites. Application engineers supported and input most of the data into the Lotus Notes databases; for example, the sales bulletins, the product problem data, and so on. With the general accessibility of the Marketing Information Central Web site, it was hoped that much of the work of inputting new product status data would be taken over by the entities responsible for the original data such as the product lines and so on.

Creative Tension and Development of Digital's Corporate Web Presence

The success of user-led development of Digital's intranet systems had unintended consequences for the development of the company's Internet IS. Digital wished to implement a corporate Web site in order to execute its e-Business strategy, such as it was. External users consisted primarily of design engineers who were now provided with enhanced product search and select features in order to better meet their needs. The system would also provide a mechanism by which design engineers could order products or have samples sent to them. Internal users provided product descriptions and technical data for publication, on one hand, while customer preferences and future product needs (in terms of design and manufacture) could be obtained from customer interaction and used by sales and corporate/product line marketing functions. The IS function, which provided technical support for the initiative, did not see itself as leading the project, that responsibility rested firmly with the VP of Corporate Marketing. The appointment of a Webmaster was a pivotal factor in the success of the Web project. The Webmaster acted as a user project manager whose role was to provide leadership and guidance for the ongoing development, operation and use of Digital's Internet presence. Previously she was involved with the Computer Products Division (CPD) application support center at Norwood.

Enthusiastic as many of the management team were by the exciting new possibilities for customer contact and marketing new and existing products using the Internet, others were less enthused as they perceived that tried and tested methods of communicating with customers were to be discarded and replaced by indirect, impersonal technological mechanisms. Predictably, this led to friction between the various groups involved, particularly the sales and marketing functions. Take, for example, this admission by the Webmaster: "I know that the Web site will continue to be an emotional thing and not everyone will be happy." Nevertheless, elsewhere she admitted that the Web site was jointly developed with cross-functional teams from these constituencies, indicating that the difficulties mentioned were overcome — at least on a formality.

One of the major difficulties that arose in relation to the implementation of this Web-based IS centred on the manner in which product details were prepared for publication on the Web. In a move that paralleled the intranet policy at Central Applications, the Webmaster shifted the emphasis from authorship and ownership of all new product data to the product lines. The early successes in deploying what was a new technology led some senior managers to believe: (a) that traditional mechanisms of customer contact were now obsolete; (b) that existing business processes were under threat; (c) and that catalogs, CD-ROMs, and sales engineers were now of little value.

The perspectives of IS function managers on the issue of IT support for promoting product data to customers are summed up by a comment from the IS manager for the Internet project:

> The [Central Applications Manager] does this on the intranet internally, [the Webmaster] is on the Internet site: I think maybe that there is some competition there, I don't think that is organizationally clear who is responsible for this — it just hasn't been defined. I don't think Digital works like that, [Central Applications] have done this for a long time and now [the Webmaster] needs to do this externally. The choices are "I can use his stuff or I can do my own thing"; [The Central Applications Manager], I think, gets and maintains it himself, while [the Webmaster] has the product line people do it for her. [Central Applications are] facing field service engineers while [the Webmaster] is facing the customer.

Thus, the absence of an overarching policy on the management of the customer interface at Digital (one direct, the other via sales and field service engineers) led to competition and tension between two important organizational functions. However, this proved beneficial and led to optimal outcomes for customers and field service and sales engineers, as the Web team and Central Applications unit both wished to be perceived as the nexus of corporate knowledge. It must be said, however, that unequivocal top management support helped mitigate many of the problems mentioned and others that arose elsewhere in the organization regarding the new Internet IS, and thereby led to a successful development outcome.

CURRENT CHALLENGES/PROBLEMS FACING THE ORGANIZATION

This section describes the problems and challenges facing the organization in relation to IS development and governance of IT infrastructures, and, in particular, the issues confronting its IS function and engineering-oriented business 'communities-of-practice' in the Sales, Corporate Marketing, and Standard Linear Products divisions. The following challenges/problems are discussed with reference to the preceding case report.

Business users in engineering 'communities-of-practice' were committed to leveraging IT to transform core business processes and to be innovative in delivering products and services using IS. It is evident that they will continue to do this with or without the help of the IS function. Hence, in order achieve their objectives, they will exercise as much control over the development of IS and the governance of IT infrastructures as is possible. On the other hand, the IS function is committed to bringing order and professionalism to the mayhem caused by the organic and uncoordinated approach to IS development and IT infrastructure deployment by engineers from the business divisions. Factional interests will continue to exist as engineers in business 'communities-of-practice' form alliances with others to achieve their ends. However, if the IS function continues to operate from a relatively weaker power base, it will need to form potent alliances to obtain its goals. The challenges for the organization's leadership would be to maintain what is good in Digital Devices' culture, structure and processes, while transforming how the company deploys and governs IT infrastructures and develops and implements IS. These challenges are now detailed.

At the time this study ended, the company faced several major options in addressing what were its main problems: the marginalization of the company's IS function and the power asymmetries this created with the business community in terms of IS development and governance issues. The first option concerns the challenge of changing the company's structure for the purpose of establishing a new division based on the IS function. From IS managers' perspectives, the key challenge is to have the IS function emerge from beneath the wing of the Finance Division and become an autonomous organizational unit with a CIO of equal standing to the VPs of business divisions, as is the case with almost all large multinational organizations. The challenge for the IT-literate, engineering-oriented, business 'communities-of-practice' would be to gracefully cede control over the design, development, implementation and operation of IT infrastructures so that a uniform and aligned approach could be adopted in the provision and deployment of IS. This would involve a change in power relationships and commitments. Hence, the challenge for business and IS managers here would be to address the fallout in terms of the perceived loss of control by business managers over the design, development and evolution of the IS they depend on to conduct business.

An alternative to this option would be the challenge of creating a business-specific IS function within each division with direct reporting relationships to a senior business executive: for example, the IS manger for the Standard Linear Product Division would report to, and receive budgetary resources from, a senior executive or the VP of that division. Overall strategy could then be formulated by a corporate IS function. Thus IS personnel could participate with business users as members of the same 'community-of-practice' and the culture of user-led development in the organization would not need radical change. The problem here is that if corporate IS remained under the umbrella of the Finance Division, then the CIO could not be said to be unbiased in terms of strategy formulation, the allocation of IS budgets and the prioritization of IS projects. Hence, the corporate IS, whatever its size, would need to be focused exclusively on strategy, but with a CIO that had VP status reporting directly to the CEO. This would enable the CIO and his IS executives to address, for the first time, the challenge of formulating an IS strategy that was aligned with business strategies and needs across the organization, thus IT-enabled support for business processes could be delivered more effectively and efficiently. Indeed, the absence of a coherent IS strategy throughout the 1990s was a significant problem for the company and its IS function.

Another problem highlighted by IS managers, and evident from the case, was the limitations on IS performance in its inability to deliver timely solutions to business due to a shortage of IS staff, especially those with competencies in particular areas such as Internet and intranet technologies. If recruiting new staff was going to be problematic, due to the high demand of IT professionals at the time, the challenge for IS managers would be to choose between outsourcing, consultancy or customizable-off-the-shelf software approaches, or implement hybrid solutions involving a mixture of all three. These could be integrated with the above options. However, there will remain the significant challenge in convincing an IT-literate business 'community-of-practice' that IS is best placed to do this, as many business managers, such as the Manager of Central Applications, are already contracting consultants, and so on. Whatever strategy is selected, there remains the challenge of confidence building in the business community in regard to the IS function, as IT-literate business managers already had a long-standing role in providing for their own IS needs.

If management at Digital Devices address the aforementioned challenges and solve related problems, there remain several issues to be addressed in the short term. As an IS manager pointed out, having a single IS unit serve the IS needs of both the Sales and Corporate Marketing divisions was causing problems. The challenge of senior management would be to merge the two divisions, as the existing structure lay at the root of many of the IS development-related problems being experienced by the IS function in providing joint solutions. Sales and marketing strategies could be then be aligned more effectively so that agreement could be reached on integrated IS applications. This was important given that a number of sales and marketing engineers were fearful of the company's radical change of strategy in planning to use Internet-based systems to replace established means of meeting customer needs. The challenge was to use the Internet as an additional sales and marketing tool, while not abandoning tried and tested business processes — only then could the 'doubters' be won over. Then there was the problem of business managers in the Sales and Marketing divisions thinking that they knew better than IS managers as to which IT platform was the best IT-based solution for their IS needs, as indicated in the case. Even if agreement was reached on a particular IS solution, change management problems tended to arise that could only be solved by business managers. For IS managers, the solution to these and other problems was to draft Project Charters that delineated the roles and responsibilities of all stakeholders and which would provide agreement to implement the agreed project outcomes. The challenge for the IS function is to have this introduced on a corporate-wide basis.

Several of the major issues facing Digital Devices related to matters of IT governance and adherence to standards. One such problem facing the organization will be resolving issues relating to the IS function's support for the Microsoft Windows platform and the engineering 'communities-of-practice' allegiance to UNIX-based systems. Take, for example, that Linux, the free Open Source Software operating system, now comes with a client suite of personal productivity tools (Open Office) and enterprise-wide system software utilities that rival Microsoft's offerings (Apache, MySQL, etc.). Then, there is the competition between Microsoft's .Net and Sun's Java 2 Enterprise Edition (J2EE) in the application development space. Interestingly, engineers in product line divisions were early adaptors of Java technologies and are committed to their use, as J2EE applications run on Windows, Mac and all UNIX variants, while .Net applications run on Windows only. Also, it will be interesting to see whether the company will continue with its insistence on Windows client and server operating systems in the face of the lower total cost of ownership (TCO) of Linux-based Open Office and server side utilities, especially given the range of UNIX-based competencies in the organizations.

Finally, while Digital's intranet strategy was an undoubted success, it had two obvious weaknesses. First, the heterogeneous nature of the Web and data servers meant that it would be more difficult for the IS function to quickly roll-out anti-virus and worm upgrades across different platforms (e.g., Microsoft's Internet Information Server (IIS), Lotus Domino, Apache, etc.). Thus, weak links could exist that would compromise the company's local and wide area networks (LANs and WANs) and cause data loss. The challenge here for the IS function would be to implement a strategy that migrated non-standard servers to the corporate standard(s), and introduce automated anti-virus upgrades and other means to protect valuable corporate data repositories. Second, the case description of Digital Devices' intranet and Internet infrastructures indicates that the company's knowledge resources were not well integrated, in that there existed islands of knowledge stored in diverse data repositories — something that is in contravention of knowledge management practice. Problems of duplication of effort and data inconsistency aside, a major challenge for Digital's IS function is to protect this learning organization's most valuable resource, knowledge of its core business processes and products.

REFERENCES

Abrahamsson, P. (2001). Rethinking the concept of commitment in software process improvement. *Scandinavian Journal of Information Systems*, *13*, 69-98.

Butler, T. (2003). An institutional perspective on developing and implementing intranet- and Internet-based IS. *Information Systems Journal, 13*(3), 209-232.

Butler, T., & Fitzgerald, B. (2001, January/March). The relationship between user participation and the management of change surrounding the development of information systems: A European perspective. *Journal of End User Computing,* 12-25.

Cavaye, A. L. M. (1995). User participation in system development revisited. *Information and Management, 28,* 311-323.

Jasperson, J., Carte, T. A., Saunders, C. S., Butler, B. S., Croes, H. J., & Zheng, W. (2002). Review: Power and information technology research: A metatriangulation review. *MIS Quarterly, 26*(4), 397-459.

Keen, P. G. W. (1981). Information systems and organizational change. *Communications of the ACM, 24*(1), 24-33.

Kling, R., & Iacono, S. (1984). The control of information systems after implementation. *Communications of the ACM, 27*(12), 1218-1226.

Markus, M. L. (1983). Power, politics, and MIS implementation. *Communications of the ACM, 26*(6), 430-444.

Patton, M. Q. (1990). *Qualitative evaluation and research methods.* London: Sage.

Sabherwal, R., Sein, M. K., & Marakas, G. M. (2003). Escalating commitment to information system projects: Findings from two simulated experiments. *Information and Management, 40*(8), 781-798.

Selznick, P. (1949). *TVA and the grass roots.* Los Angeles: University of California Press.

Selznick, P. (1957). *Leadership in administration.* New York: Harper and Row.

Stake, R. E. (1995). *The art of case study research.* Thousand Oaks, CA: Sage.

Winograd, T., & Flores, F. (1986). *Understanding computers and cognition: A new foundation for design.* Norwood, NJ: Ablex Publishing Corporation.

ENDNOTE

[1]   The product data sheets contained detailed descriptions and specifications of products; it is therefore a vital component in making sales, as customers require this information to match products to their specific design needs.

Tom Butler is a senior lecturer in Information Systems at University College Cork, Ireland. Before joining academia, Dr. Butler had an extensive career in the telecommunications industry. His research is primarily qualitative, interpretive and case-based in nature and has two related major streams: IT capabilities and the development and implementation of information systems in organizations; and knowledge management systems. Other research interests include hermeneutics, e-learning, educational informatics, IT education and the digital divide. Dr. Butler received his PhD from the National University of Ireland at UCC, where his doctoral research examined the role of IT competencies in building firm-specific IT resources in knowledge-intensive organizations.

This case was previously published in the *Journal of Cases on Information Technology,* 7(3), pp. 18-36, © 2005.

Chapter XII

Changing the Old Order:
Sequencing Organizational and Information Technology Change to Achieve Successful Organizational Transformation

Chris Sauer[1], The University of New South Wales, Australia

EXECUTIVE SUMMARY

This chapter describes the transformation of the motor vehicle registration and driver licensing business of the Roads and Traffic Authority of the Australian state of New South Wales. At the heart of this transformation which took place between 1989 and 1992 is a system called DRIVES. The project was innovative in the technology platform it devised and in the CASE technology it used to build the application. The new system has paid for itself at the same time as transforming the Roads and Traffic Authority's way of doing the business. In addition it has generated new strategic opportunities. The iterating sequence of steps, or looped path, by which the Roads and Traffic Authority achieved its organizational transformation is compared with the more traditional top-down path. The looped path helps prepare the organization for the information technology change, makes risk more manageable by reducing the dependence between steps in the path, and leads to strategic benefits after the organizational changes have been mastered. Thus, we say that the particular order in which change was undertaken led to the new organizational order.

BACKGROUND

The state of New South Wales (NSW) is situated in the south east of Australia. It is an area 15% larger than Texas with a population of six million. The state capital is Sydney which is the same size as Los Angeles with a population of 3.7 million. For most of the 1980s the government of New South Wales administered roads and their use through two separate departments. The Department of Main Roads planned, built and maintained roads. It was a major spending department with a billion dollar budget. The Department of Motor Transport registered and licensed the vehicles and drivers who used the roads. It collected revenues for the state Treasury amounting to approximately the figure spent by the Department of Main Roads. Although running very different types of business, the two departments were both old-fashioned in their conduct of business. The Department of Main Roads was strongly influenced by its established engineering culture rather than business values. The Department of Motor Transport was viewed as a bureaucratic backwater from which bright managers sought to escape. Staff described its business practices as "Dickensian."

As the 1980s progressed, the climate in government and public administration began to change. Governments reduced the scope of their activities and increasingly imposed commercial values and practices on their major service providing departments.

In 1988, the government decided to merge the Department of Main Roads, the Department of Motor Transport, and the much smaller NSW Traffic Authority which was responsible for road safety. In January 1989, the Roads and Traffic Authority (RTA) came into existence as a super department of almost 12,000 employees and a budget in excess of $A1 billion. The head of the Department of Main Roads, Bernard Fisk, was appointed Chief Executive of the RTA.

SETTING THE STAGE

Our concern in this chapter is confined to the vehicle registration and driver licensing part of the RTA's business. Initially, the RTA had no choice but to continue to operate the Department of Motor Transport's existing business processes. These separated the delivery of licenses and registration from back office administrative processing. Delivery was through the RTA's 138 motor registries which are locally situated shopfronts at which members of the public pay their fees and obtain their licenses and registration documents. Registries perform a wide variety of tasks related to registration and licensing. They also administer driver's tests.

Each registry has its own manager who is responsible through line management to a regional director. In 1989, at the time of the merger, a typical registry had 12 to 15 staff each of whom carried out highly specialized tasks. For customers this specialization resulted in a frustrating lack of customer service. They were required to join one queue to submit their application and renewal forms and then another to pay. If there were difficulties with their paperwork they might have to join other queues as well. After all that, there was a strong possibility that the registry would be unable to resolve the problem and so would have to refer them to the central administrative processing unit at Rosebery in inner Sydney which dealt with problems and handled all the data collection forms and computer processing.

In the old business process, customer records would take around 10 days to be updated and customers could sometimes wait weeks for new registration documents to reach them in the post. For the police, it was hard to enforce registration and licensing law because offenders could claim that their missing documentation was "in the mail." There were insufficient controls to detect corrupt practice in the registries. An inquiry by the New South Wales Independent Commission Against Corruption found "endemic corruption in a number of motor registries in the Sydney metropolitan area." Some driving examiners were systematically accepting bribes from driving schools to pass students and certain registry staff were falsifying or selling license and registration information.

The central computer system operated by the staff at the Rosebery unit consisted of two IBM 4381 mainframes. The application software was 14 years old and prone to intermittent failure. Much of it was written in undocumented Assembler and had been so heavily amended to cope with legislative and administrative changes that the programmers were doubtful they could continue to change it without making it more error prone.

The CEO was acutely aware of his legacy: "Something had to be done. Any query was a matter of using a group of specialist programmers, it would take a long time, and there was always the danger that the system would fall over in seeking to extract that information. The Minister wanted better information on which to base policy and I wanted better service to motor registry customers."

The task of determining what should be done was assigned to the RTA's General Manager of Information Services, Geoff Deacon, who had joined the Department of Main Roads in 1987 as Head of Information Technology (IT). His work in trying to bring order to the Department of Main Roads' different systems and technologies was to prove important for the new project in that he came to recognize the potential of an open systems platform, "I . . . started to get a feeling that Unix was to be the way of the future. We wanted to move towards a single integrated network and open systems were definitely the way to go. We figured an open system approach would ensure that new technology could be implemented with minimal disruption as it became available." His technology choice was a Fujitsu mainframe running the UTS/M version of Unix. This was unconventional in that the accepted Unix configuration involved multiple minicomputers.

Deacon was faced with the choice of an application rewrite or implementing a new system. Rewriting was nearly impossible because the system was so poorly documented. He therefore proposed a new system under the name DRIVES (DRIver and VEhicle System).

The RTA's chief executive did not wait for DRIVES to be implemented to start a program of organizational change. He was conscious of the new mood in government to improve public perceptions of government services. He therefore moved quickly to position the RTA strategically as a more customer responsive body.

Fisk's first change was to structure the RTA into regions both for its road development responsibilities and its registration and licensing business. The new structure transferred accountability and authority from Head Office to the field and reduced levels of management. In the process, Fisk refilled managerial positions to ensure that his strategy would be in the hands of staff who were up to the challenge.

The RTA then set about changes that would be evident to the public. It transformed the registries from a highly differentiated workplace with many grades of staff to a multi-skilled workplace with just two grades of customer service officer, and a supervisor and a manager. Intense specialization was replaced by a more customer oriented flexibility. While the registries had to continue to use the old business systems, this new flexibility made it possible for managers to make some immediate improvements in customer service.

PROJECT/CASE DESCRIPTION

The DRIVES project had two main objectives. The first was to replace the old application technology with a robust, modern system which would eliminate the risk of an irrecoverable failure. The second was to remove the need for the central processing unit, thereby saving $A20 million per year in staff costs and at the same time providing a swifter service to registry customers. Other benefits included enhanced accuracy and timeliness of records, improved security of data, flexibility of access to data, potential to expand, rapid communications and better management information. In providing for flexibility and the ability to grow and develop as the business and the technology changed, the RTA was preparing itself for the future.

In late 1989, the RTA approved a budget of $A28.6 million for building a new licensing and registration system. The CEO signaled his desire for a quick implementation by renaming the project DRIVES '90 : "I deliberately set an unrealistic timeframe, I had to keep the pressure on Geoff [Deacon] to perform because I was scared of the existing system falling over."

The RTA decided to build DRIVES itself because Deacon was unable to find an adequate package solution. Success required that the RTA be able to manage technology, application, and organizational challenges. Technology challenges included developing the technology platform; adopting the unproven pairing of Unix on a Fujitsu mainframe; and learning to use a Computer-Aided Software Engineering (CASE) tool which itself had to be converted from IBM's MVS operating system to suit the RTA's environment. Application challenges included the size and complexity of the application, changes to the data model, and the difficulties involved in converting records because of the poor quality of the data. The main organizational challenge was the management of change in the motor registries. One task was to change registry staff attitudes — "We were trying to change a group whose whole focus was to get the money off the customer, stamp something and then put the paperwork in the background for somebody else to fix, into a culture where we said you have the power and the responsibility to do it at the front counter with this complicated system." Registry change was also complicated by a continuing industrial dispute between the RTA and a union which was trying to avoid losing its position to a competitor.

Deacon managed the technical, application, and organizational challenges in a number of ways. His innovations included establishment of a Change Management Team. In the course of the project, this team undertook a refurbishment of the registry offices and trained 1,500 customer service officers.

Deacon was particularly helped by the support he received from his CEO. Fisk's support for resourcing the project meant that Deacon could quickly build up the project organization with good quality contract staff and technical specialists employed by suppliers. This meant that technology challenges could be tackled by technically proficient staff. When delays occurred, Fisk accepted them but continued to push for system delivery. When the project ran into any difficulty he made resources available to help solve it. When the budget was exceeded, his view was, "If I can't find a spare five to ten million dollars, there is something wrong." His evident commitment convinced both Fujitsu and Texas Instruments that it was worth putting in extra effort to solve technical problems. According to Fujitsu Australia's Managing Director, his company was happy to continue to make special efforts because it was confident of Fisk's commitment to the project: "The management team from Bernard Fisk down were absolutely convinced that they had made the right strategic decision and they knew the benefits they were going to get."

Support from the top extended even further in the case of the industrial dispute. When the union launched a campaign of public criticisms in the press, not only did the CEO appear on a local radio program and Deacon invite journalists to a briefing, but also the RTA's minister, Wal Murray, made strong statements of support in parliament. In the face of such a solid reaction from the RTA, the criticism quickly died away.

CURRENT STATUS OF THE PROJECT

In September 1991, the Licensing component of DRIVES was implemented in the registries. Ninety staff at the central administrative processing unit left the RTA in accordance with the terms of an earlier agreement resulting in immediate staff savings. In June 1992, the Registration component was implemented, and the remaining 400 employees left under the same terms thus yielding the full, expected staff savings of $A20 million per year.

Both phases of implementation experienced teething problems. The registries experienced a number of start up problems with the Licensing data which caused delays at the counters with a build-up of queues in the registries but which were overcome in time. Registration which is a high volume transaction initially struggled to achieve a satisfactory processing throughput. Response times at the registries averaged 6 to 10 seconds. For a period, customers were openly dissatisfied at the long queues they faced. The combined efforts of the DRIVES Systems team, assisted by Fujitsu specialists gradually brought performance up so that response times were close to target by December 1992. Once Fujitsu delivered its multi-processor Unix in January 1993, response times fell to around two seconds, the target envisaged in 1989.

Since 1993, the RTA has been able to further develop the applications and to maintain them without significant difficulty. New versions of the software have been installed smoothly without adverse effects on business processing.

SUCCESSES AND FAILURES

DRIVES has been a major success. The RTA has met its two objectives of replacing the old system and achieving productivity gains leading to $A18 million cost savings[2] and an estimated $A5 million revenue increase annually. In the process the RTA has transformed the way it does registration and licensing business, giving it organizational, business, and technological benefits. At the same time, it has created new strategic opportunities. DRIVES has resulted in improved service in the motor registries which are now able to complete customer transactions at a single counter position and solve problems on the spot. Surveys conducted by an independent research company have shown that customers appreciate the changes in terms of reduced waiting times, better service, fewer queues and improved registry appearance.

DRIVES has also speeded up essential registry activities such as banking. Before, a separate cashier handled the registry's takings and did a manual daily balance. Now, DRIVES automatically balances each officer's cash drawer. What used to take two clerks up to an hour to complete at the end of each day is done in 15 minutes.

DRIVES has also helped the RTA combat corrupt practices both by limiting opportunities and exposing misconduct. DRIVES contains a high level of auditability and is protected through a combination of passwords and access levels. The RTA is able to detect and investigate unusual patterns of usage. RTA employees found to have engaged in corrupt practices have been swiftly dismissed and prosecuted on the basis of DRIVES information.

With the safety of corporate information assured, the RTA has been able to evaluate opportunities such as installing DRIVES terminals in car-dealer offices and at motor auctions. This move would allow cars to be registered at their point of sale while administrative savings would be made by both the RTA and the dealers. The range of other opportunities includes outsourcing the entire licensing and registration operation, using information available through DRIVES to lower the state's $A70 million fine default bill, and introducing phone-in license and registration renewals or do-it-yourself booths at large shopping centers.

DRIVES has improved the identification of stolen and unregistered vehicles, and assists police with driving and vehicle offenses. In the future, DRIVES could be used to get unregistered vehicles off the road more quickly through electronically exchanging information with external stakeholders such as the Police and the Traffic Infringement Processing Bureau.

Safe-T-Cam is an example of a truly innovative project enabled by DRIVES. It is a system for electronically collecting data on heavy vehicles. As trucks or semi-trailers pull up to weighing stations on the highways of NSW, their image is captured and their number-plates read. This information is transmitted to DRIVES which returns an alert if a vehicle is over-weight or unregistered. Problem vehicles are called into the station and the others are waved on. Safe-T-Cam sites on major highways permit automatic checks on long distance speeding. Safe-T-Cam is able to access DRIVES to obtain up to date owner information. The State saves money through a reduced accident bill while the road transport industry benefits from the decrease in driver delays at the weighing stations.

Various technological benefits have also emerged. As well as permitting easy upgrade and enhancement, the open systems platform has allowed the RTA to explore mid-range alternatives to its mainframe technology without having to rewrite its systems. It is thus able to keep up to date and to explore newer technologies such as client/server without incurring major overheads.

Against such a substantial success, the project's downside pales into insignificance. Budget and schedule overruns were financially significant, but they did not prevent the project from giving a net positive return on investment within two years. From the organizational perspective such budget and schedule problems were negligible. The CEO did not expect the project to come in on time, rather he used the schedule to maintain the pressure to achieve implementation at the earliest possible moment. The strategic importance of the new system was such that he was prepared to fund the budget overrun. The system performance problems were essentially just teething problems. They had a short term effect on customer satisfaction but the improvements to registry service have in the longer term far outweighed initial dissatisfaction.

EPILOGUE AND LESSONS LEARNED

Popular writers on organizations and management have made much of IT's potential to transform organizations. The DRIVES experience shows that organizational transformation is not the outcome of a technology project alone. DRIVES' contribution to the transformation of the RTA was one part of a larger program of corporate renewal. A successful technology project on its own would have yielded benefits by removing the threat of the old system failing catastrophically, but the RTA was able to transform the way it did business because of the interaction between the technology and the other organizational change that took place. It is important therefore (1) to recognize that technology is most effective when it is complemented by other organizational change, and (2) to understand IT management in this wider corporate context.

In the past, those IT professionals who have recognized the importance of the interrelationship between technology and organization have recommended that IT systems should *fit their organizational context* (Ein-Dor & Segev, 1981; Keen, 1981). Unfortunately, this has been interpreted to mean that systems should be developed and implemented for the existing state of the organization rather than that IT and the organization should be managed in a mutually complementary fashion.

More recently, proponents of IT-based organizational transformation have tried to locate IT developments in the context of a configuration of organizational elements which includes strategy, structure, management processes, and individuals' roles and skills (Walton, 1989; Scott Morton, 1991; Henderson & Venkatraman, 1992). On this view, technology is one component among several, *all of which must fit each other* for substantial performance benefits to be achieved. The conventional view of how to achieve this is to tackle the organizational change sequentially taking a top-down path. This path (Figure 1) proceeds from strategy to structure, then to technology and on to management processes, and roles and skills (Scott Morton, 1988, 1991; Yetton, Johnston, & Craig, 1994; Yetton, Craig, & Johnston, 1995). In starting from strategy and proceeding downwards, this order of change is rationally appealing. However, it is also limiting in that it can encourage a view of technology as exclusively driven by a strategic vision which foresees the technology's full potential. It can also encourage the technologist's view of the technology project as a project-in-isolation (Abdel-Hamid, 1993), because strategy and structure are taken as givens, decided by business managers in advance of technology investment, while roles, skills and management processes are finer detail which technologists expect lower level managers to change to fit the technology.

Recent research has demonstrated that successful transformations can and do occur when rather different paths of change are followed. In some cases the technology leads the rest of the organization while in others it lags behind (Ciborra, 1991; Yetton et al., 1994, 1995; Burn, 1994). One of the advantages of recognizing the value of different paths is that management of IT is seen less in isolation and more as part of the management of the whole organization. The DRIVES case demonstrates a different path and explains how it contributed to the RTA's success.

Figure 1. The top-down path to IT-based organizational transformation

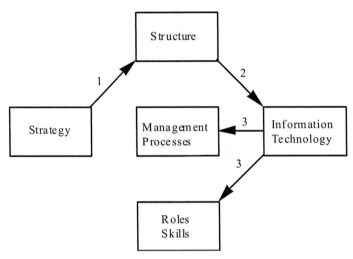

Figure 2 illustrates the path taken by the RTA. It goes from the strategy of developing quality of service to customers, to structuring geographically to achieve greater customer focus, to introducing restructuring and multi-skilling in the registries, to implementing DRIVES, to acquiring and mastering the skills to work with DRIVES, to improved management control in the registries, to the exploration of new strategic opportunities. It differs from the top-down path in including two loops. The small loop depicts change to roles and skills in the registries both before and after DRIVES was implemented. The larger loop starts with strategy and revisits strategy after all the other major changes have been completed.

We can identify several lessons from the RTA's looped path to organizational transformation. First, by introducing multi-skilling and de-layering at the registries in advance of the implementation of DRIVES, the RTA reduced the organizational change subsequently needed to work effectively with the new system. Once these changes had been made in the registries, DRIVES made more sense as a work technology than the old system. Thus the sequence of organizational change eased the path for DRIVES so that on implementation, customer service staff could concentrate on learning to use DRIVES. Had the RTA waited for DRIVES to be implemented to make its organizational changes in the registries the implementation which was taxing enough might have easily become intolerable for the staff because too great a burden of new learning would have been placed upon them.

Second, the initial steps through strategy, structure and roles and skills were worthwhile in themselves. They generated benefits for the RTA independently of the new system. This both helped sustain the momentum of transformation and made it easier to manage because each step was not dependent on others yet to be taken.

Third, new strategic opportunities arose at the end of the RTA's path of change not because they had been identified in a detailed strategic vision years earlier, although

Figure 2. The RTA's looped path to organizational transformation

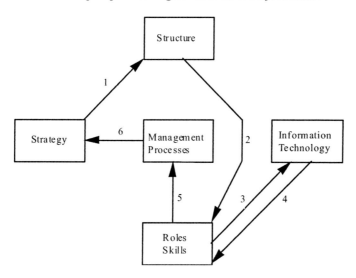

DRIVES had been designed as a platform for the future, but more because as the RTA developed the technology and learnt its characteristics and possibilities it was able to recognize and subsequently explore new opportunities. Thus, effective implementation of both technological and organizational change can create a platform for the emergence of opportunities. But these are discovered through familiarity with the new organizational way of working rather than by inspired acts of creativity at the time of conception of either strategy or technology.

Organizational transformation is a risky business as the proponents of business process reengineering have always made clear (Davenport, 1993; Hammer & Champy, 1993). Risk is at its most extreme if the path of change is sequenced such that none of the benefits of transformation are reaped until every step of the path has been successfully completed. Risk is more easily managed if it can be confined to individual steps (Yetton et al., 1995).

The RTA's path helped it manage the risks it faced. The substantial benefits in multi-skilling and restructuring the registries meant that risk was reduced because these steps were not dependent on the success of DRIVES. Risks associated with the technology step were managed in part through the CEO's active support for the project. That support was a natural consequence of DRIVES' being an integral part of the RTA's strategy of improving quality of service. Had the strategic benefits of DRIVES been purely emergent, that is, had strategy only appeared last in the path in Figure 2, then it is likely that the risks of such an innovative project would have been harder to manage.

The RTA case demonstrates the importance of the order in which organizations undertake change to change the old organizational order. It shows advantages to sequences of change which vary from the top-down path. In particular, sequences which yield pay-offs independent of the technology and which permit important learning to take place prior to implementation reduce the burden of learning and risk associated with implementation.

QUESTIONS FOR DISCUSSION

1. What was DRIVES' strategic importance to the RTA in 1989?
2. What is the value of changing structure, roles and skills before technology?
3. Why were so many benefits emergent rather than planned?
4. How did the order in which the RTA undertook change help it to manage its risks?
5. Is the RTA's experience transferable to the private sector?

REFERENCES

Abdel-Hamid, T. K. (1993). A multi-project perspective on single-project dynamics. *Journal of Systems and Software, 22*, 51-165.

Burn, C. J. (1994). A "R"evolutionary stage growth model of information systems planning. In J. I. DeGross, S. L. Huff, & M. C. Munro (Eds.), *Proceedings of the 15th Annual International Conference on Information Systems* (pp. 395-406). Vancouver, BC.

Ciborra, C. U. (1991). From thinking to tinkering: The grassroots of strategic information systems. In J. I. DeGross, I. Benbasat, G. DeSanctis, & C. M. Beath (Eds.), *Proceedings of the Twelfth International Conference on Information Systems* (pp. 283-291). New York.

Davenport, T. H. (1993). *Process innovation: Reengineering work through information technology.* Boston: Harvard Business School Press.

Ein-Dor, P., & Segev, E. (1981). *A paradigm for management information systems.* New York: Praeger.

Hammer, M., & Champy, J. (1993). *Reengineering the corporation: A manifesto for business revolution.* New York: Harper Collins.

Henderson, J. C., & Venkatraman, N. (1992). Strategic alignment: A model for organizational transformation through information technology. In T. Kochan, & M. Useem (Eds.), *Transforming organizations* (pp. 97-117). New York: Oxford University Press.

Keen, P. G. W. (1981). Information systems and organizational change. *Communications of the ACM, 24*(1), 24-33.

Scott Morton, M. (1988). Strategy formulation methodologies and IT. In M. J. Earl (Ed.), *Information management: The strategic dimension* (pp. 54-67). Oxford: Clarendon Press.

Scott Morton, M. (Ed.). (1991). *The corporation of the 1990s: Information technology and organizational transformation.* Oxford: Oxford University Press.

Walton, R. E. (1989). *Up and running: Integrating information technology and the organization.* Boston: Harvard Business School Press.

Yetton, P. W., Craig, J. F., & Johnston, K. (1995). Fit, simplicity and risk: Multiple paths to strategic IT change. In J. I. DeGross, G. Ariav, C. Beath, R. Hoyer, & C. Kemerer (Eds.), *Proceedings of the Sixteenth International Conference on Information Systems,* Amsterdam, Netherlands (pp. 1-11).

Yetton, P. W., Johnston, K. D., & Craig, J. F. (1994). Computer-aided architects: A case study of IT and strategic change. *Sloan Management Review, 35*(4), 57-67.

ENDNOTES

[1]   The author is grateful to Wendy Jones for her part in researching and writing up the case on which this chapter is based.

[2]   While DRIVES savings are $A20 million per annum, $A2 million is usually subtracted as the cost of maintaining the system.

Chris Sauer is currently senior research fellow at the Fujitsu Centre for Managing Information Technology in Organisations at the Australian Graduate School of Management in Sydney. He researches general management issues in IT-based organizational transformation. His first book Why Information Systems Fail: A Case Study Approach *was published in 1993. He is co-editor with Philip Yetton of* Steps to the Future: Fresh Thinking in the Dynamics of IT-Based Organizational Transformation *to be published by Jossey-Bass in 1997. In addition he has published various papers on his research and on IT educational issues.*

This case was previously published in J. Liebowitz & M. Khosrow-Pour (Eds.), *Cases on Information Technology Management in Modern Organizations*, pp. 48-56, © 1997.

Chapter XIII

Adoption and Implementation of IT in Developing Nations:
Experiences from Two Public Sector Enterprises in India

Monideepa Tarafdar, University of Toledo, USA

Sanjiv D. Vaidya, Indian Institute of Management Calcutta, India

EXECUTIVE SUMMARY

This case describes challenges in the adoption and implementation of IT in two public sector enterprises in the postal and distribution businesses respectively, in India. In spite of similarities in the scale of operations and the general cultural contexts, the IT adoption processes and outcomes of the two organizations were significantly different. While one failed to implement IT in its crucial processes, the other responded effectively to changes in external conditions by developing and using IT applications for critical functions. The case illustrates how differences in organizational factors such as top management commitment, unions, middle management participation, capabilities of IS professionals and specific aspects of organization culture resulted in such differences. The case is interesting and significant because it is representative of experiences of many government-aided organizations in India, which have undertaken IT modernization as a response to external changes and government mandates. The findings can also be generalized across similar organizations in other developing countries.

ORGANIZATIONAL BACKGROUND

Introduction

The adoption of IT in large public sector organizations poses some interesting challenges and issues. These are related to specific characteristics of these organizations with regard to their entrenched processes, culture, the role of bureaucracy, performance measurement criteria and decision-making processes (see for example, Caudle et al., 1991). This case describes challenges in the adoption and implementation of IT in two public sector enterprises in India. The enterprises were in the postal and distribution businesses respectively.

Public sector enterprises (PSEs), in the context of the Indian economy, are companies that are largely administered and supported by the government. They exist in different areas such as transportation, goods distribution, postal services, telecommunications, and other manufacturing and service sectors of the economy. There are different types of PSEs (Mathur et al., 1979). Some of them are statutory corporations established through legislative resolutions of the Parliament. The Parliament is the executive branch of the Government of India, similar to the House and the Senate in the United States. Many other PSEs are departmental agencies, functioning directly under a particular department of the government. Others are established as companies with limited liability under the Companies Act of India. A few PSEs, like those in the Railways sector, function exclusively under one ministry of the government.

The government plays an important role at the strategic level, in activities such as policy making and financial outlay. At the operational level, PSEs run directly by government departments are staffed through a cadre of bureaucrats and administrators. In PSEs that are established through legislative acts, professional managers and technical specialists manage the operations. These bureaucrats, administrators, professional managers and technical specialists are responsible for achieving annual objectives in terms of activities accomplished and budgetary goals. Policy implementation with respect to modernization and IT adoption is the responsibility of organizational employees, who have autonomy over operational details of the implementation process, within a broad framework specified by the government.

National Couriers Limited (NCL) was in the business of providing postal, courier and information transfer services to different parts of India. It functioned directly under a government department. The company also provided limited banking services such as money transfer, insurance and certificate of deposit services. It had about 90,000 employees working in offices in various states in the country. Eighty-five percent of the personnel of the company were unionized and were either unskilled or clerical level workers. The remaining were professionally trained administrators.

National Traders Limited (NTL) was a distributor of agricultural products, particularly food grains, to different parts of the country. It was created by a Parliament resolution. It provided services such as procurement of these products from producers, their storage and management in warehouses, and distribution to non-producing consumers through retail outlets. During the 1970s and 1980s, the organization had played a key role in encouraging farmers to increase their production, by providing them with an assured market and stable purchase prices. Subsequently, the major function of the company had been to collect part of the surplus agricultural produce, and suitably store and distribute it, so that it could be used during lean production seasons and in places where emergencies and natural calamities happened. The organization procured, distributed and transported about 22 million metric tons of produce, annually. Most of the purchasing centers were located in the northern part of the country. Consumers were located all across India and also in the islands off the southern part of the country. NTL had about 63,000 employees, 95% of whom were unionized.

Services and Processes: Brief Description

Both NCL and NTL were service organizations. The major processes of NCL were collection, sorting and delivery of articles. Articles were collected from more than half a million collection centers, sorted in 550 sorting offices and delivered through more than 100,000 delivery offices. Other processes included activities related to banking, money transfer and information transfer functions.

Some financial details about the operations of the company are provided in Table 1.

All these functions involved managing and processing significant amounts of information. In this context, the head of the operations of the eastern region observed:

> *The sheer volume of information and articles that is required to be handled is tremendous.*

The major activities of NTL related to the distribution of agricultural produce. Relevant figures in this context are provided in Tables 2 and 3.

There were four critical activities for NTL, as described next.

Table 1. Background information for National Courier's Limited

	1992-93 million	1993-94 million	1994-95 million	1995-96 million	1996-97 million	1997-98 million	1998-99 million	1999-2000 million
Total Mail (no. of articles)	13,400	13,051	13,607	13,957	15,096	15,750	16,790	17,430
Money Transfer (no. of transactions)	105	99	102	106	111	111	120	122
Money Transfer (Rs. mn) [i]	29,124	31,825	33,555	37,872	41,018	44,654	47,450	48,790

[i] *45 INR (Indian Rupee) = 1 U.S. dollar*

Table 2. Procurement of food grains from different parts of the country

Year	PROCUREMENT OF FOOD GRAINS (in * 100,000 tons)	
	WHEAT (April –March)	RICE (October – September)
1999-2000	120	185
2000-2001	150	220
2001-2002	200	215
2002-2003	185	160
2003-2004	150	170
*(As on 27.02.2004)		

Table 3. Movement of food grains moved in different parts of the country

Year	Movement of Food Grains (in Million Tons)
1996-97	25
1997-98	20
1998-99	22
1999-2000	20
2000-2001	15
2001-2002	19.5
2002-2003	26.8
2003-2004 (up to Nov'03)	15.3

1. **Purchase of agricultural produce from producers:** This was done through a network of purchase centers all over the country.
2. **Storage of the purchased produce in appropriate places and under appropriate environmental conditions:** NTL had a network of storage depots for this purpose.
3. **Interfacing and maintaining liaison with administrative authorities in different states:** This was required in order to plan for state-wise requirements of produce.
4. **Distribution planning and transportation of produce:** This function involved the transfer of produce from purchase centers to storage warehouses and then to the numerous distribution centers. It required access to good transport infrastructure, and liaising with professional transport agencies.

The overall processes of both organizations were therefore similar, in that they involved the transfer of physical goods and the accompanying information to and from different parts of the country. They also involved interfacing with government authorities at the state and national levels.

Organization Structure and Characteristics

The bureaucracy in India is typically the administrative arm of the central government and is largely responsible for turning legislation into policies and policies into practice. Bureaucrats therefore have a wide range of functions in many sectors of the economy, including the government departments. Their responsibilities can be broadly visualized in terms of two types of functions.

One, they are responsible for assisting in policy formulation in the different ministries and departments. They are also charged with the direct running of the day-to-day government functions like general administration, law enforcement, resources disbursement and tax collection. Two, they are also required to head government controlled PSEs in different industries such as utilities, postal services, nationalized banks, railways and public distribution systems for food grains. Both NCL and NTL, being public sector enterprises, were headed by a senior member of the administrative arm of the bureaucracy. They also had bureaucrats in different top management functions.

The operations of NCL were divided into four regions. Each region was headed by a regional office, with the regional manager as the executive head of the region. The regional manager was a member of senior management who supervised a team of middle management. Each region was further divided into districts, with a district office supervising the operations of each district. The head of each district office was a member of middle management. Members of junior management worked in the regional and district offices. There were about 200 districts and each district supervised the operations of a given number of collection centers, sorting offices and delivery centers, which were staffed by unionized employees and clerks. At the apex, there was one head office, from where the top management and company policymakers operated.

In a similar manner, NTL also carried out its operations through a network of administrative offices across the country. There was one central administrative office from where the top management functioned. The operations were divided into five zones and 17 regions. Each zone had a Zonal Administrative Office and each region had a regional administrative office, supervised by a zonal manager and regional manager, respectively. The regions were divided into a number of districts and each district was administered through a district office, which managed the functions of a number of purchase centers and storage warehouses. There were 123 districts. There were 12,000 purchase centers and 1,700 depots and storage warehouses. Zonal managers belonged to senior management cadre. Regional managers and district managers were middle managers. Junior managers also worked in all these offices. All employees in the management cadre were professional administrators. The company also had a number of clerical employees to carry out low-skilled functions in the different offices, purchase centers and warehouses.

The scale and scope of the operations of the company were very large. One of the senior managers in the company observed:

The scale of operations is among the largest for any organization in the country. The amount of information required to be processed is tremendous.

Although the particulars of the organizational hierarchy such as specific office names and designations of managers were different, the broad organization structures of the two organizations were similar, as shown in Figure 1. There were five levels of hierarchy and the decision-making processes were largely centralized. The top management in the apex (central) office and senior management in the zonal and regional offices was responsible for overall policy setting and strategic planning. All new initiatives and programs were designed at the higher levels, and were subsequently communicated through orders and directives to the middle and lower levels. Implementation strategies were planned by the senior management in consultation with middle management and implemented by middle management. This kind of planning and implementation structure is often a feature of public sector enterprises. This is because public sector enterprises usually operate on a large scale and scope, and hence it is more efficient to decide on policy at the top and leave the implementation to the middle managers in the various regional offices. The role of middle managers in policy implementation is therefore crucial (Caudle et al., 1991). In India, the accountability of the public sector to the people of India only further enhances the justification for rigid bureaucratic procedures. Such procedures lead to this rather strict division of labor between the senior management and the middle management.

Traditionally, both organizations were similar in that they were large and centralized, and had historically functioned in stable economic and business environments. They had been largely supported by the government and had not seen any major changes in their business strategies or processes for the past 20 years. Between 1980 and 1987, the top management of both companies was indifferent towards the use of IT and there was no commitment on the part of the organizational leaders to deploy IT in any of the functions. Further, most employees did not have any knowledge or awareness about IT, and tended to associate technology with loss of jobs. This observation has also been recorded in other organizations in India during the 1970s and 1980s. During this time, the Indian economy was a closed one and most organizations did not have any exposure to the use of IT (Nidumolu et al., 1993; Tarafdar & Vaidya, 2002b; Wolcott & Goodman, 2003).

SETTING THE STAGE (1987-1991)

External Conditions

The government financially aided NCL and, to a large extent, decided the rates for its services. NCL catered to both urban and rural segments of the population. During this time, the rural and semi urban segments accounted for over 70% of the customer base, and the company was a monopoly in this segment. Entry barriers were high because a vast distribution network was required to handle the volumes and reach in order to operate on a national scale. In the urban retail and corporate segments, the first major changes in the environment came in the late '80s and early '90s when a number of private

Figure 1. Decision hierarchy and organization structure at National Couriers Limited and National Traders Limited

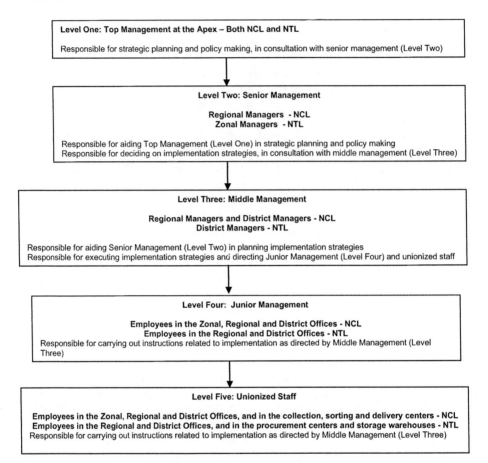

companies were set up which provided faster deliveries, although at much higher prices. Hence there was some competition in this category. However, these new competitors were too small to pose any threat to NCL on a nationwide basis. Even then, NCL did have an internal drive towards business innovation. It introduced special premium "Speed" services in 1987, which were faster and more expensive than their regular services. Corporate customers were interested in efficient and reliable service and accounted for a majority of the high value transactions through the premium services. According to a senior manager in the eastern region:

> *The products and services prior to 1987 were standard. There were no innovations. However, after 1987, we could sense some of the then happening and some impending changes in the competitive environment. Hence, even*

though we were a monopoly in the rural retail segment, we introduced new services directed towards the urban corporate and retail segments.

NTL was financially aided by the government and many of the policies regarding purchase price, selling price, and distribution requirements were decided in consultation with the government and representatives of the producers. The company was required to interact with a number of external agencies such as distribution and transport service providers in order to carry out its functions. All interactions with these external organizations were through established procedures. For example, producers were given a fixed price for their produce, and customers also paid a fixed price. Similarly, transporters were selected on the basis of tenders. There had been no significant change in most of these processes over the years. Therefore, the external environment had remained stable. In case of calamities such as floods and drought however, the company faced tremendous pressures because produce had to be rushed to specific places at all costs. The regional manager of one of the regions observed that:

Normally there are no pressures on us. We function in a regulated and financially supported environment. However in times of emergencies, we have to deliver at all costs.

Such instances however, were few and had occurred once in two or three years on an average. Moreover, in such times, NTL and other similar companies were given financial support from the government and also used their own slack resources. On the whole, NTL did not have any innate drive for business innovation. For example, it did not initiate efforts for introducing changes in its processes in a proactive manner. Its managers functioned within the parameters laid down by the government. The performance of the company was measured by the amount of produce purchased, the manner of quality control of stored produce and effectiveness of distribution. There was scope for performance slack because the company was financially supported by the government. In this context, one senior manager who had been with the company for 30 years observed:

Everyone follows standard procedures. There is no inherent drive to change and improve.

Process Descriptions and Information Processing Requirements

The primary processes for NCL included the logistical activities of sorting and transferring articles. The company also carried out limited operations related to banking functions such as money transfers and money orders.

Information processing had to be carried out quickly because article delivery times depended largely on the speed with which articles could be sorted and transported. Organizational processes were standardized through the use of standard operating procedures. Procedures were laid down for collection, sorting, delivery, after-sales activity like enquiry handling, refund, lost articles or other specific customer complaints. Tasks were structured and routine and, the context in which information had to be processed was clear. The presence of bureaucratic procedures, along with inherently simple tasks, did not leave much room for decision support requirements in the day-to-day operations. Decision making followed predictable patterns. There were well-defined rules for communicating information. All official communication was in written format. Information required for decision making was mostly available.

A senior executive explained the situation in this manner:

> *There are fixed procedures that we are trained to follow. All possible requirements can be anticipated because there is a limited set of options that customers can choose from.*

Organizational processes for NTL included functions like packing, storing and handling of the produce. These were routine, standardized and well documented. There were written instructions and well-defined procedures for different activities. For instance, there were norms for storing bags in the warehouses, for deciding how many bags would be placed in a stack, how they would be stacked, how they would be issued for distribution and so on. There were specifications for the way in which warehouses were to be constructed. There were standards for preserving the produce in the warehouses according to the desired purity and quality levels. Information regarding relevant parameters such as humidity, temperature and cleanliness were clearly specified. All official communication was in standardized formats, formal and always recorded on paper.

One of the middle managers in a regional office in the eastern region said:

> *All tasks are standardized and we have to follow standard operating procedures. There is no ambiguity.*

As far as information processing was concerned, some aspects of the company's operations required information to be processed within a given period of time. For instance, all the purchasing activities had to be completed within two to four months from the time that the produce was plucked and harvested. Transport and logistics operations involved coordination of activities across many geographical regions, and the produce had to be distributed to specific areas within a very short time, in case of disasters. The manager of one of the districts in the eastern region said:

> *There is a short span of two to three months within which we have to finish off all the purchase and storage activities. This is a time of great pressure for all of us.*

Both organizations functioned in a stable environment and were financially supported by the government. This led to the possibility of having extensive bureaucratic procedures and well-defined processes. Thus, there was not much room for ambiguity and decision support. This is a common feature in public sector organizations, and has been found to influence the adoption of decision support aids in these organizations (Mohan et al., 1990). All policy decisions regarding the adoption of new innovations were taken by the top management team in consultation with representatives of the government and communicated clearly within the organization. However, there were some differences. NCL was widely regarded as one of the best public sector organizations in India, and within the broad framework of government-mandated policies, there was considerable scope for small-scale, local-level initiatives and innovations by its middle and junior managers. NTL, on the other hand, was more prone to functioning within the confines of government mandates, and there were not many opportunities for local innovation.

IT Adoption During this Period

Basic computerization was first introduced in both these organizations in the mid-to late-1980s. This period was also marked by commencement of similar initiatives in other public sector enterprises in India (such as nationalized banks). These initiatives were largely driven by policies of the central government. To begin with, both NCL and NTL went in for applications like payroll and financial accounting at their respective central administration offices. These were later extended to their different regional offices. Overall, the IT infrastructure during this time was quite elementary and did not have any significant impact on their critical operations.

Soon after, NCL took steps to introduce some additional IT applications as well. In 1989, money transfer pairing machines were first introduced in each zone. Hitherto, all the money transfer order slips originating in a particular region and bound for all other regions were collated separately and sent to each region. This was done by all the regions, so that a number of slips changed hands everyday between all the regions. With the introduction of the computerized pairing machines, instead of counting off individual slips for each region, each region's outgoing sum was simply netted off against the incoming sum. This was a spreadsheet application in which the total amount of money ordered for each zone was collated on a spreadsheet and paired and matched for each zone. Also in 1989, counter operations for article booking were computerized in the largest office in the two largest cities. Stand-alone PCs were given to the counter clerks at these offices. This significantly reduced the waiting time for the customer and rationalized queues at the counters. Although these applications were introduced in a limited manner, it was an important step for NCL in that it had proactively implemented some IT beyond the overall parameters suggested by the government. Although the monetary investment in IT during this period was small, it nevertheless set the stage for the implementation of IT in more critical processes, in subsequent years. Further, it also served as a pilot project for demonstration and learning purposes.

Impending Changes in the External Environment

Government policies form an important aspect of the external environment for public sector organizations. Changes in these policies have often been the cause of IT deployment in organizations in developing nations in general (Albadvi, 2002; Li et al., 2002; Molla & Licker, 2002) and in India in particular (Tarafdar & Vaidya, 2002a).

In 1991, the Government of India took a policy decision to liberalize the Indian economy. This decision resulted in an increase in external pressures for public sector undertakings in many industries including telecommunications, steel, banking and transportation, among others. The resulting changes in the business and economic environment had implications for adoption of IT in both NCL and NTL. There were also overall pressures for process re-engineering, modernization and human resource development.

CASE DESCRIPTION (1992-2000)

Changes in the External Environment

Economic liberalization in the early 1990s resulted in changes in the external and competitive environment for both organizations. Liberalization provided enormous opportunities for firms from developed economies to set up manufacturing, service or distributing units in India. This resulted in the entry of many of these companies in a number of Indian industries including banking, financial institutions and the manufacturing sector (see for example, Cavusgil et al., 2002; Joshi & Joshi, 1998; Tarafdar & Vaidya, 2002, 2003). Many of these companies had advanced IT-enabled processes. This created pressures for improved performance of processes among Indian organizations. There were also pressures from different customer segments for more flexibility and better service.

As far as NCL was concerned, private companies — from both India and outside — that provided courier and fax services entered the urban markets, and targeted the retail and corporate segments. There was also an increase in the volume of business related mail. Some customer segments like businesses, government organizations and institutional bodies required faster delivery, even if it was at a higher cost. Thus, increasing competition gave rise to a need to segment customers on the basis of specific needs and provide customized service options. Therefore, a Business Development Cell was set up in 1996 to design and develop a market for value-added premium products for specific customer segments. New services were introduced for corporate customers, and the accent was on speed and reliability rather than on cost. Utility payment and e-mail services were also introduced.

That the organization perceived the pressures to be somewhat high can be gauged by the following statement, which appeared in the Annual Report of 1997-1998:

> *... will spend 65% of its plan budget on the induction of technology with a view to improving and upgrading the quality of service...developing and providing new value added services and products. NCL will continue to look at the technology options so that the postal products and services can be re-oriented to the needs of the customers.*

The second change as a result of economic liberalization was related to the role of the government. As mentioned before, the government can, through its policies and regulations, influence the adoption of IT (Nidumolu & Goodman, 1996; Rainey et al., 1976). Toward the later part of the eighties, the government laid down certain policies and mandates for adoption of IT in all major public sector enterprises in India, across different industries. Public sector banks, manufacturing units and service organizations embarked upon IT modernization programs. These organizations typically generated and processed huge volumes of transaction data due to their large scope of operations. Consequently, the most pressing requirements were for transaction processing systems.

Initiating and Implementing IT Adoption:
Two Contrasting Approaches

Both NCL and NTL initiated a program for organization-wide computerization in response to the government's mandates.

According to Caudle et al. (1991), there are four major concerns that are required to be addressed for adoption and implementation of IT in public sector organizations. The two organizations addressed these four factors in different ways.

1.   **Goals of IT adoption and identification of information requirements:** Market signals and profits guide companies in the private sector. In contrast, the public sector faces different goals, many of which are not necessarily related to financial performance. These could be related to efficiency and quality of customer service, scale of operations, the different kinds of customers served, social objectives and addressing political influences (Caudle et al., 1991). Thus, it is not always possible to directly link the adoption of IT with financial parameters, particularly for public sector enterprises. Hence, one of the ways to approach IT planning is to identify improvements that are required in concerned critical processes, and implement IT in the individual activities entailed in those processes. Identification of information requirements thus forms an important part of the planning for IT adoption and implementation in public sector organizations.

National Couriers Limited

Interviews with the head of the eastern region illustrated the process of identification of important information processing activities and requirements at NCL:

> *We had already implemented computerized transaction processing systems in the payroll and financial accounting functions, starting in 1988. After the government mandates in 1991, we identified three critical areas in order to focus our computerization efforts. The first was the handling of and sorting registered mail articles. This process was the key to speed, efficiency and customer satisfaction in our operations. The second was the transfer of information related to the status of mailed articles, money transfer and banking services. Information transfer processes formed our second largest area of operations after mail handling. The third focus for computerization was information exchange activities within our offices. These included sharing of files, data and other resources such as printers. Our computerization efforts during the period 1992-1999 were concentrated largely in these three areas.*

Between 1992 and 1999, a number of new information technologies were introduced at NCL. In 1992, computerized mail handling and sorting was introduced in the two busiest centers in the country. This reduced the time required for sorting and directing articles by half. Computerized systems for article booking, tracking and delivery systems for select cities were introduced in 1997-98 in select cities (refer to Figure 2). This sped up the booking and delivery procedure, and enabled customers to keep track of their articles.

Figure 2. Computerized booking, tracking and delivery system at National Couriers Limited

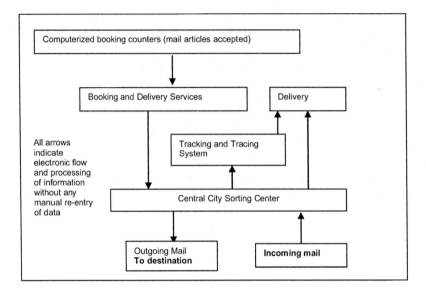

A VSAT network consisting of 75 terminals was installed for this purpose. The articles would be booked with the help of a computerized system at the booking office, and the information would be transferred via a modem connection to the Central City sorting center, where the tracking system was installed. This center was connected through the VSAT network to other sorting centers. Customers could call up at the sorting center and find out the status of the booked articles. Computerized money transfer services were introduced in 1998. This was also done through the VSAT network. Individual offices were connected to the network through a leased line modem connection. This reduced the transit time of money orders from nearly a week to a few seconds. In 1997-1998, office operations were computerized and put on a WNT-based local area network. This enabled the sharing of files, data and other resources, and significantly enhanced the efficiency of office operations.

The approach used by NCL has been referred to as the "functional approach" to IT planning (Nidumolu & Goodman, 1996). Organizations that follow this approach believe adoption of IT is desirable because it can improve the timeliness of information flow and reduce process cycle times. NCL was able to respond effectively to the external conditions and government mandates through deployment of IT applications and infrastructure in many critical functions. The financial expenditure on IT between 1990 and 1999 was INR 1000 million,[1] which was 75% of the total expenditure on modernization during this period and about 2.75% of the organization's revenues. This was relatively much higher than that during the previous 10 years.

According to the head of operations of the eastern region:

For the first time, substantial budgets were being allocated annually, for the computerization process.

A senior manager in the eastern region further described the possible financial implications in the following way:

The areas that we targeted for IT adoption covered 65% to 70% of our operations. So we expected to see significant cost savings in around 70% of our functions.

National Traders Limited

A member of the top management, who had been with the organization for more than 30 years, described the overall phenomenon of IT planning and adoption at NTL in the following manner:

We tried to follow the general instructions from the government, in identifying potential areas of IT adoption. The first step in this regard was the computerization of all high volume transaction processes. We decided to begin by computerizing the payroll and financial accounting processes.

In the mid-1990s a UNIX mainframe system was installed at the central office. This was used in batch processing applications for calculation of accounts, reporting of produce inventory and stock positions, and payroll accounting. In the late 1990s, the mainframe system was converted to a PC-based LAN. An ORACLE-based client server system was installed and the mainframe data were transferred to this. The administrative offices in the different regions carried out the same functions at the regional level using PC-based dBase applications.

In 1998, NTL connected its central administrative office, five zonal offices and 17 regional offices through VSAT links. The district offices were connected to the respective regional offices through dial-up modem connections. At the time of the study, there were about 50 PCs at the central headquarters, four to five PCs in each zonal office, two in each regional office and one in each district office. The depots communicated with the district offices through postal mail and the districts communicated with the regional offices through modems. Forty percent of the data transferred between depots and district, regional and zonal offices related to the inventory and stock position. Forty percent related to financial information and 20% to payroll data. Stock and inventory data were sent in by the depots and district offices to the regional and zonal offices manually, or through leased line modem connections. The regional and zonal offices consolidated the data and then transferred them to the central administrative office through VSAT as well as on paper. Data from all the regional and zonal offices were again consolidated at the central office. Reports about stock positions and requirements were generated for senior managers at both the head office and the regions. The transfer of stock-related information took place on a weekly basis from the depots to the zones and subsequently to the headquarters. A central server housed the consolidated data from all the regions. All the communication links were backed up by traditional mail and fax systems. The IT infrastructure is shown in Figure 3.

The investment in IT acquisition, maintenance and training during the period between 1992 and 1999 was INR 35 million, which was less than 5% of the total capital expenditure during this period.

2.   **Management of bureaucracy and paperwork:** The public sector produces a lot of paperwork that results in a proliferation of forms and paper (Caudle et al., 1991). All these records need to be computerized in an integrated manner during the process of computerization, in order to make electronic transfer of information possible between offices and minimize manual re-entry of data. Hence it has been suggested (Mohan et al., 1990) that a central governing structure be set up. This structure should oversee the integration of IT management with records management and other information resource management areas.

For NCL, the different systems were designed such that seamless integration and flow of information between different functions was possible, in a limited manner, as shown in Figure 2. For instance, in the computerized booking and tracking system, article information generated at the time of booking was transferred using electronic means through intermediate stages, all the way to the central sorting centers. Similarly, office information related to administrative activities was shared electronically within each office. These capabilities were also planned to be extended to cover electronic transfer among different offices.

For NTL, information transferred from the depots and district offices was manually reentered at the regional offices prior to consolidation and transferred to the Head Office, as shown in Figure 3. At the Head Office also, information was partly reentered manually before the generation of management reports.

Figure 3. Information technology infrastructure National Traders Limited

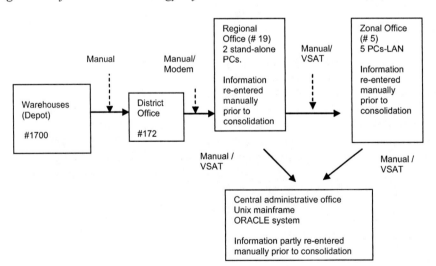

3.   **Role of top management:** The top management plays a key role in deciding the thrust and direction of IT adoption in public sector organizations (Nidumolu & Goodman, 1996). This is because the planning and decision structure with respect to implementation of changes is usually centralized.

National Couriers Limited

At NCL, there was a change in the top management in 1991 as a new CEO joined the organization. The new top management team was favorably disposed towards IT adoption and took many proactive initiatives in this regard. NCL was a member of the Universal Postal Union, and hence information about the latest IT applications in similar organizations around the world was available to the top executives. It was the thinking, planning and drive of top management that led to the introduction of the early IT initiatives. A middle manager in the eastern region office described the new priorities of the top management in this manner:

After 1991, a number of new thrusts towards IT adoption have been generated at the central office. Our new CEO is enthusiastic about the introduction of IT, and is aware of the possible areas of application. Seminars are often organized to educate and inform us about the use of IT in postal services worldwide.

All decisions regarding IT planning and deployment were centralized. However, the implementation of IT initiatives was decentralized. According to a member of the top management at the central office:

We tell the regions what the overall plans are, regarding the purchasing of hardware, installation of software and the applications required to be used. Broad decisions regarding all IT applications, hardware and software are taken at the headquarters in consultation with the regions and communicated to the zones and regions. The zones and regions have the power to make their own implementation decisions and purchases within given financial limits.

National Traders Limited

At NTL, the top management was not, in principle, unfavorably oriented towards IT. They did realize the benefits that could accrue from the use of IT, in view of the size of the company and its scale of operations. However, they were not proactive about identifying areas where the company could benefit from IT. The senior managers and policy makers were typically professional administrators and bureaucrats, and the average age was more than 50 years. They did not have any knowledge of emerging IT applications and their use by similar companies around the world. Nor were they comfortable with the use of computers. They were content to depend on the government for direction and instructions on IT adoption.

One of the middle managers who had worked in the organization for the last 15 years said:

...If the government had not made certain suggestions, computerization might have come to NTL even later than the late 1980s.

Interviews with some of the senior managers revealed attitudes that varied from measured tolerance for IT, "It seems to be useful, but it is not indispensable," to downright rejection, "Computers are just expensive typewriters."

4. **Role of middle management in driving IT implementation:** There is evidence that middle managers play a very critical role in driving IT implementation and use in public sector organizations (Caudle et al., 1991). This is because these organizations are usually large, with multiple levels of decision hierarchy (Figure 1), and it is not possible for top management to oversee the details of the implementation processes. Further, middle managers have considerable bureaucratic power in the individual departments and units. Hence, while the top management is responsible for policy setting and strategic planning with respect to IT adoption, it is the middle managers who play the most crucial role in driving the implementation processes within different organizational units.

National Couriers Limited

The middle management influenced IT adoption at NCL in two ways.

First, they were actively involved in framing the specifics of IT adoption policies and driving implementation initiatives within their units. They used their collective organizational power to frame implementation schedules and timelines. They also developed programs for end-user training and education. This was a crucial aspect of the implementation process, given the large number of unskilled and unionized employees in the organization, who viewed IT as a potential threat to their jobs. In this context, one of the middle managers observed:

> *We encouraged the clerical and low skilled employees to get familiar with the PC, and start out by just playing games. We hoped that once they became comfortable with the use of PCs, they would be able to appreciate the benefits of computerization. We also conducted education programs regarding the use of IT in organizations. Further we took steps to assure them that their jobs were safe. Throughout the entire computerization process, there was not a single day in which there was a loss of working hours because of union problems.*

In this connection, studies in the domain of IT adoption suggest that IT acceptance and innovation at the grassroots levels in different end-user units are crucial to the adoption of IT by an organization (Agarwal & Prasad, 1998; Nambisan, 1999; Rockart, 1988; Vaidya, 1991). In many developing countries, IT is seen to be the cause of reduction in opportunities for employment, and there is a hostile attitude to IT adoption and acceptance, not only at the level of semi-skilled and unskilled employees, but also by middle management. This has been a crucial factor in the introduction and management of IT in developing countries (Jantavongso & Li, 2002; Tarafdar & Vaidya, 2003).

The middle management also played an effective role as IS professionals. While the overall head of the IS function was a member of the senior management, IS activities in each regional and district office were supervised by middle management. These managers were also responsible for IT implementation in the delivery and sorting centers. In other words, middle managers were the IS heads in their respective functional departments. They supervised teams of junior managers who were responsible for installing and maintaining the hardware and software. These junior and middle management members had received technical training and were hence capable of managing the technical aspects of project implementation and systems maintenance. This kind of an "indigenous" implementation strategy is often followed in public sectors. This is because in such organizations there are constraints on hiring and firing employees. Hence existing employees are retrained and reallocated to the newer functions (Nidumolu & Goodman, 1996). Thus there was no separate IS department in NCL. Members of middle and junior management were responsible for IT implementation.

The middle management IS professionals also played an important part as IT champions. The role of IT champions in driving IT adoption has been well documented (Beath, 1991). The middle managers in NCL were credible and commanded authority by virtue of their positions. They had a good working relationship with the top management as well as the unskilled and clerical workers in the company. They were powerful enough to influence decisions at the higher levels, and saw to it that the resources required were made available. Initially there was considerable resistance — especially from the unionized staff — but this was neutralized through the efforts of middle and junior managers. In fact, in many instances, some of the unionized staff subsequently became advocates of the IT-related changes, after having gone through the training processes. They became IT champions themselves and saw to it that strong resistance groups were convinced and neutralized.

Various studies have explored the role of IS professionals in influencing the adoption of IT. IS professionals have a positive impact on IT adoption in the organization when they are technically aware of the possibilities from IT, are competent at developing new IS and maintaining existing IS, and are capable of promptly solving end-user needs (Al-Khaldi et al., 1999; Dvorak et al., 1994; Swanson, 1994). At NCL, the IS professionals influenced IT implementation through their traditional organizational power as middle managers. They were able to effectively carry out project management and end-user training; they were also able to ensure that resources were available. This case therefore illustrates a new dimension of the role of IS professionals in driving IT adoption and considerably enhances similar preliminary findings by Caudle et al. (1991).

National Traders Limited

The central IS department at NTL was headed by a senior manager who reported to the head of the finance function. He was somewhat aware of the possibilities of IT and had some limited ideas of its usefulness for the company. He supervised a team of 60 central IS employees. Out of these 60 people, 10 had a diploma or some other professional training in different aspects of software development, and could develop applications on dBase, MS Access and ORACLE. About 30 people were data entry operators, whose tasks were to key in and consolidate the data from the zonal, regional and district offices. All these employees had received the requisite training and looked after various functions in the IS department. They worked in the central administrative headquarters, and were responsible for centralized consolidation and collation of data from the regions. They also designed and implemented training programs for data entry staff in the different regions. They looked after incremental modifications to the existing applications. Further, they managed third-party vendors who carried out maintenance of existing hardware and the development of new applications.

The IS departments in the zones and regions comprised junior-level employees who had been transferred from other departments after training. They had no formal education in computer hardware or software. They were responsible for entering and consolidating the data received from the districts and depots, and generating relevant reports for senior managers at the zonal offices. At the time of the study, about 200 such employees, mostly staff and junior managers, had been trained in various applications, and had later been shifted to dedicated IS functions. They themselves were reluctant to use computers. Third-party vendors carried out the maintenance work.

The IS manager was not powerful and senior enough to convince top management to make resources available for any IT initiative other than the most basic applications. He had no significant power to independently make important decisions relating to IT deployment. Moreover the IS professionals at the central office did not have any control over whether or not the regional heads would actually implement specific IT applications. The IS department had not met with much success in this regard and there had been stiff resistance in many cases. This greatly hindered the penetration of IT because regional heads had independent authority over IT implementation initiatives in their areas.

The chief of the central IS function said:

The implementation and use of computers in the offices is completely decentralized. We cannot force anyone to start using computers. Ultimately the extent of IT use depends on the policies of the respective regions and zones.

There were more than 60,000 employees in the company, 85% of whom performed low skilled and clerical jobs. Similar to the situation at NCL initially, employees were not favorably biased towards IT, because they feared that they would lose their jobs. Hence they tried various ways to express their opinions in this regard. For example, very often, when reports were not made available on time to senior managers, subordinate junior employees would excuse themselves by saying that the computers were not working or the relevant officer in charge of taking the print-outs was not available. They would even suggest that such problems did not exist before computers were introduced. The reluctance of employees to use computers is exemplified by the fact that those who used them had to be given monetary incentives. Further, most of the middle mangers and even some of the senior managers in the regions were against the deployment of IT. There was limited penetration of IT into the user departments. Senior managers did not directly use computers. They would ask data entry operators to enter data and furnish printouts.

The similarities and differences between the two organizations have been described in Table 4.

Table 4. Similarities and differences between NTL and NCL

	National Couriers Limited	National Traders Limited
Similarities		
Size	90,000	63,000
Overall Organization Structure	Multiple levels of hierarchy, centralized planning	Multiple levels of hierarchy, centralized planning
Public Sector Enterprises and the accompanying characteristics	Having functioned in stable business and economic environments. Historically supported by the government. Working under overall policy directives of the government. Subject to the IT adoption and modernization plans of the government. Staffed by bureaucrats. Professional managers and technical specialists who were responsible for tactical and operational tasks.	Having functioned in stable business and economic environments. Historically supported by the government. Working under overall policy directives of the government. Subject to the IT adoption and modernization plans of the government. Staffed by bureaucrats. Professional managers and technical specialists who were responsible for tactical and operational tasks.
Service Organizations	Postal Sector	Distribution Sector

CURRENT CHALLENGES AND PROBLEMS (2000 AND BEYOND)

In spite of similarities in their overall nature and scale of operations and historical and cultural contexts, the IT adoption processes and outcomes in the two companies were considerably different. While NTL failed to implement IT in its crucial processes, NCL was able to respond effectively to the external conditions and government mandates through organization-wide deployment of IT applications and infrastructure in many critical functions.

National Couriers Limited

The computerization process at NCL took place in two distinct phases. In the first phase, from 1987 to 1991, computerization was limited and driven by the requirements of high-volume transaction processing. During this period, the company used IT for very basic and rudimentary transaction processing operations. It was in the Support Mode (McFarlan et al., 1983) or Delayed Sector (Earl, 1989). These two modes are the first stages

Table 4. Similarities and differences between NTL and NCL (cont.)

	National Couriers Limited	National Traders Limited
Differences		
Goals of IT adoption	Based on systematic identification of critical processes (Article handling and sorting, Information management of mailed articles, Information exchange within offices) and their computerization. IT investment between 1990 and 1999 was INR 900 million, which was 70% of the total expenditure on modernization.	Followed general instructions from the government and did not attempt to identify critical processes. Computerization aimed at basic transaction processing, and not at critical processes. IT investment between 1992 and 1999 was INR 35 million, which was less 5% of the total expenditure on modernization
Management of paperwork	Different systems were designed so as to try to enable seamless integration and information transfer through electronic means. This was a consequence of an integrated approach to records management	In absence of an integrated approach to records management, information transferred from the depots to the district offices was re-entered manually before the generation of management reports.
Role of Top management	Favorably disposed towards IT adoption. Kept abreast of the latest IT developments in similar organizations in other countries. Resources were allocated to new IT thrusts.	Not, in principle, favorably oriented towards IT. Not proactive about identifying areas that could potentially benefit from IT, beyond the obvious high transaction areas. Not comfortable with the use of computers and depended on the government for instruction and directions on IT adoption.
Role of middle management and the IS department	Actively involved in framing IT adoption policies and driving IT implementation efforts, schedules and timelines. Supervised IS activities in the regions and districts, and took on the role of IS professionals. Acted as IT champions, generated grassroots awareness and interest, and developed management and union buy-in for IT adoption efforts.	IS department was headed by a senior manager who reported to the head of the finance function. Junior level employees were responsible for data entry, data consolidation and report generation. The IS head did not have any control over the implementation issues and schedules in the regional offices. Middle management was reluctant to use computers and depended on junior management to provide reports. They did not participate in or influence the IT adoption process in any way.

of IT adoption in organizations where IT is not fundamentally essential for the smooth running of operations of the company. It is used to accomplish nonessential and noncritical tasks, and the IS department functions as a back-room support department, with no participation in functions like strategic planning and implementation.

The second phase of computerization between 1992 and 2000 saw an acceleration of the computerization process. The acceleration was partly in response to government mandates and partly as a result of the enthusiasm of the new leadership about IT. During this period, NCL went through the Turnaround Stage (McFarlan et al., 1983). IT became increasingly crucial to the future development of the organization. There was a change in focus, as far as IT planning and implementation were concerned. New applications were developed and there was an increase in IT investment. At the time this study was conducted, different applications had been introduced in a limited number of offices, and covered about 40% of the operations of the company. The Annual Report of 1994-95 described the induction of computerization in this manner:

> ... NCL has made a gradual and phased attempt to introduce information technology into the postal system, so as to provide better services to its customers ...

The most important impact of IT had been to increase operational efficiencies, and IT was accorded a high priority by the top management. Hence the organization was well positioned to move to the next level of IT use, that is, the Factory Mode (McFarlan et al., 1983) or the Dependent Sector (Earl, 1989). This would include the extension of current applications to more offices and the development of more sophisticated applications. The challenge before NCL was therefore to transform from a Turnaround organization into a Factory organization. One of the most important aspects of the Factory Mode is to ensure that IT is delivered efficiently and reliably. This implies that resource requirements and budgets be correctly estimated (Earl, 1989). In this context, Mohan et al. (1990) suggest that since public sector organizations operate under fixed and often tight budgets, an inability to logically derive and clearly communicate IS budget requirements is a primary reason for these organizations not allocating adequate resources for IT adoption. A similar problem existed at NCL also, in that there were no budget-driven planning processes that could broaden the scope of the existing IT applications.

National Traders Limited

NTL was an interesting organization to study because it was large and there was significant potential for the use of IT. However, the organization did not use IT for any but the most basic functions. This was because there was a strong overall negative inclination towards IT adoption and use among the middle and junior management. For instance, none of the departmental heads at the head office or in the regional and zonal offices used computers for the latest available inventory positions. They would ask their secretaries for the relevant paper files or would simply ask their immediate subordinates over the phone.

One senior manager observed:

Anyway, I have to ask for most of the information over the phone or through fax. So what is the use of the computer in tracking the movement of the stock?

Lack of enthusiasm among managers in public sector enterprises for using IS has been documented by Mohan et al. (1990). The primary reasons for this are a low comfort level with the use of computers and a lack of awareness of applications relevant to the organization. Nidumolu and Goodman (1996) suggest that perceptions towards IT can change from unfavorable to favorable, as more projects are undertaken and more functions are computerized.

At the time this study was conducted, IT was used for routine administrative tasks, and not for any critical activities like logistics and distribution planning. Hence IT was not crucial to the achievement of the strategic objectives of the firm. Moreover, all electronic information was also stored in paper format. Transfer of information was both electronic and paper based. The challenge for NTL therefore was to move from the Support Mode to the Turnaround Mode (McFarlan et al., 1983), and increase the scope of existing IT applications. At the time of writing, they were pilot testing the use of a software for managing distribution and storage of food grains.

Change Management Issues

Change management has been suggested as an especially important issue in government organizations because of their entrenched processes (Caudle et al., 1991). In fact, the adoption of IT in the nationalized banks in India, which commenced in the mid-1980s, had been fraught with issues regarding acceptance of process changes and the fear of job losses due to automation. Employee unions, perceiving that their concerns had not been adequately addressed, had offered considerable resistance and had significantly slowed the process of IT adoption in the banks (Joshi & Joshi, 2002). Hence it is anticipated that change management issues would be crucial to the continued infusion and diffusion of IT at NTL and NCL.

The first aspect of change management had to do with overcoming resistance at different levels of the two organizations, especially at NTL. In a study of e-government initiatives in the Indian state of Kerala, Kumar (2003) reports that top management drive has been an important issue in driving IT adoption in various government departments and has facilitated the acceptance of IT at lower organizational levels. In this regard NCL had so far been able to manage differences between the various units and had been able to convince unions and clerical staff about the benefits of IT adoption, largely through the efforts of its middle and top management.

This process had been more difficult at NTL, given that the top and middle management themselves were not quite convinced about the usefulness of IT and that they had not proactively driven its adoption. As Joshi and Joshi (2002) have pointed out, it is relatively easier to work towards middle and lower management commitment after top management commitment has been secured.

It has been observed that supervisors may often be reluctant to adopt IT in their departments because of possible reductions in head count, which might lead to a decrease in their span of control. This may partially explain the reluctance of middle and junior management cadres to adopt IT, especially in NTL. The middle mangers were afraid of losing headcount in their departments as a result of the junior management receiving training and getting relocated to IT-based functions. Similarly, junior management was apprehensive about the reduction in the number of unionized employees, the resultant loss in their own power and possible backlash from the labor unions.

The second aspect of change management was that of managing the work environment during the change process. Studies by Amabile (1996) have suggested that the work environment often becomes negative in times of new technology implementation and significant business process changes. This is because the difficulties associated with adjusting to the changes often result in collective cynicism and confusion. Such conditions stifle creativity and motivation. This was observed in NTL, where the new IT was met with collective skepticism from all levels of the organization.

Public sector organizations are characterized by complex performance measurement criteria. The lack of a clearly defined bottomline in most cases leads to a focus on inputs and budgets, rather than on outputs and productivity measures. Economic liberalization in India has resulted in an emphasis on service quality, process efficiency and overall modernization in both the public and private sectors (Wolcott & Goodman, 2003). The challenges before NCL and NTL would be to use IT for enhancing their service quality, for increasing the efficiency of their operations and to appropriately manage their IT adoption processes. In absence of such an effort, both organizations would be burdened with high-cost operations and increasingly dissatisfied customers.

REFERENCES

Agarwal, R., & Prasad, J. (1998). The antecedents and consequents of user perceptions in information technology adoption. *Decision Support Systems, 22*(1), 15-29.

Al-Khaldi, M.A., & Wallace, R.S.O. (1999). The influence of attitudes on personal computer utilisation among knowledge workers: The case of Saudi Arabia. *Information and Management, 36*(4), 185-204.

Amabile, T., Conti, R., Coon, H., Lazenby, J., & Herron, M. (1996). Assessing the work environment for creativity. *Academy of Management Journal, 13*(5), 1154-1184.

Beath, C.M. (1991). Supporting the information technology champion. *MIS Quarterly, 15*(3), 155-371.

Caulde, S.R., Gorr, W.L., & Newcomer, K.E. (1991). Key information systems management issues for the public sector. *MIS Quarterly, 15*(2), 171-188.

Cavusgil, S.T., Ghauri, P.N., & Agarwal, M.R. (2002). *Doing business in emerging markets: Entry and negotiation strategies.* CA: Sage Publications.

Dvorak, R., Dean, D., & Singer, M. (1994). Accelerating IT innovation. *The McKinsey Quarterly,* 123-135.

Earl, M.J. (1989). *Management strategies for information technology.* London: Prentice Hall.

Jantavongso, S., & Li, K.Y.R. (2002, May). E-business in Thailand: Social and cultural issues. In M. Khosrow-Pour (Ed.), *Issues and Trends of IT Management in Contemporary Organizations. Proceedings of Information Resources Management Association Conference* (pp. 443-446).

Joshi, V.C., & Joshi, V.C. (2002). *Managing Indian banks* (2nd ed.). CA: Sage Publications.

Khera, S.S. (1979). Public sector management. In B.C. Mathur, K. Diesh, & C.C. Sekharan (Eds.), *Management in Government*. Government of India, Ministry of Information and Broadcasting, Publications Division.

Kumar, A. (2003). E-government and efficiency, accountability and transparency: ASEAN Executive Seminar on e-Government. *International Journal of Information Systems in Developing Countries, 12*(2), 1-15.

Lachman, R. (1985). Public and private sector differences: CEOs' perceptions of their role environments. *Academy of Management Journal, 28*(3), 671-679.

Li, Q., Zhang, X., Sun, C., & Wang, S. (2002, May). Strategies of securities electronic commerce in China: Implications of comparative analyses between China and other countries. In M. Khosrow-Pour (Ed.), *Issues and Trends of IT Management in Contemporary Organizations. Proceedings of the Information Resources Management Association Conference*, Seattle, WA (pp. 1080-1083).

McFarlan, F.W., McKenney, J.L., & Pyburn, P. (1983). The information archipelago: Plotting a course. *Harvard Business Review, 61*(1), 145-156.

Mohan, L., Holstein, W.K., & Adams, R.B. (1990). EIS: It can work in the public sector. *MIS Quarterly, 14*(4), 435-448.

Molla, A., & Licker, P.S. (2002, May). PERM: A model of e-commerce adoption in developing countries. In M. Khosrow-Pour (Ed.), *Issues and trends in IT Management in Contemporary Organizations. Proceedings of the Information Resources Management Association Conference,* Seattle, WA (pp. 527-530).

Moynihan, T. (1990). What chief executives and senior managers want from their IT departments. *MIS Quarterly, 14*(1), 15-25.

Nambisan, S. (1999). Organisational mechanisms for enhancing user innovation in information technology. *MIS Quarterly, 23*(3), 365-395.

Nidumolu, S.R., & Goodman, S.E. (1993). Computing in India: An Asian elephant learning to dance. *Communications of the ACM, 36*(4).

Nidumolu., S.R., Goodman, S.E., Vogel, D.R., & Danowitz, A.K. (1996). Information technology for local administration support: The Governorates project in Egypt. *MIS Quarterly, 20*(2), 197-224.

Rainey, H.G., Backoff, R., & Levine, C. (1976). Comparing public and private organizations. *Public Administration Review, 36*(2), 233-244.

Rockart, J.F. (1988). The line takes the leadership: IS management in a wired society. *Sloan Management Review, 29*(4), 57-64.

Swanson, E.B. (1994). Information systems innovation in organizations. *Management Science, 40*(9), 1069-1091.

Tarafdar, M., & Vaidya, S.D. (2002). Evolution of the use of IT for e-business at century financial services: An analysis of internal and external facilitators and inhibitors. *Journal of IT Cases and Applications, 4*(4), 49-76.

Tarafdar, M., & Vaidya, S.D. (2003). Challenges in the adoption of information technology at Sunrise Industries: The case of an Indian firm. *Annals of Cases in Information Technology, Volume 6* (pp. 457-479).

Vaidya, S.D. (1991, December 26-29). End user computing: An Indian perspective. *Proceedings of the Indian Computing Congress* (pp. 533-541).

Wolcott, P., & Goodman, S. (2003). Global diffusion of the Internet in India: Is the elephant learning to dance? *Communications of the Association for Information Systems, 11,* 560-646.

ENDNOTE

[1]   45 INR (Indian Rupee) = 1 U.S. Dollar

Monideepa Tarafdar is assistant professor at the University of Toledo in Ohio. She has an undergraduate degree in physics and a graduate degree in telecommunications & electronics engineering from the University of Calcutta, India. Her doctoral degree is from the Indian Institute of Management Calcutta. Her current research and teaching interests are in the areas of strategic information systems management, management of IT, enterprise systems and organizational aspects of IS. Her teaching has been in the areas of management information systems, data management, data communications and e-commerce. Her research has appeared in the Journal of Information Technology Cases and Applications, Journal of Global Information Technology Management *and* System Dynamics: An International Journal of Policy Modeling.

Sanjiv D. Vaidya is currently associate professor with the Management Information Systems Group at the Indian Institute of Management Calcutta, India. He holds a BTech in electrical engineering from the Indian Institute of Technology Bombay, and an MBA and doctorate from the Indian Institute of Management Calcutta. He has spent several years in Indian industry and has held positions in the operations and IT functions. He has also worked in the capacity of a principal advisor on strategy matters for a leading IT organization in India. His research interests are approaches and processes for information systems strategy formulation, impact of IT on organizations, end-user computing, DSS and knowledge management and e-business. His research work has been primarily of the theory building type. He has publications in Indian and international conferences and a book of strategic use of IT. His teaching interests are IS/IT strategy and management, and e-business strategies. He also participates extensively in training corporate executives.

This case was previously published in *Journal of Cases on Information Technology*, 7(1), pp. 111-135, © 2005.

Chapter XIV

Mobile Technology

Paul Cragg, University of Canterbury, New Zealand

Prue Chapman, Mobile Technology, New Zealand

EXECUTIVE SUMMARY

Mobile Technology (MT) is a small/medium-sized electronics manufacturer that has been very successful and grown rapidly in recent years. Its innovative products are exported to many parts of the world. The firm relies heavily on information technology and has many staff with very sophisticated computer expertise, yet it has no IS department and has only just appointed an IS manager. The firm's IS staff are part of an EDP team that provides IS services to all parts of MT. However, the firm is soon to be restructured into nine separate business units. This case focuses on where the firm should place its IS staff following this restructuring. The main alternatives facing management are for either a centralised or decentralised IS department.

BACKGROUND

Mobile Technology is based in Christchurch, a city that has become a major centre for electronics manufacturing in New Zealand. MT specialises in the design and manufacture of radio communications products, particularly trunking systems, base stations, mobile radios and hand held radios. Its products are used by police forces, utility organisations, transport fleets and taxi operators in many parts of the world. MT is part of an electronics industry that has grown at a high rate; electronics exports from New Zealand averaged 30% growth per year during the 1990s.

Company History

James Caddick started designing and assembling mobile radios in 1947 after returning from World War II. This small business was the predecessor of Mobile Technology, which James Caddick founded in 1969 with a staff of 12 people.

During the mid-1970s those initial products developed into an award-winning mini-phone series of mobile radios, and by 1979, it also included handheld radios and base stations. At this stage over 25% of production was being exported, staff numbers had risen to approximately 220, and the first wholly-owned subsidiary was opened in the UK. The company experienced further growth during the 1980s and released several new products, completed major investments in advanced production technology, and opened three new overseas subsidiaries.

By the firm's 25th anniversary in 1994, the head office remained in Christchurch, New Zealand, but the number of wholly-owned, offshore subsidiaries had grown to seven, with 90% of products being exported to over 80 countries worldwide. The remaining 10% was sold through the eight branches of the New Zealand subsidiary MT Communications. The subsidiaries also sold complementary products from other firms. By 1998 the total MT Group employed over 800 staff worldwide. The Group continues to work at increasing market share in well established markets, as well as fostering customers in new markets, such as Asia, Russia, and South Africa.

Mobile Technology is a privately owned company, which in recent years has experienced sales growth exceeding 25% per annum. It has consistently traded very profitably and invests most profits back into the business. The company won the 'Exporter of the Year' award presented at the New Zealand Trade Development Board awards ceremony in 1994. Growth is forecasted to continue at 20-30% per year, requiring significant investment in new product development and manufacturing capability.

MT Products

Mobile Technology (MT) has had a philosophy of design excellence and of manufacturing quality products. Its success is due to a long-established commitment to produce world-class mobile radio equipment, second to none. As a result, MT has become known for providing reliable and effective radio communications.

MT products use conventional analogue transmission, trunking technology, and quasi-synchronous communication systems. MT products can be integrated to provide a complete system solution. Its major radio telephone competitors are the world giants of Motorola, Philips, and Nokia.

MT Operations

MT business operations include research and development of new products, importing electronic componentry, manufacturing, marketing, exporting, and distributing radio communications equipment.

As a privately-owned business that has grown from a small operation, Mobile Technology has managed to maintain a family firm atmosphere through the personal touch of James Caddick. This is an unusual balance among a team of highly skilled professionals, which is slowly being lost as the company grows.

Differences in business culture exist across the firm. This is particularly noticeable between the manufacturing area and the engineering area. Most employees in manufacturing clock in and out of work and follow written procedures in order to build a quality product. Most employees in engineering tend to work more flexible hours and find each project they work on is different from the last.

Internal challenges are most often addressed on a team basis, with the active encouragement of cross-functional team members. Plenty of teams exist, with many new ones being formed. The internal structure is relatively flat, and involvement in continuous improvement programs is encouraged at all levels to help gain ownership of procedures and policies.

Research and development is an essential and ongoing aspect within the electronics industry so MT invests 10 to 12% on R&D. Skilled employees and sophisticated IT and other equipment are vital for innovation and keeping ahead of competition. MT employs a large multinational design team of engineers, scientists, and technicians. Products are designed using computer-aided design (CAD) tools, and undergo rigorous in-house tests by MT Type Approval before being certified by external organisations in order to meet international standards. In 1995, the MT Type Approval division was certified to test products to the standards required by government regulating bodies in New Zealand and Australia.

Manufacturing facilities include computer-integrated manufacturing (CIM), automated surface mounting of electronic circuit board components, soldering, and final product testing. In 1992, the purchase of their NZ$1.5 million surface mount equipment took MT to the leading edge of this technology. MT staff developed interface programs between their CAD system and the surface mount software. MT Technology has passed ISO 9001 accreditation, and consider consistently high quality to be one of their manufacturing strengths.

MT products are sold and supported by eight wholly-owned subsidiaries, as well as authorised representatives in 65 countries. Some systems design functions are carried out by subsidiaries, although smaller subsidiaries serve purely as distribution channels for MT products, as well as selling complementary non-MT products.

Information Systems

MT has a number of computer-based systems, with the most significant being used for computer-aided engineering and design (CAE and CAD), accounting, production planning, computer controlled surface mount device (SMD), and quality control. They are heavily dependent on information technology from the initial design through to manufacturing, managing and controlling.

They have a LAN with 300 users, an IBM 4361 mainframe running Unix-based CAD and quality control systems, and a Wang VS8470 handling FACT accounting and manufacturing software. The LAN involves a mix of hardware including Unix servers and workstations, Windows NT servers and workstations, and Novell servers, as well as proprietary systems for production machinery and testing.

Mobile Technology first implemented FACT software on Wang hardware in 1987. The Wang system is a proprietary one for both hardware and operating system, making modification inflexible, integration across the whole firm difficult, and upgrading expensive. The FACT software includes: sales ordering and analysis, manufacturing requirements planning (MRP), purchasing, inventory management, distribution, and the associated accounting functions of accounts payable, accounts receivable, fixed assets and general ledger. Since 1987 users had requested features that were not available on the FACT software, particularly project management, online product configuration, distribution requirements planning, and service and warranty tracking.

In addition to the Wang system, there are a variety of stand-alone PC-based applications that have been developed on a departmental basis to meet specific requirements. This has to some extent meant duplication of records and nonstandardisation of systems. For example, the Wang/FACT system does not automatically integrate with other systems such as bar-coding, quality statistics, CAD, SMD, stock management, and engineering project management.

MT Subsidiaries

Each MT subsidiary has different and independent computer systems. Most rely on stand-alone PCs with some e-mail links through the Internet. These systems range from Lotus spreadsheets for monitoring financial performance, to fully integrated business software including sales ordering, purchasing, warehousing, distribution, and associated financial modules including general ledger.

MT Communications (MTC), New Zealand

MTC implemented new software in April 1996. This did not live up to expectations. The software was found to contain an unacceptable number of bugs, and significant time and effort was expended to make the software workable. The software supplier was no longer in business from April 1997, leaving MTC with very limited support.

MT Radio Ltd (MTR), England

MTR currently uses a financial system that has general ledger, sales order entry and limited inventory management. From January 1998 MTR's software ceased to be supported.

Mobile Technology Australia Pty Ltd (MTA), Australia

MTA operates FACT on a UNIX platform. They have grown to a size where they often require information systems expertise, but have no staff dedicated to IS.

Information Systems Staff

By early 1997, MT employed five staff dedicated to information systems. They were referred to as the EDP Department. The EDP manager and a programmer managed the Wang/FACT system and reported to the MT accounting manager (who reported to the financial controller). The other three IS staff were network administrators who concentrated on their functional divisions of manufacturing, engineering, and trunking. Manufacturing included CIM, and engineering included CAD. Each network administrator reported to their functional head, i.e., the manufacturing manager, engineering manager and trunking manager, respectively.

In addition, various experts resided within departments. Many were initially tech-nicians or engineers who had developed IS skills and provided assistance to others when necessary. In the subsidiaries, responsibility for information systems typically lay with the subsidiary's accounting manager. None employed any staff dedicated to IS.

INFORMATION SYSTEMS STRATEGY

Triggered by MTC implementing new software in 1996, the MT management team could see that existing software and hardware was becoming obsolete and considered two basic options for structuring IS for the whole group:

1. **Continue with each subsidiary operating their own system:** This would allow subsidiaries to act independently. There was a strong desire for them to concen-trate on their core competencies and not individually pour resources and effort into IS. As computer systems generally required major upgrading every five-eight years, this would require a system upgrade in one or more operations each year. This problem was likely to compound as the company grew.
2. **Implement a standard system across the group:** Although each subsidiary was different they were all primarily involved in sales and service. MT would provide sufficient capability and resources to support subsidiaries. This could involve a pre-loaded system plus training, all ready to implement to each new subsidiary.

Option 2 was favoured by the MT management team, although that was not a consensus view across the subsidiary managers.

MIS Upgrade Project

During late 1996, MT decided to plan an upgrade of their information systems. The MIS upgrade project fell under the responsibility of the group financial controller, who initiated and led a steering committee of senior managers. Although this was considered a major project, the financial controller was not relieved of any of his regular responsi-bilities. Time pressures of this and other work prevented a written strategy from being completed. The steering committee met irregularly.

As an upgrade to the current FACT software would not be a straightforward process and was unlikely to meet the majority of the requirements, a Request For Information (RFI) was developed by Azimuth Consulting Limited with assistance from the MT Financial Controller. The 30-page RFI was published in March 1997. The RFI indicated the need for systems that would be capable of use in all MT organisations. They wanted to minimise the total effort and cost within the group of choosing and implementing systems. A system was sought that facilitated inter-company transactions as well as distribution to customers, and was capable of handling further company growth. Their vision was for all overseas staff to be able to access data and be able to communicate electronically with customers. A ballpark price for hardware and software licences for a system of this size was NZ$1.5 million. MT recognised that they would incur additional expenditure for implementation, training, modifications and upgrades in the three years following the purchase.

Replies to the RFI closed at the end of April 1997, and an initial list of selected suppliers presented demonstrations and discussions in three-four hour sessions. The steering committee selected a short list of three products (FACT I2, ManmanX and Symix) to be demonstrated in depth to IS staff and key users throughout the company. Between 30 and 40 staff attended at least one of the demonstrations.

The steering committee concluded that each of the three products could provide a step forward for MT, but perhaps only a small step, which would require major expense and effort to achieve. Further negotiations were carried out. Four months went by, the heat dropped out of the discussions and some managers and information systems staff began to lose interest and/or became disheartened at the continual rescheduling of deadlines and lack of tangible progress. A corporate IT manager was appointed in May 1998 to get the project back on track. The IT manager had been a member of the MIS upgrade steering committee in his role as supervisor of engineering documentation, which included CAD and other systems. He became one of the corporate management team at MT, with no staff reporting to him. He was given the responsibility to lead the upgrade project, including system selection and implementation.

NEW ORGANISATION STRUCTURE

During the latter part of 1997, another major project was brewing within the company. A strategic decision had been made to change the MT organisational structure. This was another project that vied for the time and energy of senior managers.

The major factor in this decision was the rate of growth of the company. "As the volume of business increased we had to set up systems and procedures in order to 'process' the demands. This resulted in a lack of, or reduction in, flexibility, ownership of problems or outcomes, and customer focus. The proposed structure provides for a high degree of flexibility and diversity to meet present needs and more importantly is sufficiently adaptable for as yet unclear future needs." (Group General Manager, 1997).

The group general manager was often quoted as using the analogy "the elephant was having difficulty jumping through the hoop!" MT had grown very large and was not able to perform in a way that many wished. In particular, they were concerned about late deliveries, unresponsive product development, and poor customer support. Managers in some units expressed a desire for greater independence. They had plans for their operations to improve and grow but felt restricted by existing processes.

MT management decided to restructure the business into nine separate business units. They opted for a decentralised rather than centralised structure for the business. They expected this to improve their ability to compete by being more flexible. The primary benefits of the business unit structure were seen as stemming from each unit being product focused. Units would be able to allocate specific resources to each product family, allowing each business unit to control their own destiny, and place their own priorities in response to the needs of their customers.

In some ways, the restructuring reflected the policies of the New Zealand government. During both the 1980s and the 1990s, New Zealand had moved to a free-market economy. Trade restrictions were lifted, industries were deregulated, Government subsidies and other interventions were removed, and some publicly-owned operations were privatised. In general, businesses were expected to survive on their own merits.

Each unit would have a board, and the unit manager would report to that board. The corporate unit would be headed by the group general manager, who would report to the MT group board of directors. The decision to move to this structure was made by the senior management team of Mr. Caddick, the general manager, and the managers of each functional area: finance, manufacturing, engineering, quality, human resources, purchasing and marketing.

MT employees learned about the restructuring in a number of ways:

- **State of the nation:** Every three months the general manager addresses all employees, split into three or four groups. These addresses include financial performance, forecasts, and any major decisions for the group.
- **Team briefing:** Every month, senior managers are briefed on current progress, people, procedures, and policy. This is generally a half-hour session, which is repeated to those who report to each manager, and so on down the structure, within 48 hours.

In addition, there are noticeboards and team meetings.

The restructure decision was made over a period of months, discussed in team meetings, and largely travelled the grapevine. It came as little surprise to most staff when the decision was confirmed and announced at team briefing in April 1998.

Under the new structure there would be nine business units of widely varying size; two manufacturing focused, two systems design/build and distribution, two distribution, and three internal services, including corporate. The two manufacturing focused business units would sell product to the other four distribution business units and to MT subsidiaries.

Each business unit would: be led by a manager, with a range of responsibilities and reportees; be required to undertake and publish product and financial plans for its area of activity; be measured individually on its performance; produce full monthly financial results to income statement and balance sheet level. As a general rule, it was envisaged that each business unit would be responsible for all the operations of that unit, as if they were a separate company. Thus functional responsibilities would be replicated by business units, with the exception of Corporate, the Advanced Technology Group, and the Type Approval division, which would charge their services to the individual business units.

Corporate would provide overall direction and guidance to the new management teams. The Advanced Technology Group would research and complete initial development of new technologies, ensuring compatibility of new products across the group, and maximising the skills of highly specialised engineers. Type Approval would complete initial testing of new products to the standards set by different governments, prior to products being sent to approved testing houses, and complete final tests for products to be sold within Australasia. Radio Infrastructure and Trunked Networks were to move to new premises (200 metres from the existing building) in the third quarter of 1998.

Most administration positions within MT were affected, including accounts, IS, purchasing, manufacturing, planning, and stores. Being the largest business unit, Mobile Radio was expected to continue to provide some administration resource to other business units on a charge-out basis until each unit was fully established and operational.

Even at the senior management level there were mixed views on whether this was the correct structure for the company. Some still felt there should be more central services, in particular the purchasing manager felt strongly about the benefits of bulk buying, with a centralised team of experts to complete the best contracts for the company as a whole. Thus reactions to the restructuring varied. Many staff saw opportunities for further career development, so were enthusiastic and fully committed to the new structure. Others were unsure of change and slow to warm to the idea. Ensuring the staff continued to feel secure and comfortable in their roles, was something to be considered.

CURRENT CHALLENGES AND IS

The business unit structure was planned to be in place on 1 June 1998. The largest business unit (Mobile Radio) would continue to use the existing computer systems. However, other business units may decide to use other systems.

Mobile Radio, Radio Infrastructure and Trunked Networks were expected to quickly gain IS staff from the existing staff, as well as other administrative staff, e.g., accountants. The EDP manager and programmer were expecting to become part of Mobile Radio. Also, the network administrator in Trunking expected to become part of Trunked Network, but there was no natural place for the other two network administrators to reside.

Smaller business units were expecting to share some staff resources, e.g., one accountant between them. They also recognised restructuring provided significant opportunities. This included managing in ways that made them more responsive to customers. Thus they may acquire new information systems that were more suited to their needs. They would also be free to appoint new staff who could be dedicated to their division. Furthermore, they could choose to insource or outsource activities.

Sales between business units meant each was a customer of the other, requiring sales order and analysis, and accounts receivable systems. Also, as some customers would do business with different units, the same stock item could be held at a different standard cost by the manufacturing business unit to that held by the distribution business units. Some staff wondered whether data access would be given to staff working for other divisions.

Another consideration was the shared use of the surface mount equipment by the two manufacturing divisions. The existing FACT software was not designed to handle two separate operations within one database. Sharing machinery that held reels of thousands of components added to the complexity of stock ownership, control, and valuation.

The June 1998 start date for the new business unit structure was fast approaching, leaving little or no time for selection and implementation of any new information systems or to appoint new IS staff. Decentralised information systems and staff seemed most suited to the proposed new business structure as each unit would be free to operate as it wished. Thus they could plan, acquire and recruit to meet their specific needs. In addition, they could consider new IS management practices like outsourcing. However, some managers were concerned that decentralisation may be neither effective nor efficient, particularly for the smaller units as managers would have to address IS issues as well as other business issues. They may have to acquire hardware that was underutilised in another part of the firm. Also, there were concerns that decentralisation may make it difficult for units to attract, support and retain IS staff. While many IS staff in firms that have centralised IS departments take on specialist roles, a decentralised structure would require generalists. In addition, decentralisation could reduce the potential for introducing new technologies. Thus some IS staff wondered if new recruits could feel their responsibilities ranged beyond their areas of expertise with no-one to turn to for support, while experienced staff could feel that the scale of their unit provided little opportunity to develop new expertise. Thus MT management pondered how information systems should be incorporated into the new structure.

FURTHER READING

Buchanan, D., & Hvczynski, A. (1997). *Organizational behaviour: An introductory text* (3rd ed.).

Cole, G. A. (1996). *Management theory and practice* (5th ed.).

Currie, W. (1995). *Management strategy for IT: An international perspective*. Pitman.

Earl, M. J. (1989). *Management strategies for IT*. Prentice-Hall.

Earl, M. J. (Ed). (1996). *Information management: The organizational dimension*. Oxford UP.

Hicks, J. O. (1997). *Information systems in business: An introduction* (2nd ed.).

Martin, Brown, DeHayes, Hoffer, & Perkins. (1999). *Managing information technology: What managers need to know* (3rd ed.). Prentice-Hall.

Mullins, L. J. (1996). *Management and organisational behaviour* (4th ed.).

Reynolds, G. W. (1992). *Information systems for managers* (2nd ed.). West.

Robson, W. (1997). *Strategic management of information systems* (2nd ed.). Pitman.

Ward, J., & Griffiths, P. (1996). *Strategic planning for information systems* (2nd ed.). Wiley.

APPENDIX

Company Structure: April 1998

MT Board of Directors Managing Director General Manager							
Trunking Manager	Corporate Team Engineering Manager, Manufacturing Manager, Financial Controller, Purchasing Manager, Human Resources Manager, Marketing Manager, Quality Manager						
Trunking Division	Engineering	Manufacturing	Finance	Purchasing	Human Resources	Marketing	Quality

Trunking was the only truly separate division as they had their own engineering, manufacturing and administrative staff, including purchasing, finance, etc.

Company Structure: June 1998

MT Board of Directors								
Managing Director								
General Manager								
Mobile Radio # 380 manufacturing	Radio Infrastructure # 114 manufacturing	Trunked Network # 41 design	Applications Engineering # 12 design	Mobile Data # 9 distribution	Mobile Export # 9 distribution	Advanced Technology # 37 service	Type Approval # 6 service	Corporate # 10 service

 # indicates number of employees

Paul Cragg is an associate professor in information systems in the Faculty of Commerce at the University of Canterbury, New Zealand, where he teaches on the MBA programme, as well as within the BCom, MCom, and PhD degrees. Previously he was on the staff at the University of Waikato, New Zealand, and before that at Leicester Polytechnic, England. His research centres on small firm computing. Current studies focus on IT alignment, benchmarking, IT sophistication, and adoption and use of the Internet. He has published in many international journals including MISQ, EJIS, Information & Management, *and* JSIS.

Prue Chapman graduated from the University of Canterbury with a Bachelor of Commerce, and is a member of the New Zealand Institute of Chartered Accountants. She has 15 years experience in finance and information systems, in a variety of industries, including electronics, tourism, and publishing. Her strengths are in leadership, organisational development, and change management. In the past six years she has been in the electronics industry focusing on information system planning, implementation and enhancement.

This case was previously published in the *Annals of Cases on Information Technology*, Volume 3/2001, pp. 169-178, © 2001.

Chapter XV

Technological Modernization of Peru's Public Registries

Antonio Diaz-Andrade, ESAN, Peru

Martín Santana-Ormeño, ESAN, Peru

EXECUTIVE SUMMARY

This study describes the strategy and information technology adopted by Peru's National Superintendent of Public Registries (SUNARP) to meet its organizational goals. SUNARP was created in 1994 to become the ruling entity of all public registry offices in Peru, which to that time had been working in an isolated fashion. The case describes the projects already completed, their respective success and their deployment across the organization's bureaus across the nation. The Registry Information System (SIR, in Spanish) and the consequent online registry publicity service are worthy of noting. It takes account of the fact that many of these projects were originally initiated in the largest Registry Zone, the former Lima and Callao Registry Office. Moreover, the paper mentions the future challenges faced by SUNARP in its efforts to provide online registration services.

ORGANIZATIONAL BACKGROUND

Since the dawn of humankind it was important to have an evidence of who was the owner of certain plots of land and what were the boundaries of such land. Depending on each civilization, the ways to register the transactions made on land could go from oral statements, which could be easily invalidated, to private contractual documents, which could be lost and destroyed, besides being susceptible of forgery. With the development of civilization, the need to create a political entity to guarantee the right to use lands became necessary (Buscher, 2003; Judicial Greffe, 1999). To balance society's interests and private property rights, the concept of title emerged as a document used to determine the legal situation of a specific property (Buscher, 2003).

As a whole, from a juridical standpoint, public registries are entities created by the government to register titles and documents that reflect the transactions made between private parties or between private parties and the government. Registering titles and documents means perpetuating them and making them public to provide certainty and effectiveness to transactions. Publishing transactions registered in titles and documents is a fundamental activity to guarantee their validity before a third party. This means that only if contract has been recorded in the public registries shall it have legal value.

For a society faced with underdevelopment and a lagging economy, a state guaranteeing juridical stability becomes one of the essential conditions for development. In this respect, it is critical for economic agents to feel not only that they are protected by the law, but also that they can avail themselves of the legally registered information. This registered information allows them to make accurate decisions when transacting their real properties, vehicles and general assets, and in making corporate and capital increase decisions, among other issues. Public registries thus become a tool to promote a market economy.

Peru's National System of Public Registries has undertaken the task of maintaining and preserving the unity and coherence of the registry function across the country. Law N° 26366, dated October 16, 1994, established the National Superintendent of Public Registries of Peru (SUNARP). Since then it has been the ruling body of the National Public Registries System. In consequence, SUNARP's main functions and powers include designing technical and administrative policies and rules for the public registries. It is also in charge of planning, organizing, governing, directing, coordinating and supervising the inscription and publication of deeds and contracts filed in the registries comprised in the National Public Registries System. Generally, as has already been mentioned, this system is aimed at "maintaining and preserving the unity and coherence of the registry function across the country. It aims at providing specialized, streamlined, integrated and modern services, procedures and management of all the registries comprised in it."

SUNARP performs an essential social role by linking property registration to the use of registered assets as tools for economic and social development, as registration both increases the value of assets and reduces transaction costs. Its great challenge is to create citizens' awareness of the importance of formalizing real properties and all juridical deeds in a country where, for example, 53% of the urban population and 81% in rural areas population occupy unregistered properties, the value of which may reach US$74 billion (De Soto, 2000). SUNARP's senior management are aware of their crucial social role and are therefore interested in improving the quality of their services, including reducing service costs and broadening coverage to get closer to users, in particular poorer ones.

SUNARP's mission is "granting juridical security and providing certainty in relation to the ownership of various rights registered in it, while supporting its development on the upgrading, simplification, integration and specialization of the registry function nationwide, on behalf of the nation."

Figure 1. Peru's superintendence of public registries organizational chart

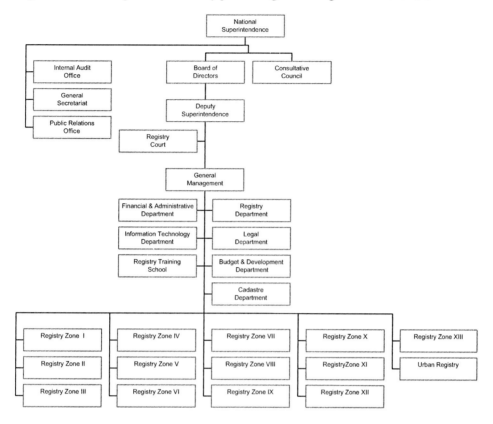

SUNARP's vision statement reflects the organization's ambition to become a world class organization, namely to be "a highly efficient and effective organization, through a modern and democratic service coverage to foster the nation's economy and to turn it into an organizational and management model for Peru's and Latin American's public sector."

To fulfill its mission, SUNARP develops two main functions: registration and publicity. The registration function demands registering the different juridical acts that could be executed, such as buying-selling movables or real estate, mortgage on these goods, incorporation of companies, mergers between corporations, capitalization, granting of powers of attorney, and wills, among others. The publicity act requires providing services, such as the issuance of simple copies, authenticated copies and/or certificates regarding previously registered acts.

Figure 1 shows SUNARP's organizational structure.

SUNARP registers deeds brought before it by individuals or organizations. It also makes registration of deeds public by granting deed records at request, searching records to determine deed inscription, delivering copies of registration files and certificates, and providing access to its book and deed archives. Contrary to a non-registered deed, registered title enjoys juridical status supported by the registration principles of legal status, authenticity, value as evidence, publication and priority, among others.

The registries under SUNARP are of various types, including:

- **Real Property Registry:** that registers, conveys, modifies and abrogates real property rights.
- **Mining Registry:** including the Mining Rights Registry, Mining Contracts Registry, Mining Pledge Registry, Mining Persons and Company Registry, and the Mandates Registry.
- **Fishing Vessels Property Registry:** for recording vessel sales, pledging, seizures, leasing, name changes, ship characteristics, and other features of fishing and other vessels.
- **Aircraft Public Registry:** which records all deeds, contracts or decisions to establish, convey, terminate, limit or otherwise modify the property or possession rights over airplanes or airplane engines. It likewise records the disablement, inoperability, loss, disappearance, abandonment, destruction and grounding of airplanes, and the agreements to use them.
- **Organizations Registry:** responsible for programming, organizing and supervising the registration process and the publication of the resulting deeds filed in the registry's records for associations, foundations, committees, cooperatives, peasant and indigenous peoples' communities, community properties, grassroots organizations, government companies, foreign based companies, foreign company branches in Peru, powers granted by foreign companies not residing in Peru, companies created through a Congress law, and individual proprietorship companies. The Organizations Registry includes all matters related to hydrocarbons properties.
- **Persons Registry:** to register mandates and powers of attorney granted to individuals, and their assignment, modification, revocation and termination; inheritances without a will, including the observations and court decisions relating to the heirs, and the Wills Register for individual will awards, extensions and annulments.
- **Individuals Registry:** for recording the capacities of individuals as relates to deeds and contracts, such as exclusions, prohibitions, insolvency, and court appointment as tutors, among others. Also registers the marital status and estate condition of individuals, including legal separation, divorce or division of estates.
- **Real Property Registry:** including the Personal Property Registry, the Vehicle Property Registry (for circulating vehicles), the Installments Sales Fiscal Registry (for private property conveyances on an installments basis) and the Pledges Registry, which in turn includes the Industrial Pledge Registry, the Farm Pledge Registry and the Global and Floating Pledge Registry.

The National System of Public Registries comprises 58 operating offices, organized in thirteen registry zones distributed throughout the country (see Appendix A). The most important of all these by number and amount of transactions is the Registry Zone No. IX (former Lima and Callao Registry Office), with jurisdiction over both the city and region of Lima.

Although all registry offices enforce similar procedures, SUNARP officials have identified the lack of a shared organizational culture. Instead, there are as many "cultures" as there are registry offices. Furthermore, the personnel and compensation policies are not uniform, opening a potential for internal issues including potential labor conflicts. Additionally, Peru's exacerbated centralism is reflected in the extreme differences in service fees paid by users (see Appendix B) with the consequence of revenue streams that occasionally fail to meet operating costs.

SUNARP and its thirteen registry zones' operations are financed by their own sales revenues for the services they provide. Previously they also benefited from a budget allocation from the Ministry of Economy and Finance that was interrupted in 2002. SUNARP's head office receives 20% of the total amount collected for registration fees; 8% goes to a compensation fund and 12% is allocated to operating expenditures. However, the 1% designated for the compensation fund is insufficient to upgrade public registries nationwide, while 2% of fees charged are not enough to cover operating expenditures. Given that the registry offices frequently fail to finance their budgets from their own revenues, a number of regulations allow transferring surpluses from some offices to under-funded registries. This procedure was introduced to allow the even development and overall efficiency of registry services nationwide.

Registry offices have the following powers and duties:

(a)   Planning, organizing, directing, executing and controlling internal registry and administrative activities in their respective jurisdictions.
(b)   Preparing and maintaining updated registry statistics.
(c)   Entering into agreements for performing registry functions. Agreements with private entities for supplying registry services on behalf of and for the public registries require the prior authorization of SUNARP's board, pursuant to its by-laws.
(d)   Correctly performing the registration functions, pursuant to the regulations in force.
(e)   Proposing to the national superintendent changes of the organization's structure, who will determine its approval.
(f)   Promoting the use of technology and upgrading of the registries' functions.
(g)   Preparing the organization's annual budget and timely sending it to SUNARP's general manager for its approval before it is included in the organization's general budget.
(h)   Organizing and maintaining an updated land registry for their respective territorial jurisdictions.
(i)   Assigning the public registrars pursuant to law.
(j)   Resolving in first instance the filed claims, reports and complaints.
(k)   Issuing decisions in their fields of competence.
(l)   Other functions.

SETTING THE STAGE

To develop the above mentioned registering and publicity functions, two fundamental concepts are handled, the concept of entry and the concept of title. An entry is an information unit with a register sense. For example, a company's incorporation causes a registry entry. Everything that happens or modifies the said company (entry) needs to be registered in that entry. In this way, the entry starts with the registration of the company's incorporation, if the company increases its capital, a second registration will be made to record this new fact, and, if later on, the company incorporates new shareholders, this fact will also be registered in the entry. Registration provides dynamism to entries. Now, every registration act on an entry needs to be duly grounded on a title. In this regard, titles are just the documents required by the registrar to execute the registration. To follow with the company example, to register its incorporation, the registrar requires the incorporation deed, to register the capital increase, the registrar will demand the documentation certifying said increase; and to register the change in shareholding, the registrar will verify the new shareholders' titles. Figure 2 shows the example explained here, while Appendix C shows in detail the registration process that used to be applied at SUNARP (before modernization).

The title registration process has been described up to here. However, the other SUNARP's fundamental function is the publicity service of registry entries. To be able to check them, SUNARP charges a rate. Its amount depends on if what is requested is a simple copy, an authenticated copy or a certificate. The publicity process is shown in Figure 3.

Since the public registry functions were established in Peru more than one hundred years ago in 1888, the ways and means to register have suffered several modifications. The first title entries were handwritten on heavy and huge volumes. In 1971, registry cards started to be used as the means to register entries. These cards meant an important progress, since they permitted the management of information in a more orderly way.

When SUNARP was formed in 1994, five general policy principles were established to guide its activities: modernization, simplification, specialization, integration and organizational image building. All of them get careful attention from management. Modernization is seen as a comprehensive process with measurable objectives and goals, which aims at improving the quality of registry services. This principle includes the ongoing introduction of new infrastructure and technologies, and automation of registry and administrative processes. Process streamlining requires ongoing assessment of registry office processes, procedures and registry administrative stages to

Figure 2. Title registering process in a registry entry

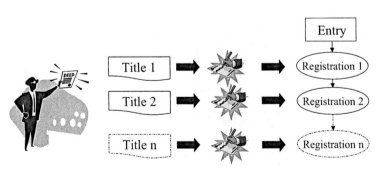

Figure 3. Process of publicity for a registry entry

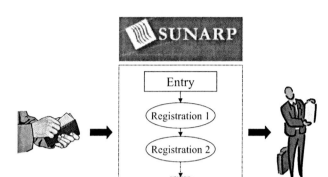

identify and eliminate redundant requirements and reduce delivery time. SUNARP recruits highly qualified personnel with high ethical standards and provides them with ongoing training. It also seeks the integration of registration offices dispersed in other government agencies by bringing them together under a single legal umbrella to create a unified registry system for Peru. Finally, SUNARP is concerned with building a reputation for organizational efficiency and good service.

However, integration and unification of the information in the different public registry offices in the whole country, procedure standardization, incorporation of new technologies and the fact of having to become subordinated to a single entity (Grönlund, 2001) meant great challenges for the newly incepted SUNARP. Standardized registration procedures ensure that all registry offices will create identical records and will enforce identical regulations and guidelines in doing so. After recognizing the need to unify its activities, since September 2001, SUNARP has identified its various area processes. It thus aims at improving service quality and getting ISO-9000 certification.

Due to the nature of the services it provides, SUNARP generates substantial amounts of information that may be classified as specific registry information and management information. Board directors are aware that information makes control easier. They have therefore taken the initiative to carry out an Intranet project to centralize and save all information concerning the National System of Public Registries and management issues.

Until SUNARP was created, there were different platforms for different types of registries (property, vehicles, commercial, among others) that were developed independently by the different registry offices scattered along the country. Through its IT department, SUNARP has completed its IT plans every year included in the organization's overall strategic plan. The initial nationwide IT policy was outlined in 1998. It has subsequently been updated to suit technological changes. A fast-track standardization plan introduced already that year reduced the number of IT platforms. Also that year, a work plan prepared together with the Administration and Finance department allowed the set up of an integrated management system, initially at SUNARP headquarters and then in bureaus across Peru.

Thanks to centralized control through the IT department, much progress has been made in standardizing the registry system across the nation. Preserving high levels of standardization requires introducing new developments, purchasing new technologies and adapting the applications necessarily through the IT division. Thus, IT functions — such as user and technical support — will be provided by the IT department in individual registry bureaus to suit each registry's specific functions.

Before 2001, the former Lima and Callao Registry Office, which performs 50% of the registration actions in Peru, had relative freedom in introducing the technological initiatives, and led all technology projects within SUNARP. Those initiatives earned the Lima bureau local and international recognition including Creatividad Empresarial Awards in 1996 and 1999, and the prize given to the best IT project in government by Common Peru 1999. In October 2002, the Guatemalan Treasury and State Properties Bureau expressed their gratitude for SUNARP's contribution to modernizing the administration of that nation's government-owned properties.

Despite its short life, SUNARP has become the leader of IT projects for all registry offices in Peru. Each registry may still introduce innovative IT projects. However, to make the most efficient use of available resources, emphasis is given to individual registry initiatives that may be replicated at other bureaus. In this regard, the efforts deployed by SUNARP fall within the class of a parallel electronic government development program. This means that although it has nationwide reach, it is handled independently from other electronic government projects that other State agencies might be developing, and that it does not necessarily obey an electronic government centralized strategy (Ronaghan, 2002). Independently from the approach followed by SUNARP's technological modernization project, it complies with the service efficiency and quality characteristics that Grönlund (2002) analyzes from different perspectives.

CASE DESCRIPTION

SUNARP's modernization project represented a huge challenge for the organization. On the one hand, the digitalization of all entries and their respective registrations was necessary, and on the other hand, it was indispensable to use a technology to guarantee juridical security or the inviolability of said entries. The modernization process required digitalizing the books and cards from 1888 to date, and to register electronically from then on.

In 1996, the Lima bureau launched an ambitious modernization project, with the strategic planning of the National Superintendent of Public Registries (SUNARP) as its starting point. The plan would be developed in stages. Introduction of the Registry Information System (SIR, in Spanish), including real property, company and individual persons modules at the Lima bureau in October 1997, allowed substituting electronic filings for paper filings. The electronic filing system was introduced in other head offices of the then-named Lima and Callao Registry Office in the department (state) of Lima. By May 2001, the Registry Information System (SIR) and the appropriate adaptation and training plans had been introduced in all registry offices in Peru. To digitalize the entries registered in the books and cards a specialized company was hired and US$5 million was

Figure 4. Evolution of Peru's public registries

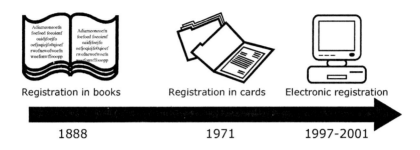

Registration in books   Registration in cards   Electronic registration

1888   1971   1997-2001

invested, all covered with revenues coming from the rates charged for registry services ("Sistema de interconexión," 2003). Figure 4 represents the different ways in which public registry information was managed in Peru from 1888 to 2001. Thanks to digitalization of public registries, Web capability was attained.

In December 2000 and January 2001, SUNARP bought state-of-the-art equipment and software capable of supporting image technology for storing of information on optical media. These acquisitions enhance juridical security and provide adequate support for implementing the Registry Information System (SIR). Standardization proceeded nationwide in 2001 and 2002, and provided the necessary platform for the ongoing national interconnection project. Figure 5 shows the SUNARP's technological infrastructure.

A major step to enhance registry development and security, this initiative provided IT support for all the physical information stored in public registries. SIR is a major technological breakthrough that includes database administration systems, fingerprint identification devices, image administrators and optical disks systems that provide additional legal security and help to standardize paperwork. The WORM (Write Once Read Many) technology was used. It permits only the registrar, recognized by his/her fingerprint, to register and to keep entries unchanged thereof. Figure 6 illustrates the procedure followed for electronic registration. Data is updated every day and stored in optical disks and support tapes. Stored data are safely kept outside registry premises. Appendix D shows how the whole registry procedure is after the SIR implementation.

SIR has nonetheless encountered some roadblocks along the way. They include personnel resistance to change work routines, in particular in the larger bureaus. In many instances, the registrars did not feel they owned the process, as they had been excluded from its development. A number of functional bugs were identified and had to be removed. Both issues were addressed through basic training provided. Likewise, IT personnel nationwide received training to use the new tools provided by the project's technological platform.

For vehicle property registration almost all registry offices in Peru used an application supplied by the Ministry of Transports and Communications in 1999. An obsolete DOS technology did not allow sound and safe integration with database. Moreover, it was designed as an administrative tool rather than from a juridical perspective, as it was

Figure 5. SUNARP's technological infrastructure

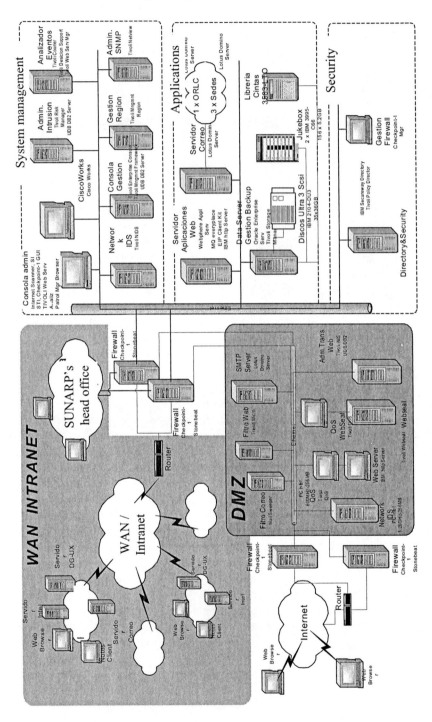

Figure 6. Electronic registration procedure

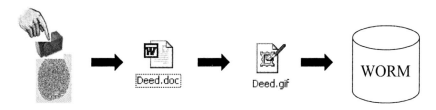

needed. Only the Lima and Callao, Arequipa and Trujillo registries have developed their own systems.

Rural Properties Divisions at individual registry offices use other software versions that are a legacy of the previous registry system in force at individual bureaus before the Registry Information System (SIR) was set up nationwide. Local bureaus based on non-standardized local criteria and under severe budget constraints developed rural property registry systems. A system running Oracle and PowerBuilder technology on a Unix platform was launched in 1997-1999, as a part of the first stage of the Land Titling and Registration Project. The system should be in place and ready to start production in the second half of project implementation, after it has been scrutinized for adapting it to local environments at each registry nationwide. Consideration will also be given to the need of functionally adapting this system to the Registry Information System (SIR), the Vehicle Property Registry and subsequent systems.

For their administrative systems, registries still use SUNARP software developed in 1997 aimed at creating a single information structure to integrate the administrative from the entire national system. The accounting system of this device was developed on a non-visual environment, while the other systems were developed on a Windows (FoxPro) environment, since at the moment of its development, the two resources were available at most registry bureaus. It is now considered that this device has completed its useful lifecycle. It is now necessary to develop a solution that considers the present registry system platform and use of a database manager that guarantees the safe management of information.

To get closer to citizens, the DATAFONO REGISTRAL call center gives clients automated (recorded) and customized (personal) orientation on paperwork, requirements, costs and duration of the different registry processes nationwide. This service was initially launched in August 1998 when the Lima and Callao Registry Office set up Datafono, an automated orientation toll-free telephone line that gave clients information on registration procedures of their choice. Although not a toll free call service anymore, the concept has been replicated in all the head registry zone offices.

Likewise, multimedia modules were set up in the Lima and Callao Registry Office premises through which the users may get instant paperwork information. For example, if a person wishes to know how to carry out an intestate succession, pressing the corresponding touch screen button will provide a printed listing of all required docu-

Figure 7. SUNARP offices interconnection

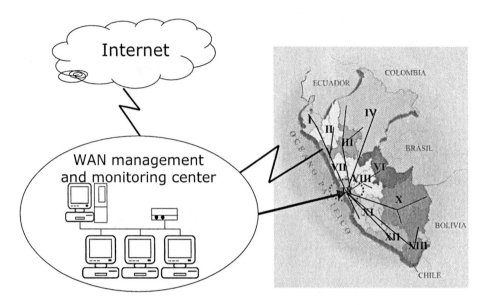

ments, costs and duration of paperwork. These initiatives were concurrent with the citizen service strategy engraved at SUNARP. Only in 2002, the organization served 529,000 people who went to SUNARP seeking direction, since they did not have the means to pay for a lawyer's or a notary's services ("Hay 23 mil," 2003). However, the most significant advances came in 1999 when the Lima bureau Web site started giving users the option to track registration paperwork.

Since July 2000, the former Lima and Callao Registry Office has provided information online in the jurisdiction of Lima Department, including Internet based access to information about electronic records and certificates. SUNARP adopted and enhanced the project through improvement of security systems and, thanks to the interconnection of registry offices all over the country through a WAN, launched it to the public on January 30, 2003 ("Hay 23 mil," 2003). Figure 7 represents SUNARP'S WAN. Another major step forward, this registry publicity service allows citizens to search SUNARP's files from their homes for a fee.

As pointed out by Lenk, Traunmüller and Wimmer (2002), SUNARP's initiative is adjusted to the four perspectives an electronic government strategy must follow. First, there is the citizen perspective, which becomes the central element of any project. Second, the process perspective required redesigning the organization, including the incorporation of information technology to create synergies. The cooperation perspective complements the former one and is directed to the cooperative efforts under a ubiquity environment. Finally, the fourth perspective, knowledge, highlights the importance of understanding and managing information to provide services.

CURRENT CHALLENGES/PROBLEMS FACING THE ORGANIZATION

The registration process has been clearly simplified as compared to the traditional registration process. Although the submission of physical documents is still necessary, registration is now totally electronic, complying with methods that guarantee juridical security. Having digitalized the entries and their respective registrations, SUNARP was just one step from offering the online publicity service and, in fact, it did so. The online publicity service adds a virtual character to it. Figure 8 shows SUNARP's homepage, which centrally resides in a single server located in the city of Lima.

The Registry Information Service (SIR, in Spanish) has permitted SUNARP to take many of the physical processes to the virtual world. However, it is still necessary for a person to go to SUNARP's office corresponding to the jurisdiction where he/she wants to register, for example, a house. If this person lives in Iquitos and wants to register a property in Trujillo, he/she will have to travel to this city to submit the documentation required by the registration process. SUNARP also wants to give citizens the option to file registrations of different types and to register capital increases of companies online. A series of difficulties must be overcome, however, mostly of a personnel management nature, rather than specific technological issues. The project requires restructuring the registrars' workload at registry head offices in order to avoid, on the one hand, work overloads, and on the other, excess idle capacity. In this way, to follow with the aforementioned example, the Iquitos registrar will receive the required documentation,

Figure 8. SUNARP's homepage

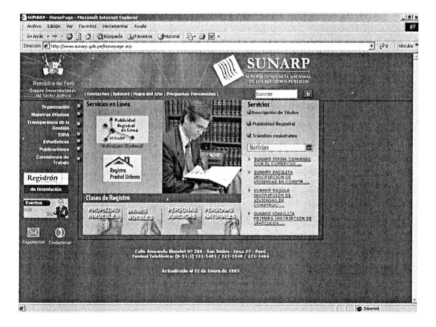

Figure 9. Registration process

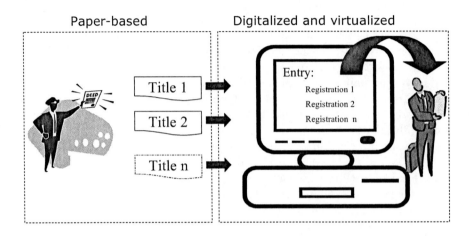

will digitalize it to register it in the Trujillo public registries and the person will not have to travel. When this is attained, we will be able to state that the title registering process will have become virtualized to a certain extent. However, it would also require measures to ensure open and safe registrations.

Figure 9 permits to differentiate digitalized and virtualized processes from those that are still performed physically.

Carlos Noriega, IT Manager, is satisfied with SUNARP's success; however, he recognizes there is a lot of way to go. Although the possibility of users enquiring online dramatically reduces transaction costs, the poor technological infrastructure existing in Peru is still one of the major access barriers (Díaz-Andrade, 2003). The online publicity service is particularly useful for lawyers and especially for notaries, since these are intensive users of this kind of information to develop their professional activities.

To access the online publicity service through the Internet, the user currently has three different payment alternatives. The first one is going to any one of the 58 registry offices in the country and paying to obtain the service; the user will receive a password that will permit him/her to access SUNARP's databases. The second option is to pay online by using a VISA credit card. As in the former case, the user will receive a password that will permit him/her to access SUNARP's database.

The third payment option merits some more analysis. Peru has a low index of computers with access to the Internet, since less than five computers per 100 inhabitants is estimated (Telefónica, 2002). However, Peru is one of the countries with the most public access to the Internet through public booths. It currently ranks 13 in the ranking of countries with most public access to the Internet (Harvard University, 2001, quoted by Telefónica, 2002). On the other hand, the use of credit cards as a means of payment is quite reduced. Until 2000, only 9% of homes in Lima were estimated to have a credit card (INEI, 2000). Before this panorama, SUNARP's management decided to sign an agreement with the ec-cab public booth network. In this way, those who do not have access to the Internet in their homes and do not have a credit card can access online services offered by SUNARP through the ec-cab booths. In this case, the user must pay the public booth administrator and he/she will provide him/her access to the online publicity service. However, there are only nine ec-cab booths, all of them located in the city of Lima ("Ec-cab booths permit...," 2003). Carlos Noriega reflects about how to facilitate access to online publicity services nationwide.

Another still pending challenge is the fact that prints of downloads from SUNARP's Web site lack legal validity and would not be admitted in a court proceeding. At present, the IT team is working to improve the certified publicity service.

Setting up the Registry Information System (SIR) across Peru also revealed some deficiencies that will be addressed through the Single Registry System (SUR) project underway. Also to be addressed is the need to integrate the land registry systems operated by various local (municipal) governments and government agencies that use SUNARP's database. This large-scale project fits the e-government plans promoted by the Cabinet Chief's Office of which the Electronic Government Head depends.

Carlos Noriega finally states:

These projects put us before many technical difficulties and budgetary constraints; however, I am persuaded that the main problem we have is changing the mindset of all the involved agents, including the registrars, lawyers, notaries, judges and public at large. Although Peruvian laws accept electronic documents, we still reject or give little value to anything that is not printed on paper. I think this change will be very long in coming. We must rethink the way in which we perform our activities, starting from the fact that technology exists and that we have it available.

REFERENCES

Buscher, G. J. (2003). *A brief history of the land court.* Retrieved April 14, 2003, from http://www.state.ma.us/courts/courtsandjudges/courts/landcourt/lchist3.html.

Buscher, G. J. (2003). *The nature and evolution of title.* Retrieved April 14, 2003, from http://www.state.ma.us/courts/courtsandjudges/courts/landcourt/evolution_title.html

Cabinas ec-cab permiten consultar registros públicos. (2003, January 29). Retrieved March 17, 2003, from http://www.elcomercioperu.com.pe/ECCab/

De Soto, H. (2000). *The mystery of capital.* London: Bantam Press/Random House.

Díaz-Andrade, A. (2003). A B2C development model for electronic commerce in less developed countries: The Peruvian case. *Proceedings of the IRMA 2003 International Conference*, Philadelphia, Pennsylvania.

Grönlund, A. (2001). Building an infrastructure to manage electronic services. In S. Dasgupta (Ed.), *Managing Internet and intranet technologies in organizations: Challenges and opportunities.* Hershey, PA: Idea Group Publishing.

Grönlund, A. (2002). Electronic government: Efficiency, service quality and democracy. In A. Grölund (Ed.), *Electronic government: Design, applications and management*. Hershey, PA: Idea Group Publishing.

Hay 23 mil nuevas empresas. (2003, January 30). *El Comercio*, b5, p. 5.

INEI. (2000). *Tecnologías de información y comunicaciones en los hogares en Lima Metropolitana*. Lima: Instituto Nacional de Estadística e Informática.

Judicial Greefe. (1999). *A short guide to the public registry*. Retrieved April 2, 2003, from http://www.judicialgreffe.gov.je

Lenk, K., Traunmüller, R., & Wimmer, M. (2002). The significance of law and knowledge for electronic government. In A. Grönlund (Ed.), *Electronic government: Design, applications and management*. Hershey, PA: Idea Group Publishing.

Ronaghan, S. A. (2002). *Benchmarking e-government: A global perspective. Assessing the progress of the UN Member States*. New York: United Nations for Public Economics and Public Administration/American Society for Public Administration.

Sistema de interconexión favorecerá a todos. (2003, January 30). *El Comercio*, b5, p. 5.

SUNARP - Superintendencia Nacional de los Registros Públicos. (2002). *Plan estratégico 2002-2006*.

SUNARP - Superintendencia Nacional de los Registros Públicos. (2002). Retrieved from http://www.sunarp.gob.pe

SUNARP - Superintendencia Nacional de los Registros Públicos. (2003, February). *Pulso Registral*. Retrieved April 12, 2003, from http://www.sunarp.gob.pe/data/pulsoregistral/46.pdf

Telefónica del Perú. (2002). *La sociedad de la información en el Perú: Presente y perspectivas 2003-2005*. Lima: Servicios Editoriales del Perú.

APPENDIX A
Registry Zones and Registry Offices

Registry Zone N° I	Piura (main head office), Sullana, and Tumbes.
Registry Zone N° II	Chiclayo (main head office), Bagua, Cajamarca, Chachapoyas, Chota, and Jaén.
Registry Zone N° III	Moyobamba (main head office), Tarapoto and Juanjuí.
Registry Zone N° IV	Iquitos (main head office) and Yurimaguas.
Registry Zone N° V	Trujillo (main head office), San Pedro de Lloc, Chepén, Sánchez Carrión, and Otuzco.
Registry Zone N° VI	Pucallpa (main head office).
Registry Zone N° VII	Huaraz (main head office), Chimbote, and Casma.
Registry Zone N° VIII	Huancayo (main head office), Huánuco, Selva Central, Tingo María, Tarma, Cerro de Pasco, and Satipo.
Registry Zone N° IX	Lima (main head office), Callao, Barranca, Huacho, Huaral, Cañete, San Juan de Lurigancho, San Juan de Miraflores, Los Olivos, and Santa Anita.
Registry Zone N° X	Cusco (main head office), Apurímac, Madre de Dios, Quillabamba, and Sicuani.
Registry Zone N° XI	Ica (main head office), Chincha, Pisco, Nasca, Ayacucho, Huanta, Huancavelica, Andahuaylas, and Puquio.
Registry Zone N° XII	Arequipa (main head office) and Camaná.
Registry Zone N° XIII	Tacna (main head office), Moquegua, Ilo, Puno, and Juliaca.

Source: www.sunarp.gob.pe
Prepared by the authors

APPENDIX B
Revenue for Service Fees (February 2003)

Registry Zone	Main head office	Revenue (US$)
Registry Zone N° I	Piura	91,775
Registry Zone N° II	Chiclayo	113,247
Registry Zone N° III	Moyobamba	30,044
Registry Zone N° IV	Iquitos	27,459
Registry Zone N° V	Trujillo	125,210
Registry Zone N° VI	Pucallpa	20,921
Registry Zone N° VII	Huaraz	49,311
Registry Zone N° VIII	Huancayo	110,587
Registry Zone N° IX	Lima	1,628,971
Registry Zone N° X	Cusco	76,552
Registry Zone N° XI	Ica	66,934
Registry Zone N° XII	Arequipa	136,781
Registry Zone N° XIII	Tacna	90,224
Total		**2,568,016**

Source: http://www.sunarp.gob.pe/data/pulsoregistral/46.pdf
Prepared by the authors

APPENDIX C
Internal Registration Procedures in Public Registries Before SIR Implementation

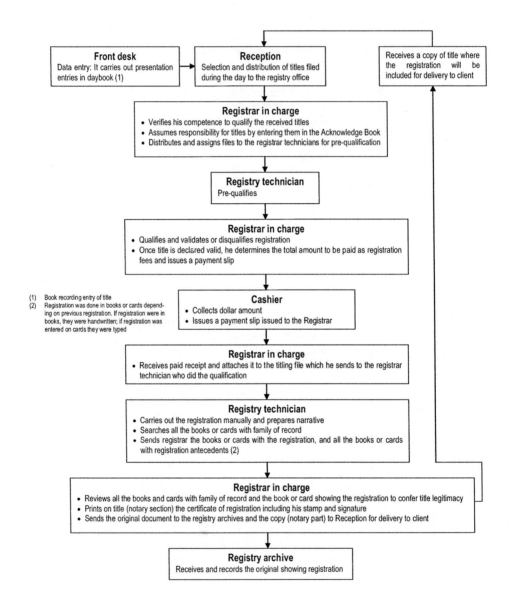

Front desk
Data entry: It carries out presentation entries in daybook (1)

Reception
Selection and distribution of titles filed during the day to the registry office

Receives a copy of title where the registration will be included for delivery to client

Registrar in charge
- Verifies his competence to qualify the received titles
- Assumes responsibility for titles by entering them in the Acknowledge Book
- Distributes and assigns files to the registrar technicians for pre-qualification

Registry technician
Pre-qualifies

Registrar in charge
- Qualifies and validates or disqualifies registration
- Once title is declared valid, he determines the total amount to be paid as registration fees and issues a payment slip

(1) Book recording entry of title
(2) Registration was done in books or cards depending on previous registration. If registration were in books, they were handwritten; if registration was entered on cards they were typed

Cashier
- Collects dollar amount
- Issues a payment slip issued to the Registrar

Registrar in charge
- Receives paid receipt and attaches it to the titling file which he sends to the registrar technician who did the qualification

Registry technician
- Carries out the registration manually and prepares narrative
- Searches all the books or cards with family of record
- Sends registrar the books or cards with the registration, and all the books or cards with registration antecedents (2)

Registrar in charge
- Reviews all the books and cards with family of record and the book or card showing the registration to confer title legitimacy
- Prints on title (notary section) the certificate of registration including his stamp and signature
- Sends the original document to the registry archives and the copy (notary part) to Reception for delivery to client

Registry archive
Receives and records the original showing registration

APPENDIX D
Internal Registration Procedures in Public Registries After SIR Implementation

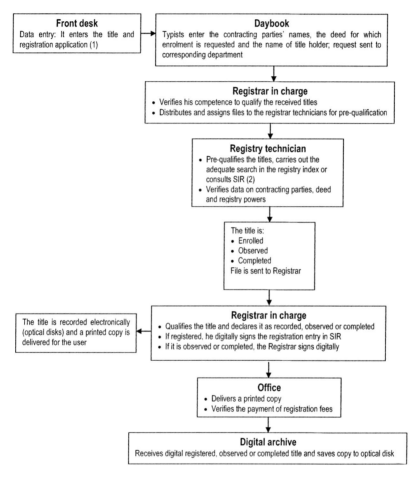

(1) A bar code on the registration application includes a sequential service number
(2) Search carried out in the Registry Information System including all the digitalized book and cards

Antonio Diaz-Andrade holds an MBA from Escuela de Administración de Negocios para Graduados (ESAN) in Lima, Perú, and a BSc in mechanical-aeronautic engineering from Escuela de Ingeniería Aeronáutica in Córdoba, Argentina. His areas of interest are the use of information technology in less developing countries, as well as e-business and the strategic use of information systems for supporting organizational planning and control. As a former officer, he worked in flight simulators projects for the Peruvian Air Force and was the Quality Control Department deputy manager at Servicio de Mantenimiento (SEMAN-PERU). Currently, he works as a research assistant in the information technology area at ESAN.

Martín Santana-Ormeño is associate professor of MIS and the director of Academic Affairs at the Escuela de Administración de Negocios para Graduados (ESAN) in Lima, Perú. He received his PhD in business administration from Florida International University in 1997. He also holds a MSc in management information systems from École des Hautes Études Commerciales in Montreal and a BSc in industrial engineering from Universidad de Lima. His current research interests are in electronic business, systems development (especially for the Web-centric applications) and technology-supported learning. He has published in the areas of international use of information technology, methods in software development, and strategic management of information systems.

This case was previously published in the *Annals of Cases on Information Technology,* Volume 6/2004, pp. 259-277, © 2004.

Chapter XVI

Information Systems and Technology Outsourcing:
Case Lessons from 'Travel Track'

Jeremy Rose, Manchester Metropolitan University, UK

Ray Hackney, Manchester Metropolitan University, UK

EXECUTIVE SUMMARY

This case concerns an information systems and technology (IS/IT) action research intervention into a train operating company in the newly privatized rail industry in the United Kingdom. Having operated for many years as a nationalized industry under government control, but outside the strictly commercial sector, the new company found itself in the position of having many of its important IS/IT systems being run by separate companies — it was outsourced without ever having made an outsourcing decision. The project involved information management in the maintenance wing of the company. After the event, analysis of the problem situation revealed the extent of the company's IS/IT management difficulties. Many of these problems were directly attributable to privatization and the outsourcing arrangements imposed upon the new company. The lessons from the case cast serious doubts upon the long-term benefits of outsourcing key systems and are believed to represent a significant learning vehicle relating to IS/IT adoption and exploitation.

BACKGROUND

Until quite recently the UK railway system was run as a state public service (British Rail) on behalf of the government. British Rail was privatized by the Thatcher government in an attempt to capture better efficiency and value for money through the exploitation of free market principles. The privatization took the form of franchising British Rail into a number of independent profit-making companies, with the government reserving the right to appoint the franchisees. The company commissioning the IS/IT study (here referred to as RTOC — Regional Train Operating Company) was one of the passenger train operating companies; other independent companies managed the track and supplied freight train services, rolling stock or heavy maintenance. Also privatized was the former systems development wing of British Rail, which had been responsible for developing and managing the IS/IT systems underpinning the rail industry. This left RTOC in the position of being *de facto* outsourced, without ever having made any decision to outsource. Most of their key operating IS/IT were still the systems developed by British Rail's development wing, which was now split into separate commercial enterprises with which RTOC was obliged to develop contractual relationships of a form that had previously not been necessary. External suppliers were now responsible for providing the mainframe services upon which RTOC relied. New IS/IT, in the future, would have to be commissioned or developed in-house.

The action research team was asked to advise on the management of information for fleet maintenance. The perceived problem was the high frequency of unscheduled delays caused by mechanical defects with the train units. This led to many operational problems, customer dissatisfaction and high maintenance costs, and attracted penalties imposed by TravelTrack (the track operating company) whose service was disrupted. It was argued that better analysis of the data captured during repairs would allow better targeting of maintenance, and better preventative maintenance. If it could be established which defects caused the majority of the problems, it was assumed, that these could be fixed during regular servicing. Mechanical problems would be better diagnosed and anticipated, prophylactic action taken, problematic components would be replaced before they failed in service, and the delays could be greatly reduced.

The project involved an extensive study of IS/IT systems and associated information management processes at three different sites. Contacts with the company lasted over three years, with the main body of work being undertaken over the period September 1996 to October 1999. The action research was undertaken using Soft Systems Methodology (Checkland, 1985; Checkland & Scholes, 1991; Checkland & Holwell, 1997). Over 50 personal and telephone interviews, meetings, workshops and presentations were conducted, at every level in the company from engineers and train drivers to the board of directors.

SETTING THE STAGE

Precise definitions of IS/IT outsourcing differ in the literature (Glass, 1996) but there is general agreement that it is the carrying out of IS/IT functions by third parties (Kettler & Walstrom, 1993). Expenditure on IS/IT outsourcing is considerable, with much of it placed with a few companies (Clark et al., 1995). However, there has been only a small (but increasing) number of empirical studies of IS/IT outsourcing, a feature noted by several authors (e.g., Sobol & Apte, 1995; Arnett & Jones, 1994). In particular, there have been few British studies (Willcocks & Fitzgerald, 1993; Cronk & Sharp, 1995). Several conceptual frameworks have been used to underpin outsourcing research including transaction cost theory, organizational politics (Lacity & Hirschheim, 1993) core competencies, agency theory and partnership (Hancox & Hackney, 2000). Much of the research has centered around the outsourcing decision; for instance Lacity and Hirschheim (1993) studied the outsourcing decision-making process in 13 companies. Their research highlighted the political nature of this decision making, as well as its cost efficiency focus, and served to demonstrate how complex it was to make objective decisions about the subsequent success or failure of the decision. At RTOC, no outsourcing decision was ever taken — the company simply became outsourced as a result of privatization. The researchers were involved in trying to take meaningful action in this context, and able to observe over a long period, and in considerable depth some of the difficulties that were encountered.

The Railway Industry

The July 1992 White Paper 'New Opportunities for the Railways' set out HM Government's proposals for the restructuring and privatization of the railway industry in Great Britain. These included:

- separating the management of the railway infrastructure from the provision of train services;
- the creation of a new regulatory regime; and
- the transfer to the private sector of the ownership of the railway infrastructure and the provision of train services.

The White Paper also recognized that some passenger services would continue to require subsidies. The legislation necessary to enable the implementation of these proposals became law in November 1993. The restructuring of Britain's railway industry has split British Rail into a number of new industry participants, which included:

- TravelTrack, who owns the railway infrastructure;
- passenger train operating companies (TOCs);
- freight train operators;
- rolling stock companies, who own the rolling stock (ROSCOs); and
- heavy maintenance suppliers, who maintain the rolling stock.

The systems development wing of BR, responsible for the development and maintenance of the company's IS/IT systems, was also split up into private companies. The activities of the industry participants are overseen by:

- the rail regulator, who grants licenses to operators of railway assets, monitors and enforces compliance with the terms of those licenses and regulates the access to track, stations and light maintenance depots, including the level of access charges; and
- the franchising director, who awards passenger rail franchises and monitors the performance of the services provided by the franchisees. He is also responsible for paying subsidies to franchisees.

The Railway Company

RTOC was one of 25 new passenger train operating companies. British Rail continued to take overall responsibility for these companies until franchising was completed in March 1997. Essentially RTOC operated as a private company in a regulated market, leasing rolling stock and buying services from the other industry parties. It was structured in a conventional way into functional directorates, and continued to run its own maintenance depots under the control of the director of technical engineering. The personnel, structure and management of the company continued without major changes until it was franchised. The new franchise holder immediately replaced the managing director and several of the board, and the company's name was changed to Regional Trains (RT).

Defect and Maintenance Management at RTOC

The maintenance effort was largely concentrated at the maintenance depot and took the form of regular examinations (like a car service) and much unscheduled work. Fitters at stations helped to resolve faults (defects) that arose on trains in service. Maintenance controllers organized the response to problems in service in order to keep the trains running. Information collection was very complex: Defects could be reported in a number of paper forms, verbally, or by radio or telephone via a number of other distinct routes; as shown in Figure 1.

However, defects reported were not necessarily those which had caused the problem (due to poor diagnosis by nonspecialist staff such as drivers and guards). Terminology relating to delays in service was also complex: 'incidents' 'were sometimes a 'technical failure' to distinguish them from nontechnical causes of delay (such as vandalism); a technical failure causing more than five minutes delay became a 'casualty.' The depot's principal reporting parameter was a statistic called 'miles per casualty' — a ratio of how far a type of train unit had traveled against the number of casualties. Work done was largely recorded on pieces of paper; the data was entered into the maintenance system Rail Vehicle Records (RAVERS) anything up to a month later.

Maintenance supervisors at the depot were responsible for allocating work and entering some data into the IS/IT systems, with clerks following the paper trail and entering the backlog of detail. A number of these systems were in operation - mainly dating from the pre-privatization days of British Rail. The principal systems investigated were GEMINI, which was at the hub of managing operations, and RAVERS (Figure 2), a system designed to help record maintenance data.

Although apparently independent, these pre-relational menu-driven mainframe databases were designed to interface and update each other. For instance, data collected in GEMINI about distances traveled by train units in service was relayed to RAVERS to prompt maintenance examinations. A totally independent system, TRUST, operated by TravelTrack, contained data about incidents and delays. PC based clients with more attractive interfaces (Micro RAVERS, Micro GEMINI) which downloaded data to the mainframe at night were available, and used in some places. In most cases, Windows-style front ends had been, or were in the process of being developed. The systems were built, improved and maintained by companies which had once been the IS/IT systems wing of British Rail, but were now independent. Development of the systems was overseen by a committee of representatives from all the train operating companies and the independent development companies. RTOC had its own IS/IT staff, but they specialized in the development of PC-based financial systems, and had little expertise in the mainframe systems beyond keeping the networked client stations

Figure 1. RTOC defect reporting: Primary information flows

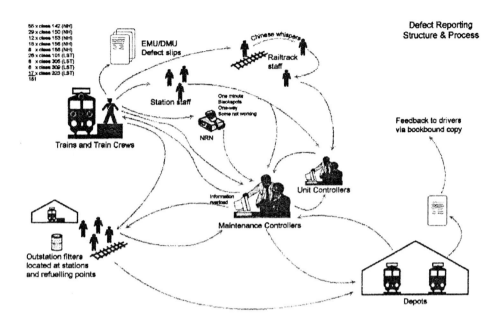

running. The status of this unit was rather low, and its leader reported to the accounting director, rather than having a seat on the board. The only staff member with any detailed mainframe knowledge left for a better post in a different industry during the course of the project. The team also encountered at least a dozen other related IS/IT systems (Figure 3). Although these systems produced a number of standardized reports, data linking delays with defects was not available— delay data was in TRUST, defect data in RAVERS and there was no way of interfacing the two systems. The designing of ad-hoc reports was exceptionally complex. A piggyback system intended to facilitate reporting by building queries to the database (FERRIT) had been recently abandoned because it was too complex for the engineers to use. Despite repeated requests, RTOC was not able to produce any hard data in a form (such as a floppy disk) that would have enabled statistical interpretation. Analysis of defects was also dependent upon the system of coding used; an additive coding system was available, but it was not used in any depth, and much of the coding was done by clerks with limited technical knowledge. Relationships between data providers (train crew) and data users (maintenance engineers) were poor, with little feedback. RTOC was not in the habit of costing defects, and little relevant financial information was available.

The project aims and objectives were originally negotiated and agreed as follows:

- Improve fleet maintenance to reduce the cost of fleet failure/delay for RTOC
- Improve the quality of maintenance data collected
- Advise on more flexible hardware/software systems
- Provide analysis of failure data and of causal variables

- Provide appropriate guidance for required change management
- Assess the cost (financial, HRM, and customer satisfaction) of fleet failure

The project was conceived in three phases. This was due to perceived difficulty and complexity. At the suggestion of the team it was agreed to report to the board of directors at the end of each stage and secure authorization to continue. As envisaged, the team made a formal report and gave a presentation to the board of directors at the end of Phase 1. Nearly a year of low level contact (negotiating and seeking approval for the next phase) now passed before serious work on the project was resumed. During this period the outcome of the franchising exercise became known, with a general sense of relief that the winner was an experienced train operating company. Phase 2 objectives were negotiated as follows:

- Refocus maintenance control with a view to linking defects and delay information at that level
- Improve data quality
- Reduce duplication of reporting
- Improve information support at depot

The most visible sign of the new franchise was the replacement of the managing director. Over the next months several other directors were also fired. The technical engineering director, to whom we reported, survived. A new focus on customer service was advertised. Relations between the consulting team and the company became strained. The manager of the depot was aggrieved by perceived criticisms in the report, while the team was irritated by the delay and by rival initiatives taking place in the company which excluded them. The focus at Rail headquarters meanwhile changed. TravelTrack (the company operating the rail infrastructure) was allowed to charge penalties for delays on its tracks which were caused by train defects

Figure 2. RAVERS schema

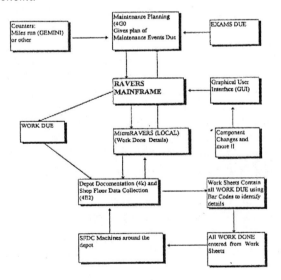

Figure 3. RTOC and Railtrack IS/IT systems case description

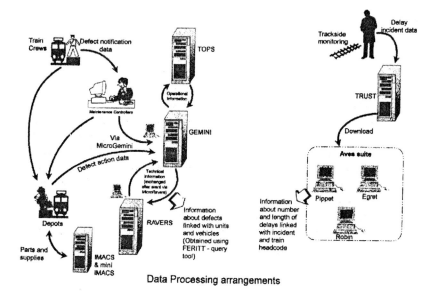

— the bills were large and management wanted to reduce them. Much effort was going into tracking the delays and challenging their attribution. However, analysis showed that there was no simple relationship between penalties and defects. The amount of the delay, and therefore the size of the penalty, was affected by many variables, including how many trains were stacked behind the failed unit, and how close to a competent fitter the unit was. The result of one of the rival initiatives was the purchase of a IS/IT system called ROBIN. This system was designed to sit on top of RAVERS and TRUST, and to integrate data about delays and defects. Unfortunately, its operation required a minor change to a database field in RAVERS which proved difficult to effect. The depot, meanwhile, looked at a Windows style front end for RAVERS, but decided that it lacked the necessary functionality. The only member of the information services staff with technical knowledge of RAVERS and GEMINI left to take up a post in Edinburgh. Levels of cooperation were much reduced, and the team found it difficult to get into people's diaries. The participants couldn't understand the long delays and apparent lack of progress and wanted quick fix solutions. Problems perceived by the consultancy team included lack of motivation, lack of understanding of RAVERS and how to use it, and a general lack of direction. The researchers put together a strategic review for the Board of Directors, which outlined the problems, and offered, in a short document entitled 'Vision for the Millennium' a description of optimized maintenance information management, based around a modern relational database system with sophisticated reporting functions.

The main proposals were for:

- A customer service rationale
- A revised message from senior management: zero tolerance of delays
- One method of reporting a defect

- Re-organization of maintenance focusing on the managing of information
- Modern IS/IT systems
- Real-time data entry at the depots and the outstations
- Greater use of the resulting management information

The board of directors welcomed the presentation and report and a vigorous debate ensued. However, the project began to run into difficulty as the researchers realized that the company had no way of achieving such a system. The team did not submit a proposal for Phase 3, nor were they asked to by the company.

RTOC — Strategic Level

RTOC was locked into its outsourcing arrangement by the market. Although there were other companies who could have provided the hardware management facilities, no other companies had the experience of developing the software in the railway industry, because, historically, British Rail had catered for its own needs. The newly privatized software companies were small and likely to be taken over by bigger software houses with much more experience and aggressive commercial instincts. There was little guarantee of future security in the outsourcing arrangements for RTOC. Within the company there was no experience of managing IS/IT outsourcing contracts, often regarded as a key ingredient of outsourcing success (Hancox & Hackney, 2000). The contracting was thought of as an administrative burden. IS/IT was regarded at board level as an expensive service, not as a source of competitive advantage or a revenue generator, and the IS/IT director did not report at a high enough level to influence this thinking. There were no strategic plans for the development of the maintenance service with which IS/IT strategies could be aligned. More over the board room was highly politicized by the franchising decisions, which resulted in a new franchisee and the replacement of the managing director and several of the board.

RTOC — Tactical Level

The predominantly engineering culture at the depot legitimated 'oily hands' engineering work, but viewed information work as an irritating overhead. Although RAVERS was efficient at transaction processing, its reporting interface was extremely poor, and it was very hard to use for the statistical interrogation of data sets characteristic of sophisticated management practice. The data kept in it was rather unreliable, because of poor information management practice. Management at the depot claimed 'too much information' and did not value any opportunities offered by the querying of accurate datasets.

There was no effective control over or influence upon the development of the mainframe systems operated by the newly privatized systems firms. It was exceptionally complex even to implement minor changes; they had to be approved by the overseeing committee made up of other independent train operating companies, each pursuing their own strategic direction. Some of these companies were in direct competition with RTOC. There was no in-house systems development effort in these operations and maintenance areas. The absence of any local systems development work in these arenas tended to mean that a 'magic bullet' attitude was adopted. The independent systems companies developed new systems without visible consultation, and RTOC responded only by purchasing or not purchasing, after cursory evaluation. One such system was intended to aid the management of examinations; it was demonstrated in a presentation but had little relevance to the company's perceived problems.

Another system (a Windows-style front end to RAVERS) was evaluated on site. The graphical user interface was a much needed improvement, but the developers had omitted important functionality, and the system was not adopted. A third system, called ROBIN, was intended to sit on top of RAVERS and connect incident data (collected by TravelTrack in a different system) with defect data. This system was purchased, but its implementation was dependent on a fudge — an alteration to an unused field in RAVERS. This ten minute programming job was held up in the overseeing committee. Of course any rival company which was already using this field for its data would have no incentive to agree to such a change. ROBIN was still unused when the researchers ended the project. Because of relative lack of experience of information work, the depot had problems establishing criteria for evaluating new systems, articulating requirements for new systems, or even with committing resources to these activities.

RTOC — Operational Level

A number of problems were very obvious. Reporting of defects was inconsistent and incomplete, relationships between controllers, engineers and drivers were poor, maintenance controllers in the control room were focused on the 'sexy' job of keeping the trains running rather than the less glamorous job of carefully reporting defects, maintenance data was coded and entered by untrained clerks a month after it was produced, and engineers were interested in heavy metal technologies, not silicon information ones. Though the databases were outdated, with rather clumsy interfaces, they might have been efficient transactional systems had they been used properly. In fact, the systems were rather poorly understood and utilized. For example, GEMINI, the system designed to manage the operation of the train service, and RAVERS, the maintenance system, were interactive. When a train failed in service, a maintenance controller would designate it a 'casualty' in GEMINI. Whilst the train is flagged as a casualty it cannot be to put back in service on a route for obvious safety reasons. This generated an entry in the 'work needed' file in RAVERS and an automatic print out at the depot, advertising the work that needed to be carried out. When the work had been carried out, the designers' intention was that a maintenance supervisor at the depot, using RAVERS, would 'clear' the casualty—thus releasing the train for service. Unfortunately the maintenance supervisors at the depot did not know how to clear a casualty, and in any case the work-done forms were entered into RAVERS several weeks later by a clerk. Trains were released into service by phone calls to the maintenance controllers at headquarters. When the situation got desperate, a clerk rang an operator at the development and management company (in another town) and asked him to run a batch file which cleared outstanding casualties. Here the users simply did not understand the set of interactions that was intended by the IS/IT system designers. Another example: at a certain outstation, the fitters needed hard copy instructions. All problems that were destined for this outstation were entered by the maintenance controllers as casualties, whether or not they had caused the statutory five minutes delay. This was because a 'casualty' report generated an automatic printout, whereas a 'defect' report did not. Here the operational need generated bad information practice and erroneous data. Maintaining good data was not regarded a priority. A third example: the language of defects (a mechanical problem delaying a train unit) and casualties (defects causing more than five minutes delay) was embedded in the IS/IT system and could not be changed. However, delays in service of more than three minutes attracted penalties from TravelTrack. It was decided to revise the definition of a casualty to a defect causing three minutes delay. However this immediately made nonsense of the depot's reporting statistic — miles per casualty.

CURRENT CHALLENGES

As part of British Rail, RTOC had always had its IS/IT needs supplied internally. Now as a newly privatized company, it found itself a partner in an outsourcing arrangement. However, there is little evidence that that arrangement is likely to benefit the company. Rather, it seems likely to perpetuate and exacerbate the company's existing difficulties. These difficulties can be summarized as follows.

Low Status and Visibility of IS/IT

The low status and low visibility of IS/IT is reinforced by outsourcing. IS/IT is confirmed as a nonessential service and a cost burden, contracting as an administrative burden, and skilled IS/IT professionals are left out of the company's core decision-making processes. Key operating systems (keeping the trains running) are afforded only minor importance.

Reactive Management

Management responds to problems rather than setting agendas. IS/IT is employed to help solve a problem, rather than aligned with business strategy to gain competitive advantage. Outsourcing reinforces the nonstrategic characterization of IS/IT systems

Skill Shortage Leading to Poor Information Management

Information management practice at the maintenance depot was poor. These practices went unrecognized largely because there were few skilled IS/IT practitioners available to challenge them. Outsourcing reinforces the skill shortage by taking the skilled practitioners off-site and making their time chargeable.

No Close Working Relationships Between Developers and Users

Outsourcing degrades the already poor communication between developers and users. The systems users developed many poor uses of the systems simply because they had no way to change the systems as their needs changed. Similarly the systems developers built systems which were of no great value to the company because they did not investigate the users' business needs

Difficulties Achieving New Systems

New systems or substantial modifications were urgently required, but the outsourcing situation made them particularly hard to achieve. Staff at the company depot don't have the expertise to specify or evaluate new systems. They may not even be able to recognize that they need them. The development companies were too remote to recognize these needs or provide useful systems. Outsourcing takes IS/IT skilled staff out of the decision-making and agenda-setting loops.

The emergent picture is of poor information management practice. This was partly caused by the low priority it was afforded, but also partly caused by inappropriate design of the IS/IT systems, lack of understanding of the how they were intended to be used, and great difficulties involved in changing the systems to reflect changing business conditions. RTOC experienced a catalogue of information management problems. It did not have the necessary mechanisms for articulating or achieving IS/IT requirements. There was no relevant technical expertise, no experience in managing contracts, no awareness of systems possibilities. Management tended to work around the information that was laboriously provided, rather than specifying its information needs. Bad data management procedures went unrecognized and there was no effective way of making changes to existing systems. Nor was there recognition of problems with the existing systems which would have served as a platform for learning about requirements for new systems. Everyone thought that they should have a new system, but that it was someone else's responsibility to make it happen. There were no ways of specifying a new system, or developing criteria for choosing an off-the-shelf solution, had such a thing existed. There was no board member with overall responsibility for IS/IT, and no formal or informal decision-making and consensus-building communities. There was no in-house system development expertise in the relevant area, and no functioning development relationship with the software supplier companies.

RTOC's problems were directly attributable to the company's history; no serious criticism of managers or staff is implied. By and large they simply struggled with the legacy of privatization and the difficulties inherent in their situation. However, we characterize the end result as dysfunctional paralysis by outsourcing. RTOC found itself an outsourcer by historical accident and struggled to deal with the unfortunate consequences. However, companies involved in or contemplating outsourcing, perhaps in search of short-term cash savings, would be wise to learn some of the lessons identified within this case.

REFERENCES

Arnett, K. P., & Jones, M. C. (1994). Firms that choose outsourcing: A profile. *Information and Management, 26*(4), 179-188.

Checkland, P. B. (1981). *Systems thinking, systems practice.* New York: Plenum.

Checkland, P. B., & Holwell, S. (1998). *Information, systems, and information systems.* Chichester: Wiley.

Checkland, P. B., & Scholes, J. (1990). *SSM in action.* Chichester: Wiley.

Clark, T. D., Jr., Zmud, R. W., & McCray, G. E. (1995). The outsourcing of information services: Transforming the nature of business in the information industry. *Journal of Information Technology, 10,* 221-237.

Cronk, J., & Sharp, J. (1995). A framework for deciding what to outsource in information technology. *Journal of Information Technology, 10,* 259-267.

Glass, R. L. (1996). The end of the outsourcing era. *Information Systems Management, 13*(2), 89-91.

Hancox, M., & Hackney, R. A (2000). IT outsourcing: Conceptualising practice and perception. *Information Systems Journal, 2*(9), 45-59.

Kettler, K., & Walstrom, J. (1993). The outsourcing decision. *International Journal of Information Management, 13*(6), 449-459.

Lacity, M. C., & Hirschheim, R. (1993). *Information systems outsourcing: Myths, metaphors and reality.* Chichester: Wiley.

Sobol, M. G., & Apte, U. (1995). Domestic and global outsourcing practices of America's most effective IS users. *Journal of Information Technology, 10,* 269-280.

Willcocks, L., & Fitzgerald, G. (1994). *A business guide to outsourcing information technology.* London: Business Intelligence Ltd.

Jeremy Rose was born in Manchester, won an exhibition to read English at Cambridge and subsequently trained to be a musician at the Royal College of Music in London. After working for some years for the Rambert Dance Company and Music Projects London his career was cut short by injury and he retrained at Lancaster, gaining his MSc in information management with distinction. He then took up his present post as senior lecturer in business information technology in the Faculty of Management and Business at the Manchester Metropolitan University. He continued to collaborate with Peter Checkland on research projects, and has more recently worked with colleagues at the University of Aalborg. He has published in management, systems and IS forums. Doctoral work at Lancaster related the themes of action research, information system development, soft systems methodology and structuration theory. Other research interests include IS evaluation, systems methodology, actor network theory, BPR, knowledge management, the health service and Inter/intranet development. He is currently visiting associate professor in the Department of Computer Science at the University of Aalborg.

Dr. Ray Hackney is director of business information technology research within the Manchester Metropolitan University, UK. He holds a Cert. Ed, BSc (Hons), MA and PhD from leading universities and has contributed extensively to research in the field of information systems with publications in numerous national and international conferences and journals. He has taught on a number of MBA programmes including MMU, Manchester Business School and the Open University. He leads the organizing committee for the annual BIT and BITWorld Conference series and is a member of the Strategic Management Society and Association of Information Systems. Dr. Hackney has served on the board of the UK Academy for Information Systems since 1997 and has served as the vice president research for IRMA (USA), associate editor of the JGIM, JEUC, JLIM and ACITM. He has also been a reviewer for a number of publishers, journals, and conferences, and was an associate editor for ICIS'99. His research interests are the strategic management of information systems within a variety of organizational context.

This case was previously published in the *Annals of Cases on Information Technology Applications and Management in Operations,* Volume 3/2001, pp. 141-152, © 2001.

Chapter XVII

Enterprise Information Portals:
Efficacy in the Information Intensive Small to Medium Sized Business

Wita Wojtkowski, Boise State University, USA

Marshall Major, Moffatt Thomas and Co. Law Firm, USA

EXECUTIVE SUMMARY

The focus of this case study is a successful regional law firm (an information intensive enterprise) that integrates information technology to improve the timeliness and quality of their work product. The firm uses information technology as an efficient and productive tool allowing them more time to understand their clients' needs and envision where their businesses will be tomorrow. Their information services professionals evaluate new technologies with an eye toward improving delivery of legal services: the goal is to build an atmosphere where complex business is handled with ease. In this case we explore the issues related to the implementation of an enterprise portal. The issues are both technological and behavioral.

ORGANIZATIONAL BACKGROUND

MT is a successful law firm providing legal services to the Pacific Northwest and Intermountain region since 1954. With offices in Boise, Idaho Falls, and Pocatello, Idaho, the firm is strategically situated for direct contact with the governor's office, the legislature, federal and state administrative agencies, courts, and international and national corporations engaged in business throughout the region.

MT has 41 attorneys, 11 paralegals and 60 support staff serving clients in the full-spectrum of business, litigation and regulatory areas. Their attorneys focus on the realities of their clients' continually evolving business needs. Whether they are working with a small start-up company or an international corporation, they take a teamwork approach in responding to legal issues with practical and innovative legal solutions.

To improve the timeliness and quality of their work product, the MT law firm attempts to deliberately integrate information technology in their practice. The firm is very cognizant of the fact that technology is only as good as the people who use it. To that end they employ a group of information services professionals who evaluate new technologies with an eye toward improving the delivery of legal services. These professionals also provide updates and educate attorneys and staff on the use of the firm's technology.

Like their clients, the firm uses information technology as a productive tool, allowing them to understand where their clients' businesses will be tomorrow. MT firm realizes that because Idaho is located in the heart of the Intermountain West, long distance transactions are a fact of life. MT's clients do business in all 50 states and internationally. To meet the physical challenges of the Intermountain West location, they aggressively utilize technology. Beyond being accessible to their clients through e-mail, voice mail and fax, every attorney office and workstation has Internet access, together with research services and access to firm-produced documents. These technology capabilities are further enhanced by a commitment to old-fashioned hard work: 24-hour word processing, 11-hour business days and Saturday morning business hours. They use technology every day to be more efficient, responsive, accessible and prompt. This firm's goal is to build an atmosphere where complex business is handled with ease. MT firm strives to continually improve on the ways they utilize information technology in their practice. To that end, the firm looked into the development and utilization of the enterprise information portal.

Enterprise information portal is a presentation methodology for information that exists in computers "out there somewhere." From the end-user perspective, an enterprise information portal is customizable Web page that contains pertinent information from the enterprise databases and data warehouses, e-mail and calendars, enterprise's messaging systems, stock quotes, news headlines, corporate communications, reference links, and relevant, for a given user, task resources (Collins, 2001).

The typical computer user does not care where the information comes from. They basically want everything they need to be easily accessible so that they may perform their job correctly (Malhorta & Galetta, 1999; Melbourne, 2002). Portals deliver on this ability to organize and present information from many sources, including the Internet, databases, document repositories (directories or document management systems) and organizational intranets (Finkelstein & Aiken, 1999).

Portals, since their inception in 1998, have been successful in e-government and large corporations (Baldwin, 2002). The question that is asked in this case study is whether a portal is appropriate for small businesses that are information intensive.

SETTING THE STAGE

MT is an information intensive enterprise. Many documents are generated and many documents have to be accessed during the daily work of this firm. Information is the lifeblood of business such as this law office. MT, although operating in 50 states, can be considered a small business. It employs a little more than 100 people. Its permanent IS staff, referred to as the IS Services unit, is composed of four professionals: MM - the IS Team Lead; CG - Applications Analyst; JH - Desktop Analyst; and MF - Desktop Specialist. The firm also employs part-time personnel. Organizational structure of the IS services in the firm is shown in Figure 1.

Functionally, the IS personnel operates as follows. Desktop people (analyst, specialist and part-time personnel) are responsible for fixing software problems, answering Help Desk questions, fixing all hardware problems, software installation and the array of day-to-day information systems related problems. This team takes all the incoming calls, but they are not necessarily able to respond to all. Some of the tasks are often deferred to other resources, either at MT or to one of their support vendors. Application personnel's task is to enhance the performance of software in current use: be responsible for productivity improvements, documentation, procedures, and the optimal use of, for example, Word and WordPerfect macros, templates, and software training.

IS Team Lead in MT firm (Mr. MM) has also the title of Visionary/IS Manager. MM is where the buck stops with regard to technology. It is his job to make sure that technology is being used intelligently, efficiently and cost effectively. His current focus is on the following areas. First, he has made it a high priority to improve productivity by increasing the reliability of all hardware and by addressing the IS Team's escalated Help Desk calls. Secondly, his focus is on leveraging existing investment in technology to provide the firm with a competitive advantage. In this he is looking at ways to deliver

Figure 1. Organizational structure of the IS services in the MT firm (HR — human resources)

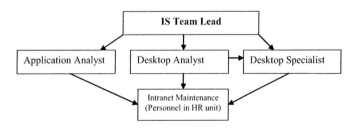

information to the firm in creative and (what may appear to the user) effortless ways. Information in the context of this firm is wide ranging: from GroupWise, to daily national news, to firm's news, and general and specialized legal news. The following text appears on the firm's Web page accessible to firm's attorneys:

> *The technology is touching every area of our business and as a result, it must be used creatively within the firm to deliver services to you and our clients in ways that weren't possible five years ago. We're here to harness the creative nature of technology and offer it as a tool to each of you. Please contact MM to learn more about using of technology to benefit your practice.*

The following text appears on the firm's Web page accessible to firm's personnel as well as to firm's clients:

> *The IS Team is working hard to be an effective and efficient service organization. We believe that you are our clients and that we are here to serve you. Please provide the Team Lead, MM, with feedback as to how we are doing (good or bad) and if you have any ideas on how we can deliver our services better, faster or more effectively. The most critical thing that we need is your communication. If you have a problem, let us know. The only problems we can't solve, resolve or work around are the ones we don't know about.*

The Reality

Information services reports directly to JJ - Office Administrator. Office Administrator, in turn, reports to senior partners — all lawyers. Office administrator is the top non-lawyer in the firm. He always walks the fine line between attorneys, (who in a law firm are what is called a "billable unit," bringing in money), and those who support them. Support personnel are not "billable units," and are thus treated as second-class citizens who to do not directly bring in money to the firm. There exists an undercurrent of tension between these two groups. The firm's personnel structure is shown in Figure 2.

A very interesting organizational dynamic is at work in the firm: the firm's top non-lawyer (Office Administrator) is quite cognizant of the needs of the attorneys and what the support staff requires for their daily work. He politically maneuvers, as much as possible, to keep both factions happy. The office administrator very rarely offers any opinions (even though he is an accounting expert) and is not given a lot of latitude (by the firm's senior partners) in decision making. Nevertheless, the closer a person is to the production of legal documents, the more respected they are in a law firm. In this firm for example, a "wordprocessor" with 20 years of experience has the ear of many of the senior attorneys. However, regarding wordprocessing technology they may need, lawyers still discount what that "wordprocessor" may require. Often they assume that this 20-year veteran is "whining and just wants to go home early."

It is important to realize that law firms use word processing differently than any other type of business. Legal documents, other than letters, are typically long (50-70 pages) and include table of contents, automatic numbering and extensive outlines. In addition,

Figure 2. Organizational structure of the MT firm

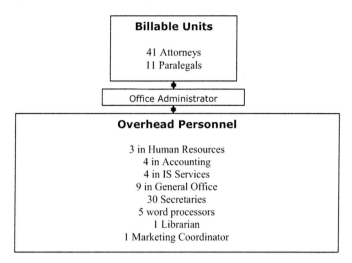

there are generally two to five people who want or need to have input on a document. Depending on the complexity of the document, the contributors may be many. For example:

- **Administrative assistant (secretary):** Creates the framework of a document including addresses, headers, and signatures. The secretary may also search in the document management system for documents that are similar to what the attorney will be doing. If similar documents are found, the secretary will give those documents to the attorney so they can identify valuable components and reuse them. This reuse process greatly lowers the cost to clients for document production.

- **Attorney:** Puts text into the body of the document through copy/paste, typing or dictating.

- **Legal assistant (paralegal):** At any time, depending on the complexity of the document or case, a paralegal might be called in to work on content, research or review of other documents. Paralegal does the "grunt work" on many documents and summarizes them for the attorneys.

- **Word processing or administrative assistant:** Type from dictated tapes into the document or otherwise prepare document for a first draft.

- **Another attorney:** Either an older mentor or another attorney gives a second opinion on the document.

- **Client:** Receives the document via fax or e-mail for review. If sent via e-mail, the law firm first sends the document in Adobe Acrobat PDF format so that modifications will be difficult.

- **Administrative assistant:** Incorporates any changes.
- **Attorney:** Approves final draft.

Attorneys are not good business people generally: they do not make decisions the way decisions are made in a typical business. The reasons are many. For example, the litigating attorneys are dreadful business people as they are trained (by definition) to analyze and criticize *everything.* As a result, any decision making process in a firm moves very, very slowly. Moreover, the shared ownership model of the law firm spreads power in a way that is incredibly complex and creates difficulty with information sharing and withholding. Very often senior partners withhold information because they see it as an opportunity to control power even in *trivial contexts.* For example, the IS Team was trying, for the longest time, to get permission to communicate to the support people in the firm that they are moving from the WordPerfect platform to Word platform in about six weeks. However, one of the senior managing partners (for political reasons) decided that the IS Team should not communicate this specific information. So, when beset with questions like "What is the status of moving to Word?" IS personnel responds that they are still working on it (although they know the precise rollout time). With trivialities like these one, much energy is often spent working against the business.

Nevertheless, the IS group mandate is to bring into play the most current information technology in such a way that the complex business of the firm is handled with ease. That is why the firm's IS Team Leader proposed to implement an enterprise information portal.

CASE DESCRIPTION

The project started with only IT Lead involved. MM's reasoning went as follows: in our law firm we deal with variety of information and a variety of documents which have to be accessed and delivered by our legal professionals, non-professional personnel, and our clients. All should have access to the Internet as well as to the specific documents, specific information, and applications they need.

The portal is the aggregator and presenter of information to a widely varied group of users. A single portal can look differently depending on what device is attached to it and what role the user holds within our firm. Since the portal is a collection of technologies (i.e., HTML, XML, Web services, LDAP directory, and databases) that function together as a presentation tool, we may consider the efficacy of its use in our firm. MM envisioned the "ecology" of a portal for the firm, and visualized it as shown in Figure 3.

To assess in more detail the need for a portal in his firm, MM consulted work on corporate portals by Collins (2001, pp. 50-51). He prepared the above table of attributes and problems.

MM considered all these and came to the following conclusions:

For attorneys, our portal can deliver dynamic lists of custom financial reports based upon login as well as links to legal resources on the Internet. To minimize the potential that the planned portal will not be used as intended (always a problem with professional staff who see information technology as an intrusion), MM considered important to plan for special approach to training (to be delivered by the IS Team) customized expressly for the attorneys in the firm.

For the paralegals, the portal can deliver personal reports of hours billed, sharing of legal research ideas, and centralized information sharing.

For the administrator, in addition to all other information, the portal can deliver dynamic lists of custom financial reports based upon login.

For the human resources (HR), the portal can allow self-service HR through the Intranet, where benefit summary and forms can be easily found.

The portal can be used by the accounting department in a customized fashion since accounting department administers all bills sent to clients and provides financial reporting information.

With a portal, IS Team can deliver technology training, technology tips, and complex information via the Intranet.

For clients, it will be possible to give logins and passwords and allow them access to customized Web pages with financial and other pertinent information.

Now, the IS Team got involved. To assess further the efficacy of a portal, the IS Team conducted semi-structured interviews with 10 administrative assistants (secretaries). The goal of each interview was to find out how they worked day-to-day, if they used the current intranet, and if so, what parts of the intranet they used. (The firm currently uses GroupWise 5.5 for e-mail, collaboration, calendar, and document management and WordPerfect 9 and Word XP for word processing. The secretaries spend roughly 95% of their day in GroupWise and word processing programs.)

Overwhelmingly, the secretaries let IS Team know that they would like to know "all the resources and features available" and that they would then incorporate what was relevant to their desk. Many similarities were found in actions they took and the processes they use to create new complex documents, such as, for example legal

Figure 3. Possible ecology of a portal for the MT firm

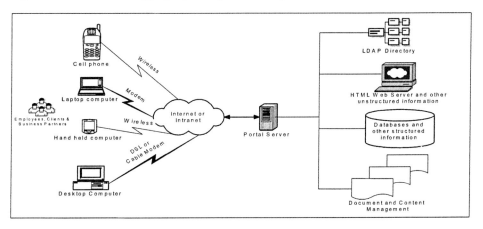

Table 1.

Attribute	Problem
Consistency	Employees need consistent information to make routine decisions.
Centralized Data Access	Senior partners need information from many different systems to make strategic decisions.
Web-Based Applications	Employees need to be able to access firm's information from an intranet site through a browser and complete most firm-related activities online.
Centralized Data Access	Paralegals and support personnel must access information from multiple data sources and applications to complete their assigned activities.
Filter Information Overload	Many employees are not aware of information or resources available to complete their responsibilities. Some cannot locate or navigate efficiently through company information or the intranet site.
Consistent Interfaces and Just-In-Time Training	Professional and support staff require extensive training to use portions of the applications and systems they need to use to complete their responsibilities

pleadings. However, despite all their similarities, almost every secretary was quick to point out that every "desk" is different because of the personalities of the attorneys to whom they are assigned. This need to feel unique amidst the common functions of their jobs hints at the potential value for personalization a portal may offer.

Because MT is a small business, MM looked into simple portal products intended for small businesses or functional departments of large organizations. Such portal products are relatively easy to deploy and are often free, included with an operating system, or low cost (less than $8,000 for 100 users). Examples include IBuySpy (a free Microsoft .Net portal at http://www.asp.net/), Novell's Novell Portal Services (included with NetWare 6 at http://www.novell.com/products/portal/), and Microsoft's SharePoint Portal Server ($8,000 for 100 users) at http://www.microsoft.com/sharepoint/).

MM pondered and pondered his options, and, taking into consideration the professional, organizational, and technical context in which he operates (for more details see also Appendix), MM settled on the Novell Portal Services (NPS) portal. When all is said and done, his decision was really based on the economic considerations. With the NPS there were no additional expenditures for software. MM's decision was based on the following reasoning: the firm has invested in the Novell Technology (NetWare 6, eDirectory, and GroupWise); NPS is already included in the NetWare 6; with the adoption of NPS no additional charges are to be incurred.

Brief on the Novell Portal Services Architecture

NPS is an enterprise information portal that is bundled with Novell's NetWare 6. It is a servlet application that runs on Apache Tomcat. It uses Novell's eDirectory version 8.6.1 and above as the directory of resources and groups, as well as for LDAP authentication. The Novell NetWare 6 server is currently running Apache Web Server version 1.3.20, Apache Tomcat version 3.3 and Sun's Java SDK 1.3. NPS can run on Novell's eDirectory on Red Hat Linux 7.0, Sun Solaris version 8, Windows 2000 or NetWare 6. NPS requires the correct versions of Apache Web Server, Tomcat Servlet and Java, and then it will run on any of the network operating systems in use in the firm. Other Web servers' configurations that will work include IIS .50 and iPlanet 6.0 and JRUN and WebLogic. The architecture of NPS is written in Java, XML, XSLT, and HTML. The entire portal exists in a subdirectory off of the tomcat\webapps directory.

CURRENT CHALLENGES/PROBLEMS FACING THE ORGANIZATION

Thus at the MT law firm, a generic and inexpensive portal was selected. A decision was made to pick a product that does not need to tie in into the existing accounting system. The basic reason for this choice was this: although the accounting system vendor offered a portal product that might tie in with their accounting system, this product was very expensive.

Yes, the firm currently has an elaborate and well working accounting system. To generate automatic reports from this system IS Lead and a member of the accounting staff designed an Access database that would generate dynamic Web pages filled with URL links to a Crystal Reports server. The Crystal Reports server produces reports that the authorized employees consider necessary. Those who need the reports are required to log into this dynamic reporting system — through the generic portal, they can be automatically logged into it. Of course, this saved a login for the user and offered a clear example of how a generic portal product can be used as a gateway to simplify access to other information resources in the firm.

Nevertheless, at the firm, the enthusiasm for the portal has been disappointing. Perhaps this is only natural since change is difficult, no matter what the context (Brown & Duguid, 2000). IS Lead is still questioned by the senior partners in the firm why time is being spent on this "unimportant" tool. In reality, the business owners still do not see the value in self-service and capture of tacit and explicit information relevant to the daily business of the firm. Even though NPS does not require additional expenditure for software, it became clear that the firm's organizational dynamics needed to be carefully considered.

What we have here is perhaps a failure to communicate. In an information intensive business such as a law firm, the need to communicate face-to-face, as opposed to electronic communication through e-mail, must be balanced (Crowther & Goldhaber, 2001). MM has been communicating with the firm's board via e-mail, and to his surprise he came to find out that he did not have the rapport that he thought he had. What is more, in the MT firm, appropriate communication is essential. With secretaries, IS Team can talk in terms of giving them additional training on a product (GroupWise, for example) to help them work more efficiently. Such an approach should not be attempted with attorneys; the habitual attorneys' answer to a proposal for a possible training is "I don't have time for that." Instead, if IS Team communicates that "Let's save you 30 minutes a day" or "How about not driving into the office on Saturdays and just work from home," they obtain consent. Although this represents simply repackaging the same training, communicating the relevance (as perceived by a given person) is crucial. Essentially, the IS Team discovered that if they "paint the appropriate picture," then they have greater success.

When all was said and done, the fact that MM had eight years of technology management experience didn't matter to the board of directors. The board makes decisions about what is important, and subsequently, where money should be spent for technology. Their decisions are based upon limited information, a modest amount of knowledge, and a limited circle of people who assemble around them. Such a situation often leads to dysfunction (May, 2003). At MT, for example, one of the board members makes all technology recommendations based upon the information his secretary provides to him. It turns out that his decisions are essentially based on her viewpoint. If she is having a bad day (her computer crashes, let us say) and that happens to fall before a board meeting, then all IS purchase decisions are stopped, and IS Team's credibility is put into question. Conceivably, this is a situation where the experts in one field (law) do not want to look like they do not know what they are talking about (in computing), and attack (with fervor) every small problem. MM concluded that the members of the board do not generally look at the larger picture, and do not take a single negative event associated with technology with a grain of salt. Perhaps the problem is similar to that expressed by T. May in his *Computerworld* article (May, 2003):

> *Most Suits (executives) don't deserve success from their investments in IT. They haven't laid the groundwork or done the homework necessary to develop good IT judgment.*

When the IS Team communicated face-to-face with the leaders in the organization, it became apparent that a continuous work on the portal was not where they should be spending their time. The allocation of IS resources to the portal would have been a poor political move at the time when the secretaries working for the members of the board of directors kept complaining about crashing computers and sluggish productivity with WordPerfect product. So, the team communicated to the board of directors that they will concentrate on another project: moving the firm from WordPerfect as the primary word processing program to Word, because uniform documents production is so important to the firm. MM finally realized that perhaps they need in this firm something similar to "Maslow's Hierarchy of Needs" pyramid (Maslow, 1968; Griffin, 2001) for information technology, and that reliability is somewhere at the base of such a pyramid.

MM now knew that a buy-in to portal involved a new way of thinking about firm's information, resources, data and processes. Essentially, MT firm will be forced to rethink how data is captured and stored so that it can be presented through a portal.

He also realized that organizations that implement portal technologies will find the greatest return when they focus on adding value or capitalizing on the difficult to replace, high value added employees (Stewart, 1997). The fact is that in this law firm, the producers, the billable units, are king (high value added employees). IS Services are a necessary and valuable resource that exists to support the firm in its primary goal and, as long as the technologists remember that fact, they can continue to deliver high quality and high value results. It is when they lose track of what their purpose is that they waste time on initiatives, which do not bring a high enough level of perceived value to the firm.

The lessons learned by MM involve both sides of the portal equation, technical and organizational. Do you have executive support? How to communicate the technical issues? Does the culture of the organization support and encourage the capture of knowledge? Does the portal work with the accounting system to provide needed financial information? The firm used Crystal Reports to create a dynamic reporting system, and this has been more successful than they had imagined.

The firm has taken on a few custom Web applications for current Intranet and they have all failed. One was a database of experts; it has been in full working condition for over six months, and it is still unused. The reason is simple: there is still a disagreement as to who is responsible for the input and maintenance. Typically, the IS people will assume responsibility, however, due to an increasing workload, this is now not possible, and the rest of the organization does not have time to dedicate. And MM discovered that the generic portal would still require a lot of effort to maintain.

REFERENCES

Baldwin, H. (2002). How integration needs are driving portals growth. *ZDNet Technology Update*. Retrieved December 8, 2002, from http://www.zdnet.com/filters/printerfriendly/0,6061,2855550-92,00.html

Brown J. S., & Duguid, P. (2000). *The social life of information*. Boston: Harvard Business School Press.

Collins, H. (2001). *Corporate portals*. New York: AMACOM.

Crowther, G., & Goldhaber, G. (2001). Face-to face or e-mail: the medium makes a difference. *Communication World, 18*(5), 23-26.

Finkelstein, C., & Aiken, P. (1999). *Building corporate portals with XML*. New York, NY: McGraw-Hill Professional Publishing.

Griffin, E. (2001). *A first look at communication theory*. New York: McGraw-Hill.

Malhotra, Y., & Galletta, D. F. (1999). Extending the technology acceptance model to account for social influence: theoretical bases and empirical validation. *Proceedings of the 32nd Hawaii International Conference on System Sciences*.

Maslow, A. H. (1968). *Toward a psychology of being*. New York: D. Van Nostrand Company.

May, T. (2003). Save the suits from themselves. *Computerworld*. Retrieved April 2, 2003, from http://www.computerworld.com/printthis/2003/0,4814,79119,00.html

Melbourne, L. (2002). Who knew? People hold the key to the enterprise portal. *KMWorld*, S14-S15.

Stewart, T. A. (1997). *Intellectual capital*. New York: Currency/Doubleday.

APPENDIX

The MT Firm

Law firms primarily produce documents to aid their clients. The MT law firm does about 40% business transactional work. This type of work is comprised of contracts, negotiations, business agreements, securities filings and other paperwork needed to transact business. The remaining 60% of the firm is litigation. This is where the firm represents clients in defending lawsuits brought against them. The firm described in this case specializes in representing companies rather than individuals. Much of a litigation legal practice involves filing documents with a court. Examples of documents filed with a court include briefs and pleadings. Beyond document production, lawyers also charge their time by the hour. Depending on the size of the law firm, the type of law practiced and type of billing requirements of the clients, the accounting functions can be very complex. MT law firm has a very sophisticated time and billing system to accommodate the needs of its corporate clients.

Organizational Data for the MT Firm

Billing Units
>   41 Attorneys
>   11 Paralegals

Personal reports of hours billed; research idea sharing; centralized information sharing
Total: 52

Overhead
>   1 Administrator
>   Oversees all non-attorney functions- primarily an accounting and managerial function.
>   3 HR
>   Human resource functions. Employee benefits administration and annual reviews. One part time employee from HR function maintains the current intranet.
>   4 Accounting
>   Billing, AR, AP; administration of all bills sent to clients and provision of financial reporting information. Over last 9 months reporting has been shifted to Crystal Reports
>   4 IS
>   Technology implementation, strategy, troubleshooting, limited support in complex legal matters, technology training
>   9 General Office Staff
>   30 Secretaries
>   5 Wordprocessors
>   1 Librarian
>   1 Marketing Coordinator

Total: 58

Hardware and Software in Use in TM Firm

In their daily work IS Team primarily supports Windows 2000 professional desktops running WordPerfect 9 and GroupWise with its Document Management System.

Hardware

95 — Dell Pentium III 933 desktops
20 — Dell Pentium 4 2.0 Ghz desktops
7 — Dell Pentium 1.13 Ghz laptops

4 — Dell servers including one quad processor, ZEON 700
10 — "white box" 1.8 Ghz utility servers for backend processing such as spam filtering and Crystal Reports
4 — Compaq servers
1 — Compaq DL380 packaged cluster — two computers and a shared storage array with 12 x 36.4 Gb hard drives for 360Gb of hard drive space.
This is the new GroupWise server.

14 — printers, all HP, ranging from LaserJet II to 4300 and 8550
These produce approximately 120K pages a month
7 — copiers — all different brands — approximately 145K pages per month

Server OS

The quad processor Dell server is Windows NT 4.0 for accounting system with an Informix database

Two of the "utility servers" are Windows 2000 Servers that run DNS,DHCP, Intranet and Terminal Server with Citrix

10 servers are Novell NetWare 6 and one server is Netware 5.1.
The Novell Portal Services portal runs on a utility server
    SpamAssassin — spam filtering
    Guinevere — GroupWise e-mail scanner for virus, spam (with SpamAssassin)
    Crystal Reports GroupWise 6
    Desktop OS is Windows 2000 Professional

Desktop Software

GroupWise 6 and 5.5 with GroupWise's document management system in use with over 500,000 documents

WordPerfect 9 (primary word processing program)

Microsoft Office XP (Word as secondary word processing program)

Carpe Diem (Billable Time entry)

Elite (Accounting system for professional services firms)

DB Textworks (case management)

Adobe (Reader, Acrobat (7 copies) and Approval (20 copies))

Norton Antivirus 8.0 Corporate Edition

15 legal research CD-ROMs in addition to Internet legal research

About 100 other utilities like WinZip, WSFTP, QuickView Plus, Conversions Plus and Visio, and so on.

Wita Wojtkowski is a full professor in the Department of Networking, Operations and Information Systems at Boise State University, Boise, Idaho, USA. She received her PhD from Case Western Reserve University (Engineering). Her current research interests are in systems development (especially for the Web-centric applications), examination of the relationships and interactions between information technology and organizations (especially object-oriented technology), and implementations of electronic commerce in all its forms. She is program co-chair of the International Conference on Information Systems Development and a member of the IEEE Computer Society and the Academy of International Business.

Marshall Major is the IS Team lead and IT visionary at Moffatt Thomas Barrett Rock & Fields, Chartered, where he is responsible for shifting IS team culture to a service-based approach. As the IS Team Lead, he is responsible for Novell NetWare and Microsoft Windows servers and wide-area-network for this 115 person law firm. As the IT visionary, he assists clients internally and externally to leverage and optimize technology. Major has 11 years of technology consulting experience and four years of technology staff management experience. His consulting focus is on troubleshooting, resolution, training and technical guidance for small- and medium-sized businesses. He is a Certified NetWare Engineer, holds both a BA in business and an MA in MIS, and is a member of IFIP.

This case was previously published in the *Annals of Cases on Information Technology,* Volume 6/2004, pp. 90-103, © 2004.

Chapter XVIII

Implementation of Information Technology in a Job Shop Manufacturing Company:
A Focus on ManuSoft

Purnendu Mandal, Marshall University, USA

EXECUTIVE SUMMARY

ABC Engineering is a Melbourne-based job shop manufacturing company. The company attempted a major improvement in the information technology area by implementing and enhancing the capability of a MIS software package called 'ManuSoft'. The general manager of ABC Engineering felt that the implementation of this commercially available package would enhance the productivity and help managers in the planning process. The company carried out a detailed study on various IT tools and information systems softwares that are applicable to the job shop manufacturing situation. Considering the prevailing company situations, it was decided that 'ManuSoft' would satisfy the information requirements. A project team was set up to study the scope of IT improvements and implement the required IT/IS system.

BACKGROUND

ABC Engineering Limited is a precision engineering jobbing company, which provides precision machining, fabrication, toolmaking and assembly services to a wide range of industries. The company began as a two-person business in 1971 and since then expanded to become one of Australia's largest precision engineering companies. ABC Engineering employs over 250 personnel with a turnover of A\$78 million in 1999. All machine operators are skilled tradesmen, or trades apprentices, fully capable of manufacture from drawings with a minimum of supervision.

As can be seen from the company organizational structure, shown in Figure 1, the management structure is flat and product orientated. The general manager reports to the board of directors and the manager of each functional section reports directly the general manager. The production managers (Aerospace, Projects, Manufacturing and Operations) are responsible for customer liaison as well as general project and work management.

The main operation at ABC Engineering centres around two units: the Tool Room and the Press Shop. This study is concerned with the Tool Room, as it represents the job shop environment in its most dynamic form. The Press Shop is also a job shop but is far more batch orientated, providing a relatively simple manufacturing environment. A schematic view of the factory layout is shown in Figure 2.

The ABC Engineering Tool Room makes parts to customer-designed order. The company provides a machining service to many types of industry. The parts made have been loosely categorised into eleven major 'product streams' by management. The categories are defined primarily for business control and reporting purposes. Every part made by ABC Engineering is pre-required by its customers, none are made for stock.

The eleven product streams, as defined by ABC Engineering management, are: Canning and Packaging, Wire Cut, Large Machining, Small Machining, Jigs and Fixtures, Large Press Tools, Small Press Tools, Mould Tools, Refurbishments and Repairs, Design Only and Major Projects. The definitions of the products attempt to provide management with a picture of the demand on shopfloor resources made by a particular job, or group of jobs. ABC Engineering's customer profile is also reflected in the product stream definitions.

The Canning and Packaging product stream provides the canning and packaging industries with high precision tools for repetitive manufacture of containers such as beverage cans and food tins. This is a highly evolutionary market. The demand of the large food and beverage organizations for innovative packaging, along with wear on existing equipment, provides a steady demand on ABC Engineering for high precision tooling. The tooling for this product stream makes use of leading-edge materials technology to produce the properties required of parts for repetitive manufacture. The principle properties required of such parts are hardness, toughness and surface finish. To machine such parts successfully requires state-of-the art facilities. Although the requirements of the canning and packaging industries are highly dynamic, this is the most repetitive market for ABC Engineering and provides a large proportion of the few repeat jobs manufactured.

The Wire Cutting stream primarily provides punches and dies for customers in the metal stamping industries. Intricate parts are also cut for the biomedical industry. The technology allows intricate through-cuts in almost any material. The cutting process does not detrimentally affect

Figure 1. Organizational chart

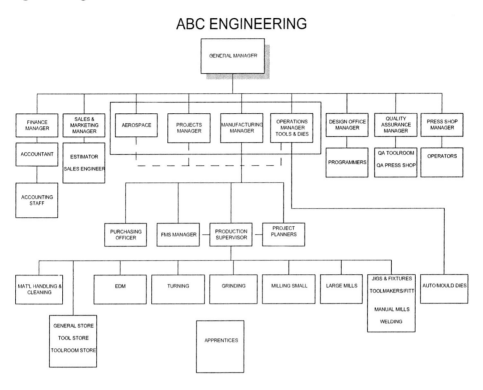

ABC ENGINEERING

the properties of pre-hardened materials, as the heat produced is minimal and confined to an extremely small area.

The Small and Large Machining streams provide machined parts for many types of industry. These product streams can service any organization that requires metal parts such as a shaft, brackets or other simple components. An example of a customer for these product streams is the machine manufacturing industry, which often requires precision parts for specialised machinery. Maintenance departments of large manufacturing organizations also require parts for machine upgrade and repair.

The three Tooling streams primarily provide the automotive industry with metal forming press tools and the plastics industry with injection moulding tools. The building of press and mould tools is a complicated process. Parts for the tools are made throughout the factory drawing on many resources. Once the parts have been made, they are fit together to form the tools. The tools are then tested and refit in an incremental fashion until the products they produce are satisfactory. The process of toolmaking requires precision machining, skilled fitting and close customer liaison to achieve satisfactory results.

The Refurbishment and Repairs product stream provides work on highly specialised machinery for a wide variety of industries. It involves the stripping and rebuilding of

Figure 2. Layout of Work Centers at ABC Engineering

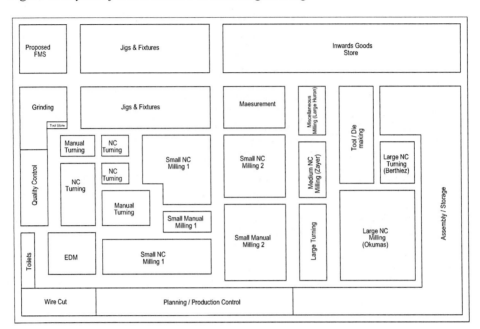

complex machinery. This can be the most complicated product stream, as the work requirements are often not known before work begins. Refurbishment of a machine could include simple rewiring, grinding or a complete remake of all machine parts and components.

The Design Only product stream is for work that involves the manufacture of CAD files or drawings only. Digitising sample parts most commonly does this. The first stage of building a tool to manufacture a plastic part is often producing a 3D CAD model of a solid part model made from clay or wood. This technique can also be used to analyse parts made by competitors within the plastics or metal forming industries.

The Major Projects product stream principally provides the automotive and aerospace industries large and precise jigs and fixtures. Products in this class are often multimillion dollar operations that involve on-going customer relations such as installation and maintenance. Major projects have a significant effect on the manufacturing resources of ABC Engineering. They often require internal services from many work centres.

As ABC Engineering provides a customer service the distinction between part categories is often difficult to make. Approximately 65% of parts are produced on a one-off basis for a wide variety of industries in the manufacturing arena. Manufacture in this environment requires a highly flexible facility. From information requirement's point of view, ABC Engineering exhibits the behaviour of a very dynamic environment. Clearly, the company needs an integrated and powerful information system to be successful in this rapidly changing environment.

SETTING THE STAGE

In the early 1990s the company installed an MIS software package called 'ManuSoft,' but the package remained underutilized. Some of the reasons for poor utilization of the software package cited are:

- ManuSoft is not user-friendly.
- The software works on DOS operating system, which is considered to be obsolete in today's computer technology environment.
- Shortage of computer skilled manpower in the company.
- The senior managers do not consider the IS a value-added activity in the organization.

However, with the change of leadership in 1995 the new general manager realized the importance of an IS in his organization. He commissioned a project team to investigate the state of IT and was keen to develop an appropriate system that would meet the information requirements for managers at various levels in the organization. We discuss here developments in the IT area, how these developments affect the existing IS at ABC Engineering, to what extent ManuSoft meets the information requirements and what could be done to alleviate the situation.

IT/IS Developments

Manufacturing organizations across the board are struggling to keep step with the aggressively dynamic computer industry. Apart from general hardware, the largest area of expenditure in the hardware field has been in client/server technology. A survey conducted in 1995 in the USA amongst 2,400 organizations showed that, of the many companies moving to client/server technology, 41 percent planned to increase mainframe purchases (Miles, 1995). The survey also showed that 49 percent of the responding companies that did not have client/server strategies planned to boost their purchases of mainframes.

There is a definite view in the manufacturing arena that it is necessary to remain up to date with evolving computer hardware technology, and that it is not clear as to what type of platform, client/ server or mainframe, is best suited to MIS development. The roles of computer technology in manufacturing are evolving as the technology itself evolves. The traditionally separate MIS systems (for example, MIS designed for financial applications only) handling few data types with high volumes per data type, and manufacturing systems handling highly dynamic data subject to great changeability and timeliness, are being blended together into comprehensive systems that can be applied company wide (Ronen & Palley, 1988).

Client/Server Technology

Client/server architecture is an approach to cooperative processing where the functions of an application are shared between multiple computers on a network. A user's workstation in a client/server architecture is called a client which is linked to the server on an interactive basis. The client serves as a user interface, processing time-consuming tasks to distribute the computing load from the server. Software that is run on client/

server technology typically makes use of open operating systems developed by vendors such as Unix or Microsoft. One of the main strengths of client/server technology is that they allow users to interface various software applications by multiple vendors and build a MIS environment that suits an organization. There are however a number of weaknesses in client/server technology. The high powered clients that act as the user interface are expensive to purchase and maintain, and the process of integrating data between software applications supplied by independent vendors can also be time consuming and costly.

Mainframe Technology

Mainframe technology focuses on the power of the server, using one highly developed machine to handle all of the data processing and storage tasks. Users access data via inexpensive 'dumb' terminals, which in themselves have no processing power, but allow access to the mainframe. Mainframe operating systems are usually proprietary, developed specifically for a particular hardware configuration, with hardware, operating system and software applications developed by a single vendor or through joint ventures between the hardware and software development teams. The main strengths of mainframe systems lie in the consistent 'data warehousing' that is a result of having only one data storage area, the pure processing power of the mainframe computers, and the fully integrated solution supplied by a proprietary system. The major weakness of mainframe is that proprietary systems typically make it difficult, if not impossible, to interface to systems from other vendors. As users find areas that the proprietary software applications do not handle well (e.g., spreadsheet reporting), small independent data warehouses are developed on personal computers throughout an organization, destroying the integrity of a single database.

Mixed Systems

Traditionally MIS has utilized mainframe computers for corporate transaction processing using vendors such as IBM, Unisys, or Hewlett-Packard. The large process manufacturing industries typically favor proprietary systems by DEC, Fisher Controls, Foxboro, Honeywell, Allen Bradley and Cincinnati Milacron. Smaller manufacturing organizations have traditionally used minicomputers and more powerful workstations on client/server networks for applications such as CAD (Laudon & Laudon, 1991; Piszczalski, 1992). Mainframes were generally run with a refusal to share the knowledge that bestows power on manufacturing staff. Because of this users became frustrated with mainframe technology and rushed into client/server technology. However, studies suggest that many corporate respondents who invested heavily in client/server networks are yet to see the cost savings, improved efficiencies and increased productivity they expected (Miles, 1995).

As computer technology develops, users from the various industries can see that they are less restricted by the limitations of the technology available and are more interested in utilizing the strengths of both client/server and mainframe systems. Hybrid systems that incorporate the strengths of both client/server and mainframe technology were the tools typically being sought by manufacturing organizations in the late 1990s. One such system was the AS/400, originally developed by IBM as a midrange, mainframe server running the OS/400 operating system also from IBM.

The question of which system is best suited to a manufacturing environment still remains unanswered, however it seems that a balance must be struck between the processing power of mainframes and the flexibility of client/server systems. Factors such as cost per user interface and processing times are important. The importance of these factors varies with the size and structure of organizations. It must also be kept in mind that with the current rate of technology development the factor of processing time, a strength of mainframe technology is decreasing in importance on an almost daily basis.

It seems that the industry is heading towards the mixed system approach to make use of the flexibility of client/server architecture. Vendors of software for such hardware environments must be aware that this flexibility is also an important factor in software selection. The flexibility provided should run all the way through the systems, from hardware compatibility to user interfaces.

Networking and Communications

Whether a mainframe using 'dumb' terminals, a client/server, or some hybrid system is used as the backbone of an MIS, a means of connecting the machines together and controlling data transfers between them is necessary. The means is termed 'networking' and the type of network used defines the method, speed, consistency and accuracy levels of data transferrals.

For communications within a single plant, a local area network (LAN) is the commonly used type of network. The technology of LANs has been the subject of a great deal of development because of their vital importance in computer-integrated manufacturing; the commercial opportunities have been recognized by vendors. Any implementation of a LAN has many different solutions. Therefore, the design and implementation must be given careful consideration.

Software Developments

A continuing major argument in the literature is one on the topic of 'off-the-shelf' software versus 'home-grown' applications. There are convincing arguments on both sides. Some benefits of standard software are that it is usually cheaper than writing company-specific software, can be seen in use by other companies before being purchased and will generally take less time to introduce (Kochan & Cowan, 1986). The major drawback is that off-the-shelf software will rarely suit any manufacturing organization completely.

Software development is the number one technical challenge associated with implementation of CIM systems (Meredith, 1987; Ettlie & Getner, 1989). The application of MIS-orientated software design tools and methodologies to manufacturing applications have generally resulted in poor performance in manufacturing systems. Problems with software not only arise because of the complexities associated with driving and controlling various elements of the factory, but also in interfacing manufacturing with both engineering and business software. Software development practices found in a manufacturing environment are typically poor, and lead to major problems in software maintenance. In the press for timely implementation, software "fixes" can be temporary "band-aid" solutions, where the intention is that the correction will be completed later. This rarely happens. Subsequent modifications or upgrades in the software can prove extremely difficult due to the nature of typical manufacturing program development (Ettlie & Getner, 1989).

The application of MIS software has developed considerably over the years. The seventies were characterized by a transition from the structured (pre-defined) management reports of the sixties to new concepts in data modeling and decision support. The need to respond quickly to changing circumstances — corporate and government responsiveness — became a key factor in the design of MIS, leading to the rapid adoption of productivity aids, such as data dictionary/directory, fourth generation languages and database management systems (DBMS).

Major Commercial MIS Packages

Several software vendors can be said to have succeeded at various levels of the MIS market. When comparing vendors of software and the applications themselves, it must be kept in mind that it is an extremely dynamic business environment. Many of the major applications such as BPCS, Movex and Manugistics are being programmed or reprogrammed in object-oriented languages and most now employ external databases. Most of the larger applications can also run on many different external databases such as Oracle, DB2, Informix, and SQL. The larger application developers place great importance on keeping up with the latest available technology, but smaller developers such as ManuSoft can often fall behind.

Table 1 presents a comparative assessment of seven large MIS vendors and their products. The seven products, listed in Table 1, represent a range of technology that are all very successful in their own field.

SAP: R/3 Application

One of the undisputed giants of the enterprise resource planning software development world is Systems, Applications and Products in Data Processing (SAP). Founded in 1972, in Walldorf, Germany, SAP is the leading global provider of client/server business application solutions.

By collaborating with business, IT executives and partners worldwide, SAP developed a unique understanding of the challenges faced in implementing technology solutions for business users. They developed software that could help companies link their business processes, tying together disparate business functions and helping the whole enterprise run more smoothly. The versatile, modular software could be quickly and easily adapted to new business processes. As a business grew, so did the capabilities of the software.

SAP's innovative approach soon made it the top software vendor in Germany. Today, SAP is the largest supplier of business application software in the world and the world's fourth largest independent software supplier, overall. SAP's sales revenue increased by 38% to US$2.39 billion in 1996. SAP's customers are served by more than 10,000 employees worldwide.

The R/3 software is built with a fully integrated modular structure, making it flexible and scalable. After installing R/3's core modules, additional modules can be selected as needed, and added to the system over time. The incremental modules fully integrate with the system as soon as they are installed, providing immediate enterprise-wide functionality. More than 1,000 business process modules are included in the R/3 model.

Table 1. Software developers and applications

Vendor	Software	Origin	Software Sales Revenue 1996 ($ million)	Major Server	Major Client(s)	Manufacturing environment			
						Software Description	Size of business	Database	Caters for job shop environment?
Systems Applications and Products in Data Processing (SAP)	R/3	Germany	2390	Various	Various	ERP/MRP	Large/medium	External - various	✓
Marcam (MAPICS)	MAPICS XA	USA	197	AS/400	Windows	ERP/MRPII	Large/medium	External - various	✓
System Software Associates (SSA)	BPCS	USA	340	Various	Windows, UNIX	ERP/MRPII	Medium/large	External - various	✓
Intentia International	Movex	Sweden	167	AS/400	OS/2, Windows	MRPII, JIT	Medium/large	External- DB2/400	✓
Baan	Tritan (Baan IV)	Netherlands, USA	388	Various	UNIX, Windows	ERP/MRPII	Medium/large	External - various	✓
Manugistics	Manugistics	USA	82	UNIX Windows NT	Windows OS/2	Supply-chain management	Medium/large	External - Oracle, Informix, Sybase	✗
Datalogix International Incorporated (Under Oracle)	GEMMS	USA	835 (Oracle)	UNIX	Windows	ERP/MRPII	Medium/large	External - Oracle Various	✓

Marcam: MAPICS XA Application

Like SAP, Marcam is a giant in the enterprise resource planning software development field. However, their major system, MAPICS XA, a modular family of products, currently provides a selection of only 35 application modules for custom configured solutions, as compared with SAP's 1,000 plus business process modules.

Successful industrial and distribution companies worldwide, ranging from producers of soft drink concentrate in Ireland, ball bearings in India to horse trailers in the United States, have formed strategic business partnerships with Marcam and Marcam's MAPICS enterprise solutions. The manufacturing industry's long-term confidence in MAPICS has created one of the largest installation bases of any enterprise software system. Nearly 15,000 Marcam customers are supported in more than 141 locations in 60 countries. A corporate staff of 1,200 employees and 1,530 sales and support affiliates throughout North America, Europe, Africa, the Middle East, Asia Pacific and Latin America are supplemented by 24-hour-a-day call-in centers based in Best, The Netherlands; Kuala Lumpur, Malaysia; and Atlanta, Georgia. The confidence in Marcams' software comes through flexibility and choice of modular, adaptable, inclusive, integrated solutions.

Introduced in 1978, the MAPICS product family was the industry's first comprehensive manufacturing resource planning (MRP II) system. Expanded and quickly changing customer requirements fuelled accelerated market responsiveness when Marcam acquired MAPICS in 1993. Numerous enhancements and additional applications, including client/server processes, EDI and Windows-based screen presentations, have made MAPICS a functionally advanced system. Continued expansion and evolution is the foundation for confidence in today's MAPICS Extended Advantage, MAPICS XA. MAPICS XA modules can be purchased, installed and added in almost any sequence or combination.

Despite possessing a smaller application range compared to R/3, MAPICS XA is a functionally rich solution for enterprise requirements and the Windows-style interfaces make it easier for those users who struggle with proprietary systems.

SSA: BPCS Application

System Software Associates Incorporated (SSA) targets manufacturing companies with annual sales of $100 million to $500 million. SSA's business planning and control system (BPCS) is designed to run on IBM's AS/400 but is also currently being ported to Unix. The BPCS client/server is a comprehensive set of integrated client/server applications which address the core system needs of industrial sector companies. The BPCS client/server is the worldwide standard for the process industries. It offers integrated electronic commerce and EDI capabilities through a strategic partnership with Harbinger and the BPCS Data Gateways.

While designed to run on the AS/400, BPCS can also be configured for the HP9000, RISC SYSTEM/6000, DEC and ALPHA servers and can be run on Windows NT and UNIX operating systems in client/server mode as well although it will probably be two to three years before the software is tested and running well on Unix. Many companies are committed to going to Unix because it offers a more open solution.

Intentia International: Movex Application

The Movex software developed by Intentia International, a $110 million Swedish software company, is a relatively new entry in the MIS market. Intentia has developed applications for the mid-range market to run on client/server architecture. The suite of applications is developed to run on the IBM AS/400 and include integrated financial, manufacturing distribution and inventory applications. It is being sold in the United States through value-added resellers focused exclusively on the AS/400 market. Intentia has licensed the software to 1,500 companies, which have implemented it at more than 3,000 sites worldwide. In the USA, the Movex system is targeted at similar companies to BPCS, i.e., manufacturing companies with annual sales of $100 million to $500 million. Advanced Manufacturing has estimated that in 1996 about one-third of the 100,000 U.S. companies with 100 or more employees will decide to purchase enterprise software. Movex operates simultaneously in 22 different languages and supports both discrete and process manufacturing functions. It also contains an executive performance measurement feature that allows business users to individually configure the data they want to track on a regular basis. A plant manager, for example, can set the system to track inventory turns without the intervention of the information systems department.

Baan: Triton Application

Dutch developer Baan Corporation is aiming its Unix-based enterprise client/server software at a few key vertical markets, the first of which is the automotive industry. The $122 million company also has teamed up with a handful of niche software companies to boost the functionality of its suite of manufacturing and financial applications known as Triton (Baan IV). Baan is developing Triton as a low-cost alternative to SAP. Compared with SAP's R/3 software suite, Baan software is typically 20% to 40% less costly to purchase. It is believed Baan is more receptive to the practice of customizing the product, as opposed to a supplier such as SAP, whose strength lies in its ability to cover most situations with pre-developed applications through its R3 software.

Manugistics: Manugistics Application

Manugistics, in Rockville, Maryland, another leading player in the client/server manufacturing software arena released Manugistics a complete reworking of the company's applications across its supply chain management suite of distribution, manufacturing, and transportation planning applications. The new release is built on a three-tier architecture that allows in-house developers to create Manugistics applications. The new architecture also allows several sites to access the applications at once. The software's new architecture provides networking performance gains and better support for remote applications. Manugistics is also continually developing software applications to improve the scope of their product such as the demand-planning module that provides tools for forecasting supply-and-demand ratios as well as analyzing the impact of changes in variables such as price, promotions, and delivery problems. Manugistics supports OS/2, Windows 95 and Windows NT clients. Manugistics is one of the new generation applications that work with programs such as Unix versions of Oracle7, Sybase SQL Server, Informix On-Line Dynamic Server, and IBM's DB2 to manage their data, rather than going through the process of designing and maintaining software-specific databases.

Datalogix: GEMMS Application

Datalogix International Incorporated is a successful vendor of client/server manufacturing software, with the release 3.2 of GEMMS — Global Enterprise Manufacturing Management System. The package includes a key piece of software that funnels data from the factory floor into enterprise systems that process business data. GEMMS runs on Windows 3.x clients and Unix servers. The system works with any open database connectivity-compliant database. Datalogix, in Valhalla, New York, also has a partnership with Oracle Corporation to pair Oracle's SmartClient line of financial and distribution client/server applications with GEMMS even though Oracle has begun releasing its own manufacturing application line.

In summary, from the array of available products and solutions it is obvious that one-size software, or even one method of obtaining a software solution, cannot fit all businesses. It is also unlikely that any single developer will meet all of a company's computing requirements.

One of the fastest ways to distinguish among systems and find a 'best fit' to an individual company is to find out what is required to adapt the software to a particular (and sometimes peculiar) method of doing business. Flexibility translates into the ability to customize fields, screens and relationships of data. The systems by the large developers, offer full customization of fields, screens and layout. As flexibility increases, price tends to go up. But low price does not always translate into loss of flexibility. Many systems at the low end of the price range have some flexibility. The names of miscellaneous fields may be changed, or perhaps unwanted items can be masked, and in some cases custom screens can be added. But, how much customization does an organization truly need? Today companies are forced to distinguish between "must have" requirements and "nice to have" components (O'Connell, 1995).

Along with the operation of the MIS, companies must decide which MIS tools are important (e.g., financial management, materials control, personnel management or production control), and choose or develop an MIS that suits their specific needs. It must also always be kept in mind that a MIS is a management information solution, not a management solution.

An example of development of system-user interfaces is given in this case study. In order to make the understanding of the steps/logics easier to follow, a description of a commercially available MIS software — ManuSoft — and the actual company on which it was applied are discussed next.

ManuSoft Management Information System

ManuSoft is a modular package similar to its larger competitors R/3, MAPICS XA and BPCS. There are five modules in the complete package:

- Quoting and estimating system (QES)
- Production scheduling and control (PSC) system
- Manufacturing control system (MCS)
- Manufacturing inventory control (MIC) package
- Materials requirements planning (MRP) package

When all five modules are implemented the system presents a fully integrated MRPII system, with information control from order to dispatch. The system can be installed in total or in separate modules. The modules used will be dependent on the requirements of the user.

The ManuSoft system is designed specifically for the DOS operating system. When recording data it locks only individual records for update so the rest of the file is open for multiple user access. This overcomes multiple user difficulties that can be encountered by programs running on DOS.

Any IBM-compatible PC with 4Mb memory and an 80386 processing chip (or higher) can handle its operation. To operate in the multi-user configuration, it is preferable to run from a more powerful computer, although this is not a requirement, only a recommendation.

The most important technology for ManuSoft with respect to operating speed is the server hard-drive. This is because the ManuSoft system, to allow multiple users to operate simultaneously in the DOS environment, must write all transactions that may cause changes in the state of its database directly to disk.

As with any system, memory is a valuable asset, in ManuSoft's case specifically for output operations. When compiling reports, the ManuSoft system writes and sorts many temporary files in order to organize data. As these files and the output reporting functions do not make any changes to the database files, the system can make use of main memory for these processes.

ManuSoft recommends the program be run on an ethernet local area network (LAN), controlled by Novell Network software. ManuSoft's original design was for this platform, although use of most networking systems is conceivable. Earlier versions of ManuSoft would not run on Windows networking systems, NT or Windows 95. The powerful caching tools of these systems over-rode the record-locking facilities of the MIS, causing system failure. ManuSoft has overcome these difficulties in later versions but only through robust, proprietary programming measures. Unfortunately these measures also slow down the system.

The ManuSoft system can collect data from the shop floor in three different ways: 'touch screen' technology, bar code readers or manual keyboard entry. ManuSoft have developed a factory control system that operates primarily through a network of touch screens that allow shopfloor workers to interact with the system to correctly choose priorities and to update work progress. The touch screens are nothing more than simple DOS-based PCs with touch sensitive displays.

However, the ManuSoft system has certain disadvantages.

- The structure of the data files makes it necessary to write specific operation programs for every data file. It also means that users are presented with a partially rather than fully integrated relational database.
- The operation of the index system makes it impossible for a user to define or restructure the search priorities or configure specific tracking of items.
- The combination of the Ethernet networking and the DOS operating system makes it unlikely that ManuSoft will ever run advanced data collection and distribution routines using CAD data for example.
- The user interface for system operation is inflexible forcing users to follow specified steps to produce outputs whether or not the user requires the steps.

- The structure of the data files makes comprehensive and flexible reporting to management requirements very difficult to achieve. The system's inability to arrange and convey required information inhibits its ability to meet the information requirements of an MIS.

CASE DESCRIPTION

As mentioned earlier, ManuSoft remained largely under-utilized in the company. In order to investigate the truth in this allegation the project team as the first step inquired into to what extent ManuSoft meets the information requirements for mangers at various levels.

Senior management has many requirements of an information system at the strategic level in order to make informed decisions on the direction of the company. Expenditure to upgrade current equipment and recruiting new people to meet production demands are just two examples. Unfortunately the ManuSoft MIS is not capable of fulfilling many of the information requirements of this level.

ManuSoft provides no way in which to compare actual costs with sales values, on the same report, for a number of jobs. To perform such an analysis for a group of jobs, reports have to be produced from the job cost reporting system and the invoice reporting system, and the results manually collated.

However, ManuSoft does provide information on work centre loading, but the interface provided to generate reports is so cumbersome that nobody is willing to learn it. The loadings charts produced by ManuSoft are half A4 page in size and are fixed for a three-month period. The information is far too detailed and complicated for a manager.

ManuSoft, being a text-based system, does allow a middle-level manager to view both the present and future loading of resources, but not on the same screen. In fact an entirely different section of the program must be accessed to go from current loading to future loading. On top of this the format of the interface provided is such that no more than 12 jobs per work centre could be listed. This makes comparison and prioritising of jobs extremely difficult.

As managers at the middle level are responsible for maintaining the efficiency of each work centre, they need to have access to an effective information system. Decisions that can affect the efficiency of a work centre involve innumerable variables such as personnel, maintenance and tooling. It is vitally important that management has a means by which to record and measure the effects of any decisions made. Without a process to provide feedback information on such decisions efficiently, management at the planning level will have no means with which to monitor and ensure improvement.

Supervisors, at lower level management, are responsible to allocate individual jobs to resources based on the priorities set by the middle level managers. Deciding which job should go on what machine and when is a highly complex decision making area. Any job that has a milling operation can be performed on any milling machine, but certain preconditions need to be satisfied. As such ManuSoft is good in providing information required by supervisors. In spite of that the supervisors are not using the ManuSoft primarily due to issues related to motivation.

The factors related to motivation in using the ManuSoft are not addressed in this case study. The project team investigated the avenues to improve the usage of ManuSoft through user-interface development. Designing software interfaces that fit the work environment is a success factor proven by many researchers. A key factor to successful IS implementation often cited by IS researchers is the teamwork between the developers and the end users of the system. When IS developers work closely with the end users of the software the fit of software to the application is much better.

In order to develop MIS-user interfaces the information requirements were assessed at strategic, planning and operations levels. Staffs were interviewed to discuss reporting requirements and preferences at each level. The requests for information showed that the ManuSoft system caters well for the operations level of the business, but the strategic and planning levels required a great deal of work.

In total 20 program files were developed to meet the shortfalls of information requirement. Table 2 provides a brief description of the program purpose and file names.

To describe the development of the interface programs and their operation this section examines three examples; *Delivery performance*, *Production by cost centre*, and *Invoicing performance*.

Delivery Performance Interface (Program 3)

The delivery performance program file is an example of early interface development. The program simplifies the production of the required reports immensely. At the introduction of this project ABC Engineering had no measurement of delivery performance. Developing a management interface capable of such measurement therefore was high priority. The importance of delivery performance measurement was reflected in a survey of customers carried out by ABC Engineering's general manager in 1995, which ranked 'on-time' delivery as the number one requirement of a good supplier.

Delivery performance is an area that is important to companies' worldwide, not only small job shops. Surveys of manufacturing executives in large successful companies in Europe, the USA and Japan repeatedly rank dependable and fast delivery among their top five competitive priorities.

The problem of tardy deliveries can be tackled on many levels — company wide, by product type or on an individual job-by-job basis. The frequency of reports varies depending on which level the report is aimed at. As there was no delivery performance measurement available at ABC Engineering before this project the global delivery-reporting task was priority. The reports are required on a monthly basis. Two delivery reports were developed to meet the management requirements at ABC Engineering. The first is a delivery trend line as percentage of 'on-time' deliveries on a monthly basis. The second is a summary report in graphical format, product code wise.

Production by Cost Center Interface (Program 2)

The production by cost center report was one of the first 'direct access' interfaces developed. The user is not required to interface with the ManuSoft system at all. The program accesses the complex JOBCOST.DAT file directly and extracts data from the file to the appropriate areas on the final report. It is important for the accounting department at ABC Engineering to be able to keep track of hours worked at various cost centers on the shop floor between set dates. This allows a labor recovery value to be assigned to each work center for that period and produces a part of the performance evaluation of the individual cost centers.

Table 2. Developed interface programs

Program Number	Program Description	Program File Name
	Strategic Level	
2	Work by cost centre	COST_CEN.XLS
3	Delivery details for a period	DESP_R2.XLS
5	Invoices by product code for a period	INVOICE3.XLS
8	Hours by product code with orders, reworks and invoices	NIGHTLY.XLS
9	Monthly order intake report	ORDER.XLS
11	Hours, rework, invoices and orders by planner for a period	PLANNERS.XLS
12	Hours, rework, invoices and orders by product code for a period	PRD_CODE.XLS
14	Progress claim information for a period	PROGRES2.XLS
15	Financial information on completed jobs for a period	RJS_COMP.XLS
20	Open orders at a point in time, with data on costs and sales.	OPENSALE.XLS
	Planning level	
1	Highlights sub-assemblies on the order book for which the final-assembly has been despatched. Such sub-assemblies must be removed manually.	SUBASS.XLS
4	Find the planner given a job number	FIND_PL.XLS
6	Download labour list from ManuSoft	LABOUR.XLS
10	Download parts and processes from ManuSoft	PARTDOWN.XLS
13	Manufacturing production sheets	PROCESS3.XLS
16	Information on hours worked by sub contractors for a period	SUBBIES.XLS
17	Presents the hours spent by employees on non-productive work activities such as cleaning machines, training and maintenance	ZEROP2.XLS
18	Presents machine loading and work scheduled to a chosen work centre in a graphical format.	SCHED3.XLS
19	Highlights by responsible planner, discrepancies between hours estimated and actual hours taken to produce the job on the shopfloor.	EST01.XLS
	Operations level	
7	Adjust Nightshift Clock-offs to the correct period	NIGHT.XLS

Various management divisions such as the board of directors or general manager require data from the Accounts department on cost center hours for company evaluation. This data may be required at any time depending on its application and usually it is required instantly. Often the Accounts department is tasked with providing evaluations for specific time periods with durations of anything from days to years. The report provides data for each work center. All data required for this report is contained in the ManuSoft JOBCOST.DAT file and as such requires only a simple program to extract the data. There is not even a need to use the ManuSoft indexing system.

To gather the information from the ManuSoft system would require the running of 27 reports (one for each cost center) from the job cost reporting section then transferal of data to a spreadsheet. Each report from that particular section of ManuSoft takes approximately 15 minutes to run (a total of approximately seven hours), while accessing the data through this interface takes only 15 minutes in total. The logic of the program is simple. It compares the operation dates recorded in the job cost file, for each of nine possible operations, in every job cost record. If a date falls between the user-defined reporting dates, the program then records the work center of operation and converts the time, recorded in base 90 code, to hours. Finally the work center is located on the report spreadsheet and the converted time is added to any time previously recorded.

Invoicing Performance Interface (Program 5)

The invoicing performance report reflects the development of auxiliary programs allowing the design of interfaces that automatically access a number of the ManuSoft data files. This program draws on data from three different data files, sorts, summarizes and presents the final report through a 'one-touch' interface.

The senior management of a jobbing shop requires data from the invoice reporting system to help answer many important questions. For example, is there enough money this period to pay everyone? Is there a strong market for product C, or should the business concentrate on product D? The data on invoicing alone cannot answer all of the questions, but it can provide information on money due to come into the business. This information can then be compared with data from cost reporting systems to give an indication of financial progress.

To gather information required by management at ABC Engineering for the monthly invoice report through the ManuSoft system, would require the generation of 12 reports from the selective invoice file printout. Such reports require approximately five minutes each followed by manual data transfer to a spreadsheet for presentation. This process would not only be time consuming but would run a high risk of error due to manual data handling. To overcome these difficulties a program was written to access the ManuSoft databases directly and produce a 'one-touch' report that could be run by any staff member with access to the appropriate equipment in a manner of minutes.

CURRENT CHALLENGES

As stated in the beginning, ABC Engineering was facing the challenge of making its existing information system more effective to users at various levels in the organization. The MIS ManuSoft, which was introduced to ABC Engineering prior to the start of this project, could not provide the right information to different levels of management at the appropriate point in time. So, what were the remedies? The development of the interface programs was one of the ways to solve this critical problem at ABC Engineering.

The system/user interface development in this case is considered to be a short-term measure of a possibly long-term problem. The business and work environment of ABC Engineering is very volatile, and to satisfy its vast amount of data storage and analytical requirements, one would perhaps advocate a much more powerful information system than the ManuSoft system. However, the development of interfaces by object-oriented programming provided an extra lease of life to the existing system, and much-needed cost savings.

While this case study concentrated on the provision of business information to management in small manufacturing organizations, it did not tackle the problem of data collection and data integrity. This is an extremely difficult area in practical installations of an information system. The collection of data — for example, hours spent on a job throughout the working day — is no simple task. Reconciling the reported data with actual data can cost an organization thousands of dollars every year; yet it is this information that drives an MIS. If the input information is not accurate, the information supplied to all levels of management will not be accurate. The outputs of the MIS may then be useless, and possibly even damaging to an organization.

The method of data collection also poses a challenge. In the job shop environment, where at present a great deal of work is still done manually, the data collection method presents an even greater challenge than interfacing to management. Because there is little benefit to workers on the shop floor, there is no incentive to them for accurate data entry. This motivational problem is generally overcome by making the data entry process (e.g., clocking on and off jobs) as part of shop floor work requirements. Research needs to be done into this side of MIS development.

At the time of writing this case study the company is going through a process of take-over bid, and most likely ABC Engineering will be sold to a large manufacturing corporation. If that happens, the information systems at ABC Engineering will certainly attract a fresh look, which will pose a great opportunity as well as challenge to the new management.

ACKNOWLEDGMENT

The author gratefully acknowledges the contribution of Matthew Sweeney in the preparation of this case study.

REFERENCES

Ettlie, J. E., & Getner, C. E. (1989). Manufacturing software maintenance. *Manufacturing Review, 2*(2), 129-133.

Kochan, A., & Cowan, D. (1986). *Implementing CIM, computer integrated manufacturing.* IFS (Publications) Ltd.

Laudon, C., & Laudon, P. (1991). *Management information systems: A contemporary perspective* (2nd ed.). New York: Macmillan.

Meredith, R. (1987). Implementing new manufacturing technologies: Managerial lessons over the FMS life cycle. *Interfaces, 17*(6), 51-62.

Miles, G. L. (1995, August). Mainframes: The next generation. *International-Business*, 14-16.

O'Connell, S. E. (1995, July). HR systems: Does higher price mean a better product. *HR Magazine*, 32-3.

Piszczalski, M. (1992), Power struggle: Can MIS rule the shop? *Corporate Computing, 1*(3), 217-19.

Ronen, B., & Palley, A. (1988), A topology of financial versus manufacturing management information systems. *Human Systems Management, 7*(4), 291-8.

FURTHER READING

Mandal, P., & Baliga, B. (2000). MIS-user interface design for job shop manufacturing environment. *International Journal of Operations and Production Management, 20*(4), 468-480.

Manufacturing Systems. (n.d.). *Top 75 ranking*. Retrieved from http://manufacturingsystems.com/software/1_10.html

SAP. (n.d.). *R/3. Better information, faster*. SAP AG. Retrieved from http://www.sap-ag.de/aboutus/sapr3.html

Purnendu Mandal is an associate professor of MIS and his current teaching interests include principles of MIS, database management, electronic commerce and strategic MIS. He taught in England, India, Singapore, Australia and the USA. He published over 100 refereed journal and conference papers. His works appeared in International Journal of Production and Operations Management, Industrial Management and Data Systems, International Journal of Quality and Reliability Management, Intelligent Automation and Soft Computing: An International Journal, Logistics Information Management, European Journal of Operational Research, *etc. Dr. Mandal serves in a number of professional bodies and currently is on the editorial board of three international journals.*

This case was previously published in the *Annals of Cases on Information Technology*, Volume 4/2002, pp. 103-118, © 2002.

Chapter XIX

Software Vendor's Business Model Dynamics Case:

TradeSys

Risto Rajala, Helsinki School of Economics, Finland

Matti Rossi, Helsinki School of Economics, Finland

Virpi Kristiina Tuunainen, Helsinki School of Economics, Finland

EXECUTIVE SUMMARY

This case describes evolution of a small software company through three major phases of its life cycle. During the first phase, the business was founded within a subsidiary of a large multinational information technology (IT) company. In the second phase, the business evolved as a spin-off from the initial organization through a MBO (management buy-out) into an independent software vendor. Finally, in the third phase, the business has established itself as a vertically-focused business unit within a publicly-quoted company operating in software and consulting businesses. These three phases are termed introduction, growth *and* maturity *as defined by Cravens (1987, 376).[1] The company described in this case, called TradeSys, Inc. (pseudonym), develops and sells software for trade unions and unemployment fund organizations. The business model of TradeSys, Inc. (later TradeSys) has evolved through a typical life cycle of product-oriented software companies in Finland. First, it was comprised of business information systems consultation and a proposition of systems solution to a few major customer organizations. This led to customer-initiated product development. Consequently, the deliverable of the very first project was developed as a solution to the needs of a single customer, which was later worked into a universal software product along with several customer projects. During all three major phases, the company had to rethink its business model and value propositions. At each stage, the ownership of the business has also changed. This case highlights the challenges of a business in the three major turning points in its life cycle and the major changes in the business model accordingly.*

INDUSTRY AND ORGANIZATIONAL BACKGROUND

Finland is a small but characteristically open market for software companies. In this Northern-European country, there are a little more than five million citizens and over 220,000 companies. Since 1995, Finland has been one of the member states in the European Union. During the past decades, Finland has rapidly shifted from being a producer of forestry and industrial goods into an exporter of high technology goods and services. According to Statistics Finland, the proportion of high technology exports surpassed 23% of all the exports of Finland in 2000 (Statistics Finland).

General readiness to adapt new technologies and a good established IT infrastructure characterize the Finnish market for software products and services. Many large foreign or multinational companies, though, have traditionally considered Finland as too small of a market for building up local operations and support networks for software businesses. This is especially true with companies providing software for narrow market segments. While Finland might not be that attractive market area for foreign companies, Finnish software companies are typically seeking to expand their operations abroad and, hence, concentrating on narrow solution domains to focus their efforts. Thus, as compared to their international rivals, local vendors focusing on narrow domains might be able to sustain superior competitive advantages related to software deployment, local support and insight into customers' needs.

In this case, we follow the evolution of TradeSys, a Finnish software vendor that has focused its operations on developing and selling software for Finnish trade unions and unemployment fund organizations. Development of TradeSys products started within a local business unit of a U.S. information technology (IT) giant, Unisys, in 1996. Around 1996, when Unisys was globally re-directing its strategy from product-orientation towards IT servicing, the management team of the current TradeSys decided to acquire the rights to the assets that became the core product of their business. The co-founders of TradeSys believed in the business and the product they had been creating and made a Management buy-out (MBO) to prove that the ideas they had been developing could be turned into profitable business. With the MBO, the business including software licenses as well as project liabilities were transferred to the two co-founders of TradeSys. Also, eight of the key persons having been part of the development team within Unisys transferred to the new company as old employees. Now, since April 2000, the company has been part of PublicSys, Inc. (a pseudonym). PublicSys is a publicly quoted information systems consulting house, which has actively acquired small- and medium-sized software companies since it became listed at the Helsinki Stock Exchange in Finland in 1999.

LEARNING OBJECTIVES

This case is intended for Master's level students. The case highlights the challenges facing a software production company in various stages of its life cycle. We discuss the evolution of the company, its product offerings and consequent changes in its business model.

In this case, we use a systematic framework, derived from earlier literature and verified with empirical research in companies, for evaluating the business model of a software product company. This business model framework, which is documented in (Rajala et al., 2001) is based on Kotler's (1991) whole product concept and Cravens' (1987) product life cycle ideas, and used to analyze the options available for a software company. After completing the case, students should be able:

- To define the business models of software companies
- To evaluate the options available for a given company, related to its:
  - product development model
  - revenue logic
  - distribution and sales model
  - servicing and implementation model
- To discuss both growth and product strategies of software companies

CASE DESCRIPTION

The company introduced in this case has its origins in the Finnish subsidiary of an American IT giant Unisys, within which the two soon-to-be-founders of TradeSys worked on information systems consultation projects for trade unions.

The trade unions have had a long established relationship with payment institutions in Finland, because the trade unions have collected their membership fees as a deductible from the salaries of members, who have given their permission for doing this. The move to this arrangement happened at the same time as larger companies started to favor the payment of salaries directly into workers bank accounts instead of cash or cheques. The companies and trade unions soon noticed that they need systems for handling the transactions and balances, and banks seemed to have systems that could be utilized here. The trade unions turned towards the state owned bank called Postipankki, which was quite happy to handle the account movements. The trade unions and unemployment funds had, at that time, practically only this one choice for a system supplier that could manage all the functions related to their membership-service needs and payment transactions. Postipankki had developed over the years a comprehensive set of tools for handling these. The bank exercised its monopoly position and bundling of the service to charge premium prices for the transactions from the trade unions.

Trade unions in Finland have a quite large member base (in some cases in hundreds of thousands) and they need different kinds of information services, not just the payment management. The first consultation projects by the co-founders of TradeSys (at that time working for Unisys) were carried out in 1993 to improve the management and handling of membership data of a trade union organization.

One of the TradeSys co-founders describes the situation as follows:

Other banks and trade union organizations were tired of the situation, where there was only one supplier of the trade union operations management systems in the market. The system was provided by a state-owned bank which had bundled the information system with its banking services and, thus, forcing the customers [trade unions] to keep their money in that particular bank's accounts.

The developers went ahead and developed a competing package. However, its introduction was far from easy. The state owned bank did not want any competitors and it tried to undermine the developments in various ways. Also, the trade unions were (and in many cases still are) quite conservative organizations, and they did not see the need to change the existing ways of doing things.

The development of this emerging business was, however, not straightforward as the parent company was not interested in this type of software product business. On the contrary, Unisys re-directed its strategy from product-orientation into IT servicing and consulting, and began cutting out all the businesses that were outside its strategic focus in 1996. A small vertical market in a small country was not seen lucrative enough by the U.S. head quarters. The head of product development (one of the co-founders) at TradeSys describes the situation as follows:

The development of a product business like this just did not work in a big organization, which was not committed to a product business like ours — even if we managed to carry out the first customer cases with at least reasonable success. Our customers were eager to continue and even one of the biggest banks in Finland was interested in seeing the development of our solution in order to benefit from a competitive solution in the existing market situation.

The strategic change of mind of the international information technology conglomerate forced the co-founders of TradeSys to consider their personal career ambitions as opposed to the corporate management's will to divest all its product businesses. The founders strongly believed in the product that had already been formed out of the consulting assignment, and there were potential buyers for the package. The following quotation is from the head of product development at TradeSys:

That time I had a difficult position at Unisys, which was cutting off all its product businesses and I had just committed to start consulting a solution with some big customers in the trade union segment. This consulting contract had led into a continuous development of a solution, and was emerging into a product concept.

So, the TradeSys co-founders were confident that they could run this as an independent business. They wanted to be able to introduce a competitive solution for the industry. Furthermore, one competing bank was willing to finance the new venture. They wanted to exploit the opportunity, because the new system gave the trade unions the possibility to use any bank of their choice for the transactions. So they went ahead and acquired the business to their possession in 1996 to prove everybody — including themselves — that the product ideas they had been developing could be turned into profitable business.

They proved to be right, as they were able to gain a market share to a degree that TradeSys has become a major player in its market segment. After the MBO, the turnover of TradeSys has grown steadily from a very small start into over 1.8 million Euro in 2000. Concurrently, the company has grown from a small product team of ten persons to a leading vendor of trade union software and the second largest unemployment fund systems provider in Finland with about 20 employees in 2000.

TradeSys was sold later in 2000 to a publicly quoted software company PublicSys. The owners of TradeSys became shareholders and members of the board of directors at PublicSys. Currently, they continue to develop the business facing the challenges of growth and maturity of the current market segment.

Evolution of the Business Model

TradeSys was founded around a business proposition for a narrow and clear market niche. The original business model evolved around the identified opportunity to serve the initial customer's information system needs by a software solution. The business model then focused on personal sales and very close customer services, because the success of the business relied on the implementation of the system projects together with the first customers.

Later, especially after the MBO, the company has been actively seeking for more customers and implementing a clear product-oriented business model in the selected vertical market segment, where it aimed at being a market leader. As a matter of fact, the company is already the leading software vendor in its segment of operations management systems for trade unions in Finland (see Figure 1). To strengthen its efforts in both product development and customer services, the organization was divided into separate teams specializing in product development, customer support and customer projects.

Currently, since TradeSys has become a part of PublicSys, the strategic focus of the company has shifted to maintaining profitable business and a reasonable market share in its selected product areas. The management has realized that the current small vertical market is not sufficient considering future growth, and, that new customers are needed to keep up funding the continuous product development.

In the following, the evolution of the business model of TradeSys is discussed by the four key elements (presented in more detail in the Appendix: (1) product development approach, (2) revenue logic, (3) distribution model, and (4) servicing and implementation model.

Products and Product Development

The initial idea for TradeSys' product development came about through customers' needs that were discovered along with first customer projects for trade unions. However, even in the first phase of the business life cycle, when the business was conducted within Unisys, the basic idea was not to develop customer-specific solutions, but more universal or at least parametrizable software products for several customers. The founders of TradeSys say that the main emphasis of the product development was put

Figure 1. Market share (%) of TradeSys and its competitors

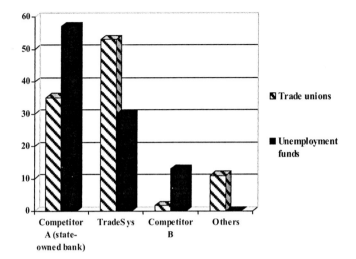

on the development of parametrized systems based on Oracle RDBMS (Relational Database Management System). In the second main phase, as the business was separated from Unisys and growing as an independent software house, main focus was directed to developing product development methods in order to be able to deliver universal solutions to customers in different customer projects.

The head of product development of TradeSys says that the aim to bring about software products was clear from the very beginning of the business:

> *Even if the first deliverables were based on direct solutions to customers'*
> *needs, we had the idea to bring about universal solutions to the marketplace,*
> *to be sold as software packages to customers with similar needs.*

So, right from the start TradeSys has emphasized the use of good software engineering principles. This has meant that the developers have been guided to use development method and case tools while developing the systems. Also the components and their interfaces have been carefully designed and the development management has enforced their use. This approach to product development has been challenged many times throughout the history of the business. In the first major phase of the business, for instance, it would have been alluring to reduce overhead costs of the company by just answering customer's core needs without investing in product development. On the other hand, much determination was needed in the growth phase to carry out careful deployments of the products and not to invest in product development only, even if the growth through successful product development seemed lucrative. In the mature phase, questions have risen whether or not the selected market segment is sufficient to justify the focus of product development efforts to that solution domain only.

The current product family of TradeSys consists of integrated system solutions for associations, trade unions and unemployment funds. The systems Alpha and Beta are designed for trade unions and the system Theta for unemployment funds, each including subsystems that can be hidden or taken into use by system parameters. These parameters allow the slight modification of the final system along with the delivery and installation of the products.

The software products **Alpha** and **Beta** form together an integrated information system designed to fulfill the various information management needs of trade unions, associations, organizations and various other societies. They provide trade unions with a view to managing information on union members, their employers and the organizational hierarchy, as well as the collection of union membership dues.

Software product **Theta** is an integrated system designed for unemployment funds. The system manages the calculation and payment of member benefits.

The whole product family of TradeSys is based on the same technology. The software is mainly developed with Oracle Developer (Forms & Reports) and utilizes Oracle RDBMS as a host database. All the development is done using proven software engineering principles and a systematic modeling approach. This has kept the product family easy to maintain and left possibilities open to develop it further to suit the needs of new markets.

The **system Alpha/Beta** includes subsystems for member management, employer management, organization services, and membership fee management. It also includes extensions for election management, course management, vacation management and magazine subscriptions. Some customers also need the extension for strike coordination and different Web services for member organizations.

The **system Theta** contains modules for operation management of unemployment fund organizations, including member management, benefit payment management and statistics. It can be extended with subsystems for telephone services, mobile phone

Figure 2. *The product line of TradeSys*

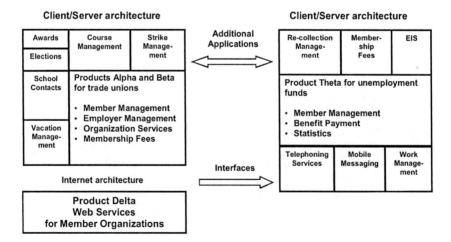

User Interface: Oracle Developer (Forms & Reports)
Database: Oracle RDBMS

messaging, electronic mail, and task management. Also, it includes extensions for claim management, various Web services and executive information subsystems, all directed for the operations management of unemployment funds.

The product-oriented offering is what differentiates TradeSys from its direct competition. The main competitor, a state-owned bank, provides an outsourcing model with large mainframes and terminals located in a service center. The director of product development of TradeSys believes that the approach of TradeSys allows for a more holistic service portfolio and better responsiveness to changes in customers' needs, while a outsourcing or service providing model may be initially less demanding for the customer. However, as compared to the competition, the TradeSys solutions enable unions and funds to deal with their daily routines by themselves. The software also enables the use of a centralized database via the Internet.

TradeSys has always stressed the quality of its development process and clear definition of the modules and their responsibilities. One of the cornerstones of TradeSys's approach has been continuous enhancement of the development processes. The company has tried to streamline its process by avoiding the need to develop tailored solutions for individual customers. Instead, the needed modifications have been implemented as options for the base package.

Revenue Logic

Profitability has been a clear business target throughout the entire history of TradeSys. Growth of business, instead, has been a secondary target. Does this seem like risk avoiding strategy? Maybe, because the steady but modest growth of TradeSys has always been financed with the operating revenue of the product business. It is worth mentioning that Finland was experiencing a severe recession in the early 1990s, and it was not as easy to raise funding to finance a rapid growth of a small software vendor operating in a narrow vertical segment as it later was for a number of start-ups in Internet business. So, creation of revenue and right pricing of offering have been important issues all the time in maintaining growth and, simultaneously, financing all development work. It is notable that all along, the company has priced its offerings based on the *value of the service*, rather than on the basis of the effort put into the development of the products.

Software license sales have formed the foundation of the revenue logic in the growth phase of the business as shown in Figure 3. The product offering has been priced so that the initial purchase equals approximately to 100,000 Euro per customer organization. Maintenance and support creates then an annual cash flow of about 15-20% of the initial purchase. Other sources of revenue such as training, accessory sales, in which revenue comes from selling books, manuals, CDs, etc., seems to have been be of minor importance during both the introduction and growth phases. This is apparently due to the small number of end users (and small installed base of software) in the early stages of the business life cycle. In the maturity phase of the business, the proportion of license sales has not grown as rapidly as during the earlier stages. Furthermore, in the recent phase the fraction of consultation has diminished, whereas training and support have grown in importance.

Figure 3. Sources of revenue (fractions of turnover in percentages) at the growth phase of business

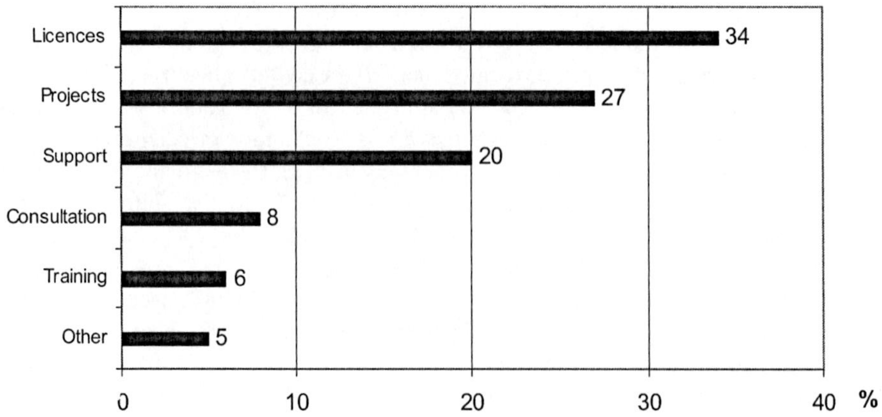

Distribution and Sales

The small vertical market of TradeSys allows the company to keep sales highly centralized. In fact, the managing director takes care of the marketing and sales functions almost alone, utilizing the resources of both customer services and product development units in different marketing occasions. Throughout its entire history, TradeSys has maintained direct contacts with its customers without any middlemen.

The sales model is strongly based on personal relationships and a good general understanding of customers' needs. This may have its advantages in creating an in-depth understanding of customer's needs in the selected domain, but, simultaneously, it raises questions about growth opportunities, because direct contact with customers is highly labour intensive from the software vendor's point of view.

Despite of the fact that the selling approach of TradeSys is very customer-oriented, it aims at selling only solutions that can be implemented on the basis of the existing, uniform products and not customer-specific or tailored solutions. The head of product development of TradeSys explained that in the vast majority of customer organizations, the products are customized only if the customer-initiated modifications can be turned into standardized features or add-ons in the existing products, or into new products of the product family.

Servicing and Implementation

The management of TradeSys has focused on the servicing and implementation part of their business model from the very early stages of their business. This part includes all the installation and deployment activities required to achieve working solutions based on the software products. For large systems, like the ones that TradeSys sells, this is an essential part of the success of the product. It can also make a major portion of the revenue in the latter stages of the product life cycle. In the early phases of the business of TradeSys, the product development engineers and the technical specialists in the customer service were actually same individuals or at least belonged to the same organizational unit.

Due to the fact that TradeSys is carrying out all the customer projects, including software installations and training, by itself and without employing any partners, the individual responsible for customer projects have been encumbered with several delivery projects, simultaneously. In the growth phase, a customer project organization of one to seven system specialists was detached from other operations to carry out all the delivery and implementation projects with customers.

The project organization has carried out various integration projects in which the software products of TradeSys have been integrated to customers' existing systems. However, as said earlier, no customer-specific tailoring has been made to the products so far.

Especially in the growth phase of the business, main focus areas of the customer support and project operations of TradeSys have been in the successful deployment of TradeSys' products to customer environments. Also, systematic gathering of customer feedback to further development of products, maintenance of high quality standards of product deliveries and the development of deep insight into solution domain in all customer operations have been the key objectives of the customer project organization. In the latest phase, maturity, the project organization is facing new challenges in generating continuous cash flow from software maintenance and support functions with the existing customers.

CURRENT CHALLENGES
FACING THE ORGANIZATION

TradeSys faces now a dilemma: it has acquired a dominant position in its vertical market and there are very few growth opportunities there. So, a choice has to be made between staying in that market and focusing on customer service and service contracts making the current customer relationships deeper and so by increasing the average return per user (ARPU), or moving into new markets, meaning either new vertical markets, or the same vertical market in different market areas.

Staying in the acquired niche assumes very little growth, but as TradeSys products provide clear benefits for the customers and switching costs are relatively high, this is also a relatively safe choice. The company can expect modest growth through selling new features to the existing customers, and, on the other hand, steady stream of service fees.

To expand, the company has two choices:

1.   **Diversifying into new markets:** One possibility to expand is to diversify into new markets with software packages that are general enough to be sold to other types of associations that have to manage their membership and payments. These could be, for example, large trade associations, national youth or sports associations, etc.

2.   **Exporting to foreign trade unions and unemployment funds:** The other possibility to expand is to export the software into European markets and try to acquire market share there. However, the different national legal frameworks as well as business traditions need to be accounted for.

Technically, the systems of TradeSys are componentized in such a way that it would be possible to develop new features needed in either of the new markets suggested above. The current technical challenges involve moving the services to Web-enabled and mobile environments.

REFERENCES

Cravens, D. W. (1987). *Strategic marketing*. Homewood, IL: Richard D. Irwin.

Kotler, P. (1991). *Marketing management: Analysis, planning, implementation and control* (7th ed.). Englewood Cliffs, NJ: Prentice Hall.

Rajala, R., Rossi, M., Tuunainen, V. K., & Korri, S. (2001). *Software business models, a framework for analyzing software industry: 76*. Helsinki: TEKES.

Statistics Finland. (2002). Retrieved from http://www.stat.fi/tk/tp/tasku/taskue_yritykset.html

FURTHER READING

McHugh, P. (1999). *Making it big in software — A guide to success for software vendors with growth ambitions.* Tiverton, Devon, NW: Rubic Publishing.

Moore, G. A. (1991). *Crossing the chasm: Marketing and selling high-tech products to mainstream customers.* HarperBusiness.

SEI, The Software Engineering Institute. (2000*). A framework for software product line practice — Version 3.0.* Carnegie Mellon University. Retrieved January 26, 2001, from http://www.sei.cmu.edu/plp/frame_report/what.is.a.PL.htm

Shapiro, C., & Varial, H. R. (1999). *Information rules, a strategic guide to the network economy.* Boston: Harvard Business School Press.

Steinmueller, E. W. (1996). The U.S. software industry: An analysis and interpretative history. In D. C. Mowery (Ed.), *The international computer software industry: A comparative study of industry evolution and structure.* New York: Oxford University Press.

ENDNOTE

[1]   Cravens has adapted this analysis from Ben M. Enis, Raymond La Grace, and Arthur E. Prell, "Extending the Product Life Cycle," published in Business Horizons 20 (June 1977), Copyright by the Foundation for the School of Business at Indiana University.

APPENDIX

Software Business Model Framework and its Key Concepts

This conceptual business model framework is best represented in practice in the customer interface of a software vendor by the activities related to its product and service offering. Within the business model, the focus is on four basic elements distinguishing different business models from each other. These elements are product development approach, revenue logic, distribution model, and servicing and implementation model (for more details, see Rajala et al., 2001).

Product Development Approach

The product development model describes the core product offering of a software venture and the way it's product development work is organized. Inside the product development model, there are several alternative approaches in developing the product offering. These options include pure *project*-oriented model where customers' needs are responded to with customer-specific system projects. At the other end, there are pure *product*-oriented models including options for creating universal software products, parametrized system products, or a product family of universal software components, and so on.

Revenue Logic

The revenue logic describes the way the software venture generates its revenue and profit. The alternatives inside this business model element include effort-driven pricing of software projects, sales and leasing of software licenses, profit sharing agreements between software vendor and its customers and/or sales channel partners, different loss-leader and media models and hybrids based on them.

Distribution Model

The marketing model describes the way marketing of the software venture's product and service offering has been organized and who are its sellers and marketers. The sales model also characterizes the outcome of the sales process, or the agreement reached between the vendor and a customer about the characteristics of the solution provided: Will it be based on uniform products sold for other customers as well, or is it a tailored solution to one customer only, or something between these alternatives?

Servicing and Implementation Model

The servicing model describes how the product offering will be dispatched or delivered to the customers as working solutions. The possibilities range from consulting by the vendor to self-service by the customer. This is an important part of the equation for the software producer, because more tailored and specialized its offering is, the less there are possibilities for exponential growth.

Between the several alternatives of these basic elements there are supposed to be interdependences that limit the constellation of feasible choices within one business model. The choices are presented as a matrix in the Appendix. The matrix can be used to position the company, or its individual product offerings and it can be also used for discussing the future possibilities of the company.

Risto Rajala, MSc (Econ) is a PhD student in the Helsinki School of Economics (HSE) majoring in information systems science in Finland. His current research is focusing on business models and product development strategies and methods of software businesses. Prior to his doctoral dissertation project he has been working as a software development practitioner at the Nokia Research Centre and Fujitsu ICL. As a co-author he has recently published a technology review: "R. Rajala, M. Rossi, V.K. Tuunainen and S. Korri: Software Business Models — A Framework for Analyzing Software Industry, Tekes Technology Review 108/2001."

Matti Rossi, PhD (Econ) is an acting professor of information systems at Helsinki School of Economics (HSE), Finland. He received his PhD in business administration from the University of Jyvaskyla in 1998. He has worked as research fellow at Erasmus University Rotterdam and as a visiting assistant professor at Georgia State University. His research papers have appeared in journals such as Information and Management *and* Information Systems, *and more than a dozen of them have appeared in conferences such as ICIS, HICSS and CAiSE. He was an organizing committee member CAiSE'95 and ECOOP'97, organizing committee member and technology chair for ICIS'98 and minitrack chair for Hawaii International Conference on Systems Sciences 98-01. He has been the principal investigator in several major research projects funded by the technological development center of Finland and Academy of Finland.*

Virpi Kristiina Tuunainen is professor (act) at the Department of Information Systems Science and director of GEBSI (Graduate School for Electronic Business and Software Industry) of Helsinki School of Economics (HSE), Finland. She received her PhD (Econ) from the HSE. She has been a visiting scholar at the Erasmus University Rotterdam (The Netherlands) and University of Texas at Austin (USA), and a visiting researcher at the Business School and at the Department of Computer Science of University of Hong Kong. Her research focuses on electronic commerce, inter-organizational information systems and economics of IS. She has published articles in journals such as MIS Quarterly, Journal of Management Information Systems, Journal of Strategic Information Systems, Information & Management, Journal of Global Information Technology Management, International Journal of Electronic Markets, Australian Journal of Information Systems, Information Technology and People, Information Technology and Tourism *and* Scandinavian Journal of Information Systems. *Her research papers have also appeared in a number of international conferences. She is member of the editorial boards of* Scandinavian Journal of Information Systems, JITTA, *and* EM Electronic Markets.

This case was previously published in the *Annals of Cases on Information Technology*, Volume 5/2003, pp. 538-549, © 2003.

Chapter XX

The Foreign Banks' Influence in Information Technology Adoption in the Chinese Banking System

Michelle W. L. Fong, Victoria University, Australia

EXECUTIVE SUMMARY

Foreign direct investment has been a common conduit of technology transfer for the locally funded enterprises in the host country to adopt foreign technology. In addition, it could be a powerful agent in affecting technology adoption within a technologically backward host country. By contrast, foreign direct investment has not been a significant source of information technology transfer into the Chinese banking system. Neither has it been an effective agent in affecting technology adoption in this system. The priority and concern of the Chinese government in protecting, and retaining control of, its domestic banks and financial market have kept foreign direct investment in the banking industry at a relatively modest level. The controlled industry, the long wait for full market competition, and the inadequate infrastructure and operating framework have inhibited the foreign banks from adopting highly sophisticated information technology for their restricted business operations and from being an effective conduit in technology transfer.

BACKGROUND

The Chinese Economy

The Chinese economy's GDP (gross domestic product) has been riding on a positive growth phenomenon, since the initiation of its economic reform program and its transition from a command to a market-based economy in 1979. The new direction undertaken by the Chinese government has definitely propelled the growth of the economy between the pre-reform and reform periods, as shown in Graph 1. The real GDP growth between 1979 and 2000 (in the reform period) was at an average annual rate of 9.25%, superseding the average annual growth of 5.3% experienced between 1960 and 1978 (in the pre-reform period). Although the growth had lost its vigor between 1992 and 1999, many economists and observers remained optimistic in the potential of this emerging market economy.

The Chinese Banking System

Prior to 1979, the financial flows in the Chinese socialist economy were largely governed by the predetermined central plan. Under this system, the state-owned banks were the most active and important financial agents in the economy. They provided the amount of money required to produce the predetermined amount of output and super-

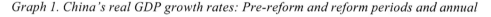

Graph 1. China's real GDP growth rates: Pre-reform and reform periods and annual

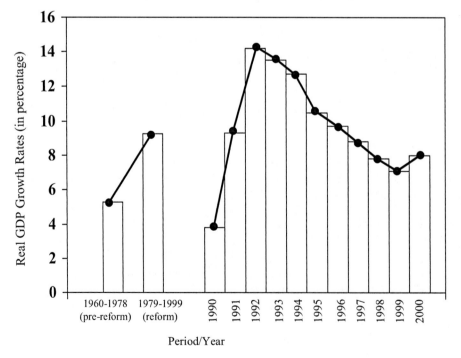

vised the utilization of funds in accordance with the requirements of the central plan. The banks virtually had no independent role in the creation of either money or credit from the funds deposited by the households and the state-owned enterprises. They merely acted as financial agents of the Ministry of Finance, and the inflow and outflow of money effectively belonged to the latter. The banking system at that time was a monobank system in which a single bank, the People's Bank of China (refer to Appendix for a brief history of this bank), undertook the roles of central and commercial banking. As compared to the capitalist system, the financial intermediary activity level and role of the Chinese socialist banking system was very limited and noncompetitive, and deliberately simple and passive. In terms of information technology adoption, there was less demand and incentive for banking technology applications.

The decision made by the Eleventh Central Committee of the Chinese Communist Party in 1978 to transform the socialist country to a market economy has resulted in the implementation of the economic reform program. Since then, the economic reform program has been conducted on a gradual and experimental basis, with emphasis on opening economic sectors (at varying degrees) to market forces, trade and foreign investment. The Chinese government recognized that the support of a well-developed and active financial industry is one of the requisite conditions for the full operation of a market economy. Hence, the financial sector became one of the initial sectors selected for reform and for eventual full foreign participation. The ultimate aim of the reform of this sector is to achieve a sound financial system that is capable of deploying scarce capital resources in the most efficient way that supports economic growth. The admission of foreign banks is regarded as a key attraction not only for foreign capital but also banking expertise to boost the growth of the fledgling market-based financial sector. As a result, several changes in the financial industry were targeted during the reform period, propelling the financial industry to play an active and pivotal role in the development of the economy.

Effectively, the banking sector has been the central focus of financial reform because of its relatively established standing as the active financial intermediary in the economy since the pre-reform period. The reform of the banking sector has resulted in the People's Bank of China becoming the country's official central bank and the abolishment of competition restriction among its state-owned banks. Four Chinese state-owned banks dominated the banking sector during the pre-reform period and the reform period of the 1990s, and they are the Industrial and Commercial Bank of China, the Bank of China, the Agricultural Bank of China and the People's Construction Bank of China (refer to Appendix for a brief history of these banks). The high market share of these four state-owned banks is a legacy from the past monopoly position of each bank in the pre-reform period, being the exclusive banking unit to specific market segments. These four banks executed the credit allocation plans of the economy during the pre-reform period and have continued to play a primary role in the provision of financial intermediary services during the reform period. The high market share is also due to the fact that these banks have been relatively effective direct channels for the government in managing, controlling and regulating the economy since 1979. However, it is expected that as the reform of the financial system develops, the market dominant position of these banks will be dissipated in the long run by the entry and active participation of other financial units. Table 1 depicts a diminishing financial intermediary role played by the four state-owned banks over time. However, in the interim, the state-owned banks are expected to remain

Table 1. The extent of the financial intermediary role played by the four state-owned banks in China

Year	Loan	Deposit
1985	93 %	93 %
1986	93 %	93 %
1987	90 %	86 %
1988	89 %	81 %
1989	89 %	77 %
1990	88 %	73 %
1991	87 %	88 %
1992	86 %	89 %
1993	79 %	69 %
1994	67 %	68 %
1995	63 %	63 %
1998	71%	62%

the core financial units at the transitional stage of the country's movement towards a market economy.

In addition to the above-mentioned state-owned banks, there are three state policy banks[1] (State Development Bank, Export and Import Bank of China and Agricultural Development Bank of China); three state-held banks (Communications Bank of China, China Everbright Bank and CITIC Industrial Bank); three public-held banks (China Merchants Bank, Huaxia Bank and China Minsheng Banking Corporation); and over 80 city commercial banks, 3,200 urban credit cooperatives and 41,500 rural credit cooperatives in the country.

The Foreign Banking Sector in China

Below is a brief history on the foreign banking sector in China, in regard to the origination of foreign banking presence in the country prior to 1949; the demise of foreign banks during the Communist regime; and the return of the foreign banks to the newly emerged market economy in 1984, after the implementation of the open door policy.

1. Prior to 1949

Foreign financial institutions were first located at treaty ports and in Beijing in the 1840s after the opium war. These foreign financial institutions constituted a powerful influence on the direction of the Chinese financial industry development prior to 1949. This was especially so during the reign of the Manchu government. For much of the period, the operation of the Chinese financial industry was in the control of the foreign financial institutions, which even had the power to overturn rules issued by the Chinese authorities (People's Bank of China Education Editorial Committee, 1985). This extensive foreign power largely stemmed from the fact that the weak Chinese government allowed the operation of foreign financial institutions to be governed by the laws of their respective home country rather than by those of the host country. The vulnerability of the government was also reflected in the operations of joint venture banks in which the government had a capital share, for example the Russo-Asiatic Bank, Banque Industrielle de Chine, Chinese American Bank of Commerce, etc. The internal organization of these joint venture banks was completely in the hands of the foreign shareholder, irrespective of the shareholding configuration. The public accorded lesser confidence to these banks than to the independent and fully funded foreign banks in their financial activities (Lee, 1982). In effect, the fully funded foreign banking sector had a monopoly role in the economy's trade with foreign countries.

Prior to 1949, the foreign banks continued to remain powerful financial agents even despite the turbulent political events in the country. For example, after the Sino-Japanese war in 1894 to 1895 when many of the foreign banks withdrew their businesses from the country, the remaining 14 foreign banks still constituted a powerful force in the country's financial system. The power of the foreign financial banks remained strong even during the rule of the KMT government and amidst attempts to strengthen the local Chinese banking sector. This was evidenced by the shore of total assets held by foreign banks within the industry and their influence in the monetary condition of the economy. In October 1947, the 13 foreign banks located in the active financial market in Shanghai had asset holdings at 26.2% of the total overall assets in the Shanghai's financial market, whereas the 147 local Chinese banks' assets only accounted for 54.2% of the total. In August 1948, when there were only 12 foreign banks left in Shanghai's financial market; their assets were even higher than before, at 36% of the total assets. In terms of the monetary situation, the foreign banks always heavily influenced official and black market foreign exchange rates, and were very important in currency issuance. At the end of April 1949, for example, the currency issued by a foreign bank was about 5.8 billion yuan, which constituted two-thirds of the total currency issued for circulation for China (People's Bank of China Education Editorial Committee, 1985).

The foreign financial influence and power came to an end in the year 1949, when the government came under the control of the Chinese communists led by Mao Zedong. It was also the beginning of the era when the foreign banks and financial institutions, except the Hong Kong and Shanghai Banking Corporation, the Standard and Chartered Bank, the Overseas Chinese Banking Cooperation, and the Bank of East Asia, were either nationalized or had their assets expropriated or frozen by the ruling Chinese Communist Party (Wang et al., 1990).

2. 1949 to 1978

The revolutionary event in 1949 resulted in the withdrawal of many foreign banks from the scene or, in the case of the U.S. banks, they were penalized heavily (through property expropriation or the freezing of assets) for their country's role in the Korean War. However, not all the foreign banks were ousted from the Chinese banking system, as the Hong Kong and Shanghai Banking Corporation, the Standard and Chartered Bank, the Overseas Chinese Banking Cooperation and the Bank of East Asia were allowed to remain, largely for political rather than economic reasons.

Since the heavy exodus of the foreign banks, the national banking system has undergone several deliberate changes to the role of those banks that remained, mostly in accordance with the political climate. In spite of the continued involvement of the four banks noted above, the closed economy era of 1949-1979 cut off any active presence of foreign banks in the industry. Through the People's Bank of China, the government took steps to revoke the privileges enjoyed by the foreign banks in China, and consolidated and transformed private financial institutions firstly into public-private joint-venture banks and then eventually nationalized them (Yan, 1993).

3. 1979 to 1990s

With the open door policy in 1979 and the rapid growth experienced by the Chinese economy, the Chinese government declared the financial market opened to a number of foreign financial institutions[2] in 1984. Despite this declaration, barriers to foreign entry have been high and heavily restricted in their business location and activities. Nevertheless, the number of operational establishments created by the foreign financial institutions in China has been on the increase since 1979, as shown in Table 2. A majority of these operational establishments are in the banking and insurance sectors.

SETTING THE STAGE

Business Interest of the Foreign Banks

One of the main purposes of the foreign banks in establishing an early presence in the huge potential Chinese market was to provide support to their clients from their home country. The flow of foreign direct investment (FDI) into China has been on the increase as more international corporations move into this country to take advantage of its newly but gradually liberalizing Chinese economic environment. FDI in China has grown from US$636 million in 1983 to US$45.6 billion in 1998, which saw a concurrent increase in the number of foreign banking establishments in the Chinese economy. Although FDI has dropped to US$40.4 billion in 1999, the country remains one of the largest FDI recipients in the world.

Another main purpose of the foreign banks in establishing an early presence in the Chinese market was to prepare for the opening up of the local currency (Chinese yuan or Renminbi) business to them. In the Chinese culture, the propensity to save is one of the traditional virtues that have been highly regarded and upheld by the Chinese populace. The Chinese domestic savings as a percentage of GDP averaged above 30% between 1978 and 1998. In 1998, the domestic savings as a percentage of GDP stood at 32%. This Chinese penchant for savings, which has placed the country as the world leader in savings rates, spells substantial business market potential for well-established foreign banks. Although the local currency business opening has been gradual, it had been assessed by experts to be inevitable, in view of the external institutional pressure, for example China's desire to qualify for WTO (World Trade Organization) membership, and also of the evolution of a financial system that supports the development of a market economy. This assessment was in part realized in 1997, during which year nine foreign banks were permitted to deal in the local currency business in the Pudong region of Shanghai. By September 1999, 25 foreign banks located in Shanghai and Shenzhen were given approval by the central bank to conduct local currency business. However, the local currency business clientele of the approved banks is only limited to foreign corporations — foreign investors and Sino-foreign joint ventures. Foreign banks are not allowed to engage in transactions with local Chinese citizens and wholly Chinese

Table 2. Number of operational establishments created by foreign financial institutions in China

Year	Number of foreign financial institutions in China
1979	33
1987	181
1990	209
1992	304
1994	404
1995	603
1996	694
1997	702
1998	717

Source: Jinrongshibao, 1987, 1992, 1995, 1997; Dipchand et al., 1994; People's Bank of China, 1996; China Economic Information, 1997

institutions. It is expected that the foreign banks will be permitted to offer local currency services to local Chinese companies in two years, and to individual Chinese citizens in five years, after China became a member of the WTO. China is keen and resolute about joining the WTO, as evidenced by its concessions in opening financial businesses to offshore groups and giving foreign banks greater access to local currency business. Concessions such as the easing of geographical limits on those 25 foreign banks' activities and the lifting of earlier prohibitions on their lending consortia formation, related management fees, and inter-branch transfers. However, concessions have been conducted on a gradual basis, which is considered necessary by the Chinese government because the Chinese banks are not ready for full market competition with the foreign banks. The Chinese government viewed that the fledgling stage of the financial sector does not warrant the response to the calls, from the foreign governments and financial operators, for immediate full access.

Table 3 shows the types of foreign participation in China's banking industry in 1980, 1994, 1998 and 1999. A representative office merely functions as a liaison office, and is prohibited from conducting business. As a result, the staff strength is kept to a size of between three to five staff. Except for those operational branches that have license to conduct local currency business, the usual business scope is confined to foreign exchange deposits and loans, note discounts, remittances, warranties, import and export settlements and ratified foreign exchange investment. Both types of operational branches (with and without the license to conduct local currency business) are restricted to activities with foreigners and foreign-funded enterprises. To qualify for establishing an operational branch in China, the foreign bank must have a representative office in the country for at least two years, its parent company must have total assets of over $20 billion, and its headquarters are located in a country where there are sound financial supervisory and administrative systems (Chen & Thomas, 1999). On the other hand, to obtain a license to conduct local currency business, the foreign bank must have a three-

Table 3. Types of foreign bank participation

Types of foreign bank participation	Number in 1980	Number in 1994	Number in 1998	Number in 1999
Operational branches	50	100	173	175
Representative Offices	225	302	253	248

year history of operation in China, show that it has a profitable position for the past two years and have assets of value of at least US$150 million (Chan and Reuters, 2000).

The Performance of Foreign Banks

The market share of the foreign banks in China is estimated to be not more than 3%. The total value of assets of foreign-funded banks in China was US$11.8 billion in December 1994, with deposit at US$2.49 billion and loans US$7.5 billion. These amounted to 2.0%, 0.7% and 1.7% of the aggregate values for the four state-owned banks respectively. These values increased by December 1995 to US$19.14 billion, US$3.1 billion, US$12.75 billion respectively, with the relevant percentage being 2.1%, 0.7% and 3.0% respectively. At the end of 1997, 1998 and 1999, the total value of assets of foreign-funded banks in China was US$38 billion, US$34.2 and US$31.4 respectively, which is less than 3% of the aggregate values for the four state-owned banks in each year. Thus the level of participation of these foreign banking institutions remains very low.

Though a greater role for the foreign banks in the industry (in the areas of local currency denominated deposits and loan transaction) is intended, the scope of market opening will be on a gradual basis. The 1996 announcement that the Pudong district in Shanghai will be the first test city open to foreign entry has caused concern among the domestic banks. Foreign banks were known to have performed well despite the restriction imposed on their business scope and activity. When the foreign banks were not authorized to engage in local currency banking business, 90% of their income was earned from trade bills discounting for importers and exporters and fees from document processing.

One of the major banks in Shanghai has expressed the view that foreign banks will pose a serious challenge to its foreign trade settlement business, and have the potential to cut its business by 50% if full market access is granted to the foreign banks. This view is representative of the attitude of Chinese banks on foreign bank entry. The Chinese banks felt threatened by the foreign participants, especially in the international business area, and regard them as competitors with much higher levels of competitive advantage in capital resources, skills, services and technology.

The strength of the foreign banks in this business area was illustrated by the case of Dalian, where state-owned banks started to provide foreign exchange deposit services in 1988. After about seven years in foreign exchange business, the total foreign exchange deposit achieved by the four dominant local players in Dalian's financial market in 1995 totaled US$400 million. The six foreign banks, which were only allowed to deal in foreign exchange business about two years ago in Dalian, had achieved three-quarters of the state-owned banks' foreign exchange business in 1995. This has greatly alarmed the domestic banks.

The Chinese authorities have grave concerns that foreign banks may become overtly dominant if full market access is granted and lead to the repetition of the pre-1949 situation where control of the financial system fell into the hands of the foreign banks. On the one hand, the government authorities accorded heavy protection to the Chinese commercial banks, so that the protection of the interests of the Chinese banks was a priority in any new changes to be made. On the other hand, they found foreign banking participation indispensable in its emerging market economy, as China's domestic commercial banks are experiencing severe capital and credit shortages in attempting to meet all the needs of growing business activity. The Chinese government preferred to maintain control over the finance industry, rather than take the opportunity of rapid financial development offered by the full participation of the foreign banks. Therefore, to avert the loss of control over the banking industry, foreign banks were initially only allowed to serve foreign business investors in the Chinese economy. Paradoxically, the customer scope of these foreign banks — mainly limited to foreign business enterprises, Sino-foreign joint-ventures and cooperative enterprises — has precluded their involvement with the high-risk major default borrowers which are the state-owned enterprises. The relative credit standing of these enterprises may be drawn from a survey conducted by a major bank in Guangdong, in which 92% of loan default was committed by the state-owned enterprises while the remaining 8% was by Sino-foreign ownership enterprises.

The foreign funded banks have generally performed well in view of the restrictions and their constricted scope of operations. In 1996, their average return on assets was 0.6%, and their after tax rate of return on investment was reported to have increased by 31% over 1995. In 1997, their average return on assets was 0.7%. Some of the foreign banks became profitable after two years of operation in China and made profound profits. For example, 13 of the 25 foreign banks allowed to operate in Tianjin were reported to achieve a total profit of US$7.4 million with an ROI (return on investment) of 3.08 times at the end of May 1999. However, because of the many restrictions imposed on the foreign banks, their businesses are limited to small clientele base and short-term loans. As a result, their business became saturated very fast.

CASE DESCRIPTION

Information Technology Adoption in the Chinese Banking System

Prior to 1978, the level of information technology adopted in the banking system was insignificant. Since the opening of the Chinese economy to world trade and the abolishment of the monobank system in favor of a market-oriented banking system during the reform period, the adoption of information technology within the Chinese banking industry has been on the increase in line with these developments. However, the increase in information technology adoption occurred mainly in the four dominant state-owned banks, among which the Industrial and Commercial Bank of China has been the leading information technology adopter in the Chinese banking industry. Table 4 shows that this leading bank has made a profound increase in the adoption of information technology between 1985 and 1999.

Table 4. Information technology adoption in the industrial and commercial Bank of China

Forms of Information Technology Adopted	1985	1999
Mainframe computer	-	141 units
Minicomputer	7 units	963 units
Microcomputer	10 units	106,475 units
Mainframe centers	-	47 centres
Computerized business outlets	100+ outlets	41,216 outlets

The initial focus of computerization in the four state-owned banks was largely centred on the front-counter or front-desk in business and saving outlets. This is the most heavily computerized work system as compared to other work systems, some of which still rely on manual work process. As a result, 90% of these banks' business outlets have computerized front-counter or front-desk support. However, a considerable number of the small and medium banks still rely on manual mode of operation in this work system. When the overall Chinese banking system is taken into consideration, the aggregate status of information technology adoption reflects a shallow pattern of technology applications, which affects the quality of information systems.

The initiation and progression of technology adoption by the domestic banks are very much attributed to government's efforts, which have been transmitted through the reform agenda and the specific projects targeted at establishing the CNFN (China National Financial Network[3]) infrastructure for the banking system. Competition pressure from the highly concentrated Chinese banking market lacks the type of verve displayed by a developed market-oriented economy and is not forceful enough to propel rapid and strategic adoption of information technology. Strategic moves, such as using information technology to create competitive advantage and innovative positioning, do not characterize the business strategy of the Chinese banks. In addition, there are limited market opportunities for the strategic use of information technology in the industry. The bank customers still perceive banking services in very traditional terms and have not been able to fully appreciate the benefits associated with information technology based products and services. For example, the number of bankcards on issue has been on a rapid increase since 1993, but the incidence of card usage at the automatic teller machines and the point-of-sale systems remains low.

It has been assessed that the status of technology adoption in the Chinese banking system is equivalent to the 1980s standard of the developed countries (Liu, 1999). The pattern of technology applications still constitutes islands of automation. This is evidenced by the existence of manual and dual processing modes, and the inability of the banks to configure a virtual network that is capable of comprehensive geographical coverage and extensive interbank linkage. The internal focus of the banks during applications development, has led to the construction of proprietary networks. In the mid-1990s, a panel of 38 experts examined the status of the adoption of information technology within the financial system, and pointed out that the absence of coherent strategy and policy among the banks has hindered the interoperability of the banks' corporate networks. Even though the headquarters set standards and requirements, these were not consistent across the different banks. In addition, the lack of a distinct national direction governing technology adoption strategy had led to the result of further incompatible technology applications. It was stressed by these experts that financial computerization should be listed as a national strategy, to realign adoption undertakings to ensure compatible technology applications. In 1997, the banks located in 12 major cities began to work towards an interoperable system for a unified banking system (Shang, 2000). However, banks continue to face difficulty in areas where telecommunication infrastructure is inadequate.

In areas where the telecommunication infrastructure is inadequate, banks experience a connection gap not only among their own inter-organization networks, but also connection gap with the CNFN (China National Financial Network). The non-interoperability problem has resulted in partially automated or manual work processes. It is expected that the resolution of the system incompatibility and non-interoperability problem will involve a considerable amount of time and cost which in turn, impinges on the deteriorating profit and tight financial position of the Chinese banks.

Another problem facing the Chinese banking system is the shortage of information staff. In addition to this problem, the available information staff has limited skill to cope with the complexity of advanced user applications systems and this difficulty has resulted in many different system applications. There were IBM mainframe systems, open systems, traditional systems; fund, savings and credit card systems, which were developed individually and demanded all types of different application environments. Information technology staff, who were knowledgeable in both technology application and in business organization, remained scarce and difficult to recruit. A majority of the information technology staff has largely applications skill, rather than skill in debugging and resolving problems which arose in the applied systems. An unstable information technology support force further aggravated the lack of strong skill in this area. With the new labor reform policy[4] in force, these banks faced tough competition in the labor market in attracting, as well as in retaining, a stable pool of the required talent and expertise. The banks were extremely frustrated with losing their heavily sponsored employees to companies, which could afford higher wages and benefits. Even in the Special Economic Zones, where staff resources were comparatively richer in quantity and quality than the other areas, and where the bank branches registered a higher computerization rate, the problem of shortage of higher skilled information technology personnel constituted a crucial problem.

Information Technology Adoption: The Implications for Domestic Banks

Information technology provides an opportunity for businesses to improve their efficiency and effectiveness, and even to gain competitive advantage (Benjamin et al., 1984; Earl, 1989; Ives & Learmonth, 1984; Porter & Millar, 1985; Dierickx & Cool, 1989). In the developed countries, banks are among the biggest investors of information technology and they apply leading technology to achieve unprecedented cost efficiency and competitive advantage. Some of the technology investments undertaken by these banks in the past have become necessary tools for operations and competition today, such as the Automated Teller Machine, which constitutes the minimum standard of convenience expected of banks in the developed countries. A leading information technology application that has been expected to create new standard in the banking industry is the electronic network. Intelligent electronic networks capable of processing huge transaction volume and handling a multitude of business and consumer applications are emerging in the banking world, and their capabilities are stretching seamlessly across geographic borders. Despite the problem of privacy intrusion and security risk associated with online systems, the global banking community is very positive about embracing the Internet in its future strategic operations (Sheshunoff, 2000; Davidson, 2000; Stafford, 2001). Although the types of transaction currently supported by Internet banking are limited (mainly account enquiries, money transfer, bills payment and payroll deposit), it is anticipated that full service Internet banking would become the industry standard and not the exception in the not-too-distant-future (Sheshunoff, 2000; Wilson, 2001). At present, the Chinese banks lag behind the overseas foreign competitors in using electronic networks for strategic competitiveness and the option of Internet banking in the country is still highly underdeveloped. The central bank is concerned about the impact of foreign competition on its domestic banks, particularly when China became a member of the WTO and when its financial sector is opened to full market competition. It has urged its domestic banks to gear up and gird themselves for the technological challenges that will be posed by the well-endowed foreign competitors, particularly Internet banking (Zeng, 2001).

The effective adoption and applications of information technology to every aspect of the banking operations are not only crucial for the Chinese banks to survive the challenges posed by its foreign competitors when the country entered the WTO, but also for maintaining a timely, stable and reliable financial system that is vital to the maintenance of market confidence. Furthermore, this would facilitate the Chinese banks to integrate with the rest of the banking world and exploit opportunities associated with the rising number and volume of international financial transactions.

Foreign Direct Investment and Technology Transfer: A Literature Review

Foreign participation, particularly through foreign direct investment (FDI), has been identified as an important attribute that could provide the host country with ready access to an advanced level of technologies and know-how, and also to a pool of financing resources (Conroy, 1992). There are studies that suggested FDI brought positive impact or spillovers, such as higher growth rate of productivity, higher competitiveness level and higher living standard, to a host country through technology transfer activities (Quinn, 1969; Globerman, 1979; Chen, 1983; Blomstrom & Persson, 1983; Morton, 1986; Schive, 1990; Conroy, 1992; Wang & Bromstrom, 1992; Caves, 1995; Borensztein et al., 1998; Sjoholm, 1999). On the other hand, there are studies that suggested otherwise (Cantwell, 1989; Haddad & Harrison, 1993; Aitken & Harrison, 1994; Kokko & Tansini, 1996; Perez, 1998). Explanations provided by researchers for the mixed evidence tend to be centered on the characteristics of the host country in encouraging or harnessing maximum benefits from technology transfer. For instance, Blomstrom et al.

(1994), Kokko (1996) and Sjoholm (1999) found in their respective studies that a high technology gap between the foreign and domestic firms and a low degree of competition in the market could impede the exploitation of technology transfer. They stressed that FDI is an effective conduit for the transfer of technology when there is a sufficient absorptive capability[5] of the advanced technologies in the host country (studies by Cohen & Levinthal, 1990; Borensztein et al., 1998; and Chuang & Lin, 1999, are of similar view). Otherwise, it will be difficult for the technologically backward domestic firms to close the technology gap and catch up with the foreign firms. They also stressed that the level of technology transferred via FDI is dependent on the competition pressure in the host country because foreign participants from developed countries are likely to bring in relatively modern and efficient technologies to defend their position in a very competitive market (also supported by Wang & Blomstrom, 1992; Blomstrom & Lipsey, 1996). In the process, the competition pressure may also stimulate the adoption of technology or efficiency-enhancing strategies by domestic firms due to the desire to stay ahead of competition or catch up with the technology-wielding foreign firms (Caves, 1974; Dunning 1993; Blomstrom & Kokko, 1997; Gonclaves & Duque, 1999). For a better outcome, there have been suggestions that the developing host countries, particularly those not blessed with rich endowments, implement measures to stimulate competition and concurrently build up local technological competency and infrastructure for effective transfer of technology, rather than getting the required technological capability in place before introducing full market competition (Wang & Blomstrom, 1992; Frischtak, 1989; Blomstrom et al., 1994; McKendrick, 1995).

From the above review, although the characteristics of the host country are important in technology transfer, the role of the government and the policymakers is a critical one in ensuring that their policies and actions optimize the benefits and spillovers from foreign technology transfer. Market liberalization and foreign presence can be disastrous if not managed properly, and may generate adverse impact on the domestic firms, which is feared by host governments of developing countries. Foreign participants, especially those from developed countries, generally have technological advantages that enable them to compete successfully against the domestic firms and have easier access to international capital financing for investment in sophisticated technology (Mason, 1973; Mitchell, 1989, 1991). Host governments of developing countries are cautious to ensure that the foreign participants do not become too powerful and generate a detrimental effect on the profitability and future tenancy of their domestic firms (Cowling & Sugden, 1987; Young et al., 1994). This is a reason why some of the emerging market economies such as China adopted a gradual liberalizing stance for their markets. Even so, it is important that the host country government and policymakers do not stifle the positive impact or spillovers from FDI. There are indirect benefits associated with technology transfer that need to be taken into consideration. For example, employment from FDI may expand local capabilities to the advantage of the domestic firms. Human capital investment undertaken by the foreign firms (to equip its local labor to run the operations in the host country) may ultimately benefit domestic firms in the long run, as a result of labor migration. There are studies that revealed a considerable number of managers working in the local firms in Latin American and East Asian countries received their first training through their employment with these foreign multinationals (Katz, 1987; Hobday, 1995).

Foreign participation can have a great impact on the host country. Therefore, rules and policies pertaining to the investment environment must also take into consideration of the motivations behind investments made by foreign firms because they have heavy implications on the types of incentive that will entice meaningful technology transfer from these firms. A foreign participant's commitment to technology investment and transfer is likely to be positively associated with the strategic importance of its investment and its foreign market performance (Isobe et al., 2000). The foreign firm will engage in less resource commitment for FDI if it continuously suffers poor market performance or uncertainty surrounding its investment (Johanson & Vahlne, 1977, 1990).

The Potential of Foreign Banks in Technology Transfer

According to the KPMG (1994) report, the rationale of the government's admission of foreign banks into the Chinese banking industry was to attract foreign capital and banking expertise. However the regulated nature of the industry during the reform period so far has highly constricted the scope of foreign banking institutions' participation, and the overall participation of these foreign banking institutions is very low. As a consequence, their impact on technology adoption has been insignificant. Even the Sino-foreign joint venture, which has been the most direct mean of technology transfer in other industries, is not easily accessible in the Chinese banking system. The highly confidential nature of banking business has kept this type of business formation at a low rate. About 10% of the relatively active banking business entities were established on this basis.

A primary research was undertaken on foreign banks in late 1994, to assess the role that they played in technology transfer in Beijing. This research showed that there was little opportunity for the domestic economy to tap foreign expertise in the area of banking technology from the fully funded foreign enterprises operating in China. All of the 98 main foreign banking offices located in Beijing at that time were approached, of which 67% responded to a telephone survey regarding their level of technology adoption in China.

Due to the operational restrictions imposed on the foreign banks in Beijing, the number of staff in the Beijing representative offices is being kept at a low level. Seventy-three percent of the respondents described their organization structure as involving the following simple configuration:

- Chief representative (normally expatriate from headquarters)
- Assistant representative
- Secretary
- Driver

Seventeen percent of the foreign offices surveyed did not employ computers to operate their activities and about half of this group was the Japanese banks. However, these banks were equipped with basic communication and paperwork processing equipment, such as a fax machine and copier. Word processing tasks and data processing tasks were carried out on a labor-intensive scale, via typewriters and hand-operated calculators. On the other hand, 40% of the respondents have computer facilities on a sharing basis of at least two persons to one computer, while 12% of the offices surveyed provide a single personal computer station to every staff (except the driver). The latter group tended to be American, European, and Canadian banks. Only 4 % of the banks in the survey were equipped with computers that have international communication linkage, usually linked up with the headquarters. Less than 1% had domestic communication network linkages among its affiliated offices or branches located in China.

Almost half (53%) of the offices surveyed have branches or offices in other regions of China, and almost all the business branches in Beijing and other areas that deal with business transaction, had adopted computer technology but with a low incidence of inter-organizational electronic linkage. When the foreign banks were further interviewed on their intentions concerning the future adoption of banking technology in China, the interviewees regarded the availability of technology support to be most inadequate in China and information technology staff was normally sent from headquarters. In addition, technology hardware and software tended to be sourced from overseas headquarters or from the main overseas regional office, where the application of technology was at a very sophisticated level. Business branches in most cities of the Special Economic Zone were commonly characterized by a higher number of staff members than the representative office in Beijing. Computers were adopted in business branches for transactional purposes. However, the local users were seen as having weak capability in computer usage. Training was either conducted on an in-house basis or at the overseas offices. Adoption of sophisticated technologies remained insignificant in the late 1990s because of the low level of participation given to the foreign banks and the weak infrastructure that supports the adoption of information technology. These foreign banks also experienced an unstable pool of staff. Overall, the plan to adopt further technology in these banks is dependent on the market opening for their participation and the infrastructure support (telecommunication and power) within the country.

Thus, the central issue in the availability of technology for transfer from foreign banks to the Chinese market primarily lies in the degree of market participation open to them. This ability to participate in the market is closely associated to the opportunity of business participation or expansion. The infrastructural support took on second importance in attracting foreign technology introduction into the Chinese banking system. Thus far, the opening of the Chinese market to the foreign banks has been a carefully planned and controlled process, which explains the high passivity of foreign banks in technology adoption.

On the demand aspect of this technology transfer process, the ability to integrate or absorb any available foreign technology into the domestic system is also dependent upon technical expertise and managerial skills. In the Chinese banking system, not only is the opportunity for foreign technology transfer low, but the weak capability of the labor resources has not been able to absorb or assimilate any available foreign technology in the country. Even though the labor mobility factor[6] is high, it does not benefit the pattern of technology diffusion. Because the four state-owned banks employed 95% of the employees in the Chinese banking industry, the low level of participation and highly limited employment opportunities from the foreign banks do not permit meaningful transfer of technology and knowledge to the local labor. The role of foreign banks in technology and knowledge transfer is limited in the Chinese system.

CURRENT CHALLENGES/PROBLEMS FACING THE CHINESE GOVERNMENT

If the Chinese banks are to effectively exploit and harness benefits from technology and knowledge (banking expertise) transferred by the foreign banks through greater market access, further reform efforts are needed to overcome challenges and problems within the Chinese banking system, as well as those systems that are intimately linked to it. A stable and resilient banking system, a product of successful reform efforts, has the additional benefit of allaying the government's concern about loss of market control to the foreign banks if greater market access is granted.

The major challenges and problems that have to be tackled in the far-reaching reform efforts are as follows.

Loan Default

In the Chinese banking system, the amount of non-performing loans stood at 20% and unrecoverable loans at 7%. The Chinese government is eager to clear up these massive and long-standing loans before opening the market fully to foreign competition. The default borrowers in the non-performing and unrecoverable loans were mainly the state-owned enterprises. Their failure in adapting to the market forces and poor investment management ability had resulted in huge losses and capital assets underutilization, thus their inability to meet loan repayment. The cumulating debt problem was also blamed on the absence of comprehensive bankruptcy law and lack of strong cooperation from the local government[7] during the early reform period. In addition, the lack of experience and discipline of the bank staff have contributed to the inefficiency of the system. Although China has an unusually high rate of savings by East Asian standards, it has not been efficiently use as an investment resource by its domestic banks, in view of the lack of prudence in lending decisions and the high proportion of non-performing loans. The debt situation is threatening the profitability of the domestic banks and the viability of the country's financial system. The deteriorating profit of the domestic banks has an adverse impact on their attempts in information technology adoption and capability development. To ensure that the banks are disciplined in their lending approach, the central bank has progressively implemented rules that engender prudent lending decisions. However, the remedial measures, such as 'debt-to-equity conversions' for the ailing state-owned enterprises and transferring bad debts to the newly created state asset management companies were not expected to produce effective result in eradicating the problem. More effective measures and reform efforts are needed to resolve and prevent further buildup of the longstanding loans, so that the Chinese banks can focus on establishing a modern and sophisticated commercial banking role. Otherwise, the opening of the banking industry to foreign banks will be a lengthy process.

Regulatory and Legal Framework

Although the regulatory and legal framework has been evolving to keep in pace with the transition towards a market-based economy, shortcomings remained in the supervisory, regulatory, legal and accounting systems which required further effort to bring them up to international standards. This is also relevant to bankruptcy procedure, which has implications on the accumulation of non-performing loans in the financial system.

Legislative incompetence and procedural irregularities have the effects of undermining the confidence of foreign investors. For example, the foreign banks became concerned and even more cautious when China did not bail out foreign creditors of the failed Guangdong International Trust and Investment Corporation (GITIC), which is one of the country's provincial government investment arms, when it became bankrupt on January 16, 1999 with an unpaid accumulated debt of US$4.3 billion. Foreign banks were the last in preference of payment in the list of creditors. This eroded the confidence of foreign banks and caused severe contraction and retraction of credit from foreign banks. With the added strain from the long wait in gaining full access to the local currency market, a handful of the foreign banks are closing or downgrading their presence in China at the call of restructuring by their headquarters. According to the Foreign Banks' Association in Beijing, 70% of foreign banks have scaled back in their lending or closed their branches in the past two years (Zheng, 2000).

The nascent legal and regulatory framework requires further reform efforts. A strong legal and regulatory regime is necessary for strengthening the central bank's ability to manage and control the monetary situation, tightening credit supervision of individual commercial enterprises, enhancing banks' credit discipline, and establishing an integrated and open banking system where competition is orderly and management is effective.

Infrastructure

Infrastructure is beneficial to the economy "only when it provides services that respond to effective demand and do so efficiently" (The World Bank, 1994, p.2). A sound and efficient infrastructure is fundamental to the adoption and diffusion of information technology and banking expertise. However, China is still involved in trying to overcome the problem of inadequate basic infrastructure and has yet to reach a level that is fully beneficial to the economy. The Chinese telecommunication and power supplies infrastructure impose direct constraints on potential delivery systems in the banking industry, and this in turn influences the range of possible products or technologies that can be adopted. The institutional frameworks of these two infrastructures (telecommunications and power) share many similarities. The technical and particularly institutional constraints imposed by the infrastructure, especially the telecommunication infrastructure,[8] have been impeding the ability of the Chinese banking industry in its adoption of information technology to realize benefits such as:

- cost-effectiveness in linking the Chinese banking units,
- extensive coverage of all provinces,
- international standards for open access,
- secure and reliable transmission of financial data and information,
- rapid payment settlement without information transmission delay,
- flexible structure for creation and further support of financial products and services.

The stage of infrastructure development also has an impact on the foreign banks' technology adoption position. A technology-oriented foreign bank will have to make heavy investment in information technology support to overcome the shortcomings in the infrastructure. However, such investment strategy will be made difficult by the nature of the market opening to the foreign banks and the business justification of return on the investment. Hence, infrastructure deficiencies hampered both the process of technology adoption within the banks and technology transfer to the banks.

Human Resource

The shortage of appropriately qualified human resources is one of the most pertinent issues facing the banking system in their adoption and diffusion of information technology. The foreign banks constitute one of the conduits in training and imparting banking expertise to the Chinese locals. However, their low level of participation limits this role. The government is also a critical force in cultivating a pool of the required talent. Government intervention would seem relevant in situations where market imperfections or externalities make it unfair for private participation to fulfill the entire role in training the resources.

External facilities specialized in training people for information services remained relatively scarce in China. The average skill level of the information technology personnel in China remained low. There was also a lack of individuals with knowledge of both the technical applications of information technology and the business value systems of the banks. Such individuals are in high demand for their potential in enhancing business value through the exploitation of technological capability. From 1979 till now, it has been the responsibility of the domestic banks to create a pool of information technology talent to support the technology adoption and diffusion process. For the domestic banks, this has weighed on their already tight financial position. Although the government's support for computers courses in primary and secondary education level is growing, basic education takes years. Support from the government in the area of providing external training facilities is needed. This would not only alleviate the constraint faced by the banks, but also may serve as a coherent national strategy to incorporate the concentration of scarce resources into developing indigenous technological capabilities. This is necessary to meet the immediate and pressing demand for talents in those economic systems that are already involved in information technology adoption. The consolidation of the different learning paradigms by establishing responsive and nationally coordinated training centres, for example, might not only alleviate the financial burden on the technology adopters but also have an impact on the adoption of consistent standards in technology operations and management.

REFERENCES

Aitken, B., & Harrison, A. (1994). *Do domestic firms benefit from foreign direct investment? Evidence from panel data* (World Bank Policy Research Working Paper No. 1248). Washington, DC: World Bank.

Almanac of China's Economy. (1991, 1994-1996). Beijing: State Council Development Research Centre.

Benjamin, R. I., Rockart J. F., Scott-Morton, M. C., & Wyman, J. (1984). Information technology: A strategic opportunity. *Sloan Management Review, 25*(3), 3-10.

Blomstrom, M., & Kokko, A. (1997). *Regional integration and foreign direct investment* (NBER Working Paper No. 6019). Cambridge, MA: National Bureau of Economic Research.

Blomstrom, M., Kokko, A., & Zejan, M. (1994). Host country competition, labour skills and technology transfer by multinationals. *Weltwirtschaftliches Archiv, 130*, 521-533.

Blomstrom, M., & Lipsey, R. E. (1996). Multinational firms and the diffusion of skills and technology. *NBER Reporter*, N, 11-13.

Blomstrom, M., & Persson, H. (1983). Foreign investment and spillover efficiency in an underdeveloped economy: Evidence from the Mexican manufacturing industry. *World Development*, 11, 492-501.

Borenszten, E., De Gregorio, J., & Lee, J. W. (1998). How does foreign direct investment affect economic growth? *Journal of International Economics, 45*(1), 115-35.

Cantwell, J. (1989). *Technological innovation and multinational corporations*. Oxford: Basil Blackwell.

Caves, R. (1974). Multinational corporations, competition and productivity in host-country markets. *Economica, 41*, 176-193.

Caves, R. (1995). *Multinational enterprise and economic analysis* (2nd ed.). Cambridge: Cambridge University Press.

Chan, C., & Reuters. (2000, January 25). Shanghai set to widen Yuan trade. *China Web.* Retrieved April 26, 2001, from http://www.chinaweb.com/english/cw_html/thebigissue/the_renminbi/HK1954.html

Chen, E. K. Y. (1983). Multinational corporations and technology diffusion in Hong Kong manufacturing. *Applied Economics, 309-321.*

Chen, J., & Thomas, S. C. (1999). Banking on China. *The China Business Review, 26*(6), 16-19.

China Economic Information. (1997, December 5). More foreign-funded banks set up in China. *ChinaVista.* Retrieved April 26, 2001 from http://www.chinavista.com/business/news/archive/dec/dec11-03.html

China — Foreign banks allowed enlarged business scope. (1999, August 6). *Asia Intelligence Wire*, p.1.

China statistical yearbook. (1989-1999). Beijing: Statistical Information and Consultancy Service Centre.

Chuang, Y. C., & Lin, C. M. (1999). Foreign direct investment, R & D and spillover efficiency: Evidence from Taiwan's manufacturing firms. *The Journal of Development Studies, 35*(4), 117-137.

Cohen W. M., & Levinthal D. A. (1990). Absorptive capacity: A new perspective on learning and innovation. *Administrative Science Quarterly, 35*, 128-152.

Conroy, R. (1992). *Technological change in China.* Paris: OECD.

Cowling, K., & Sugden, R. (1987). *Transnational monopoly capitalism*. London: Wheatsheaf Books.

Davidson, S. (2000, November). Internet banking: Key strategic and tactical issues for community bankers. *Community Bankers, 9*(11), 48-50.

Dierickx, I., & Cool, K. (1989). Asset stock accumulation and substainability of competitive advantage. *Management Science, 35*(12), 1504-1514.

Dipchand, C. R., Zhang, Y., & Ma, M. (1994). *The Chinese financial system*. Westport, Conn: Greenwood Press.

Dunning, J. G. (1993). *Multinational enterprises, and the global economy*. Reading: Addison-Wesley.

Earl, M. (1989). *Implementation: Management strategies for information technology*. New York: Prentice-Hall.

Frischtak, C. (1989). Competition as a tool of LDC industrial policy. *Finance & Development, 26*(3), 27-29.

Globerman S. (1979). Foreign direct investment and 'spillover' efficiency benefits in Canadian manufacturing industries. *Canadian Journal of Economics*, 12, 42-56.

Gonclaves, V. F. C., & Duque, J. (1999, July/August). Portuguese financial corporations' information technology adoption patterns. *Interfaces, 29*(4), 44-57.

Haddad, M., & Harrison, A. (1993). Are there positive spillovers from direct foreign investment? Evidence from panel data for Morocco. *Journal of Development Economics*, 42, 51-74.

Hobday, M. (1995). *Innovation in East Asia: The challenge to Japan*. Aldershot: London.

Isobe, T., Makino, S., & Montgomery, D. B. (2000, June). Resource commitment, entry timing, and market performance of foreign direct investment in emerging economies: The case of Japanese international joint ventures in China. *Academy of Management Journal, 43*(3), 468-485.

Ives, B., & Learmonth, G. P. (1984). The information system as a competitive weapon. *Communications of the ACM*, 27, 1193-1201.

Jinrongshibao. (1987-1997). Jinrongshibao. Beijing.

Johanson, J., & Vahlne, J. E. (1977). The internationalization process of the firm: A model of knowledge development and increasing foreign market commitments. *Journal of International Business Studies, 8*(1), 23-32.

Johanson, J., & Vahlne, J. E. (1990). The mechanism of internationalization. *International Marketing Review, 7*(4), 11-24.

Katz, J. M. (1987). *Technology creation in Latin American manufacturing industries*. New York: St. Martin's Press.

Kokko, A. (1996). Productivity spillovers from competition between local firms and foreign affiliates. *Journal of International Development*, 8, 517-530.

Kokko, A., & Tansini, R. (1996). Local technological capability and productivity spillovers from foreign direct investment in the Uruguayan manufacturing sector. *Journal of Development Studies*, 32, 602-611.

KPMG. (1994). *Banking and finance in China* (1st ed.). KPMG.

Lee, F. E. (1982). *Currency, banking and finance in China*. New York: Garland Publishing, Inc.

Liu, H. (1999). Bank network security. *Financial Computer of China, 116*(3), 42-46.

MacCormac, S. (1993). Foreign bank branches on the move. *China Business Review, 20*(3), 40-43.

Mason, R. H. (1973). Some observations on the choice of technology by multinational firms in developing countries. *Review of Economics and Statistics*, 55, 349-355.

McKendrick, D. (1995, September). Sources of imitation: Improving bank process capabilities. *Research Policy, 24*(5), 783-802.

Mitchell, W. (1989). Whether and when? Probability and timing of incumbents' entry into emerging industrial subfields. *Administrative Science Quarterly, 34*, 208-230.

Mitchell, W. (1991). Dual clocks: Entry order influences on incumbent and newcomer market share and survival when specialized assets retain their value. *Strategic Management Journal, 12*, 85-100.

Mo, Y. K. (1999). Strengthening the banking system in China: Issues and experience. In Bank for International Settlements (Eds.), *A review of recent banking reforms in China: BIS policy papers no. 7 — October 1999* (pp. 90-109). Basel: Bank for International Settlement.

Morton, K. (1986). *Multinationals, technology, and industrialization: Implications and impact in third world countries.* Lexington, MA: D.C. Heath and Company.

National Bureau of Statistics People's Republic of China. (2001, February 28). *Statistical communiqué of the People's Republic of China on the 2000 national economic and social development.* China Statistical Information Network. Retrieved April 27, 2001 from http://www.stats.gov.cn/english/gb/gb2000e.htm

People's Bank of China. (1996). *China financial outlook, 1996.* Beijing: China's Financial Publishing House.

People's Bank of China Education Editorial Committee. (1985). *China modern financial history.* Beijing: China Financial Publisher.

Perez, T. (1998). *Multinational enterprises and technological spillovers.* The Netherlands: Harwood Academic Publishers.

Porter, M., & Millar, V. E. (1985). How information gives you competitive advantage. *Harvard Business Review, 63*(4), 149-160.

Quinn, J. B. (1969). Technology transfer by multinational companies. *Harvard Business Review, 47*(6), 147-161.

Schive, C. (1990). *The foreign factor: The multinational corporation's contribution to the economic modernisation of the Republic of China.* Stanford, CA: Hoover Institution Press.

Shan, H. G. (1999). Realising the main objective of ICBC in computerisation. *Financial Computer of China, 114*(1), 8-10.

Shan, H. G. (2000). Consolidate the computerization foundation of ICBC for the financial gobalisation challenge. *Financial Computer of China, 126*(1), 2-4.

Shang, F. L. (2000). Speed up the development of bankcard business, drive the Golden Card Project construction. *China Credit Card, 44*(1), 4-5.

Sheshunoff, A. (2000, January). Internet banking — An update from the frontlines. *American Bankers Association Banking Journal, 92*(1), 51-53.

Sjoholm, F. (1999). Technology gap, competition and spillovers for direct foreign investment: Evidence from establishment data. *The Journal of Development Studies, 36*(1), 53-73.

Stafford, B. (2001, February). Risk management and Internet banking: What every banker needs to know. *Community Banker, 10*(2), 48-49.

The World Bank. (1980-1999). *World development report.* New York: Oxford University Press.

Wang, J. Y., & Blomstrom, M. (1992). Foreign investment and technology transfer: A simple model. *European Economic Review, 36*, 137-155.

Wang, T., Liu, H., & Zhang, X. (1990). *China finance encyclopedia*. Beijing: Economics Administration Publishing Bureau.

Wilson, C. (2000, August). Using the Internet to serve business customers. *Community Bankers, 9*(8), 16-19.

Yan, X. (1993). *China business: Financial activity directory*. Beijing: Beijing University of Science and Technology.

Young, S., Hood, N., & Peters, E. (1994). Multinational enterprises and regional economic development. *Regional Studies, 14*(4), 489-502.

Zeng, M. (2001). Internet banking urged. *China Daily*. Retrieved April 26, 2001, from http://chinadaily.com.cn.net/cover/storydb/2001/04/21/cb-2bank.421.html

Zheng, Y. (2000). Foreign banks scale back even as China pledges to open more. *China Web*. Retrieved December 21, 2000 from http://www.chinaweb.com/eng.../cw_html/thebigissue/wtodeal/HK10326.html

FURTHER READING

Chen, J., & Thomas, S. C. (1999). Banking on China. *The China Business Review, 26*(6), 16-19.

Harner, S. M. (2000). Financial services and WTO: Opportunities knock. *The China Business Review, 27*(2), 10-15.

Kremzner, M. T. (1994). Foreign banks in China: Financial sector reforms will open opportunities. *East Asian Executive Reports, 16*(6), 9-13.

Zhang, J. H., & Zheng, J. X. (1993). *Challenges and opportunities for foreign banks in China* (Policy Paper 7). Western Australia: Murdoch University, Asia Research Centre on Social, Political and Economic Change.

ENDNOTES

[1]   These banks were established to take over the government-directed or 'policy' lending functions of the four state-owned banks.

[2]   Banks, financial companies, trust and investment companies, insurance companies, insurance brokerage and agent companies, securities companies, investment banks, merchant banks and fund management companies, financial leasing companies, foreign exchange brokerage companies, and companies providing consulting services in finance, insurance and foreign exchange. However, China bans foreign entry in commodity futures, financial futures and other derivative financial services.

[3]   CNFN (China National Financial Network) is a specialized banking network that supports information system applications for information flow, transaction processing and a range of traditional and modern financial services on an intra-city, inter-city, inter-region and inter-bank basis. The CNFN is to be supported mainly by a satellite-based telecommunication network infrastructure (Jinrongshibao, 1996).

[4]   During the command era, jobs were allocated to individuals by the government. This practice was abolished in the reform period in which individuals seek

employment in the labor market and companies have to compete to attract quality labor.

[5] Absorptive capability refers to the capability to acquire, assimilate and exploit the transferred technology.

[6] The movement of labor carries the potential of knowledge flow and constitutes a potential factor in technology diffusion among economic entities in the developed overseas countries.

[7] The desire of local governments to prevent business failure or business bankruptcy, in order to ensure continuous employment for the locals, has contributed to the high level of bad debt in the banking system.

[8] Telecommunication infrastructure is a social overhead capital that has a macro influence on a firm's pattern of information technology adoption and diffusion. It constitutes telephone lines, satellite communications, broadband communications, institutions and policies, etc., that made up a nation's telecommunication framework which determines a firm's internal and external connection with other entities.

[9] In geographical localities that are below county level.

APPENDIX

History of the Major Chinese Banks

A. The Central Bank in China

The People's Central Bank of China was established in April 1948. Since its establishment, the bank has functioned as both a central bank and a commercial bank for about 35 years. From December 1948 onwards, the People's Bank of China was given the responsibility of issuing the country's standardized currency, the Renminbi, for circulation within the economy. This remains unchanged till today. In fact, the People's Bank of China has always retained its principal identity and had remained a core bank in times of mergers, demarcation or division within the banking industry. In the year 1952, which witnessed the consolidation of the socialist economy, the People's Bank of China became the monobank to regulate and manage the banking industry. The Bank of China's overseas business activities were incorporated into the People's Bank of China area of operations, while the Agricultural Cooperative Bank was dissolved. As a result, the banking structure became highly centralized and unitary, with the People's Bank of China operating as the only bank in the economy. However, the arena of the principal bank's activity was extremely limited, and was restricted to playing a subservient role to the Ministry of Finance in credit, savings and settlement activities. Lending activities were only for state-owned enterprises and in the form of working capital of a temporary and seasonal nature.

Several changes occurred in the role of this bank from 1979 onwards, transforming the bank into a vital economic unit in the economy's development path. The People's Bank of China attained its independence, separate from the Ministry of Finance, in 1983. It was also given wider discretion and independence in its lending activities. In January

1984, the People's Bank of China severed its direct involvement in commercial credit and deposit operations, and assumed the official status of a central bank. The Industrial and Commercial Bank of China was specially created to take over the severed commercial arm of this bank. Gradually, the People's Bank of China adopted the functions typical of central bank in industrialized countries.

B. The Dominant Players: The Four State-Owned Banks

1.   The Industrial and Commercial Bank of China was established on January 1, 1984 under the approval of the State Council. Although it came into existence during the pre-reform period, its significant share of market activities was derived from the lateral transfer of established business activities from the People's Central Bank of China when the latter became the country's official central bank and had to sever any direct involvement in commercial credit and deposit operations. The transferred commercial portfolio consists of urban banking business that specialized in savings deposit and lending to commercial enterprise. In term of assets, this bank is the largest bank in China and was ranked among the largest banks in the world in 1997.

2.   Bank of China was built on the foundation of the Daqing Bank in 1912. It operated as the international bank prior to its nationalization by the government in 1949. In 1953, the bank was appointed by the government to undertake and control all foreign exchange activities within the country, thus making it the economy's only specialized foreign exchange center. It operated under the jurisdiction of the People's Bank of China and was referred to as the Foreign Exchange Bureau of the Economy.

     In 1979, the Bank of China was appointed by the government to play a crucial role in the country's import and export policies. The bank underwent a restructuring exercise in order to fulfill this important assignment. In addition, it took on a new role as the clearinghouse for domestic transactions denominated in foreign currencies. Its activity in foreign exchange was further increased with the semi-floating currency system, with the Chinese yuan pegged against a basket of seven major foreign currencies, instead of just the Swiss franc used in the earlier reform period. Through this activity of pegging the Chinese currency against a basket of seven major foreign currencies, the bank became a major driving force in encouraging hi-tech import for industrial modernization and export to earn foreign exchange. It also provides financial credit to enterprises with export potential, in line with the country's trade orientation strategy. However, its prime position in foreign exchange and international transactions has been gradually eroded by the entry of new domestic banks and foreign banks.

3.   The People's Construction Bank of China was established in 1954 to handle the capital construction segment of banking activities. During the pre-reform period, it handled capital construction fund allocation and credit extension in accordance with the state budget and relevant policies. In 1958, the central government placed the bank under the jurisdiction of the Ministry of Finance as its Capital Construction Financial Division and closed all its branches. It took on a name identity as a bank again in 1962 but merged into the People's Bank of China in 1970 during the Cultural Revolution era. In 1972, it successfully regained its name identity as a bank

yet again and operated in the Department for the Ministry of Finance. Although this bank had been closed, merged and resurrected at particular times during the pre-reform period, its roles were confined to the handling of the country's capital construction. The People's Construction Bank of China's banking role developed in the 1980s and involved in deposit activity and commercial lending to the construction industry. In 1996, the bank changed its English name to 'China Construction Bank'.

4. Agricultural Bank of China. During the pre-reform timeframe, several attempts had been made to establish a specialized bank to handle the financial matters of the economy's agricultural sector. Credit cooperatives were the initial common financial institutions established since 1951 to support the agricultural sector. However, they were all closed off as part of the major banking industry restructuring exercise in 1952, during the Chinese internal movement against 'the three evils' — corruption, waste and bureaucracy. These credit cooperatives were reestablished in March 1955 to be known as the Agricultural Bank of China, but their service to the agricultural sector was lacking in strength and effectiveness. At that time, the branches of the Agricultural Bank of China were absent at the 'grass-roots' level,[9] and they were situated in popular towns and cities, above the county level. In remote agricultural areas where the Agricultural Bank of China did not have a branch, the People's Bank of China branches played a substitute role in these areas. In 1957, the Agricultural Bank of China was shut down for its role in generating inflation. The bank was reestablished again in November 1963, however the revival lasted for two years before it was then merged into the People Bank of China in 1965 (Yan, 1993).

After the various episodes of attempt and failure in establishing a specialized bank for the agricultural sector, a specialized agricultural bank was revived in 1979 and was named as the 'Agricultural Bank of China'. This bank has been responsible for financial intermediation, mainly supporting the rural areas in its agricultural activity. The most active part of its banking business covers loans to state-owned enterprises in the rural areas and loans for rural agricultural activities such as crop advances, agricultural capital investment, and farm development.

Michelle W. L. Fong is a lecturer in the School of Applied Economics, Victoria University. Prior to her academic and research career, she worked with different business systems in different corporations in Singapore, Malaysia, China and Australia. This gave her an insight into the information technology applications within these organizations, which spurred her research interest in the adoption, diffusion and leapfrogging of information technology.

This case was previously published in the *Annals of Cases on Information Technology*, Volume 4/2002, pp. 141-161, © 2002.

Chapter XXI

Enterprise-Wide Strategic Information Systems Planning for Shanghai Bell Corporation

Yuan Long, University of Nebraska - Lincoln, USA

Fiona Fui-Hoon Nah, University of Nebraska - Lincoln, USA

Zhanbei Zhu, Shanghai Bell Co., Ltd., China

EXECUTIVE SUMMARY

In response to increasing competition and technological advancement, Shanghai Bell Co., Ltd., a leading telecommunications enterprise located in Shanghai, China, carried out a major initiative to develop its next generation information technology/ information systems (IT/IS) strategic plan. The initiative was prompted by limitations of its current enterprise application systems where the systems were neither able to keep up with the evolving needs due to organizational change nor satisfy the increasing demands for information sharing and data analysis. This case describes the environmental and organizational context of Shanghai Bell Corporation, and the problems and challenges it encountered in developing an enterprise-wide strategic IT/ IS plan. The issues covered include alignment of IT strategy with evolving business needs, application of a methodology to develop the strategic IT/IS plan, and evaluation of strategic planning project success.

BACKGROUND

Shanghai Bell Co., Ltd. (herein referred to as Sbell), is a joint venture between China, the Belgian Fund for Development, and Alcatel. Founded in 1984, Sbell has become one of the pillar enterprises in China's modern telecommunication and information industry. During the past few years, Sbell was ranked among China's top ten foreign investment enterprises and China's top 100 enterprises in the electronics and information industry. In 2001, Sbell employed more than 4,800 people with an average age of 29, among which 78 percent of them have university education, including 900 with postgraduate degrees. The main products of Sbell include switching, transmission, terminal, mobile and Internet systems. Figure 1 shows the statistics on the market share of Sbell in China in the year 2000. In 2000, the sales revenue of Shanghai Bell reached 10.8 billion RMB (1.3 billion USD), which is an increase of 17 percent over the previous year. Figure 2 shows the increasing trend in after-tax sales revenue at the headquarters from 1995 to 2000. By the end of 2000, Shanghai Bell has total assets of 17 billion RMB (2 billion USD) and in May 2001 was recognized by Fortune as one of the best foreign investment enterprises in China.

Urged by intense competition and the fast-changing, dynamic environment, Sbell carried out a significant organizational innovation at the end of 2000. The company initiated a series of changes to reengineer its previous hierarchical and highly centralized management structure to a flatter and more flexible one. Four major measures were taken to establish a new matrix organizational structure, which includes six business divisions and three platforms within the overall company (see Figure 3).

First, Sbell established six new independent business divisions — switching networks, mobile telecommunication networks, data communication networks, transmission networks, network applications, and multi-media terminals — to cover the key business core. Each division was given the authority to determine its own products and materials (within the broad company context) and has some degree of financial independence. The sovereignty and flexibility of these business divisions led to speedier response to the changing environment and a closer relationship with customers.

Figure 1. Market share in China (until year 2000)

Switching
Shanghai Bell 34%
Other Companies 66%

Terminal (ISDN, NT)
Shanghai Bell 50%
Other Companies 50%

Mobile
Shanghai Bell 12%
Other Companies 88%

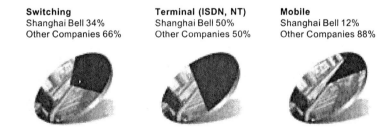

Source: Shanghai Bell Corporation

Figure 2. Sales at headquarters (from 1995 to 2000)

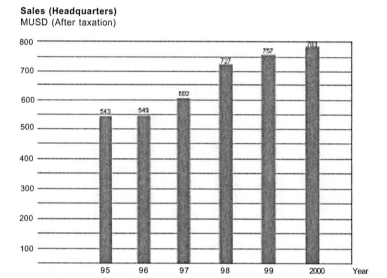

Sales (Headquarters)
MUSD (After taxation)

Group sales revenue reached USD 1.3 billion in 2000 and is expected to reach USD 1.44 billion in 2001.

MUSD: Millions of USD
Source: Shanghai Bell Corporation

   Second, a research and development (R & D) platform was set up to improve the capability for technological innovations. In order to manage the development of products efficiently, the R & D platform was organized as a three-layer structure. The first level is located at the top management level, titled as "Chief Engineering Office," which is responsible for corporate technical and product strategy, technological innovations, project management, technical/product standardization management, intelligence service, and corporate Intranet, etc. The second level is the corporate R & D department, which focuses on intermediate- to long-term R & D, and technologies that were shared among different business divisions. The third level is the Business Division (BD) R & D, which is located within each business division and is regarded as the front-line that interacts directly with customers on a regular basis. In order to enhance technological innovations, Sbell planned to increase the number and proportion of employees in the R & D department (from 34 percent in 2001 to 40 percent in 2005) as well as its R & D investment (from 9 percent in 2001 to 15 percent in 2005). Sbell believes that enhancements of research capability using advanced Information Technology would greatly benefit its long-term development.

   Third, Sbell set up eight marketing, sales and service regions in multiple distributed sites, including 32 branches in China and about 20 overseas offices, to establish a strong sales and service network across China and abroad. Instead of focusing only on sales revenue, the top managers of each region have to pay more attention to marketing and service. Both cooperation (gaining cross-regional customers and supporting nationwide promotions) and competition (pressure to minimize cost and meet budget) co-existed among these regions.

Fourth, the previously isolated manufacturing sub-divisions (such as production, planning and procurement) were re-arranged to establish a flexible and unified manufacturing platform. Both the manufacturing platform and the business divisions have the authority to determine their providers or buyers based on their unit's cost and revenue (ROI). For instance, if the business divisions find that the manufacturing platform cannot satisfy their requirements (cost, time or technology), they can choose manufacturers from outside the company. The same is true for the manufacturing platform. When the price offered by the business divisions is too low or a technological requirement is too high, the manufacturing platform can receive orders from outside the company. Competition and cooperation greatly contributed to business performance. In this way, units that have an independent accounting privilege would strive to reduce cost and increase benefits in order to avoid elimination.

To summarize, a new matrix organizational structure (as shown in Figure 3) was established. The new organizational structure was supported by six business divisions (network applications, switching networks, mobile networks, etc.) and three platforms — (1) manufacturing, (2) research and development, (3) sales, marketing and service. The six business divisions share the resources provided by the three platforms. For example, a project team can recruit technicians from BD, technology instructors from R&D, and sellers from marketing on a temporary basis to deal with a specific case. In addition, functional departments, including human resource and finance, supported the daily operations of the company.

The integration and advancement of both research and development platform and the sales, marketing and service platform contributed to the evolving business strategy of Sbell, which is a combination of "technical-oriented" and "market-oriented" strategy. A decentralized architecture enhanced sovereignty of units and increased flexibility. A

Figure 3. Organizational structure of Sbell

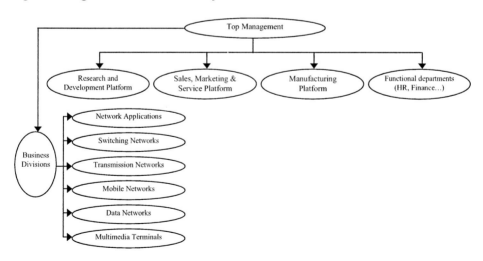

flattened structure reduced management layers and resulted in quicker response to changing customer preferences and a shorter design-to-market cycle.

IT Structure

Sbell implemented the SAP R/3 enterprise resource planning (ERP) system in 1998 as its core transaction processing system. The ERP system comprises four modules — materials management (MM), production planning (PP), financial accounting (FI), and sales and distribution (SD). According to the ERP project leader, Mr. Yunjun Xiao, "The FI module has worked well during the last few years. However, data-sharing problems existed between and within the MM and PP modules. Business processes for sales and marketing were only partially supported by the SD module." Hence, further integration of MM and PP modules as well as extensions of SD functionality were needed. Besides the ERP system, other applications were also developed, including the human resource (HR) system that was outsourced and a call center that was developed in-house.

Sbell invested several million USD to develop its computer platform and network systems in 1996 and continued to extend and improve its networks and technical infrastructure. To provide a solid high-speed network, Digital Data Network was used to connect multiple sites within Shanghai, and ISDN, ISP and ADSL were installed to link sales distributions outside Shanghai with the headquarters. Despite using advanced equipment and technology, the current networks could not satisfy the increasing needs of the distributed and continually expanding environment. Moreover, distinct operating systems (Windows 95/98/2000, Unix, Windows NT) and databases (Oracle, Sybase) existed simultaneously in the company, which resulted in data isolation and inconsistency.

The company did not have an integrated IT/IS department that was responsible for developing IT strategy, managing IT projects, and supporting and maintaining the IT infrastructure. The current IT workforce within Sbell included (Figure 4): (1) an IT department (with 10 people) that focused on providing technical support for the IT infrastructure (network, desktop, data center and maintenance) of the whole company; (2) 20 engineers in the switching business division that took charge of maintaining IBM mainframe; (3) technicians in each division who were responsible for installation and maintenance of local networks; and (4) teams established on an ad hoc basis for specific IT application projects such as the ERP implementation. There was no position similar

Figure 4. Existing IT organization in Sbell (April 2000)

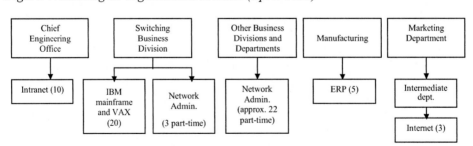

Source: Shanghai Bell Corporation

to that of the CIO, and the existing IT department provided solely technology support rather than drove IT strategy by aligning it with business goals.

SETTING THE STAGE

Because radical organizational change took place over a short period of time, many problems, including organizational and behavioral issues as well as application systems and information technology issues, arose. The challenges discussed next led the top management to initiate a strategic IT/IS plan in order to support the organizational change and to improve the capability of current IT application systems.

First of all, the current IT applications did not provide sufficient support for the revised organizational structure. For example, the two core competencies identified — *research & development, and sales, marketing & service* — were not well supported by the existing application systems. Without the help of IT, the strategic advantage that can be gained from the new organizational structure was limited.

Second, the current IT/IS structure needed significant improvement. The existing information systems could not satisfy the increasing demands for information sharing and data analysis. For example, problems in integrating legacy systems and the ERP system, and in information sharing within the ERP system, still existed. Some departments felt that the current application systems could not satisfy their specific functional requirements of day-to-day operations and decision making, thus they began to build small-scale systems within their units without waiting for or obtaining approval from the top management. These isolated systems led to serious problems such as information conflicts and functional redundancy. Furthermore, the current information technical architecture could not support the decentralized structure of the extended organization. The current systems lacked the capability to manage, control and support multiple sites, and the ability to adapt to the changing environment. Moreover, without a centralized IT/IS department, the company felt an urgent need to build an effective and efficient IT organization to help the company develop its IT strategic plan, manage IT projects, and outline specific IT policies and rules.

Third, there was a high likelihood in the near future that Alcatel would acquire Sbell by becoming a majority shareholder and develop Sbell as one of its major global information technology research centers. Although the contract was still under negotiation at the time of the case, future integration problems concerning management, organization and technology should be considered. IT should be designed to support the potential merger with Alcatel.

Facing the above problems, the top management decided to develop an enterprise-wide strategic information systems plan in early 2001 to achieve the following objectives:

- update Shanghai Bell's IT vision and strategy to align with its evolving business objectives;
- develop an appropriate application architecture that would meet its long-term growth objectives;
- develop an appropriate technical architecture that would ensure interoperability and integration between existing and emerging systems, and provide appropriate linkage to key business strategies; and

Figure 5. Organization structure of SISP project team

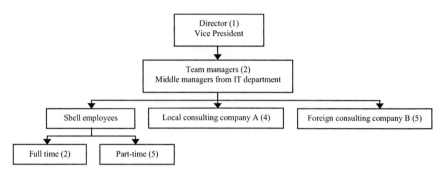

•   assess and design an information services organizational structure to help meet its long-term objectives.

In the middle of February 2001, a kickoff meeting was held among the top management to initiate the strategic information systems planning (SISP) process. A project team was set up, and was directly led by a vice president (VP) and two managers from the Information Center and the IT department of Sbell. To facilitate the implementation of SISP, the company suspended all of its application systems projects under development, and declared not to approve any IS budget until the end of the SISP project.

In March 2001, two IT consulting companies were selected to assist in the SISP project. One of the consulting companies (Company A) is a domestic company that has extensive knowledge of Chinese corporations and rich experience in developing strategic information systems plan in the telecommunication industry. The other (Company B) is a well known American-based IT consulting company that has a good reputation, an extensive knowledge base, and a proven methodology for SISP. "We selected Company A for its strong communication skills and rich experience in dealing with IT strategic issues in domestic industries," according to the vice president, Mr. Zhiqun Xu. He continued, "As for Company B, we chose it because of its strong IT background and specialization in IT strategic consulting. In addition, it is also viewed as being 'unbiased' in software and hardware selections and recommendations. Company B does not have its own proprietary application products, so it is more likely to recommend the most appropriate products rather than in line with its vested interest. We hope that the two consulting companies can work closely with our employees, to bring new concepts and ideas to the company and to educate our staff."

A vice president, two middle managers, four consultants from consulting Company A, five from consulting Company B, two full-time Sbell employees and five other part-time personnel from key departments, made up the core SISP project team (as shown in Figure 5).

CASE DESCRIPTION

At the beginning of the project, the team members, particularly employees within Sbell, did not have a clear understanding of SISP, and had little knowledge of how SISP can benefit the company and how to develop a strategic plan. Hence, the consultants spent about a week to train the employees in SISP approach.

The project manager of consulting Company B, indicated:

> *A strategic information systems plan for Sbell, can be seen as a vision with directional statements, and comprises a set of both broad and detailed guidelines that provide a framework for strategic, tactical and operational decision making. An IS strategy should also clearly link the IS goals to the strategy of a business, and provide a detailed blueprint for the acquisition, development, deployment and retirement of IS/IT assets over a multi-year time horizon.*

A strategic IS plan, according to Sabherwal and Chan (2001), comprises three types of strategies: information systems (IS) strategy, information technology (IT) strategy, and information management (IM) strategy. IS strategy focuses on systems or business applications of IT, and is primarily concerned with aligning with business needs to derive strategic benefits. IT strategy is concerned mainly with technology policies, including architecture, technical standards, security levels, and risk attitudes. Finally, IM strategy is concerned with the roles and structures for the management of IS and IT, and is focused on issues such as the relationships between the specialists and users, management responsibilities, performance measurement processes, and management controls (Earl, 1989).

The two consulting companies jointly carried out a four-phase approach (as shown in Figure 6) to accomplish the SISP project's objectives:

- **Phase 1:** Development of IT vision (2 weeks)
- **Phase 2:** Understanding the current business (6 weeks)
- **Phase 3:** Strategic information systems planning (4 weeks)
- **Phase 4:** Delivery of final report (2 weeks)

For simplicity, the SISP development process was depicted in Figure 6 as a linear flow of events. However, it would be more realistic to have a number of feedback loops included in the diagram. For example, while producing the IS plan in phase 3, the planners frequently returned to phase 2 to interview specific employees to obtain additional information.

The details of the four-phase approach will be discussed in the subsequent sections.

Phase I: Development of IT Vision

The focus during the first two weeks of April 2001 was on understanding, identifying and documenting the IT vision. It was recognized that IT should support the basic goals of the firm, thus the first thing needed was to identify the business strategy. Several

Figure 6. Strategic information systems planning process

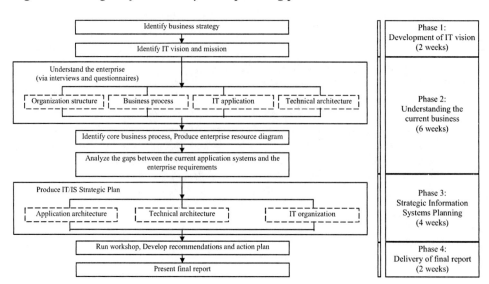

interviews were conducted at the top management level to understand strategic and organizational issues concerning short-term and long-term business goals, organizational reengineering, and IT evolution to support the necessary organizational change.

Mr. Xin Yuan, the associate chief executive manager summarized the weaknesses of Sbell as: weak in research and lack of innovative and cooperative culture within the company. "In order to survive in today's business environment and to become a global leading high-tech company," he continued, "we urgently need to strengthen **Research** and **Marketing**, which would contribute significantly to our core business competencies. Therefore, we propose changing from our current spindle structure, which focuses on manufacturing, in the middle part of the spindle, to a dumbbell structure, which focuses on research and marketing at the two opposite ends of the dumbbell."

Based on an analysis of the information gathered from the interviews, the team delivered an IT vision report outlining the enterprise environment, business strategy, IT vision, and alignment between business strategy and IT vision.

Phase II: Understanding the Current Business

"One of the most important objectives of Phase 2," emphasized by Mr. Ziqiang Pan, the project manager of consulting Company A, "is to identify the critical business process of Sbell." He continued to explain, "Core business processes are those activities flowing through the value chain of the company. They are stable and not easily affected by the external environment. Identification of core business process is the foundation for understanding the current business needs and the gaps between those needs and the functionality provided by existing IT applications. We can therefore determine the potential application opportunities and priority of application development portfolio."

Starting the middle of April, the project team was divided into five groups to conduct a six-week survey, which included a series of interviews and a semi-structured questionnaire. The objectives of this survey are two-fold: (1) to identify the current business process, and (2) to gain a better understanding of the organization, and its technical architecture and application systems. The five groups corresponded to the five business areas:

1. Manufacturing and procurement
2. Research and development
3. Sales, marketing and service
4. Functional departments
5. Business divisions

Each group, comprising one or two consultants working jointly with several Sbell employees, conducted interviews and administered questionnaires in the specific business area. These employees played an active role in bringing the consultants and Sbell employees together.

A series of interviews were conducted at the middle management level. Several meetings were held between the project team members, and the managers and representatives in the respective departments. The interviews provided the planners with an understanding of the core business process within each department, the functionality provided by existing application systems, and the future IT/IS needs of the departments. Communications between the planners and the employees also provided opportunities for employees to clarify the purpose of SISP and its approach.

The planners also administered a semi-structured questionnaire to representatives from each department. The questionnaire comprised four major parts:

1. **Business process:** concerned with relationships between processes, average execution time of each process, number of participants involved in each process, available IT support, major activities, and input and output information of each activity.
2. **Organization and management:** concerned with department objectives, organizational structure, human resources and IT resources, as well as the relationships and cooperation among units within and outside Sbell.
3. **IT application:** concerned with limitations of existing information systems, cost of each IT application, development methods (in-house or out-sourced), names and functions of each module, the scope and boundaries of business processes supported by each application, and interfaces among those applications.
4. **Technical architecture:** concerned with current IT infrastructure, platform, database and network.

At this stage, the planners spent a lot of time on collecting documentations of business processes, seeking information on undocumented but critical activities, and then combining information produce an overall view of the enterprise. This work was labor intensive and time-consuming. On one hand, the planners had to take much effort to check for accuracy of the core processes since inconsistencies might exist between the process presented in the "official" documents and those carried out in practice. On the other hand, the planners had to communicate frequently with on-site employees to seek information on undocumented but critical activities, and then produced a formal documentation (business process diagrams) based on the employees' description of their day-to-day operations.

Day-to-day operations in such a big company were so complex that the planners met many challenges. First, they found that the business processes were unstable with respect to ownership. Because of frequent organizational adjustment, work that was done by department A today might be carried out by department B tomorrow. Second, the more in-depth the survey, the more they found unclear boundary and ambiguous relationships among some of the processes.

Facing these problems, the planners decided to take a break and to discuss these issues. First, was it necessary to depict ownership as part of the business process? Organizational structure (people) is easily affected by the external environment and internal innovations, while operations, especially the core business processes of the company, would remain stable no matter who does it. Therefore, analyzing activities by ownership is not worthwhile for obtaining a stable view of the enterprise. Second, how in-depth should the planners analyze these processes? At what level of detail was it sufficient for producing the strategic plan? Realizing that the objective of analyzing business process in this case was for IT/IS strategic planning, rather than to produce an implementation design, the planners felt it would sufficient to identify the core business process, capture the general activities for each process, and more important, realize activities not supported by IT applications. Third, how should planners deal with those problems, such as information conflict and process redundancy, found in the analysis procedure? Considering that this was an SISP project, not a BPR (business process reengineering) or BPI (business process improvement), the planners decided to document the problems and provide recommendations to the company for future improvement. In this way, the planners could save time and avoid being involved in political issues such as power struggle.

By the end of May 2001 (after six weeks of hard work), the planners presented an enterprise information resource diagram showing a snapshot of the existing information resource of the enterprise. Eight core business processes were identified, including manufacturing, procurement, research and development, marketing, service, sales, human resources and finance. Among them, manufacturing, procurement, finance and part of sales & marketing were supported by the ERP system; human resource was supported by an out-sourced software; and research & development almost gained no support from application systems.

The enterprise information resource diagram is a two-tier model (shown in Figure 7).

The first layer of the enterprise information resource diagram depicts business processes that were identified through the survey. Application architecture, the second layer, describes the application systems that support specific business operations. Different colors were used to indicate different application systems that provided support for specific business processes. Therefore, from the two-layer diagram, it became fairly easy to identify the business processes that were covered by the application systems, and those that were important but only partially supported or not supported by any application.

Figure 7. Enterprise information resource diagram

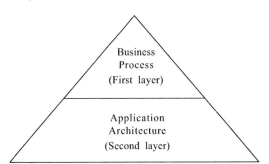

Phase III: Strategic Information Systems Planning

At the beginning of June 2001, it was time for the planners to produce a strategic IT/IS plan. The project team was divided into three groups to work on the following three areas: application architecture strategic planning, technical architecture strategic planning, and IT organization strategic planning. Much emphasis was placed on the application strategic plan; since it was considered the most critical area that needed a lot of work, nearly two-thirds of the team members participated in this group.

Application Architecture Strategic Planning

Application architecture comprises the set of IT applications (bought or built) that delivers the business process, and the technology (i.e., middleware) that integrates the various applications and links them with a coherent data model.

The enterprise information resource diagram was represented on "post-it" notes and stuck onto the walls of a conference room for others to view, critique, and make suggestions for modifications. Several employee representatives were invited to comment on the correctness and accuracy of the diagram.

First, the planners tried to identify potential application opportunities from the enterprise diagram. They found that finance and human resources were well supported by the application systems. Although manufacturing and procurement were generally covered by the ERP system, information inconsistency existed, thus system optimization was needed. Sales, marketing and service were partially supported by the ERP system and some isolated small-scale systems; research and development obtained almost no support from the IT systems. It seemed Sbell was in urgent need of the following: application for R & D (collaboration product commerce or CPC), and application for sales and marketing (customer relationship management or CRM), and optimization of the ERP system. Other application systems, such as e-procurement and knowledge management were also potential applications. CPC is a new type of software and services that uses Internet technologies to tie together product design, engineering, sourcing, sales, marketing, field service and customers into a global knowledge net (Aberdeen Group, 1999). CPC can facilitate management of product life cycle and cooperation with external partners. CRM is an integrated customer-oriented system concerned with sales management, marketing information acquisition and service improvement. Since service and support would become the competitive edge of Sbell, developing CRM would provide opportunities for Sbell to establish a closer collaboration with partners, suppliers and customers. ERP optimization includes integrating current stand-alone systems, developing additional modules, improving user training, and strengthening ERP support team. These ways can greatly increase the efficiency of the SAP R/3 system.

Next, prioritization of projects was considered due to the limited resources. The key question is: Which project was the most urgent for Sbell and should be implemented first, and which should be implemented next? The planners considered many factors in making a final recommendation. These factors included the business strategy, alignment with Alcatel (the potential merger), IT vision, budget, cost, time, technical complexity and technology trends.

Among the potential application systems, CPC was regarded as top priority for the following reasons:

1.   Lagging behind in advanced communication technology, Sbell faced the danger of decreased market share due to increased competition from both foreign companies and rapidly-growing local companies. Therefore, increasing the capability of research and development became crucial for survival and future development of Sbell.

2.   There was a high likelihood that Alcatel would acquire Sbell by becoming a majority shareholder and develop Sbell as one of its major global information technology research centers. Therefore, Sbell should build an advanced R & D platform to meet the anticipated challenge.

3.   Compared to marketing and sales, R & D was considered more urgent and crucial in its needs for IT support. Sbell has a well-organized sales force. Some operations in sales were supported by isolated or shadow systems. Although the functionalities provided by IT applications were inadequate, the system can handle basic operations. In comparison, R & D obtained little support from IT and was considered the weakest part of the company. Therefore, improvement of sales & marketing was necessary but not considered as urgent as improvement of R & D.

Other issues were also addressed in application architecture planning, such as application development alternatives (e.g., buy or build), application vendor selection, budget and implementation schedule.

Technical Architecture Structure Planning

The technical architecture is the foundation upon which the application architecture was built. The technical architecture should be further decomposed into "layers," such as application systems, database, IT service, network and platform.

Based on an in-depth survey of the current technical infrastructure conducted at the earlier phase, the planners collected detailed data and information in computing infrastructure, network infrastructure, and enterprise IT service.

A workshop was held with IT managers and users to develop a technology specification for Sbell's strategic architecture. The topics included: IT principles, platform/operating system(s), network infrastructure, middleware infrastructure, systems/network management, security infrastructure, and IT services.

After several discussions and changes, the group conducted a review session to finalize the written report detailing the IT mission, business drivers, IT principles, technology standards, and specific technology frameworks that would guide Sbell in the implementation and deployment of enterprise-wide technology and its next generation application systems.

Organizational Strategic Planning

The organizational architecture is the remaining component, which is important but often ignored in practice. The organizational architecture refers to the IT organizational structure, as well as the set of management processes or governance rules.

A series of interviews were conducted to understand the organizational and management processes in order to align the IT organization and management processes with the business strategy. The group first analyzed the current IT organization and compared it with other advanced IT organizations, and then presented a series of suggestions for IT organizational structure and project management. A workshop, which was primarily attended by management personnel, was held to present and discuss the results. The review was one day in duration and was held at Shanghai Bell's headquarters.

Phase IV Delivery of Final Report

Several review sessions were held among the consultants and the employees of Sbell to achieve consensus of the final report. A vote was taken by the top management during an application strategic planning workshop to determine the priority of potential IT applications.

The results of all phases were consolidated into a formal final report that documented the strategic and operational plans for IT development. The report addressed the following areas: business strategy and IT drivers, IT vision and mission, application architecture strategy, technical infrastructure strategy, and IT organization and management strategy. Application architecture strategy included a three-stage operational schedule for the implementation of information systems, including a potential list of applications, the priority of these applications, and recommendations on development alternatives (out-souring or in-house), vendor selection and budget. Technical infrastructure strategy and IT organization strategy provided recommendations for technical framework and construction of IT organization in Sbell.

In the middle of July 2001, after five-month of close cooperation, the project team presented a final report to Shanghai Bell's executive management at its headquarters. In summary, the suggestions included:

1. ERP optimization, CPC, and CRM were absolutely necessary for Sbell. Among them, ERP optimization and CPC were of the highest priority and needed immediate attention, while CRM was to be carried out next.
2. Establishing an independent and centralized IT organization (shown in Figure 8) is essential. This organization should be directed by the CIO and should comprise both an IT department and an IS department.
3. Building a distributed technical architecture that utilized advanced network technology.

Figure 8. Sbell IT/IS organization chart (to-be)

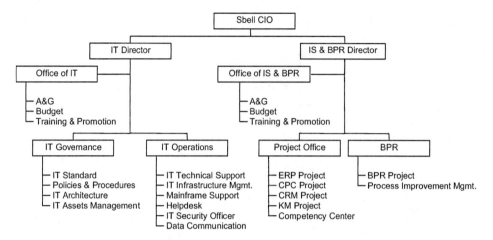

Source: Shanghai Bell Corporation

CHALLENGES/PROBLEMS
FACING THE ORGANIZATION

This case described the development of strategic information systems planning for Shanghai Bell Corporation, a high-tech company in China. Some of the key issues and challenges faced during the process are presented here for further discussion.

Issues and Challenges Faced in SISP

Issues related to evaluation. How should one evaluate a strategic IT planning project? What are the criteria for evaluating SISP success? These are hard problems with little consensus in the literature. From a practical perspective, the objective of SISP is to produce a workable schedule for approved application portfolio. Therefore, the close relationship between the strategic plan and the subsequent implementations can be considered as a key indicator of the contribution of a strategic plan. Success can be assessed by the degree to which implementations were carried out according to the strategic plan. Another indicator of success is the advancement of IT/IS positions in an organizational hierarchy. In this case, a CIO position was to be established and a centralized IT/IS department was being planned. Further, a significant increase in IT investment was planned. Could this SISP project be considered a success? What are the relevant factors to be taken into account in evaluating a strategic planning process?

Issues related to politics. The SISP project was supported and emphasized by Mr. Xi, the chairman and CEO of Sbell, and directed by one of the VPs, who was responsible for R & D. The planners received full support from the middle management within R & D, but less interest and cooperation from some departments, such as sales and finance. Insufficient communication with some of the middle management is one of the weaknesses of this project. Although this might seem to have a subtle impact on the strategic plan, it may have unexpected consequences on the implementation that follows (i.e., lack of support from middle management may jeopardize the implementation). Such problems are common for many projects. What are the steps could be taken to reduce the effect of politics and to increase participation?

Issues related to methodology. In this case, the strategic application architecture plan was based on the analysis of current business process. As we know, the business processes for a large company are very complex and it is almost impossible to capture these processes completely within a short time. At what level of analysis would it be considered sufficient? This seems to be a tricky issue to deal with. For example, if the business processes are captured at a high level of granularity, the planners might not be able to identify the key business processes, and the gaps between the business needs and the functionality provided by the existing application systems. On the other hand, if the analysis is too detailed, it would be extremely time-consuming, costly and unnecessary.

Support from top management. Support from top management is one of the critical success factors for any IT project, especially for a strategic IT/IS planning project, which primarily benefits the top management. The support from the CEO and VPs was very helpful to the planners in carrying out large-scale interviews and administering questionnaires within the company. Also, the commitment of top management is the decisive factor for subsequent implementation. Since obtaining commitment from the top management was not easy, the planners took the effort to seek opportunities to engage in regular communications with the top management. They also convinced the top management that the results have significant implications since they were developed based on a scientific methodology. What are some general recommendations and suggesting the seeking commitment from the top management? What could Sbell have done better?

Issues related to teamwork. A success factor in this case was attributed to the close cooperation among members in the project team. Three groups in the project — employees from Sbell, consultants from consulting Company A, and consultants from company — worked closely together during the entire SISP process. The team leaders (two IT managers from Sbell) and the full-time and part-time team members from Sbell played an active role in the development of SISP. They were highly regarded employees and professionals in the different departments, and they knew the business very well and had excellent communication skills. Without their help, it would be hard for the consultants to receive a fairly high level of participation in conducting interviews and questionnaires, and to obtain first hand materials in such a short period of time. The consultants in Company A possessed experience in developing IT projects in Chinese companies; they have skills to manage cultural and political issues; they also have no language difficulty in communicating with employees of Sbell. The consultants in Company B have a strong IT consulting background and they have a sound methodology and a good reputation. The three groups have their unique characteristics, and a combination of these specific strengths contributed to the smooth development of the project.

The role of consulting companies. Companies might be reluctant to hire consultants because they are suspicious of what consulting companies can really do for them. In this case, the consulting companies played a key role in developing the strategic plan, in educating the internal employees, and in promoting the IT positions within the company. At the beginning, Sbell had no idea how to develop a strategic IT/IS plan. The consulting companies brought the knowledge into Sbell, and educated the company on a scientific development methodology. The training greatly benefited employees, especially those in the project team, by providing them a good understanding of SISP. These employees became proficient in applying the SISP methodology at the end of the project and would definitely be taking an active role in future development of IT within Sbell. The communication between the consultants and the employees also led to increased recognition of the importance of the role of IT within the company. Furthermore, it prompted the top management, middle management and the staff to pay more attention to the role of IT in achieving business success. Several other lessons can be learned from this case. With rich experience and a strong knowledge base, consultants may be inclined to draw conclusions from their previous experience, which may not fit a specific company. In this case, due to the limitation of time and resource, Sbell spent little time on issues related to technical architecture, where the consultants made most of the recommendations. In the subsequent implementation (CPC and CRM), some problems emerged and the company felt the need to modify the technical architecture. Hence, Sbell learned that it should not completely rely on the consulting companies; modifications might be needed to better meet its needs before finalizing the plan.

REFERENCES

Aberdeen Group. (1999, October 7). *Market Viewpoint, 12*(9). Retrieved from http://www.aberdeen.com/ab_company/hottopics/pdf/10991290.pdf

Earl, M. J. (1989). *Management strategies for information systems planning*. Englewood Cliffs, NJ: Prentice Hall.

Sabherwal, R., & Chan, Y. E. (2001, March). Alignment between business and IS strategies: A study of prospectors, analyzers, and defenders. *Information Systems Research, 12*(1), 11-33.

Shanghai Bell Corporation. (n.d.). Retrieved from http://www.alcatel-sbell.com.cn

Yuan Long is a PhD student at the University of Nebraska-Lincoln, USA, majoring in management information systems. She received her master's degree in computer science from East-China Institute of Computer Technology. She has published articles in Computer Technology *and* Management Science *(both in China). Her current research interests include strategic information systems planning and software engineering.*

Fiona Fui-Hoon Nah is an assistant professor of management information systems at the University of Nebraska - Lincoln, USA. She received her PhD in management information systems from the University of British Columbia. She has published in Communications of the ACM, Journal of Computer Information Systems, Journal of Information Technology, Journal of Information Technology Cases and Applications, Journal of Electronic Commerce Research, Journal of Software Maintenance, Business

Process Management Journal, *and* Simulation and Gaming. *Her research interests include enterprise resource planning, human-computer interaction, individual and group decision-making, and theory building in information systems research.*

Zhanbei Zhu is a manager of information center and a team leader of CPC project in Shanghai Bell. He received his PhD in management science from Beijing University, China. He has seven year of industrial experience in information service, knowledge management, and business intelligence research and practice.

This case was previously published in the *Annals of Cases on Information Technology,* Volume 5/2003, pp.431-446, © 2003.

About the Editor

Mehdi Khosrow-Pour, D.B.A, is executive director of the Information Resources Management Association (IRMA) and senior academic technology editor for Idea Group Inc. Previously, he served on the faculty of the Pennsylvania State University as a professor of information systems for 20 years. He has written or edited more than 30 books in information technology management. Dr. Khosrow-Pour is also editor-in-chief of the *Information Resources Management Journal*, *Journal of Electronic Commerce in Organizations*, *Journal of Cases on Information Technology*, and *International Journal of Cases on Electronic Commerce*.

Index

J

job 8
job order database 126
job scheduling system 126
joint application development 125

K

knowledge acquisition 166

L

lack of communication 168
LAN (see local area network)
learning organization 61
learning organization theory 62
licensing 198
lifecycle objects 24
local area network (LAN) 297, 303
logical inferences 165
Lotus Notes 166

M

main project scheduler 129
mainframe technology 296
management buy-out (MBO) 310
management of change 200
manufacturing 351
manufacturing and procurement 357
Manugistics 301
ManuSoft 295
marketing 350
master scheduler 133
materials management (MM) 352
MBO (see management buy-out)
mining registry 248
MM (see materials management)
Movex software 301
multi-skilled 199

N

National System of Public Registries 248
networking 297
New South Wales 197

O

object 22
off-the-shelf software 297
open systems platform 199
organization and management 357
organizational alignment 63
organizational change 59
organizational culture 62
organizational dynamic 280
organizational transformation 203
organizations registry 248

P

paper production 155
path 197
persons registry 248
philosophy of technology 94
placement 8
polymorphism 23
PP (production planning) 352
process reengineering 27
process Support 67
product development model 312
production by cost center report 305
production planning (PP) 352
project coordinator 124
Public Registries of Peru (SUNARP) 246

R

R&D (see research and development)
rail industry 265
real property registry 248
registry information system (SIR) 255
relational database management system
    (RDBMS) 315
requirement analysis 125
research and development (R&D) 350
restructuring 61
revenue logic 312
risk 197
risk management 27
Roads and Traffic Authority 197